Thomas Edward Bridgett

History of the Holy Eucharist in Great Britain

Vol. 1

Thomas Edward Bridgett

History of the Holy Eucharist in Great Britain
Vol. 1

ISBN/EAN: 9783337286170

Printed in Europe, USA, Canada, Australia, Japan

Cover: Foto ©ninafisch / pixelio.de

More available books at **www.hansebooks.com**

HISTORY

OF

THE HOLY EUCHARIST

IN GREAT BRITAIN

BY

T. E. BRIDGETT

OF THE CONGREGATION OF THE MOST HOLY REDEEMER
AUTHOR OF 'THE RITUAL OF THE NEW TESTAMENT' 'OUR LADY'S DOWRY'
'THE DISCIPLINE OF DRINK' ETC.

VOL. I.

BRITONS, PICTS, SCOTS, AND ANGLO-SAXONS

𝔓𝔢𝔯𝔪𝔦𝔰𝔰𝔲 𝔖𝔲𝔭𝔢𝔯𝔦𝔬𝔯𝔲𝔪

LONDON
C. KEGAN PAUL & CO., 1 PATERNOSTER SQUARE
1881

(The rights of translation and of reproduction are reserved.)

NOTICE.

THE present volumes bring down the History of the Holy Eucharist to the Protestant Reformation. The author had collected materials to complete the History to the present day; but when he found that a third volume would be required in order to treat adequately the Reformation and post-Reformation periods, he thought it better to make the early and mediæval periods complete in themselves. His present intention, however, should he live to continue the History, is to treat in a separate volume of the Reformation and post-Reformation periods.

CONTENTS

OF

THE FIRST VOLUME.

CHAPTER		PAGE
	INTRODUCTION	1
I.	THE EARLY BRITISH CHURCH	13
	APPENDIX ON THE GALLICAN LITURGY	24
II.	SIDE LIGHTS FROM BRITTANY	27
III.	THE PICTS AND SCOTS	52
IV.	DEVASTATION	70
V.	BRITISH ISOLATION	78
VI.	ANGLO-SAXON CONVERSION	85
VII.	THE EASTER CONTROVERSY	102
VIII.	ANGLO-SAXON FAITH	119
IX.	AN HISTORICAL CONTROVERSY: ÆLFRIC	133
X.	THE MASS PRIEST	147
XI.	CHURCHES AND ALTARS	152
XII.	REQUISITES FOR MASS	167
XIII.	LITURGY AND CEREMONIAL	175
XIV.	ON SAYING AND HEARING MASS	186
XV.	INTENTIONS OF THE CELEBRANT	200
XVI.	ON RECEIVING COMMUNION	215
XVII.	VIATICUM AND RESERVATION	231
XVIII.	A RETROSPECT	241

HISTORY

OF THE

HOLY EUCHARIST IN GREAT BRITAIN.

INTRODUCTION.

How wonderful has been the history of the Holy Eucharist in Great Britain! For more than a thousand years the races that successively peopled the island regarded the celebration of this Sacrament as the central rite of their religion, the principal means of divine worship, the principal channel of divine grace. The Holy Eucharist was the great mystery of faith,[1] the object not only of fear and of love, but also of supreme adoration. Then a change came, and now for more than three hundred years this view of our Lord's institution has been rejected with an energy and perseverance which no language can exaggerate. Altars of sacrifice were broken in pieces or condemned to the vilest uses. The doctrine of masses was called 'a blasphemous fable and dangerous deceit,' the worship of our Lord beneath the sacramental veils 'idolatry.' The offering of mass by Catholic priests was punished with cruel death, the repudiation of it was required as the price of social preferment or of civil liberty. In the belief in the Holy Eucharist a test was found to distinguish between the professors of two opposite religions. Even to this day a solemn abjuration of the ancient Catholic doctrine is required when the crown is placed on the head of the most exalted ruler of the nation.

It is evident then that, whichever of these views is embraced, a history of this rite, even a partial history, professedly restricted to one country, ought to be full of interest and instruction. If the Pro-

---

[1] *Mysterium fidei*, words used in the very act of consecration.

testant view be correct, then it will be a history of idolatry in worship and consequent corruption in morals. If, on the other hand, the Catholic view be the true one, it will be the history of God's fidelity to His promises, His watchful providence over His Church, His gracious dealings with men, and we shall have many a fair page to unroll of the mutual love of the Creator and of His creatures, though those pages may be defaced with some foul blots of man's ingratitude.

It is such a history, from the Catholic point of view, that I have attempted in the present work, and the purpose of this Introduction is to explain the principles which have presided over its composition.

When the Protestant views of the Eucharist were put forth in writing in the sixteenth century, they led to many learned answers in which texts of Scripture and sayings of the Fathers are discussed with necessary yet wearisome minuteness and reiteration. With such discussions I am not concerned, and they will have no place in my volumes. Both sides in the great controversy have now grown somewhat weary of fighting about questions of grammar and rules of interpretation. Men have begun to turn their eyes to history, and to seek in it a commentary written by the hand of God on His own revelation. I am far from saying that that commentary does not itself admit of more than one reading, nor am I commending historical to the exclusion of scriptural or patristic studies: I merely say that to study a doctrine in its results is a favourite method in modern times, and I will not conceal that it is one full of interest and delight to myself. The writers of the sixteenth century to whom I am referring, occasionally, though seldom, make use of this argument drawn from history. I think I may truly say that the charges made against the ancient faith were so new, so startling, so vast, that at first Catholics could scarcely grasp all their meaning, or know on which side to turn for the best answer. It was as if the existence of the sun in the heavens were called in question, and they knew not whether to appeal to the testimony of the senses of living men, or to the effects of light and heat on agriculture, or to the records of science or of history. The doctrine of the Church on the Holy Eucharist untrue! Why, it was the doctrine of the Scriptures, the doctrine of the Fathers, the doctrine of all ages! If it were untrue, then all ages had been monstrously deceived, and the Christian Church had failed. At first an effort was made by the innovators to disguise this tremendous consequence. The Church had merely suffered a Babylonish captivity to the Bishop of Rome. This was Luther's first contention; but by degrees men grew bolder, and the theologians of Queen Elizabeth, in the crudest language they could find, condemned the Church of their forefathers as apostate and idolatrous.

The enunciation of such propositions almost took away the breath of Catholics, accustomed as they had been to look on the Holy Catholic Church as the temple of the Holy Ghost, the tabernacle of God with men, the holy city, the heavenly Jerusalem, adorned as a bride for her husband. St. Thomas of Villanova, a contemporary of Luther's and a friar of the same Augustinian order, gave eloquent utterance to the amazement and horror which seized on him: 'Good God,' he says,[1] 'if those who forsook all the riches and pleasures of the world, to live in the greatest purity and simplicity, like angels in human form, living for Thee alone, for Thy honour, for Thy service, and intent on Thy praises day and night, seeking nothing but Thee, hurting no man, doing good to all, humble, modest and pious; if such as these were deceived and lived in error and, as thinking evil of God, perfidious and sacrilegious have been condemned —who then have been saved? O God, if Thou hast despised these and forsaken them and suffered them to err—these who, beyond the limits of human strength, have lived in holiness and purity in worship and devotion to Thee—whom then dost Thou love? whom in the world dost Thou enlighten? If these have despised Thy divine Majesty, who then have found favour with Thee? For certainly none such as these in all virtue and sanctity has the world ever possessed or seen. Away, away with such a thought about God as that He should suffer to err such worshippers, such most holy lovers of His goodness; or that He should condemn to eternal death those whom only His own grace could have raised to such a height of purity and sanctity.'

More than a hundred years before these words were written the author of 'The Imitation of Christ' had pointed to the ancient faith and devotion of the Church's saints as a confirmation of the truth of their belief in the Blessed Sacrament of the Altar: 'Oh! how true and burning was their faith, and what a solid argument is it of the truth of Thy sacred Presence!'[2] So too, our own great champion and martyr, Cardinal Fisher, in his controversy with Œcolampadius brings forward as a corroborative proof of the Real Presence its wonderful effects in the lives of the saints.[3] After enumerating these, he adds: 'If anyone should attentively consider the progress and

---

[1] Concio II., *in Dom. SS. Trin.* vol. i. p. 701. Ed. 1850.

[2] 'O vera ardens fides eorum: probabile existens argumentum sacræ præsentiæ tuæ' (lib. iv. cap. 14).

[3] *De Veritate Corp. et Sang. Christi*, lib. iii. Proœm.

the decline, and the reformations of life which have often occurred in the Church, he will find that neglect or abuse of this sacrament has been the cause of decline; and, on the other hand, that faithful worship and devout frequentation of this sacrament have wonderfully contributed to progress and reform.' He goes on to show this from history, recalling how the first Christians, as the Acts of the Apostles relate, added prayer and frequent communion to their hearing of the word of God—how all the constancy of the martyrs came from their being inebriated with the Blood of Christ in holy communion—how, when persecutions and heresies ceased, the greater number of Christians fell into luxury and vice—and how the two great patriarchs of the Franciscan and Dominican orders, who revived piety and virtue, were especially devout to the Blessed Sacrament. 'And if it be objected that in these very orders there are abuses, I cannot deny it,' he replies, 'though there are also many pious and holy men. But this confirms my argument. For I am thoroughly convinced that in those communities where, in addition to holy reading and devout prayer, they are accustomed purely and sincerely to celebrate the divine mysteries, there great fruits of piety and religion daily grow; but whenever the divine mysteries are neglected or undevoutly performed, no hope of any good need be entertained.'

How were these arguments met by the innovators? They were never met. As the Jews railed against our blessed Lord without heeding His appeals to His life and works, so these men railed against the Church without heeding her appeal. If there was any attempt at a reply, it was such as the following. When Catholics quoted our Lord's promises to His Church, the Protestant Reformers replied by quoting prophecies of rebellion, apostasy, and antichrist. If Catholics pointed to the Church's saints, Protestants derisively pointed to sinners. But there was no endeavour to weigh the matter calmly, and to trace effects to causes, and to distribute impartially praise and blame. And this is why I have said that the history of the Church, or God's commentary on His own revelation, admits of more than one reading. I do not, of course, mean that there is more than one true interpretation of facts, or that the true interpretation is hard to find. I mean that there are two elements in the Church, the human and the divine, and the human element sometimes submits itself to the divine action and glorifies it, while at other times it resists the operation of God, perverts or profanes His institutions, and, by uniting a high profession with unworthy practice, 'causes the name of God to be blasphemed among the Gentiles.' 'Among the Gentiles,' says Holy Scripture—that is, among the ignorant and prejudiced, who are unable or who refuse to see things as they are, and to assign effects to their true causes. By these 'the way of truth is evil spoken of,'[1] being blamed for that which it condemns.

There are two figures under which the Divine Teacher has opened to us this mystery of good and evil. He has said that 'a good tree cannot bring forth evil fruit;' and He has told us that in the field of His Church weeds shall be found mixed with the wheat. Those who speak evil of the way of truth misapply these tests. They see the weeds with which the enemy has oversown the corn, and they attribute them to the evil nature of the field, or to the hand of Him who sowed the good seed. Others, less bigoted and bitter, do not, indeed, consider that the weeds are the genuine produce of the field, but they persist in holding—in spite of our Lord's declaration—that if the field is divine it should bear no weeds or very few. They compare the weeds that grow in this divinely hedged and planted field with the weeds that grow in the wilderness outside, and they say that they are equally plentiful and equally noxious. Thus a recent 'History of Crime in England' makes much of its prevalence in the Middle Ages as an argument against the claims of the Catholic Church. Without admitting or denying the facts alleged, I reply that our Lord's field is known neither by the absence nor by the fewness of the weeds, but by the quality of the grain. Such a harvest of sanctity as it has produced was not gathered from seed sown by the hand of man, nor was it produced by human cultivation. We must not be surprised or scandalised if we find weeds in the Church's field of a peculiarly loathsome sort. As our Lord was set for the fall as well as for the resurrection of many, so the Blessed Sacrament is death to the wicked no less than life to the good. It is certain that there are phases of wickedness and degrees of malice in Catholic countries, arising from the abuse of this sacrament, which will not be found where abandonment of faith and loss of priesthood have made this kind of sacrilege impossible. We read in the Acts of the Apostles that, as a consequence of the lively faith and piety and daily communions of the first Christians, they were fruitful in every kind of good work; yet this beautiful description is followed by the awful history of Ananias and Sapphira tempted by Satan to lie to the Holy Ghost and plotting to defraud the Church. And it can hardly be rash to attribute this terrible fall, in the midst of such examples of virtue and in the presence of countless miracles, to the blinding and stupefying effects of sacrilegious communions, when we read St. Paul's warning to the

---

[1] 2 Pet. ii. 2.

Corinthians: 'He that eateth and drinketh unworthily, eateth and drinketh judgment to himself, not discerning the Body of the Lord. Therefore are there many infirm and weak among you, and many sleep.'[1]

Could we then read aright the history of the Church in any land, we should be filled with awe at the terrible judgments of God for graces neglected and holy things profaned, as much as with joy and gratitude for graces bearing fruit in sanctity and salvation.

Let me, however, say that, although I shall not omit to note abuses and crimes, so far as may serve for warning or move to reparation, I shall seek by preference examples of piety and love. And this for more than one reason. First, because other writers have more than sufficiently gathered up tales of scandal and catalogued deeds of impiety. I cannot excuse in this respect even our old Catholic chroniclers. Instead of imitating the manner of Venerable Bede, and gladly putting on record all that could edify, or, when obliged as faithful historians to recount evil deeds, doing so with evident shame and grief, too many monastic historians, with gossiping avidity, have collected, and related with an almost prurient minuteness, the shame of monks and abbots, of priests and bishops. But these, at least, were priests writing for priests, and in a learned language; and it would be well for our modern historians to remember, when they gloat with indecent delight over the satirical pages of some mediæval writers, that those writers are all priests; that none are so unsparing of the faults of their own order as the clergy; and that the very bitterness and exaggeration which often characterise their denunciations prove the loftiness of the standard by which priestly failings were ever judged.

It is needless then for me to repeat these well-known stories. At the very beginning of the Reformation the history of a thousand years back was ransacked for dirt to fling at the Catholic Church; and from the pages of the writers whose works form the Parker Society's publications, such matters have passed into innumerable modern histories and books of controversy.

A second reason for giving more prominence to what was excellent than to what was defective in ancient piety is this: that irregularities from their very nature are salient, attract attention at the time, and get recorded for future generations; while humble, unobtrusive piety, simple obedience, and regular observance find few chroniclers. No one who has not sought diligently in ancient documents can easily

[1] 1 Cor. xi. 29, 30.

form a conception of the difficulty of gleaning information regarding matters which, from the nature of the case, must have been of daily and almost hourly occurrence. In the long series of historical books of the Old Testament, ranging through decades of centuries, how seldom is the Sabbath mentioned! If all that is said of its observance were brought together, it would scarcely occupy the space given to the relation of one enormous crime.[1] Hence the extreme fallaciousness of mere negative arguments; hence the undue prominence given to evil over good in almost every record of human affairs. Let anyone search through the five large volumes called 'Annales Monastici,' published by the Master of the Rolls, containing the chronicles of several large abbeys in different parts of England, and reaching through many hundred years, he will not find even one page describing the daily service of the church or the acts of piety of the monks. Why should the annalist describe what everyone knew and daily witnessed? It would have seemed as natural to chronicle the daily rising of the sun and the effect of its rays upon the world. Indeed, there is a singular analogy between what is said of the weather and of the Blessed Sacrament. The annalists place on record how there was an earthquake throughout England in 1089; how a comet with two tails appeared in 1097, and mock suns in 1104; how at one time the Thames was almost dried up, and how at another it overflowed its banks; how thunder was heard on the feast of the Holy Innocents in 1249, while snow fell at the end of May in 1251. They tell of eclipses, murrains, severe winters, droughts, signs and portents. But they never describe the verdure of spring, the genial heat of summer, the fruitfulness of autumn; they never describe the full river flowing peacefully, or the midnight skies covered with brilliant stars. In the same way, if a church is burnt in an incursion of the enemy, if a murder is committed within the walls of the sanctuary, if the sacred vessels are stolen from the altar, if the holy rites cease during an interdict, such events are chronicled. But the daily service of the church, the fervent communions, the prayers poured out before the altar, the acts of faith and charity—all these, as a matter of course, are scarcely heeded.

This is most natural, but it presents to us, who are not eye-witnesses, both a danger and a difficulty. The danger is that of dwelling on the exception rather than on the rule, of generalising the rare abuses as if they were the acknowledged use. The difficulty is that even those who see the folly and wickedness of such judgments

[1] As, for example, that of the Benjaminites and its punishment. (Judges xix--xxi.)

are perplexed and often baffled in their efforts to recall the genuine history of the past. There is great truth in a remark of Sir Walter Scott : 'The traditional recollections concerning the monks themselves are exceedingly faint, contrasted with the beautiful and interesting monuments which they have left behind them. The people can tell nothing but that such a race existed and inhabited the stately ruins of these monasteries. The quiet, slow, and uniform life of these recluse beings glided on, it may be, like a dark and silent stream, *fed from unknown sources,* and vanishing from the eye without leaving any marked trace of its course.'

Since the days of Sir Walter Scott a great deal has been written to illustrate the lives of the monks and the effects of their life on the laws and civilisation of the country. But it is still true that the *sources* of that silent fertilising stream have been inadequately searched. The principal source which fed the stream of Catholic life, whether among monks or laymen, was the Blessed Sacrament ; and it is to its investigation that this treatise is confined. What has been said of the scantiness of information, and the difficulty of rightly adjusting what we have, must plead for me if I have but imperfectly succeeded in my attempt.

The words of Sir Walter Scott, just quoted, remind us that the public is not equally unacquainted with every part of Catholic worship. The building is more familiar than the altar which was its principal feature; the altar and its ornaments are more generally known than the liturgy ; and the liturgy is better understood than the faith and devotion which gave life to it. I propose, therefore, to dwell principally on what is least known, though by far the most important. It will be sufficient for my purpose to touch on architecture, metallotechny, embroidery, just so far as they served devotion, since fuller details can be found in works already written and of easy access. Even to ritual and liturgy I shall give but a subordinate place. 'The end of the commandment,' says the Apostle, 'is charity from a pure heart, and a good conscience, and an unfeigned faith.'[1] Whatever can illustrate these things, however minute, I can never count trivial, and shall gladly record ; whatever neither springs from them, nor leads to them, nor teaches about them, however great, I gladly lay aside.

The history of the Blessed Sacrament is, however, mainly a secret one. Though it is the fountain-head of the life of the Church, yet the waters of life are conveyed from it by hidden channels, and life

---

[1] 1 Tim. i. 5.

and growth, even when visible in the results, are too gradual and too complicated to be observed by human eyes. Air and sunshine, water and soil, are all necessary for the plant, yet who shall trace the tender green of the leaves, the brilliant hues of the flowers, or the delicious fragrance of both to their component elements, and analyse the process of the transformation? So, in the garden of the Church, prayer and preaching, sacraments and worship, pastoral vigilance and fraternal union, joy and suffering, all work together to produce the flowers of sanctity; and among all these influences the most universal and most efficient is unquestionably that of the Holy Eucharist. But it would be in many cases a rash attempt to assign a special trait of sanctity or this or that heroic act to its operation. I shall not, therefore, venture farther than to record some works of piety, generosity, charity, and endurance which had for their explicit object this sacred Mystery; or such effects as can be unmistakably traced to it.

And here I must make a candid confession. I have been very often tempted to throw these notes aside, from a deep sense not only of my own incapacity to deal with so awful and mysterious a theme, but of the intrinsic inadequacy of the materials themselves to do justice to it, however skilfully they might be handled. Let me illustrate my meaning by what may happen to a botanist. He has spent years in collecting specimens of every variety of one class of flowers. He has penetrated forests, climbed mountains, crossed the ocean. Gradually his portfolios have been filled; his specimens, dried, arranged, catalogued, are almost complete. Two or three of the rarest known varieties alone are wanting, while several new specimens unknown to former botanists give to his collection a special value. He presents it to a museum; it will interest enthusiastic botanists like himself. Even unscientific amateurs may gaze with pleasure at certain forms and colours. But the collector himself has an experience he can never communicate. Each little dead flower calls up before him not only the brighter picture of its living self, but also the very landscape that surrounded it. He sees again the bleak moor, the dense wood, the lonely mountain where it grew. He remarks once more the nature of its soil, the state of the atmosphere, the accompanying vegetation. And besides such physical facts as he would at the time have noted down for after use in a botanic treatise, the faded blossom brings to his mind a personal vision full of joy. He remembers his weary searches, his frequent disappointments, all compensated for on that joyful evening when, just before sunset, he at last found that long-sought and unique specimen. The view from the mountain has indeed no scientific connection with the flower, nor was it one of the conditions of its growth, yet in the mind of the collector the two things are indissolubly united. The adventures of that successful day, the valleys that were searched in vain, the other flowers that were either disregarded or carefully gathered, but which do not belong to *this* collection—these things are all vividly pictured in the collector's mind. If he is a simple enthusiast, he will expect others to share in his enthusiasm. If not, he will resign himself to what is inevitable, satisfied that, though he knows that only a few trained botanists will be able to appreciate the special value of his collection, it is not a useless contribution to science. His personal adventures, his toils, his disappointments are his own affair. They had their reward, and the remembrance of them is a pleasure. But it is incommunicable.

I may say the same of my Eucharistic gleanings. I cannot hope to make others share my own enthusiasm; but I do regret that my specimens are so completely separated from their surroundings, and that I cannot show by pen or pencil where my flowers grew, and why they grew there and could not grow elsewhere. I do not regret that my readers will never know, nor care to know, how many books I have searched to no purpose, or that one little fact told in three lines of text or buried in a footnote cost more labour, greater research, than a whole chapter of wider interest—these are authors' secrets and belong to authors alone; but I do feel that an incident taken from the life of a saint loses its interest, and nearly all its teaching power, when separated from its context in that life. To many of my readers the names of Cuthbert, Aldhelm, Thomas of Hereford, Margaret of Scotland will probably be little more than names. They bring no memories in their train; so that when I tell how Cuthbert received the Viaticum in his hermit's cell, how Aldhelm by the music of his harp drew the peasantry to mass, how Thomas could not offer the Holy Sacrifice without tears, how Margaret contended against priests and bishops for the Easter communion, very little of the full meaning of these facts will have been conveyed to the reader. Their moral force or persuasiveness depends on the beauty of the characters represented by those names; but I cannot write a biography of all whom I must mention. The same may be said of national events. I am compelled to treat of them only partially, from an exclusive point of view, however diligently and impartially I myself have tried to study them.

All this may seem very egotistical, and evidence that I have not the skill to handle historic themes. Be it so! Yet dried flowers, severed from the stem, pressed, dried, grouped, and catalogued, are, at the best, a poor record of the groves and vales and hills where they grew; of the dews and rains, the days and nights, the storms and sunshine that made them what they were.

The order in which I have arranged my materials must speak for itself. It is as far as possible chronological. The disadvantage of this arrangement is that of having to dwell on the same aspect of my theme more than once; for example, I shall have to treat of the frequency of celebration by priests and of communion by the laity, first in early times, and then in later ages. But the danger of reiteration is not so serious as would be the confusion left in the reader's mind, were I to carry on one branch of my subject through all its various phases during so many centuries, and then return on my steps to do the same with another branch.

I am so far from apologising for the multitude of quotations, that I consider this the real value of my book. It is a compilation for the most part from rare works, or from works such as are out of the reach of ordinary readers. In nearly all cases I have drawn from first sources, and have carefully indicated my authority whenever I have admitted an exception to this rule.[1]

I might have called my treatise a basket of fragments; for the history of the Blessed Sacrament reminds one of that of the multiplication of the loaves related in the Gospel. 'When he had commanded the multitude to sit down upon the grass, He took the five loaves and two fishes, and looking up to heaven He blessed and brake and gave the loaves to His disciples, and the disciples to the multitude. And they did all eat and were filled. And they took up what remained, twelve full baskets of fragments.'[2] This miracle is emblematic of the great sacramental banquet which has been going on for ages, and at which so many nations have been seated in the unity of the Catholic Church. 'For we, being many, are one bread, one body, all that partake of the One Bread.'[3] St. Mark tells us that the multitude sat down in ranks by hundreds and by fifties.[4] I have not attempted to write the history of the whole banquet, but of one group only, that which has feasted in the island of Great Britain. As one

---

[1] I should most willingly here have recorded my obligations and my gratitude for literary assistance; but as my principal benefactor wishes to remain unknown, I must be content to thank the superiors of ecclesiastical colleges and religious houses who have most kindly given me access to their libraries. I have thus been able to profit by the rich collections at Ushaw, Oscott, Ampleforth, St. Edmund's (Ware), St. Thomas's (Hammersmith), St. Michael's (Hereford), and other places. My obligations to personal friends are too numerous to mention. May none of them go unrewarded!

[2] Mat. xiv. 19, 20.   [3] 1 Cor. x. 17.   [4] Mark vi. 40.

who has shared in the feast, who has eaten and been satisfied, I have helped to gather up the broken fragments which tell of the wondrous miracle. May He who said 'Gather up the fragments that remain, lest they be lost,'[1] accept the basket or handful which I offer to His glory, as a token of my gratitude, love, and adoration !

[1] John vi. 12.

CHAPTER I.

THE EARLY BRITISH CHURCH.

ST. JOHN CHRYSOSTOM, writing in the fourth century, made use of a remarkable comparison in order to illustrate the propagation of our Lord's sacramental presence throughout all centuries, and over the entire globe. 'It is not man,' he says, 'who causes the oblations to become the Body and Blood of Christ, but it is Christ Himself who was crucified for us. The priest, representing Christ, stands and pronounces the words, but the power and the grace are from God. "This is My Body," he says. This word transforms the oblations. And just as the words "Increase and multiply and fill the earth" were once spoken, but throughout all time give to our human nature the power of generation, so also the words "This is My Body" once pronounced produce a perfect sacrifice at each table in the churches, from that day to this, and from now to our Lord's second advent.'[1]

It would deeply interest us, could we discover at what period of the world's history, in obedience to the command to multiply and fill the earth, a human being first set foot on the island of Great Britain, and who was that adventurer. But this will never be known. No rifled barrow of our Celtic or Turanian predecessors is ever likely to give up this secret. And so too there is no probability that any document still awaits discovery which will solve the controversy as to who first preached Christianity in Britain, or what priest erected the first altar, and first pronounced the words of consecration which made this island not merely the dwelling-place of man, but of Emmanuel, 'God with us.'

It does not fall within the scope of this work to discuss in detail the origin and character of the early British Church, any further than regards the Sacrament of the Holy Eucharist. The Holy Eucharist is, however, so truly the centre of a whole group of doctrines, practices, and institutions, that, when the faith on that one sacrament is known, the character of the whole religion is determined.

[1] *Homil. I.*, 'On the Betrayal of Judas.'

A well-known antiquarian, the late Mr. Thomas Wright, more than once defended the singular proposition, that 'Christianity was not established in Roman Britain;' by which he meant that it had either not entered the island before the fifth century, or at least had made no progress.[1]

While he allows that this 'is a conclusion totally at variance with the preconceived notions into which we have been led by ecclesiastical historians,' he brings forward no other proof of his own view than that 'not a trace of Christianity is found among the innumerable religious and sepulchral monuments of the Roman period in Britain.' But were this literally true[2] it would neither amount to an argument in favour of Mr. Wright's negation, nor even present a difficulty to the received belief that Christianity had widely spread throughout Britain for at least two centuries before the departure of the Romans. For Mr. Wright would not deny that it had thus spread in the two centuries which intervened between their departure in 410 and the landing of St. Augustine in 597. Yet how few are the monumental evidences of the Christianity of that period! No church, no altar, no font, no chalice has been preserved above ground or dug up to testify to a period when nearly all the Roman and Celtic inhabitants of South Britain were Christians. The fires of the pagan Saxons destroyed the churches and their contents, and if anything remained it has been obliterated by the hand of man or the action of the elements.[3] It is true that we have many remains which tell of

---

[1] *The Celt, the Roman, and the Saxon*, pp. 300-303, 2nd ed. Also *Biographia Literaria*, art. 'Gildas.'

[2] This statement is exaggerated. See article in the *Archæological Journal* for September 1867 (vol. xxiii. p. 221), by Mr. J. W. Groves. In 1864, at Chedworth Wood in Gloucestershire, a Roman villa was discovered. It has on its pavement not only crosses, but the Christian monogram. This discovery seems to connect the famous Boadicea with Christianity, for on a brick is the word 'Arviri,' and on a stone 'Prasiata.' Now, Arviragus was the father, and Prasiatagus the husband, of Boadicea. The Christian monogram is also found on a tesselated pavement dug up at Frampton, in Dorsetshire. Mr. Wright disposes of this latter evidence by surmising that the proprietor possessed a taste for literature and philosophy, and that, with a tolerant spirit which led him to surround himself with the memorials of all systems, he had adopted among the rest that which he might learn from some of the imperial coins to be the emblem of Christ Jesus, who, in his eyes, might stand on the same footing as Socrates and Pythagoras.

[3] There exist a few Christian sepulchral inscriptions. See Haddan and Stubbs, *Councils and Eccl. Documents*, vol. i. pp. 162-169. There is no British church at Canterbury, though the Roman bricks of the British church of St. Martin are used in the present fabric. One reason why we have now no traces of very early British churches is that such as survived to the 7th century—and many did survive—were utilised by the converted Saxons, and have consequently, in the course of

heathen worship; but Christianity had hitherto made little use of the arts of sculpture or of working in metal, and it is no cause of wonder that its presence in Roman Britain is not testified to by any relics now in our museums.

In order to maintain his view Mr. Wright had to set aside the explicit statements of ancient historians. The short and casual allusions found in Tertullian, St. Chrysostom, St. Jerome, and others, he calls 'flourishes of rhetoric.' The testimony of Venerable Bede is derived from Gildas, and Gildas never existed, or at least his history is a mere Anglo-Saxon forgery! Such is Mr. Wright's theory, and, were it accepted, this chapter of the present work might be omitted, since Gildas is the principal witness to the faith of the British Church in the Blessed Sacrament. It is enough to say that those most competent to form a judgment have decided against Mr. Wright in every point, and that the genuineness and authenticity of Gildas's writings do not admit the slightest doubt.[1]

Gildas has been often understood to say that Christianity was spread in Britain in the time of Tiberius, but he is speaking of the propagation of Christianity in general, not of its introduction into Britain. Nothing more can be gathered from him than that it was introduced and propagated between the time of the Apostles and the year 297, from which date he really begins his history. Tertullian, however, writing in 208, says that 'the places of the Britons unvisited by the Romans were yet subject to Christ and believed in Him.'[2] Origen also, writing twenty years later, declared that 'the virtue of our Lord and Saviour is with those who are separated from our world in Britain.' These distinct testimonies of well-informed men show that the faith must have been long propagated in Britain to have spread even beyond the Roman domination, and that it was by no means confined to Roman soldiers or colonists, but had been preached to and received by the natives as well. And this contemporary

ages, been replaced. But Mr. Wright might be asked to explain why no remains of Anglo-Saxon pagan temples now exist. Would he maintain that they never existed?

[1] Lingard has vindicated Gildas in his *History of the Anglo-Saxon Church*, vol. i. note B. Mr. Green, in his *Short History of the English People*, p. 7, himself refers to his article in the *Saturday Review* for April 24, 1869. In this he dwells especially on the eminently British character of Gildas. Messrs. Haddan and Stubbs show that he employs a Latin version of the Bible unknown to Anglo-Saxons, but used by other British and Welsh writers. Mr. Pryce, in his recent *Essay on the Ancient British Church*, p. 64, points to 'his evidently undesigned use of Celtic words.' He justly calls Mr. Wright's attempt to question the genuineness and authenticity of Gildas 'absurd.'

[2] *Adv. Judæos*, 7.

evidence is quite in harmony with the later testimony of Venerable Bede as to the conversion of King Lucius, and in no way contrary to the existence of Christianity in Britain at a much earlier date.[1]

There seem to be two popular errors in the judgments formed about British Christianity. One is to suppose a great change to have taken place between that form of it preached in the first or second century and the form depicted by Gildas and Bede in the fifth and sixth. Of such a change there is no proof whatever. It was entirely unknown and unsuspected by the writers to whom we owe our knowledge; and the theory of an early corruption of Christianity is due solely to the difference between the testimony of authentic history and the preconceived fancies of certain Protestant writers as to the nature of Apostolic teaching. But, on the other hand, there are many who seem to forget how long a period was filled by the British Church, and how many changes in outward circumstances may take place in a country during the space of five or six centuries. It need hardly be said that the painted Britons described by Cæsar, living in dense forests, have very little resemblance to the civilised Britons of the fourth century, some of whom were famous for their skill as lawyers, and who in general had become unwarlike and effeminate from too much luxury. The Romans were as capable of imposing their civilisation on a country as the English of to-day; and anyone who will consider the results of English occupation of a country like India or New Zealand for a century or less, may form some conception of the changes wrought in Britain by the Roman occupation of more than three hundred years. In the Britain of the fifth century there were numerous large cities, with fine public buildings, besides many towns and fortified places. Every city had its magistrates and civil order. The imperial court had often been fixed in Britain. It is probable that some of the British princes held sway recognised by their Roman masters, as in our Indian Empire at present. 'What Calcutta is now to London, London or York was then to Rome.' Whitaker says that 'the provinces into which Britain was then divided seem to have attained a more considerable degree of refinement and to have existed in a more flourishing condition than any of them knew for very many centuries afterwards' (*i.e.* after the Saxon invasion and desolation). 'All the improvements of the Romans had necessarily been introduced. Our mines

---

[1] Though Burton calls the story of Lucius a fable, and Milman a legend, Dr. Bright considers that they had no grounds for denying it. (*Chapters of Early English Church History*, p. 4.)

were worked with the greatest skill, and our towns were decorated with baths, temples, market-places, and porticos.'[1]

Of course this does not mean that the whole country was cultivated or the whole population civilised. At the present day what wretched remains of savage tribes still linger on in the territory of the United States; and in any one of our own great cities what poverty coexists with wealth, what ignorance with science, what brutality with refinement!

Thus is explained the varying language of St. Jerome. Describing what he had himself seen, at one time he draws a fearful picture of the morals of some pagan Britons, called Attacots, a warlike tribe settled in Galloway, whom Theodosius had enlisted in his army. These were cannibals, and lived in promiscuous sexual intercourse. At another time he is full of admiration for the piety of British Christians. 'The Briton,' he says, 'separated from our world, if he has made much progress in religion, leaves the western sun and seeks Jerusalem, a place known to him only by report and the authority of Holy Scripture.'[2] And as a nation may comprise different classes, so too a Church has its different epochs. We must be careful, therefore, not to generalise hastily, or to conclude that the British Church was always in the relaxed state, as regards discipline, in which St. Gildas describes that of his own day in the middle of the sixth century.

On the other hand we may safely generalise as to its faith. If British Christians flocked to Jerusalem and Rome, it was because in those cities, and in all intervening countries, they found the same faith and the same worship which they had learnt at home. This is no conjecture. The testimony of St. Jerome, a great reader and a great traveller, is most explicit. 'The church of the city of Rome,' he says, 'is not different from that of the whole world. Gaul and Britain and Africa and all barbarous nations adore one Christ and follow one rule of truth.'[3] St. John Chrysostom is no less clear.

---

[1] *History of Manchester*, tom. ii. p. 6. Writing of Agricola's government of the natives at so early a date as A.D. 79, Tacitus says that 'paulatim discessum ad delinimenta vitiorum, porticus et balnea et conviviorum elegantiam.' Mr. Skene says: 'The natives soon began to study the Roman language and to adopt their dress, and by degrees acquired a taste for the luxurious and voluptuous life of the Romans.' (*Celtic Scotland*, i. 44.) Numerous remains of Roman baths have been found north of the Humber, no less than in the southern parts of the island.

[2] S. Jerome *Adv. Jov.* ii.; *Ep.* 44 et 84. On the Attacotti, see Skene, *Celtic Scotland*, i. 101, 106.

[3] 'Nec altera Romanæ urbis Ecclesia, altera totius orbis existimanda est. Et Gallia et Britannia et Africa . . . et omnes barbaræ nationes unum Christum adorant, unam observant regulam veritatis.'—*Ep.* 101.

'Even the British isles,' he says, 'have felt the power of the Word for there, too, churches and altars have been erected; there too, as in the extreme east, or beside the Euxine, or in the south, men may be heard discussing points in Scripture, with different voices, but not with different belief.'[1] It is true that their countryman, Gildas, accuses them of being fond of novelty and of receiving heresies easily, in allusion to the inroads made first by Arianism and then by Pelagianism. But this very accusation supposes the possession of the right faith by the majority, and of a rule of faith, common to the whole world, by which heresy might be discerned. In order also to repel the heresies, the British bishops either went abroad to take part in councils of the Church, as at Arles in 314, and probably at Nicæa in 325, and at Sardica in 347, and again at Ariminum in 359; or they sent to the continent to bring over champions of the truth, as St. Victritius of Rouen in the fourth century, St. Germanus of Auxerre, St. Lupus of Troyes, and St. Patrick in the fifth. It was hardly necessary, therefore, for a recent learned writer[2] to vindicate the orthodoxy of the Britons, as if against St. Gildas and St. Bede; for neither of those historians for a moment supposes that the Britons as a church differed in faith from themselves or from the rest of the Catholic Church throughout the world. They merely assert a tendency in the people to certain novel speculations, but a tendency which was met and overcome. Certainly at a later period, when intercourse with the continent was somewhat less frequent, instead of being prone to novelty, the Britons were found to be obstinately tenacious of even minor points of discipline.

Since then the Christianity of Britain was the same as that of the rest of the Catholic Church, even had we no explicit testimony regarding the Blessed Eucharist, we should still know the faith and practice of the British Church; and if need were we might rightly expand what is brief and implicit in the mention of British institutions by the fuller details supplied by contemporary history. Thus, when St. John Chrysostom says that in Britain there are churches and altars of sacrifice ($\theta v \sigma \iota a \sigma \tau \eta \rho \iota a$), we know the force he gives to this word by almost numberless passages in his works, where he maintains the doctrines of the Real Presence and of Sacrifice. But it will not be necessary to borrow elucidations from other countries. We have

---

[1] *Contra Judæos.*

[2] Rev. Dr. Bright, *Chapters of Early English History*, p. 12. 'It is evident that Gildas, and Bede, following him, have greatly exaggerated the influence of Arianism in Britain. Eminent doctors of unquestioned orthodoxy, in the period following the Athanasian, speak as if the distant islanders were one in faith with themselves.'

native testimony, if not great in quantity, yet explicit and far-reaching.

Take this one fact. Bishops of York, London, and Caerleon were at the Council of Arles in the year 314.[1] Among other canons they decreed that the Bishop of Rome should by letters promulgate the uniform observance of Easter through the whole world; that no one could marry again during his wife's lifetime; and that seven bishops, or at least three, should take part in the consecration of a bishop. Here then we have a church, governed by bishops, in full communion with the Holy See and with the rest of the Catholic world, in the full consciousness of unity of faith and worship, and taking measures for its perpetuity. We see the care with which the sacrament of holy orders is watched over in the persons of those fathers of the priesthood on whom depends the propagation of our Lord's sacred Body and of His mystical Body the Church; while a similar watchfulness is extended to the sacrament of marriage, on the sanctity of which rite depends the orderly propagation of society, both natural and supernatural. In the mention of the great festival of Easter we see a whole system of worship, a cycle of fasts and feasts making up the ecclesiastical year, any disturbance in which would be like bringing confusion into the movements of the planets circling in their complex harmony.

Let us look into some of the details of the system thus revealed; and in the present chapter no document shall be quoted which is not purely British, and belonging to a period antecedent to the coming of St. Augustine for the conversion of the Saxon invaders. Besides the history or letters of Gildas we have a code of penitential canons drawn up by St. Gildas in 570, and similar decrees made by St. David at nearly the same date.[2] From these we find that the British Church bore a very monastic character. Monasteries of monks and nuns abounded, and the bishops seem in general to have lived in monasteries, and probably belonged to the regular clergy. Yet there were also secular priests resident in their presbyteries.[3] We have

---

[1] Haddan and Stubbs, *Councils*, vol. i. p. 7; Pryce, *The Ancient British Church*, pp. 86-90.

[2] For the authenticity of these see Haddan and Stubbs, *Councils*, vol. i. pp. 113-120, and Preface, p. x. In their present authentic form they were not known to Lingard, and therefore are not quoted by him.

[3] This is clear from the complaint of Gildas of the conduct of some towards their female relatives who acted as their housekeepers: 'Religiosam forte matrem, seu sorores domo pellentes et externas indecenter levigantes.' There is no question either of sending away or bringing in *wives*. I make this remark because of late years many writers have affirmed with increasing confidence that marriage of priests was both common and recognised in the British and Saxon Churches.

mention of priests (called both presbyteri and sacerdotes), of deacons, subdeacons, and lectors. Among the few details of ritual we have the significant fact that the hands of the priest were anointed with chrism at his ordination.[1] And this is in harmony with the doctrine of Gildas on priestly authority, for he represents the clergy as both exercising the power of the keys and offering sacrifice to God.[2] Should priest or deacon have been put to public penance for some great crime, even after its accomplishment there remained this terrible penalty: 'Henceforward it is unlawful for the priest to offer sacrifice, or for the deacon to hold the chalice;'[3] these being then, as now, the distinguishing offices and privileges of priests and deacons.[4]

In order to offer sacrifice 'decently and in order,' a special and consecrated place had to be chosen, as soon as this was possible. How soon this was we do not know. Venerable Bede tells us that the Britons had their churches before the persecution of Diocletian, since 'after its cessation, in 313, they *rebuilt* the churches which had been levelled with the ground, founded and adorned basilicas of the holy martyrs, celebrated festivals and performed the sacred rites (*sacra conficiunt*) with clean hearts and mouths.'[5] This he took from Gildas, who, without the help of documents, could know the history of the churches which were still standing when he wrote. Most of these churches were of wood,[6] yet stone churches were not unknown. Venerable Bede speaks of St. Augustine recovering one 'built by the ancient Roman Christians' in Canterbury, which he consecrates in the name of our holy Saviour; and this appears to have been of stone, as well as that of St. Martin in the same city.[7] According to a good archæological authority, 'the Cornish churches of the fifth to the seventh centuries, built by the Irish missionaries, were generally provided, as in Ireland, with a well' (for baptisms), 'with a simple parallel chancel, separated by a low stone step' (from the body of the building), 'with a stone altar, and a stone bench table.'[8]

---

[1] Haddan and Stubbs, vol. i. pp. 138-141, and also p. 102.
[2] *Quasi passim* in his *History, Epistle,* and *Canons.*
[3] Haddan, vol. i. p. 119.
[4] The Council of Arles, at which British bishops were present, had, in its fifteenth canon, rebuked some deacons for usurping the functions of the priesthood in the celebration of the Holy Eucharist.
[5] *Eccl. Hist.* i. 8.   [6] *Ib.* iii. 4, 25.   [7] *Ib.* i. 33.
[8] Rev. Mackenzie Walcott, *Church and Conventual Arrangement.* According to Mr. Willis (*Canterbury Cathedral*, pp. 20-32), St. Augustine placed his altar at the west end of his cathedral. Dean Stanley conjectures that he did this in imitation of the altar of St. Peter's in Rome (*Historical Mem. of Canterbury,* pp. 39-41).

St. Germanus came over to Britain to preach in the fifth century. In his life, which was written by Constantius a few years after the saint's death, we read of a church of boughs being erected in the midst of the camp, in which the soldiers might celebrate the Easter festival. It was after hearing mass and receiving communion in this rural tent that the newly baptised Christians, dressed in their white robes, gained the famous Alleluia victory.[1]

But whether the church were of wood or of stone, the altar, which was its principal feature, was nearly always made of stone. It is called by Gildas *ara* or *altare*, and he adds the epithets *holy* and *venerable* ;[2] and when he is reproaching his nation, or certain members of it, for their disregard of oaths, the expression he uses is the following : 'When they have stood before the altars, pledging their oaths, they go away and think no more of it than if they had sworn upon dirty stones.'[3] In another place he inveighs against a native prince or tyrant named Constantine, who 'with his accursed sword rent the most holy altar, so that the altar-cloths purpled as with gore stained the place of the heavenly sacrifice.'[4] The shape of the altars we have no direct means of ascertaining, though they were probably not oblong parallelograms as at present, but square and small, standing on two columns, or perhaps even one.

The 'most holy sacrifice,' the 'heavenly sacrifice' (*sacrosancta sacrificia, cæleste sacrificium*), was called mass or missa, then as now. The liturgy with which it was celebrated was not in the Celtic but the Latin tongue, and this too not only during the Roman occupation, but for centuries after. It is uncertain whether the liturgy was Roman or Gallican.[5] The difference, however, between these was not con-

[1] Baptism was administered on Easter eve, and was immediately followed by communion of the neophytes, as we know from St. Augustine, *Sermon* 227.

[2] 'Inter altaria stantes'—'sacrosancta altaria'—'venerabilibus aris' (*Epistola*). These expressions suppose several altars in the same church.

[3] *Ib.* : 'Inter altaria jurando demorantes, ac hæc eadem ac si lutulenta paulo post saxa despicientes.'

[4] *Ib.* : 'Sacrosancta altaria nefando ense laceravit, ita ut sacrificii cælestis sedem purpurea ac si coagulati cruoris pallia attingerent.' He had just murdered two children. Dr. Rock seems to understand this passage as if the altar-stone were covered with silk of purple dye (*Church of our Fathers*, vol. i. p. 265). Dr. Lingard supposes that the altar-linens were purpled with the blood spilt.

[5] On this subject I must refer for a fuller discussion to the preliminary dissertation of Dr. Forbes, late Anglican Bishop of Brechin, to his edition of the *Arbuthnot Missal.* Of the northern Britons in Tertullian's time he says : 'Whatever religion they had must in form and ritual have been Roman.' Dr. Bright says : 'The original British use was apparently identical with the Gallican.' (*Chapters of Early English History*, p. 28.) Dr. Lingard sees no reason for supposing that the old British liturgy was Gallican. He considers it to have been Roman.

siderable; for when St. Augustine consulted St. Gregory about the difference in the 'custom or rite of masses' between the Roman and Gallican Churches, the Pope leaves him free either to choose between them or to modify one by the other.[1] The variations were therefore unimportant. When the saintly missionary reached Britain and asked for intercommunion and help from the British bishops, he made some complaint about their observance of Easter and also about certain baptismal ceremonies, but none about the liturgy of the holy sacrifice. One of the penitential canons of St. Gildas shows how scrupulously the forms of administration of sacraments were observed: 'If any one by mistake make any change in the sacred words *where danger is noted*, he will observe a three days' fast.'[2]

The Eucharistic rite was therefore not a mere communion. It was also a sacrifice. The very particles reserved for communion received their name from sacrifice among the Britons, as afterwards among the Saxons.[3] 'Si casu negligens quis sacrificium aliquod perdat,' *i.e.* 'If anyone by negligence let fall and lose a sacrifice,' are the words of one of Gildas's canons. Thus we should say a Host, from Hostia, a victim. And the sacrifice was believed to avail not only to those who communicated, nor to those only who were present, but to the absent also; and it could be applied according to the intention and desire of the celebrating priest. One of the canons of Gildas says: We may offer the sacrifice for good kings, not for bad ones, but priests may always offer for their bishops.'

With regard to communion on the part of the laity we have no information. A canon of Gildas, appointing a penance for a secret sin committed by a boy twelve years old, shows that at a very early age children were admitted to confession; and we know that for many centuries it was the custom even for infants to communicate. That the Blessed Sacrament was reserved for the sick is also to be gathered from the canon already quoted, speaking of letting fall the sacred particle, for it is added, 'leaving it to be devoured by beasts or birds,' which shows that the accident is not supposed to have taken place in the church during the distribution of holy communion, but on the road or in the fields when the priest was carrying it to the sick. It is also no strained interpretation of the words, if we gather from them, what we know from other sources to have been the case,[4]

---

[1] Bede, *Eccl. Hist.* i. 27.
[2] Haddan and Stubbs, *Councils*, i. 115. [3] *Ib.* i. 114.
[4] On this subject of communion under one species in the early Church, the reader may consult with advantage one of the essays in the book called *The Sacrifice of the Eucharist*, by the late Rev. Charles Garside. (Burns and Oates.)

that the sick communicated under one species only. It is certainly also a clear proof of the belief of the British Church in the Real Presence that the loss of the sacred particle, due not to deliberate sacrilege, but to accident arising from want of reverential care (*si quis casu negligens*), should merit for the priest no less a penance than a fast of three Quarantains or Lents.

These few details are almost all that has come down to us directly regarding the celebration in South Britain, previous to the Saxon conquest, of that sacrament by which our Lord's Passion was to be ever commemorated and applied to the souls of men. We are almost wholly ignorant of what we should most wish to know—the effects of our Lord's Presence on the lives of His disciples. We see indeed the monastic life in great esteem and much frequented by men and women, but we have few authentic details of the virtues practised by those tens of thousands of monks and nuns, and the penitential canons of St. Gildas speak not of virtues but of crimes— of crimes possible even to those who made profession of the pursuit of holiness, though of course the existence of a code of penal law is no proof that crime is frequent. We see bishops watching over their flocks, with zeal for faith and true pastoral solicitude, but the same glimpse reveals the ravages of two heresies most contrary to the adorable Eucharist, since Arianism denied our Lord's Divinity, and Pelagianism the influence of His grace. Almost our only authority as to the moral state of the British Church is Gildas, and it would be contrary to all fair interpretation to generalise his strong language, as if what he says of his own day applied to all the centuries that had passed, or even then admitted no exceptions. Mr. Green has drawn a true picture of Gildas : 'Ascetic, keenly religious in the whole tone of his mind and temper, clinging with a fierce contemptuous passion to the Roman tradition of the past, but vindicating as passionately the new moral truths with which Christianity fronted a world of license, steeped to the lips in biblical lore, orthodox with the traditional orthodoxy of the Celt, patriotic with the Celtic unreasoning hatred of the stranger, the voice of Gildas rings out like the bitter cry of one of those Hebrew prophets whose words he borrows, rebuking in the same tones of merciless denunciation the invader, the tyrant, and the priest.'[1] It is not, however, easy to understand why Mr. Green should call Gildas's hatred of the stranger 'unreasoning.' The pagan Saxons had surely given good reason for such hatred. He wrote his history about a hundred years after the commencement of the barbarians' invasion. He was born in 516, the year of the great

[1] Art. in *Saturday Review*, April 24, 1869.

British victory of Mons Badonicus, which stopped the progress of the invaders for a time. He was about thirty years old when he wrote, and, though those years had been a time of peace, he had learnt from men a few years older than himself what fearful sufferings had preceded them. He has described the people with their priests as taking refuge in their churches, and thereby only increasing the fury of their heathen enemies. The buildings are set on fire, and their occupants have to choose between death in the crackling flames within and death among the spears and swords outside. Wherever the heathen came, utter ruin and devastation, death or captivity, came with them.

Nor were Gildas's denunciations of his countrymen undeserved. During the fifty years of respite that were given them they fell into the vices which spring from luxury and intemperance, and provoked the anger of God to punish themselves, instead of propitiating His justice and themselves uniting in manly energy to resist the invaders. Gildas's sense of what was coming was really prophetic. He saw that the petty tyrants, without religion and without a sense of honour or of truth, would fall a prey before long to the cruel enemy. He looked to the sanctuary, and there he saw many priests living unworthily—'raro sacrificantes et nunquam puro corde inter altaria stantes.' Reverence for our Lord's Presence and devotion to the holy Mass had perished among many. Therefore Gildas knew that chastisement was at hand. Yet certainly all were not corrupt; Gildas himself was one of a company of saints. St. David was governing his Church in holy discipline. The penitential canons were being enforced, and while Britons assisted the Irish in holy legislation, many Irish saints came over to Britain, and have left their names to towns and churches and wells in Wales and Cornwall.

APPENDIX TO CHAPTER I.

ON THE GALLICAN LITURGY.

Although I do not think it proved that the Gallican Liturgy was ever in general use in any part of the British Isles, yet, as it must have been occasionally celebrated here, and was almost certainly used in Brittany, it will be useful, for the elucidation of the present and following chapters, to give a short outline of its principal features, that those who are not liturgical scholars, but are familiar with the Roman rite, may see wherein they differ.[1]

[1] Cardinal Bona first treated of the Gallican Liturgy (*Rerum Liturg.* i. 12). Then Cardinal Tommasi published three old Gallican masses. Mabillon re-

The mass began by the choir singing an antiphon, a verse of a psalm, and the Gloria Patri, &c. The preface or exhortation of the priest to worthy celebration followed. The deacon called for silence, and the celebrant sang Dominus vobiscum and a collect. Then was sung the 'Aius,' or the Trisagion (*Thrice-Holy*), in Greek and Latin, and the Benedictus. Lections from the prophets and apostles were next read, and on feast-days the acts of the martyr or confessor. The Hymn of the Three Youths (*Benedicite*, Dan. iii.) followed. Then the Trisagion while the deacon went to the pulpit to sing the Gospel, and again after the Gospel. The sermon was preached by the bishop, or a homily was read by another. Prayers were said over the penitents and catechumens, and they were put out of the church. Then silence was called, and the Body of Christ, reserved from the mass of the day before, was brought in from the sacristy in a vessel called a tower, and placed upon the altar. This particle was consumed by the celebrant at his communion, and another particle from the present mass placed in the tower for reservation. Of this ceremony St. Germain of Paris, who died in 576, wrote as follows: 'God commanded Moses to make silver trumpets which the Levites should blow when the victim was offered, as a sign by which the people might understand at what hour the oblation was made, and that all bowing down should adore the Lord, until the column of fire or the cloud should come and sanctify the sacrifice. Now, however, the Church with sweet harmony sings the wonders of Christ, not with trumpets, but with spiritual words, while the Body of Christ is being taken to the altar. The Lord's Body is carried in a tower, because His tomb was cut in the rock like a tower, and within it was the bed where rested the Lord's Body, whence also the King of glory rose triumphantly.'[1] A hymn or antiphon, called the Sonus, was sung during this procession and the offertory which followed. Afterwards the diptychs were read, which contained the names of the most illustrious dead of that Church and of those in special communion with it; then the celebrant sang the collect *post nomina*, while the people gave each other the kiss of peace, and then another collect, *post pacem*. After this followed the Preface and the Canon, which was much shorter than ours (the Gregorian). The consecration was made by the priest in a low voice. After a prayer, *post secreta*, the consecrated Host was broken and a particle placed in the Precious Blood, while the choir sang an anthem. Some more collects were sung and the 'Our Father,' in which the people joined. The blessing was given to the people before communion and with great solemnity, 'in order that the Mystery of benediction might be placed in a blest vessel,' says St. Germain. If the bishop was the celebrant, he sang three prayers for this blessing, varying with the feasts. A simple priest, in the bishop's absence, said 'Peace, faith, and charity, and the communication of the Body and Blood

published these, together with a fourth, and a full dissertation (in *Musæi Italici* tom. i.). Martene (*Anecdota*, tom. v.) published a short treatise of St. Germain of Paris on the ancient Gallic Liturgy. This, as well as Mabillon's treatise, have been reprinted by Migne (*Patrologia*, tom. lxxii).

[1] Migne, *Patrol.* tom. lxxii. col. 92.

of the Lord, be with you always.' The non-communicants then left, and while the communion was being made the choir sang a piece called Trecanus, perhaps the Apostle's Creed. A prayer was said, and with another collect the mass concluded.

There are many passages in the Gallican liturgies which have come down to us giving the clearest evidence of the belief in the Real Presence. St. Germain says : 'The breaking and mingling of our Lord's Body was evidently declared to the holy fathers by such great mysteries, that while the priest broke the oblation an angel of God was seen cutting with a knife the limbs of a beautiful Child, and collecting His Blood in a chalice, so that they might more truly repeat the word of our Lord that His Flesh was meat and His Blood drink.[1] While the priest breaks the Host the clergy suppliantly sing an antiphon, for when our Lord suffered death all the elements bore witness with a shudder.'

---

[1] The vision here referred to is related by Palladius, and will be given in a future chapter.

CHAPTER II.

SIDE LIGHTS FROM BRITTANY.

WHETHER Britain first received the Gospel from Gaul or more directly from Rome is uncertain. The latter supposition is more probable, since, according to the testimony of Tertullian, the faith had spread to the extreme north of Britain by the end of the second century, whereas it does not seem to have conquered the north of Gaul until the end of the third. But, whatever the case may have been, we know that the Christians of Britain entered into close relations with those of Gaul. British bishops passed to the continent to take part in important councils, and Gallic bishops came to the help of their insular brethren in their contest with heresy.

The British Church, towards the end of the fourth century, established a colony in Gaul—a Church in every respect similar to the mother Church of Britain, and keeping for centuries with that mother the most intimate relations. It is from the study of this Church, the Church of Little Britain, or Brittany, that I shall seek in this chapter some further illustrations of British doctrine and devotion as regards the Holy Eucharist.

Opposite to our modern counties of Cornwall, Devonshire, and Dorset, lies the great western promontory or peninsula of France still known as *La Bretagne*. In ancient times this was called Armorica, a word of Celtic origin indicating a country bordering on the ocean. The Armorican territory originally comprised the whole sea-coast, from Calais to the mouth of the Loire or perhaps even of the Garonne. It was afterwards restricted to the north-west corner of Gaul between the Seine and the Loire, and later still to the great peninsula west of our second degree of longitude. It is only with this peninsula that we are here concerned. A few words as to its political and social history will be necessary to introduce what has to be said of its religious character in the fifth and sixth centuries.

The similarity in language, appearance, character, social institutions, and religion between the inhabitants of Northern Gaul and Southern Britain was noticed by Cæsar and Tacitus; and these

Celtic features were much less modified in the Armorican peninsula by the four centuries of Roman domination that succeeded, than in the rest of Gaul. No great cities were there built, and the inhabitants continued to speak their native language, and retained to a great extent their old laws and customs, and clung to the Druidical form of worship.[1]

That the Britons from Great Britain founded a little independent kingdom in this corner of Gaul a century before Clovis and his Franks passed the Rhine, is now as uncontested a fact as the existence of the sun in the heavens, to use the language of M. de Courson, the learned historian of ancient Brittany; though Breton writers, under Henry III. and Louis XIV., had to expiate in the Bastile their temerity in maintaining such a proposition. The origin of this principality is somewhat obscure. According to William of Malmesbury, Constantine the Great rewarded many of his veteran British troops with settlements in Armorica. Malmesbury does not give his authority, but there is nothing unlikely in the statement. Further, it is certain that Maximus, the Roman governor of Britain, led an army, in great measure consisting of British youth, into Gaul in 384. According to Gildas these never returned; so the tradition that Maximus, after his victory over the emperor Gratian, settled these British troops in Armorica, is very probable. Moreover, Bede and Malmesbury state that the troops led from Britain by the tyrant Constantine in 410 took refuge with their fellow-countrymen in Brittany. This again is likely enough, for they certainly never returned to Britain, where Roman dominion was henceforth at an end.[2] But, without laying too much stress on these three military colonisations of Armorica, it is certain that, whether on the above or other occasions, there was a great and early emigration of Britons into Gaul, and that, after the invasion of Britain by the Saxons in the fifth century, this emigration continued to such an extent that the whole body of the inhabitants of Western Armorica looked on themselves as British or of British origin. There is no record of massacre or expulsion of the former inhabitants, nor of dissensions between them and the British settlers. We may therefore conclude that—except perhaps in the region of Vannes—the country was thinly populated, and that there was sufficient land for the new-comers.

As in race and language the two peoples were the same, they easily amalgamated. In one important matter, however, they differed. The

---

[1] The proofs may be seen in vol. i. of the *Histoire des Peuples Bretons*, by Aurélien de Courson.

[2] See Skene's *Celtic Scotland*, i. 108-113.

British colonists were Christians, the original inhabitants of Armorica were still heathen. St. Gatian, the first bishop of Tours, had indeed, towards the end of the third century, founded bishoprics at Rennes and at Nantes, in Upper Brittany, but the missionaries had not penetrated the great forest of Brékilien which separated this district from Lower Brittany, or at least they had failed to gain a victory over Druidism.

The British immigrants were more successful. Men who, to practise their religion freely, had abandoned Britain rather than yield to the heathen Saxons, soon made monastic and eremitical settlements in all the islands around Armorica as well as on the mainland. Their example and preaching converted the landed proprietors, who, at the departure of the Romans in 409, had become so many independent lords.[1] These lords or chiefs made grants of land for monastic institutions. From these institutions spread religion and civilisation.

Gibbon has truly said that the kingdom of France was a monarchy founded by bishops. It was indeed the Gallo-Roman bishops who built up the French nation. But in Brittany the Church and civil society were the works of monks and hermits, as their names attached to every town and village still attest.[2]

When the Roman troops were withdrawn from Britain in 409, the Britons expelled the civil governors. Their example was at once imitated by their countrymen in Armorica, and Conan Meriadec became their leader and assumed the title of king. For half a century repeated efforts were made by the Romans to subdue this rebellious district, but without success. The Britons co-operated with the Roman generals or emperors as allies, but kept their independence. British troops took part in the great battle of Chalons in 451, when Visigoths, Burgundians, and Franks joined with the Romans to resist the invasion of the Huns under Attila. After Clovis had expelled the Visigoths from Gaul, he turned his arms against the Britons in 510, but he did not invade their territory, and was satisfied

---

[1] They are called Tyerns, or chiefs, which was commonly translated into the Latin word *tyranni*, which of course has little relation to our word 'tyrants.'

[2] An old hymn runs thus :—

'Septem sanctos Britanniæ
Veneremur, et in ipsis dimiremur
Septiformem gratiam.'

These seven saints were St. Paul or Pol, St. Tugdual, St. Brieuc, St. Malo, St. Samson, St. Patern, St. Corentin. These were the apostles of Lower Brittany, called formerly Domnonée, where the Breton language prevailed, La Bretagne Bretonnante.

that their princes acknowledged his supremacy, and their ruler exchanged the title of king for that of count. Such nominal submission no more deprived them of their real independence than the acceptance by Clovis himself of the title of Roman consul proved his actual dependence on the Roman emperors. In the seventh century the title of king was reassumed by the British chief, but by the intercession of St. Eligius, in 635, with Judicael, king of the Britons, war was prevented on the condition that the British princes should acknowledge themselves tributaries of the Frankish king. It was necessary to say this much of the political and geographical position of the continental Britons, because it thus becomes apparent that they lived in the same kind of isolation in Gaul as their brethren in Great Britain after the Saxon invasion. If we study their history during the first two centuries of their establishment beyond the sea, we shall find that they had sufficient intercourse with the Gallic Church to prove their perfect identity of faith and practice, but too little to have been influenced by the ecclesiastical system of their neighbours, or to give any colour to the supposition that they had lost their primitive purity by a closer communion with Rome than was known to their insular countrymen.

The sources from which information may be derived as to the religious practices of these ancient Britons are principally two. In the first place we have Gallic Councils legislating for the British Church; and secondly we have contemporary Gallic writers who, from their special relations with Brittany, are unimpeachable witnesses. There are also many lives of the saints venerated in Brittany; but these, however important in themselves, I must here forego, in order to avoid discussion of questions of dates and authenticity.

I. To begin then with Councils. Armorica (or Brittany) belonged by ecclesiastical organisation to the province of Tours; and in the year 461, a British bishop took part in the first Provincial Council of Tours—'Mansuetus episcopus Britannorum interfui et subscripsi.'[1] The only early dedications of churches in Britain that have come down to us—at Canterbury in the south-east and at Whithern in the north-west—were to St. Martin of Tours. It is, therefore, very interesting to find the British Church of the emigration in filial communion with the see of which this great saint was the principal ornament. As no city is named as the see of Mansuetus, it is probable he was a regionary bishop.[2]

[1] Labbe, iv. 1053.
[2] On the subject of the various sees in Brittany, see Haddan and Stubbs, *Councils*, vol. ii. part i. pp. 72-80.

Nine bishops of the province of Tours met in 461 to celebrate the festival of St. Martin, and on the octave day the Council was opened under the presidency of St. Perpetuus of Tours. The fathers made thirteen canons for the enforcement of ecclesiastical discipline. As in those days it happened not unfrequently that married laymen who had won the esteem of the people in civil magistracies were suddenly elected to the office of bishop, while members of the inferior grades of the clergy, to whom marriage was lawful, were, on the promise of continence, admitted to holy orders, abuses easily crept in, such as we see alluded to by Gildas in Britain.

This council, therefore, reminds the clergy of the absolute necessity, for the ministers of the altar, not merely of conjugal chastity, but of virginal chastity or at least of continence. 'If continence,' says the first canon, 'is prescribed (by St. Paul) to the laity when they give themselves to prayer,[1] how much more to priests and Levites, who at all times must be ready with all purity to offer sacrifice, or to baptize in case of necessity.' However, for those who had been married previously to their ordination, and were unwilling to observe this discipline, the council in the second canon mitigated the rigour of the ancient councils[2] to this extent, that such clergymen were not deprived of communion; but they were neither admitted to the higher grades, nor allowed to minister in their respective functions. From the circumstance that Mansuetus the 'Bishop of the Britons' subscribes to these canons, it is evident that celibacy had been the discipline in Britain no less than in Gaul or in Italy; otherwise, most certainly, instead of consent there would have been remonstrance and indignant protest.[3] That celibacy was the discipline in Brittany is also proved from a fact mentioned by St.

---

[1] 1 Cor. vii. 5.

[2] 'Licet a patribus nostris . . . id fuerit constitutum . . . nos tamen huic districtioni moderationem adhibentes.' The decrees referred to are those of Popes Siricius and Innocent I.

[3] Mr. Haddan says (vol. i. p. 155) that 'marriage of the clergy appears to have stood in the British Church from the sixth century much as, at the same date, in the remainder of the Western Church; viz., as a common practice, but with a growing feeling against it. The only singularity of the Britons was that the practice held its ground among them more effectually than elsewhere in following centuries down to the twelfth.' I should rather say that the early practice and feeling were far more severe than the later. But the discussion of this question would be long and intricate, and does not belong to this place. The practice and feeling of the fifth century are clearly seen from the canon mentioned in the text, which was nevertheless a relaxation of the stricter discipline of the fathers. See also Concil. Arelat. (A.D. 452), can. 2, 3, 4, 43, 44, and Con. Arvern. (A.D. 533), can. 13.

Gregory of Tours in his 'History of the Franks.' A British prince named Macliarus had been tonsured and consecrated bishop. Seeing a chance of succeeding to the throne, 'he let his hair grow,' Gregory says, 'and took back his wife from whom on becoming a cleric he had separated; and for this the other British bishops excommunicated him.'[1] The remaining canons of this Council of Tours do not regard immediately the subject of this book.

Four years later a council of five bishops, presided over by St. Perpetuus, was held at Vannes, in Brittany.[2] By the 11th canon it appears that those who were called Levites in the Council of Tours, and to whom marriage was forbidden, were not only deacons but also sub-deacons. All these are forbidden to be present at marriage feasts and dances, both of which were then conducted with much indecency, and the reason given is 'that they may not defile their eyes and ears consecrated for the sacred mysteries.' The 15th canon prescribes that a uniform rite both at mass and at office—'ordo sacrorum et consuetudo psallendi'—is to be observed throughout the province of Tours.

In 511, Modestus, bishop of Vannes, took part in a synod assembled at Orleans by the desire of Clovis. The 26th canon[3] forbids anyone to leave the church when mass is being celebrated before its conclusion, and the benediction of the bishop (if he is present). By the 31st the bishop was directed to assist on Sundays in the offices of the church nearest to which he might then chance to be. Other decrees were made regulating the fast of Lent and the celebration of the great festivals. As regards Lent, some did not fast on the Saturdays, and to make up the forty days began their fast after Quinquagesima Sunday. This custom was forbidden.[4] A more serious question arose regarding the precise time of the year for the celebration of Easter, and a council was assembled at Orleans in 541, at which were representatives of almost all the ecclesiastical provinces of Gaul. It was then decided that the calculation of Victorius should be followed; that each year on the feast of the Epiphany the bishop should announce the time of Easter to his flock; and that, if any difficulty arose, the metropolitans should consult the Apostolic See (of Rome) and stand by its judgment. This was but a restatement of the principle that the British Church had proclaimed

---

[1] *Hist.* iv. 4. The event occurred in 560.
[2] Labbe, iv. 1055.   [3] *Ib.* 1408.
[4] So also in the 12th canon of the Council of Agde (A.D. 506): 'Omnes Ecclesiæ filii, exceptis diebus dominicis, in quadragesima, etiam die sabbatho jejunent.'

more than two centuries before in the Council of Arles, when, in the year 314, the bishops of York, London, and Caerleon had subscribed the canon which decreed that the Bishop of Rome should by letters promulgate the uniform observance of Easter throughout the world. Yet it appears that on one or two occasions the Britons of Armorica, like their insular brethren, preferred their own calculation to the calculation of Rome. Happily, however, we do not find this discrepancy to have led to any schism or serious dispute.

In 557, a council was held in Paris, at which were present several bishops honoured as saints, and amongst others two of British race, viz. St. Paternus of Avranches and St. Samson of Dol.[1] Though there is nothing in the decrees of this council bearing directly on the subject of the Holy Eucharist, yet the intercommunion and harmonious action of these British saints with others of Gallic or Frankish race, as St. Pretextatus of Rouen, St. Leontius of Bordeaux, St. Germain of Paris, St. Chaletric of Chartres, St. Felix of Nantes, prove that we may apply to Brittany the detailed information that we possess regarding the sacred rite as celebrated in other parts of Gaul or France.

In 567, St. Euphronius of Tours, St. Pretextatus of Rouen, St. Germain of Paris, St. Felix of Nantes, St. Chaletric of Chartres, St. Domnolus of Mans, with one or two more bishops, held another provincial synod at Tours. In this synod it was decreed that no one should consecrate a bishop in Armorica—whether Briton or Roman (*i.e.* Gallic) by race—without the consent of the metropolitan. It appears from this that political reasons were at work among the Britons making them seek independence of a see which was now in the territory of the Franks. No such claim had, however, as yet been publicly made, and the council legislated for the Britons as well as for the rest of the province of Tours. Some of the canons of this council deserve more than a passing mention.

In renewing the decree that the clergy married previous to ordination, who were very numerous in those days, should live in separation from their wives, the council laments the necessity of having to recur to this subject: 'Who could have believed that a man who consecrates the Body of the Lord would be so wickedly bold, had not such abuses arisen in these last days as a punishment for our sins?' This language was not directed against illicit

---

[1] Labbe, v. 381. St. Samson was a bishop and was abbot of Dol, but whether there was then a bishopric of Dol is disputed. The archbishops of Dol afterwards claimed metropolitan rights over Brittany in opposition to Tours, and the dispute, with appeals and counter-appeals to the Popes, lasted for centuries.

concubinage, nor against attempts to marry after ordination—for there was no question at all on such matters—but against a continuance in a lawful marriage after the voluntary separation promised in ordination. It assuredly proves not only the antiquity of the discipline, but the sublime estimate of the priesthood, and leaves no doubt as to the belief in the Real Presence of our Lord's Body, as the foundation of that estimate.[1]

In the 22nd canon the council legislates against the unworthy communions of some of the laity. A feast of the Chair of St. Peter was then kept on February 22.[2] This had been intended to replace the pagan festivals which used to be celebrated at that season by the Romans. But ancient customs are not easily abolished. The council complains that 'on returning home after mass on this feast some offered food to the manes of the dead, and, after receiving the Body of the Lord, partook of meat consecrated to the devil.' Should the priests know of any who were guilty of these or other gentile superstitions, they were to forbid them to approach the altar or even to enter the church.

There are two canons of this council which have been understood to refer to the Presence of our Lord, not in mass or communion only, but as reserved permanently in the churches. The discussion of these canons will enable me to bring together other facts and documents relating to this interesting subject.

The 3rd canon is in these words : 'Ut Corpus Christi in altari non imaginario ordine sed crucis titulo componatur.' What is to be understood by 'ordo imaginarius'? What by 'crucis titulus'? What by 'componatur'? Different interpretations have been given. That which has been adopted by some late writers is that the particles of the sacred Eucharist should be placed by the celebrant of mass on his corporal, not in fantastic arrangement, to make up certain figures, but only in the form of a cross.[3] The fathers did not think it right

---

[1] 'Si inventus fuerit presbyter cum sua presbytera . . . annum integrum excommunicatus habeatur. . . . Nullus potuit æstimare quod auderet ille, qui corpus Domini consecrat, talia perpetrare, nisi tempore novissimo pro peccatis nostris illa surrexerunt.' (Can. 19 ; Labbe, v. 858.) Anyone who reads the history of the Church of Gaul in the 5th and 6th centuries, the lives of Gallic saints or decrees of councils, will see that ordination after marriage was not a rare but a very common occurrence. A promise of continence was always required, and the consent of the wife as well as of the husband.

[2] This is now the feast of St. Peter's Chair at Antioch, and there is another of his Chair at Rome, January 18.

[3] This is Dr. Rock's interpretation, for which he claims originality ; yet I find it in Migne's *Dictionnaire des Conciles*, vol. ii. p. 1029, as adopted by others. It is made very probable by a curious treatise written in 845, and published by

that the mind of the celebrant should be occupied with such trifles, which might easily degenerate into superstition, especially in a time and country where heathenism was by no means entirely destroyed, and divination was often practised both by laymen and by clerics.

Others interpret the canon to refer, not to the mode of celebrating mass, but to the reservation of the consecrated species. They take 'componatur' to mean 'laid up' or 'reserved.' But among the advocates of this interpretation there is diversity. Some understand the fathers of the council to have prohibited the placing of the pyx with the reserved particles among the images ranged along the altar, and to have prescribed the laying of it under the cross which stood in the centre of the altar. To this interpretation Mabillon objected that images were not placed on altars till a much later period. In the sixth century they were placed in baptisteries, around the walls of churches, and, at least in the form of reliquaries, underneath or inside the altars. He therefore understands the decree to forbid the reservation of the Holy Eucharist *anywhere* among statues or pictures, as it had been the custom hitherto to place it in the baptistery, in the sacristy, in the ambreys, in the wall of the apse, or together with relics in the ark beneath the altar slab. A more uniform and honourable place was selected by this council (according to Mabillon), viz. under the canopy or ciborium which it was usual to construct over the high altar. This position is designated as *sub titulo crucis*, because the ciborium was crowned by a cross, or had one pendent beneath it, to which the receptacle of our Lord's Body—generally in the form of a tower or dove—could be attached.

In favour of this interpretation it may be said that King Charibert, by whose care the second Council of Tours was celebrated, had medals struck, on one side of which is represented what seems to be a two-handled chalice, such as those which are known to have been sometimes suspended under the altar-canopies. These chalices are surmounted by one or three small circles, which may be meant for the sacred particles or hosts.[1]

But, on the other hand, the interpretation of Mabillon seems to presuppose that a cross was invariably placed on or under the ciborium, which is by no means certain. St. Gregory of Tours makes

---

Mabillon at the end of his *Dissertation on the Use of Unleavened Bread*; for by the drawings in the ancient MS. (reproduced by Mabillon) it is seen that priests did arrange the particles in various groups according to the festivals.

[1] Engravings of these are given by Mabillon (copied from the *Treatise on French Coins* of Claude Bolerove), in his *Dissertatio de Azymo ac Fermentato* cap. 8.

mention of one as hanging over the altar,[1] and probably this was often the case, but ancient pictures and mosaics sometimes represent the ciboria without crosses. They were certainly not placed on the altars as a permanent part of the furniture until a much later period.

Independently, however, of the interpretation of the canon in question, it is known that the high altar was at least one place of reservation, though not the only one. In the fifth session of the Council of Constantinople, celebrated in 536, a complaint was read that had been made some years before by the clergy of Antioch against the heresiarch Severus. They allege, among other things,[2] 'that he did not spare the holy altars or the sacred vessels, breaking them up or melting them, that he had dared to seize on and appropriate the gold and silver doves, made to represent the Holy Ghost, and which were hung over the baptismal fonts and the altars, saying that the Holy Ghost must not be figured in the likeness of a dove.'

In the West we have a very clear testimony in a decree of St. Leo IV. A.D. 850: 'Let nothing be placed on the altar except reliquaries and relics, or perhaps the four Gospels, and the box with the Body of the Lord for the viaticum of the sick; let all other things be laid up in a clean place.'[3] This decree is of a later date than the period we are now considering; but it testifies to former ages. It is not an ordinance prescribing the reservation of the Eucharist on the altar as a new rite. It is a decree against innovations.

The box here mentioned by the Pope was often of very costly materials, and sculptured into various forms, among which a dove and a tower are the most frequently mentioned. We have just seen an example of gold doves hanging over the altar at Antioch; they are frequently mentioned in France and England. But to return to the immediate neighbourhood of Brittany. St. Felix became bishop of Nantes in 549. He built there a splendid cathedral, evidently on the model of the great churches in Rome and Constantinople.[4] Both the church itself and some of its ornaments have been described by Fortunatus, who saw the church a few years after its consecration. He wrote for the bishop an inscription to be engraved

---

[1] 'Pendebat super ipsum altare crux holychrysa eleganti opere facta.'—*Mirac.* ii. 43; Migne, *Patrol.* tom. lxxi.

[2] See Labbe, v. 159.

[3] 'Buxida cum corpore Domini ad viaticum infirmis.'

[4] Le Vicomte Edouard de Kersabiec has written a learned and interesting life of St. Felix in the *Bibliothèque Bretonne et Vendéenne*, in which he mentions (p. 34) some fragments in white marble lately discovered, which quite bear out the panegyric pronounced on this church by Fortunatus.

on a golden tabernacle or tower for the reservation of our Lord's Body. It is a testimony as much to the faith as to the ceremonial of the British Church in the sixth century.

> Quam bene juncta decent, sacrati ut corporis Agni
> Margaritum ingens aurea dona ferant;
> Cedant chrysolitis Salamonia vasa metallis,
> Ista placere magis ars facit atque fides.[1]

Which I venture to translate :

> The sacred Body of the Lamb Divine—
> A priceless pearl—demands a golden shrine,
> In wealth and art with Solomon's to vie,
> More rich, more fair to faith's discerning eye.

The 4th canon of the same council of Tours is a further testimony both to the respect shown to our Lord's Body, and the mode of showing it. It forbids laymen to stand among the clergy near the altar during mass or office. The part of the church towards the altar, separated from the rest by a balustrade (*cancellos*), must be open only to the choirs of clerics who chant the Psalms. Nevertheless 'the holy of holies' (*sancta sanctorum*) will be open to the laity, both men and women, for (private) prayer, and when they come to communion. By this canon we see that the part of the church near the high altar was considered specially sacred. It was there, then as now, that the clergy officiated.[2] The reasons for excluding the laity were not Pharisaic pride and the assumption of special sanctity on the part of the clergy, but motives of decency and order. Had the laity been admitted to the sanctuary, psalmody would have become almost impossible. Not the humble and devout, but the proud and worldly, would have coveted these 'first places in the synagogue,' and unseemly contests would have arisen, besides scandal to the poor and other inconveniences which may easily be imagined. The gates of the sanctuary were, however, thrown open at the time of communion. In this the Gallic Church differed from the Roman of this period; for among the Romans the priests and deacons went through the church giving communion to the laity. In Spain the laity received outside the sanctuary.[3]

Two or three stories from St. Gregory of Tours will illustrate this custom of the Gallic Church in the sixth century. Ursulfus, a poor man living near Tours, had been deprived of his sight while doing

---

[1] Fortunati *Carmina*, iii. 25 ; Migne, *Patrol.* tom. lxxxviii.

[2] St. Gregory of Tours speaks of the 'cancelli qui sub arcu habentur, ubi clericorum psallentium stare mos est.' (*Mirac.* i. 39.)

[3] Council of Braga, A.D. 563, cap. 13 ; Labbe, v. 841.

some work on Easter Sunday. Attributing this to God's anger, he spent two months serving in the church of St. Martin, in prayers and fasting, hoping by the intercession of this great saint to obtain pardon and relief. 'One Sunday, while assisting at mass (*dum esset ad pedes Domini et cum reliquo populo missarum solemnia spectaret*), he suddenly recovered his sight, so that he could go up to the altar to receive communion without a guide (*ad sanctum altare communicandi gratiâ*).[1] Once when St. Gregory himself was preaching during mass on the feast of St. Martin, a paralysed girl, who, day after day, for three months had been laid at the saint's tomb, was suddenly cured, and afterwards, in the presence of all the people, without assistance came forward to the holy altar to communicate.[2] On another occasion a cripple was placed at the tomb of St. Martin on the vigil of his feast, and the next day, 'when, at the end of mass, the people began to receive the sacred Body of the Redeemer, he was suddenly cured, and on his own feet without help went up to the blessed sanctuary (*beatum altarium*.)'[3]

I have quoted these passages not so much for the miracles related as for the illustration of the place and time of the people's communion; yet I will add one more story which, although it contains no such detail, refers to a Briton and shows the Britons in full religious communion and in identity of all pious practices with the Franks or Gallo-Romans who frequented the tomb of St. Martin. 'About this time,' St. Gregory says, 'there came a certain man from Brittany named Paterimanus, who was blind, deaf and dumb, and crippled in his hands. He was not born so, but a disease had so affected him, that his feet alone were of service to him. This man visited the basilica of our most powerful patron (St. Martin); he poured forth prayers, and his eyes were restored to sight, and his hands recovered their former vigour. Feeling himself cured by the power of the blessed bishop, he proclaimed the grace he had received aloud to the people. In testimony of this miracle he received gifts from many, but he spent them in redeeming captives from the yoke of slavery.'[4]

The second purpose for which the sanctuary gates were to remain open, according to the canon I am illustrating, was that the faithful might at any time go before the altar for prayer. Among the collections of sacred anecdotes made by St. Gregory of Tours, nothing is

---

[1] *De Miraculis S. Martini*, ii. 13.   [2] *Ib.* 14.
[3] *Ib.* 47. This word is generally used by Gregory for the sanctuary around the altar.
[4] *Ib.* iv. 45.

more common than the expression 'prostrate before the holy altar.'[1] And before the altar was certainly the favourite place for very earnest prayer; the faithful knew that the Blessed Sacrament was reserved there—'the priceless pearl of the sacred Body of the Lamb,'[2] the Body of Christ ever united to His Soul and Divinity, and not a dead body such as the relics of the saints.

If then the Christians of those times are frequently mentioned as praying before the altars in order to invoke the saints whose relics there reposed, we are compelled to admit that when they are represented as praying to God before the high altar where the Blessed Sacrament was reserved, it was to our Lord Himself, believed to be present in the heavenly mysteries, that this devotion and adoration were offered.

II. What has hitherto been said directly concerns the British Church in Gaul, being drawn from the decrees of councils in which British bishops sat and legislated, or which were held in their own metropolitan church of Tours. I will now add a few details which I have gathered from the writings of two bishops of the sixth century, St. Gregory of Tours[3] and St. Fortunatus,[4] the only contemporary

---

[1] 'Ingressus basilicam prostratus coram sancto altari preces cum lachrymis fudit ad Dominum.' (*De Miraculis S. Martini*, iv. 7.) 'Prostrata coram sancto altari lumen recepit.' (*Ib.* iv. 12.) 'Duas deinceps noctes vigilant. Deinde prostrati coram sancto altari, dum supplicant,' &c. (*Ib.* i. 14.) 'Ad sanctum se altare duci deposcit solo prostrata,' &c. (*Ib.* ii. 37.)

[2] See *ante*, p. 37.

[3] Florence Gregory, more commonly called by his last name of Gregory, was archbishop of Tours, and died in 594, two years before his namesake St. Gregory the Great sent missionaries to the Anglo-Saxons. By his *History of the Franks*, he has done for the French Church what Venerable Bede has done for the English. He has left also several books of miracles. It must be confessed that Gregory does not show the discretion or critical skill of Bede. Yet the truth of the alleged miracles in no way affects my subject, since the picture of manners and ecclesiastical practices, with which alone I am concerned, was of course drawn from what was familiar to him and his readers and every day before their eyes.

[4] Venantius Honorius Clementianus Fortunatus, more commonly known as St. Fortunatus, was an Italian by birth, but, out of devotion to St. Martin, made a pilgrimage to Gaul, and there spent the greater part of his life. He was made bishop of Poitiers, and died in 609. He has left an immense number of poems filled with details of civil and ecclesiastical life. There can be no rashness in applying these details to the British Church, since Fortunatus spent much of his time in Nantes with St. Felix, bishop of that city. Nantes then was not indeed in Brittany, but on the borders of that province. We learn, however, from one of his poems that Fortunatus actually resided among the Britons. Writing to his friend Druco, a deacon in Paris, he says:—

'Sequana te retinet, nos unda Britannica cingit' (iii. 33).

authors, I believe, who throw any direct light on the Church of Brittany at that time. From these two authors a very complete and minute picture might be drawn of the Church of Gaul in the sixth century, which would contain many beautiful contrasts with that dreary picture of perfidy, lust, and bloodshed which is painted by political historians of that period. It is with regret that I confine myself to the altar and its immediate surroundings. I begin with the place of sacrifice.

Since Gaul had early received the faith and at the same time enjoyed all the advanced civilisation of the Roman Empire, the whole country had become by degrees covered with churches, from the temple or basilica of the great cities, constructed of stone and splendidly decorated, to the oratory of wood built for the labourers and shepherds of the country districts. Most of the basilicas were erected over the tombs of martyrs who had died for Christ in days of persecution, or of holy bishops, hermits, and virgins who had flourished at a later period. Churches were set apart for the service of God by a solemn dedication. They were adorned with representations of our Lord, of the Blessed Virgin, and of the saints, sometimes sculptured, but more frequently painted. St. Gregory describes a picture of our Lord which was pierced by a Jew and then taken down and carried off from the church. This was, of course, a detached board hanging on the wall.[1] Representations of our Divine Redeemer hanging on the cross were as yet very rare. Mixed up as Christians were with Jews and heathens, our Lord's triumphs were a more congenial subject than His sufferings, humiliation, and nakedness, as appears clearly from what is told of a picture of the crucifixion at Narbonne. Our Lord had been represented by the artist with only a linen girdle round the loins. The people came eagerly to gaze on this unwonted spectacle. But a priest thought that he was warned in sleep by our Lord Himself, who said, 'You are all dressed, yet you gaze on Me thus naked.' The bishop ordered a veil, which was rarely lifted, to be hung over the picture.[2] It was a picture of our Lord, but probably not a crucifix, which Fortunatus describes as being venerated with tears of devotion by a holy nun :—

> Vidit forte meum quoties in imagine vultum,
> Oscula dans labiis lumine fudit aquas.[3]

Fortunatus is the author of the beautiful hymns adopted by the Church, *Vexilla Regis prodeunt*, and *Pange lingua gloriosi lauream certaminis*, which he wrote for St. Radegund when she received a portion of the cross from the East.

[1] *Mirac.* i. 22. He calls this tabula *imago* and *icon*.
[2] *Ib.* 23.   [3] Fortun. viii. 4.

The Blessed Virgin was sometimes represented as seated in a chair carrying the Holy Infant in her arms.[1] From several passages of Gregory and Fortunatus it would seem that walls and ceilings were covered with paintings. Gregory himself enlarged and decorated the church of St. Martin.

> Lucidius fabricam picturæ pompa peromat
> Ductaque quæ fucis vivere membra putes.[2]

In every church the principal object was the altar. Besides the high altar there were several smaller ones in side oratories and crypts.[3] Altars were often constructed over the tombs of saints; but in no case was it lawful to consecrate an altar without relics.[4] Some were placed immediately under the altar-stone, others in a movable ark or shrine beneath the altar.[5] St. Gregory speaks of the great crowd of priests and Levites in white vestments going in procession, chanting psalms and prayers, carrying crosses and tapers, and bearing relics, which were placed inside the altars.[6] The altars themselves, if they were of stone, were blessed and consecrated with holy oil.[7]

Before the pictures, altars, and relics, lamps were kept burning day and night. St. Gregory speaks on one occasion of a girl, on another of a devout old woman, whose office it was to trim the lamps before nightfall.[8] Fortunatus, by a poetical figure, speaks of the daylight having been shut up perpetually in a church dedicated to our Lady, from the number of lamps kept burning at night, just as the Divine Light had been enclosed in her womb:—

> Ecce beata sacræ fundasti templa Mariæ,
>   Nox ubi victa fugit semper habendo diem;
> Lumine plena micans imitata est aula Mariam
>   Illa utero lucem clausit, et ista diem.[9]

The people brought wax tapers which they lighted themselves and

---

[1] In the story of the Jewish child cast into a furnace by his father for receiving the Holy Eucharist, but saved from death by our Lady, Evagrius (*Historia*, iv. 35) merely says that, according to the child's own account, 'a woman with a purple dress' saved him from the fire. St. Gregory of Tours makes him say it was the woman whom he had seen represented in the Christian Church, seated in a chair with a child in her arms. (*Mirac.* i. 10.) The event happened in 552.

[2] Fortun. x. 6. Not only paintings, but figures sculptured in stone or wood, were so used. See Fortun. i. 13.

[3] S. Greg. *Mirac.* i. 33. [4] *Ib.* 31.
[5] Fortun. x. 6. [6] *De Glor. Conf.* cap. 20.
[7] Con. Epaon. (A.D. 517), can. 26. [8] S. Greg. *Mirac.* i. 15, 33.
[9] Fortun. i. 15, on a church built at Bordeaux by St. Leontius.

left burning before the shrines.¹ One woman, by a curious devotion very common in England in the thirteenth century, had a candle made to her own height, and prayed during the whole night before the tomb, holding it in her hand.² Another burnt incense before a shrine in her private devotion.³ A holy priest, named Severinus, used to hang garlands of lilies on the walls of his church;⁴ and St. Radegund is praised by Fortunatus, who was her secretary, because at Easter-time, when men decorated their thresholds with flowers, and women decked themselves with roses, she and the holy abbess St. Agnes used to make garlands to adorn Christ's altars :—

> Tempore vernali Dominus quo Tartara vicit,
>   Surgit perfectis lætior herba comis ;
> Inde viri postes et pulpita floribus ornant,
>   Hinc mulier roseo complet odore sinum.
> At vos non vobis sed Christo fertis odores,
>   Has quoque primitias ad pia templa datis ;
> Texistis variis altaria festa coronis,
>   Pingitur ut filiis floribus ara novis.⁵

Happily for the people, great respect was generally paid to consecrated churches. By the desire of Clovis, a council of Orleans in 511 granted to them the right of sanctuary; and it was the custom to take an oath of more than usual solemnity by coming before the altar and stretching out the hand over it.⁶ We have seen that this practice was common in Great Britain in the time of Gildas. It was also forbidden to wear arms when assisting at mass or vespers.⁷

The churches were ever open during the day for private devotion, and the public psalmody or office was performed at fixed hours during both day and night. The night office is called by St. Gregory sometimes vigils, at others matins.⁸ A bell was rung even at night to announce this service to the people, who were accustomed to assist at it, at least before great solemnities. We have an anecdote of two little boys who rose of their own accord to go to the church at the sound of the bell.⁹

---

¹ 'Dum cereos frequenter devotio Christiana deferret.'—S. Greg. *Mirac.* i. 57.
² *Ib.* i. 16.   ³ *De Mirac. S. Martini*, ii. 38.
⁴ *De Glor. Conf.* cap. 50.   ⁵ Fortun. viii. 9.
⁶ St. Gregory relates many instances of punishment of perjurers. See *Mirac.* i. 20, 33, 53, 57, ii. 19.
⁷ Con. Aurel. III. can. 29.
⁸ 'Vigilias celebrat et missarum agit festa pro liberatione populi sui.' (*Mirac.* i. 13.) 'Post peracta matutinorum solemnia media nocte.' (*De Vita et Morte Sept. Dorm.*)
⁹ *De Mirac. S. Martini*, lib. i. 28, 33, ii. 45.

The holy sacrifice of the Mass was, however, then as now, the principal act of worship and devotion, and the councils prescribed that the people should assist at this, at least on Sundays and festivals.[1] Many of the cures related by St. Gregory are said to have happened during mass, so that in this way also devotion to the saints led up to the supreme worship of God. To God alone was mass ever offered, but this could be done with a special commemoration of a saint. In a document found in the library belonging to St. Martin's church and published by St. Gregory, St. Martin is supposed to have appeared to seven saints at Tours and to have said to them: 'Call the abbot, that in honour of the Holy Trinity he may celebrate mass, making commemoration of me and of the saints whose relics are in this altar which I consecrated, and let him place a host for each one of you (*singulas hostias pro vobis singulis*), and when they shall have been consecrated, each one of you must communicate. And after the communion, and you have received the viaticum of the Body and Blood of Jesus Christ, and when the mass is finished, you shall prostrate yourselves in prayer and so die.'[2]

In another place St. Gregory relates that Queen Ultrogotha came to the tomb of St. Martin and with long fasts, many prayers and vigils, gave large alms to the church, as well as alms to the poor, and asked that masses should be celebrated in honour of the Blessed Confessor.[3]

Mass was offered for special intentions, as by a priest during a siege for the deliverance of his people.[4] It was offered not only for the living, but also for the relief of the faithful departed. A woman, having lost her husband, came during a whole year to the church of our Lady in which he was buried, having a daily mass said for the repose of his soul.[5]

St. Sigismund, king of the Burgundians, had not been free from some very grievous sins during his life. He, however, not only had made public acknowledgment of his great sorrow, but also had suffered a cruel death. The people, therefore, prayed for the repose

---

[1] *Vide antea*, p. 32. The Third Council of Orleans (A.D. 538) orders that on the great festivals the mass must not begin later than the third hour (*i.e.* about nine or ten), in order that all may meet again for vespers. (Can. 14; Labbe, v. 299.)

[2] This document is quite apocryphal; yet it is not so much a forgery as a pious romance, in which the famous story of the seven sleepers in the cave of Ephesus is repeated with modifications and transferred to Tours. It is of course no less authentic as an illustration of ecclesiastical customs than a true history.

[3] *De Mirac. S. Mart.* i. 12.

[4] *Mir.* i. 13.   [5] *De Glor. Conf.* 65.

of his soul, and were disposed to honour him as a saint. For both purposes they offered the holy sacrifice; 'in ejus honore missas devote celebrant, ejusque pro requie Deo offerunt oblationem.'[1]

The celebration of mass admitted, of course, of various degrees of solemnity. Fortunatus describes a magnificent ceremonial in which St. Germain of Paris and his clergy took part. There is a band of music, fifes and flutes, trumpets and drums, and vocal music in which both sexes have their share:

> Hinc puer exiguis attemperat organa cannis,
> Inde senex largam ructat ab ore tubam.
> Cymbalicæ voces calamis miscentur acutis,
> Disparibusque tropis fistula dulce sonat.
> Tympana rauca senum puerilis tibia mulcet,
> Atque hominum reparant verba canora lyram.
> Leniter ille trahit modulos, rapit alacer ille,
> Sexus et ætatis sic variatur opus.[2]

From a story of St. Gregory's it is clear that the whole congregation of men and women joined in some parts of the liturgy. 'A woman had lost the use of speech, but one Sunday, during mass, when the Lord's prayer was said, her mouth was opened, and she began to say the holy prayer with the rest.'[3] Very different from a mass celebrated by a bishop surrounded by his clergy in the basilica of a great city must have been a mass offered by a single priest, served only by his clerk, in a country church.

Severinus—the same priest who hung garlands of lilies on the walls of his church—had built two small churches twenty miles apart, and used to serve both, remaining three days at each. On the Sunday, having said mass in one, he used to mount his horse and ride as fast as possible that whole distance to say a second mass at the other. This interesting detail we should not have known, had he not one day in riding struck his head against the branch of a tree and uttered an exclamation of anger, which gives Gregory occasion to mention how it happened.[4] On great feast days, however, it was forbidden to say mass in the country churches without special leave of the bishop, which would be granted when they were far from the episcopal city.[5] Otherwise the country people flocked into the towns and there kept the vigil and the feast. Indeed, on great feasts there

---

[1] *Mir.* i. 75.   [2] *Carm.* ii. 10.   [3] *De Mirac. S. Martini*, ii. 30.
[4] *De Glor. Conf.* 106.
[5] In the private oratories of noblemen mass might not be celebrated at Easter, Christmas, Epiphany, Ascension, St. John Baptist, and other great solemnities. Both the nobles and their chaplains had to seek the episcopal city on those days. See Council of Auvergne (A.D. 533), can. 15; Coun. of Agde (A.D. 506), can. 63.

was a fair held outside the church, so great was the confluence of people.

The priest who celebrated mass, as well as the people who communicated, were bound to be fasting. This was an inexorable rule. So that St. Gregory mentions it as a singular and terrible crime that a certain priest, wearied by the long vigils of Christmas Eve, went into his house and drank after midnight (*post galli cantum in ipsa nocte*). Next day he dared to say mass, and was punished by a fit of epilepsy. This disease never after left him. 'The wretch did not fear, steeped in wine as he was, to do what a man who is fasting cannot do without dread.'[1]

Another chastisement for sacrilege brings us directly into Brittany. A British count suffered from pains in the feet. He could get no relief by medicine. At length some evil counsellors said to him: 'If you get from the church a ministerial vessel which is laid on the altar, and wash your feet in it, you will be cured.' 'The fools,' St. Gregory says, 'did not understand that vessels consecrated to God must not be used for profane service. The count quickly sent to the church, and obtained from the sacristy a silver paten of the most holy altar, and washed his feet in it. At once the pain increased, and he became totally unable to walk.'[2] This story shows that patens were then both large and deep, being made to hold the oblations of the people. Mabillon has proved that besides the ordinary bread and wine offered by the faithful, which was given away in alms, communicants were generally expected to bring carefully prepared hosts, made of unleavened bread, thin and round (somewhat larger than what are now used). They were baked between irons and stamped with a cross or with some sacred letters.[3]

Of communion something has been already said. It was usually received under both species. Of its frequency it would be rash to draw conclusions from isolated examples. Fortunatus, in a prose treatise on the 'Pater Noster,' writes: 'Our asking for our daily bread seems to teach us that we should receive reverently every day, if it is possible, the communion of His Body; since, as He is our Life, we cut ourselves off from the nutriment of our life, if we are slow to approach the Eucharist.' However, a pious sentiment like this proves nothing as to popular customs, and was probably intended only for the clergy, or for monks and nuns.

That communions had become very rare among some of the laity is sufficiently evident from what we know of the manner of life and prevalent disorders of society amidst continual wars and irruptions

---

[1] *Mirac.* i. 87.   [2] *Ib.* 85.   [3] *Dissertatio de Pane Euch.* cap. 8.

of barbarians. The Council of Agde (A.D. 506) was obliged to decree that 'seculars who should not communicate at Christmas, Easter, and Pentecost, should not be considered Catholics.'[1]

Yet it is with surprise that I have read the assertion of a recent learned writer[2] that non-communicants were not allowed to assist at mass. As this is an assertion reflecting on the discipline of the Catholic Church for many centuries throughout the whole world, I may be allowed to examine its foundation. The following proofs are alleged:—1. 'The care taken (in early ages) to exclude from the mysteries all who were not fit to participate.' 2. A canon of the Council of Antioch, A.D. 344. 3. The repetition of the same canon in 560 by Martin of Braga for the instruction of the Church of Spain. 4. A decree quoted by Gratian as of Pope Anacletus. Of this it is said: 'The decree is of course spurious; but it is interesting as indicating what was the law of the Roman Church at the time of the Isidorian forgeries (about 830), and also probably that the practice of non-communicating attendance had then begun—for the decree would not have been put forth without a purpose.'

I will take these proofs in the inverse order. Can this writer be serious in supposing that in Rome in the ninth century none went to mass but communicants, or that the toleration of the presence of non-communicants was an abuse just then creeping in? But as I shall have to treat of this period later on, under the history of the Anglo-Saxon Church, I will not here bring forward proofs that all were bound to hear mass on Sundays at least, and that most certainly all did not communicate. As to the motive of the author of the Isidorian decrees in forging the decree of Pope Telesphorus, it would seem to me to have been done in order to give an air of antiquity to his forgery by introducing a bit of discipline notoriously contrary to that of his own day, yet which would startle no one, since it was then as now a commonplace of ecclesiastical orators and writers to lament the decay of primitive fervour in the matter of communion.

The second and third proofs I may take together. Martin of Braga was a Greek, and made a translation into Latin of many Greek canons. It by no means follows, because he republished these, that they were all in force in his day. Nothing was more common than to set down ancient and partly obsolete canons in such collections,

---

[1] Can. 18; Labbe, iv. 1386. Agde (Agatha) was a city in an island in the Gulf of Lyons.

[2] *Dictionary of Christian Antiquities*, by Dr. W. Smith and S. Cheetham, art. 'Communion.' This article is by the editor, the Rev. Samuel Cheetham, Professor of Theology at King's College, London.

partly as a reproach to the degenerate discipline of the days of the collector, and partly as a norma or standard to which discipline should be reformed, so far as circumstances would permit. The Council of Trent declares its wish that all assistants at mass should be fit to communicate, but it is far from wishing to exclude non-communicants from assisting at mass. This course was taken by Martin in the second Council of Braga in 583, as we read in its Acts.[1] And in the collection published by Martin himself, not as a legislator, but as a canonist and teacher, there are certainly some things which he did not intend to be carried out in Spain. The decree quoted by him from the Council of Antioch need not however be considered as having become obsolete in the sixth century, nor does it prohibit the presence of non-communicants at mass. The words are these, as given by Martin: 'If anyone enters the church of God, and does not listen to the sacred scriptures, and in wantonness (*pro luxuria sua*) turns away from the communion of the sacrament, and in assisting at the mysteries (*in observandis mysteriis*) rejects the appointed rule of discipline, such a one we decree should be cast out of the Catholic Church, till he do penance, that he may merit indulgence and communion.' The original decree of the Council of Antioch seems rather directed against those who took no part in the liturgy, 'not communicating in prayer with the people.' But in both cases the denunciation is levelled, not against devout assistants though non-communicants, but against idle gazers, men who would take no part in the service.

Gallic councils of this century forbid the assistants at mass to leave before the end. They are to await the benediction of the bishop if he is present.[2] This merely proves that some who were present, being non-communicants, were impatient at waiting so long in the church. They are commanded to wait to the end, but they are nowhere commanded to communicate.

There are two sermons[3] of St. Cæsarius, bishop of Arles in the first part of the sixth century, in which he complains that many of the people went out before the sermon, some went home, many stayed outside talking and laughing and quarrelling. He tells them that prayers and reading of the Scripture are not mass; that such devotions they might have performed at home, but that only in the church are the oblations made, and the Body and Blood of Christ consecrated.

---

[1] Labbe, v. 839.

[2] Council of Agde (A.D. 506), can. 47; Council of Orleans (A.D. 511), can. 26; third of Orleans (A.D. 538), can. 29.

[3] These may be found also in the Appendix to St. Augustine (ed. Bened.), *Serm.* 281, 282. The 280th is on the same subject, but of a later date.

'Consecrationem vero corporis vel sanguinis Domini non alibi, nisi in domo Dei, audire vel videre poteritis.' He begs them to wait till the mysteries are ended, the Pater Noster said, and the blessing given. Now the bishop's blessing in the Gallican Church was given before the communion of the people. It is evident then that St. Cæsarius allowed the non-communicants to go before the people's communion, which rather followed mass then than made a part of it, but he entreats and commands all of every class to be present until then. His exhortation is that they see and hear the consecration.

But one story from Gregory of Tours will suffice to put this matter beyond all controversy. I have already quoted his account of a lady who had a daily mass said for a whole year for the repose of the soul of her husband. She was present each day, but St. Gregory says she did not go every day to communion, though she made her offering daily of a measure of the very best wine of the country. A wicked subdeacon, noticing this, used to set the good wine aside for his own use and substitute some poor wine in its place. The lady had a dream in which the soul of her husband complained of the sour wine given him to drink in the other world. The lady was astonished, but the mystery was explained when the next day she went to communion, and her teeth 'were nearly knocked out' by the sourness of the wine.[1] People may think as they like about the lady's dream or her faith in purgatory; but no one can reasonably deny that when St. Gregory wrote this (in the sixth century in Gaul) even very devout ladies did not go to daily communion, though they assisted at daily mass, and there was no irregularity in their hearing mass when they did not intend to communicate.

As to the earlier ages it is no doubt true that the heathen, the excommunicated, and catechumens were not allowed to be present at the more solemn part of the mass; but it is yet to be proved that in any age of the Church mere non-communicants were forbidden to hear mass, or that the precept of hearing mass involved the precept of receiving communion. St. Theodore, in the seventh century, declared that from his personal acquaintance with Greek and Latin customs, 'among Greeks, both lay and cleric communicate every

---

[1] 'In die qua Domino oblationem pro ejus anima delibasset semper sextarium Gazeti vini præbuit in sacrificium basilicæ sanctæ . . . muliere non semper ad communicandi gratiam accedente. . . . Ad matutinum secundum consuetudinem surrexit . . . quibus expletis, celebratisque missis, accedit ad poculum salutare, quæ tam fervens acetum hausit ex calice, ut putaret sibi dentes excuti.'—*De Glor. Conf.* cap. 65.

Sunday, and those who abstain from communion three Sundays are excommunicated. Among Latins, those communicate who will, but those who do not are not excommunicated.'[1] To discuss this matter further would take me beyond my limits. But it was necessary to correct so strange a statement as that I have been discussing, since, if it were admitted, the estimate we should have to make of the British Church would be entirely changed. For we know that those who came to mass were commanded to remain until the end. We know also that many never approached holy communion, except upon the greatest festivals. If these then were forbiddden to hear mass when they did not receive communion, it would follow that they only entered the church three or four times a year, and neither worshipped God publicly nor were instructed to do so, since mass was the great act of worship, and the sermon was always preached during mass.

Nor would the picture be less fearful were we to suppose that the great majority went to mass every Sunday and also received holy communion. For, knowing what we do of the disorders then prevalent, such a supposition would lead us to the conclusion that sacrilegious communions were multiplied beyond measure.

Happily we need accept neither of these views. The Church has ever known how to adapt her discipline to circumstances which she could not control. The conversion of the Roman Empire, and still more the sudden conversion of whole nations of barbarians, rendered utterly impossible the continuance of a discipline framed for the catacombs, or for days when persecution allowed few but the fervent to profess the Christian faith and take part in public worship. The Church could not require very frequent communion from men whose lives unfitted them for so close a union with the Holy One, however much she might lament their unworthiness and urge them to amendment. But to exclude them from assistance at the Holy Sacrifice would have been to deprive them of the most powerful means of obtaining the grace of contrition, and would practically have cast them out of the range of all her influences and driven them into recklessness and corruption. The course she really took was to exclude from the Holy Sacrifice those whom she would punish severely for a time, that their very exclusion might teach them respect for holy things. Those also who by noise and levity showed contempt for the sacred rite she would rebuke and admonish, and, if necessary, punish by removal. But she never drove from her temples those who like the publican, though standing far off from the altar as

[1] Haddan and Stubbs, iii. 186.

judging themselves unworthy to draw near, yet struck their breasts and said, 'God be merciful to me a sinner.' Such as these she would urge to make their repentance speedy and sincere, and to crown it by a worthy communion. The oftener such communions were made the more she would rejoice.

Let me sum up in a few words the results of this chapter. We have seen a system of worship in principle and general outline, as well as in most of its details, identical with the worship of the Catholic Church at the present day, but in all respects utterly opposed to Protestant belief and practice. This system of worship not only prevailed throughout Italy and Roman Gaul, but pervaded that corner of Gaul cut off by geographical position from the rest and socially and politically almost isolated. Religion alone in those fearful days of disruption and warfare bound men and nations together. But we have clearly seen that religion did indeed form an effectual link when all other ties were broken. Brittany was united with the Gallo-Roman and Frankish Church on the one side, and with Wales and Cornwall and Ireland on the other. The Gallic Church recognised the heroic virtue of British saints, whether born in Brittany, as St. Melanius, or coming over from the sister Church in Great Britain, as St. Gildas, St. Samson, St. Patern, St. Paul de Léon, St. Malo (or Maclorius), St. Maglorius. And these great teachers and apostles, bred up in insular traditions, did not find their continental brethren alien to themselves in any point of faith or worship.

The testimony of Fortunatus to certain pious practices has been frequently quoted in this chapter. It is curious how often he alludes to Great Britain as being one in faith with the rest of the world. I will content myself, however, with one passage. St. Radegund, the queen who became a nun, sent messengers to beg, through the intervention of the Emperor Justin the Younger and the Empress Sophia, a portion of the true cross. On their return Fortunatus wrote a complimentary poem. In this he congratulates the emperor on his orthodoxy, and that, instead of following the schismatical and heretical example of his predecessors and setting himself up, like Zeno and Justinian, as a teacher, he received the faith as it was proclaimed and enforced by the chair of St. Peter in Rome.

> Quam merito Romæ Romanoque imperat orbi,
> Qui sequitur quod ait dogma cathedra Petri!

'Let us return thanks to God,' exclaims the poet, 'for the new emperor holds whatever the Council of Chalcedon decreed. Gaul, O emperor, sings this to your honour. Galicia in the far west has heard it. Cantabria tells it to Vasconia.¹ The story of your faith runs to the farthest nations, and beyond the ocean the land of Britain applauds.'

> Currit ad extremas fidei pia fabula gentes,
> Et trans oceanum terra Britanna favet.²

Thus, then, twenty years before St. Augustine landed on the shores of Kent as a legate of Pope St. Gregory, the Catholic Britons thrilled with joy on hearing that far-off Constantinople no longer resisted the authority and teaching of the successor of St. Peter in Rome.

¹ These were provinces in the north of Spain, whence Arianism had been banished, and which were now Catholic.

² *Ad Justinum et Sophiam Liber.* Let me add that Fortunatus recognises British saints:

> 'Egregium Albanum fœcunda Britannia profert'

(*Carm.* viii. 4), and tells how Britain, with the rest of the Catholic world, recognises Gallic saints.

Of St. Hilary:

> 'Thrax, Italus, Scytha, Persa, Indus, Geta, Daca, Britannus
> Hujus in eloquio spem bibit, arma capit'

(vi. 7, and viii. 1). Of St. Martin (x. 7):

> 'Qui velut alta pharus lumen prætendit ad Indos,
> Quem Hispanus, Maurus, Persa, Britannus amat.'

Lastly, around the throne of our Lady in heaven, he says (viii. 5):

> 'Æthiopes, Thraces, Arabes, Dacus, Indus, Alanus,
> Aurora et vesper, Persa, Britannus adest.'

CHAPTER III.

THE PICTS AND SCOTS.

'THIS island at present,' wrote Venerable Bede in the eighth century, 'in the languages of five nations examines and confesses one and the same science of the sublimest truth and true sublimity, viz. in those of the Angles, Britons, Scots and Picts, and Latins, and this last, by the study of the Scriptures, has become common to all the rest.'[1] This testimony to the absolute unity in faith of the different churches throughout Great Britain is confirmed by every document which has come down to us from whatever source. What we have already seen in the records of the early British Church, we find again in the early legislation of the Irish Church, in the Penitential of St. Columbanus, who carried the Irish discipline over the continent of Europe, and in the life of his namesake, St. Columba, who propagated the faith which he brought from Ireland throughout the north of Britain.

We shall confine our attention in the present chapter to North Britain, called in ancient times Alban, or Albania, or Caledonia.

Bede distinguishes between the languages of the Britons, Scots, and Picts, and even attributes to these nations different origins; but it is now known that their languages were closely akin. Some have, indeed, hesitated about the Picts, thinking them to have been a branch of the Saxon family. But this is a groundless conjecture. 'The Pictish,' says Dr. Reeves, 'was undoubtedly a Celtic dialect, but more nearly allied to the British or Welsh than the Gaelic.'[2] This explains why St. Columba, as his biographer informs us, during his missionary journeys spoke to the Picts by an interpreter; though

---

[1] *History*, i. 1. Lappenberg says: 'The name, Picti, is by no means an appellation bestowed on enemies with painted bodies, but is a Roman corruption of Pight.'—*England under the Anglo-Saxons*, p. 55 (Eng. Tr.)

[2] Reeves's *Adamnan*, p. 63. For the Saxon origin of the Picts, see Dissertation in Tytler's *History of Scotland*. Robertson considers the Picts to have been not Cymrian, but Gaelic Celts, akin to the Irish Picts. (*Scotland under Early Kings*, ii. 380.) Lappenberg is of the same opinion, but Mr. Skene agrees with Dr Reeves.

on other occasions, speaking to kings or Druids, who were more cultivated, he did not need one. The Picts occupied, during the early Christian centuries, the greater part of modern Scotland. The northern Picts were those who dwelt beyond the Grampians; the southerns dwelt north of the Forth, but south of the mountains, *i.e.* in Kincardine, Forfar, Perth, and Fife. The British kingdom of Strathclyde, reaching to modern Glasgow, and the Anglian kingdom of Northumbria, reaching to Edinburgh, divided between them the southern part of modern Scotland, with ever varying boundary. The Scots were Irish who had settled in Argyle and the Isles, then called Dalraida. Scotia was the name of the home of the Scots, or the north of Ireland. It was not till the tenth century that it was given to a part of Caledonia, and three or four centuries more passed before it was extended to the whole of modern Scotland. But as Roman was a name given to one of Roman origin, whether born in Italy or in some Roman colony or possession, so Scot was the name of an Irishman, whether in Ireland or in the Irish settlement in North Britain. It has been much disputed at what period the Scots passed over into Caledonia. According to Mr. Skene they were already Christians.[1] But in any case it was from Ireland that they derived their Christianity. When first we meet with them in British history, it is as enemies and invaders of the country, leagued with the barbarous Picts. But in the period with which we are now concerned they have a very different character. They invade the territories of Britons, Picts, and Saxons alike, but not to carry devastation. They leave their own country to enlarge the bounds of the Holy Church, and to enrich others with the worship and love of Jesus Christ.

After this rough outline of the geography and history of the tribes which occupied the north of Britain when Christianity made its first appearance among them, I will now gather together the few documents which throw any light on the history of the Blessed Sacrament in those regions, beginning with the Britons of Strathclyde and the Southern Picts, and then proceeding to the Scots and Northern Picts.

I. THE NORTH-BRITONS AND SOUTHERN PICTS.

The Romans had early carried their arms as far north as the Perth Grampians, but their hold upon any part of the island north of the Firths was very precarious. According to Tertullian, Chris-

---

[1] *Chronicles of the Picts and Scots*, edited by W. Skene, Esq., for the Lords Commissioner of the Treasury, Introd. p. cli. Mr. Skene, by this introduction, and by his later work on *Celtic Scotland*, has quite superseded all earlier works.

tian missionaries had even gone in advance of the Roman arms; but whatever settlements they may have made must have been overthrown in the descents of Picts and Attacots both before and after the Roman departure in 408. It was during these troubled times that St. Ninian, a Briton of Strathclyde, went to study in Rome. He is said to have been of royal family, and was probably a Christian from his childhood. Being made a bishop, he returned to his native country. He was not contented with reviving faith and devotion in the already Christian region between the Solway and the Clyde, but preached successfully among the Southern Picts. He built his episcopal church of stone in Wigton or Galloway, and it was commonly called the White House (Candida Casa) or Whithern. His church still existed in the time of Venerable Bede, three centuries later, and was renowned as the resting-place of the body of St. Ninian and many other saints.[1] Near this church was the great British monastery of Rosnat, which was famous during the sixth century, and was much frequented by Irish scholars.[2] At the beginning of the eighth century, that part of Britain fell under the power of the Angles of Northumbria, who were Christians, and they substituted an English episcopate for the British one in the see of Whithern. Of this line Pechthelm was the first (A.D. 730), and he had several successors. The monastery of Rosnat was repeopled with English monks, though there is no reason to think that any Britons were expelled. For in the absence of detail about this British and Pictish church, the one fact which stands out conspicuously is the perfect unity of faith and worship between the Christianity planted by St. Ninian and that of the English Church of Bede and Alcuin. It is, therefore, from our intimate knowledge of this latter that we must supply what is unrecorded of the former. Bede, as we have seen, distinctly affirms that Britons, Scots, Picts, and English professed 'one and the same science of the truth.' He calls Ninian 'a most reverend and most holy bishop, who had been regularly instructed at Rome in the faith and mysteries of the truth.' A most interesting letter of Alcuin also reveals to us that there were traditions regarding St. Ninian, at the end of the eighth century, in Ninian's own church and among the English. He wrote to the monks serving the church of Candida Casa as follows: 'I beg you to remember my name and to intercede for me in the church of our most holy father, Bishop Ninian, renowned for his many virtues, as I have lately learnt from my faithful

---

[1] *Hist. Eccl.* iii. 4: 'Ubi ipse etiam corpore una cum plurimis sanctis requiescit.'

[2] See Haddan and Stubbs, i. 120.

pupils, the scholastics of the Church of York, in the poem they have sent me; and from the account they give me of his miracles I recognise his sanctity. Therefore I beg of you most earnestly that you recommend me to his intercession, that, by the pious prayers of your saintly father and your own, I may secure, through Christ's mercy, pardon of my sins, and come at last to the company of the saints who overcame the toils of the world, and have attained the crown of eternal glory. I have sent to the body of your holy father Ninian a veil of silk, that I may be remembered there and have a share in your and his intercession.'[1]

As the poem written by Alcuin's scholars has not come down to us, we cannot judge of the nature of the traditions on which he relied for his belief in the sanctity of St. Ninian. But it must be remembered that if the Britons had long been driven from the south of England when Offa built the monastery of St. Alban's in 793, this was not the case at Whithern. The Britons were still there mingled with the Angles. There had been a succession of bishops and learned monks, and in all probability many documents now lost were then in existence.

In any case the religion planted by St. Ninian was in existence and familiarly known to Bede and Alcuin and the monks at Whithern, and they saw that it was the same as their own. Yet it was certainly not derived from the Anglo-Saxons. Until the middle of the seventh century, there had been little or no communication between the churches, and the two nations had been continually at war. Those, therefore, who would maintain that the religion of Bede and Alcuin, which taught the invocation of the saints and the adoration of the Blessed Sacrament, was a corruption of primitive Christianity, must also maintain that the British Church of Strathclyde was also gradually corrupted, not by Roman or Saxon influence, but by a spontaneous process, and that these two independent corruptions resulted in a complete identity of doctrine and of practice. That this identity really existed in the seventh and eighth centuries is proved, not only by the testimonies already given, but also by other incidental evidence. In the year 680, St. Wilfrid, being in Rome, distinctly testified to the orthodoxy of the Britons, Scots, and Picts. In a synod of 125 bishops, presided over by Pope Agatho, in preparation

---

[1] Only a part of this letter was printed by Usher (*De primord. Eccl. Brit.*), and from him by Froben, i. 297. Usher omitted the latter part where Alcuin asks the intercession of St. Ninian. The whole letter has been printed from the MS. in the British Museum by Messrs. Haddan and Stubbs, vol. ii. p. 8, and by Sir T. D. Hardy, in his *Descriptive Catalogue*, vol. i. part i. p. 45.

for the Council of Constantinople of the same year, against the Monothelites, St. Wilfrid, as his friend and biographer Eddi relates, made a profession of the Catholic faith, not merely in his own name, but 'for the whole north of Britain and of Ireland, and for the islands, inhabited by Angles, Britons, Scots, and Picts.'[1] St. Wilfrid's own episcopal authority extended over many of the Southern Picts, and Eddi tells us that he ordained priests and deacons in every place for their better instruction;[2] but nothing is ever said of their being taught new doctrine or reconciled with the Church.

Again, when the Northumbrian king, Oswy, 'subdued the greater part of the Picts to the dominion of the English,' as Bede relates,[3] an English bishop, named Trumwine, was appointed to rule over them, and fixed his see at Ebbercurnig (Abercorn) on the Firth of Forth. In 685 the Picts threw off the English yoke, and Trumwine withdrew with his monks.[4] Bede, who relates these political changes, says nothing of change of faith or worship.

Lastly, in 721, Sedulius, a British bishop of Strathclyde, of Scottish race, and Fergustus, a Pict by birth and a bishop of the Scots, subscribed in Rome to a council held under Gregory II.[5]

These few facts sufficiently prove that the Pictish Church was orthodox in all points, as orthodoxy was understood by all the churches in communion with the Holy See.[6]

Notwithstanding all this, there will be some who will find it difficult to believe that such invocation of the saints as Alcuin practised towards St. Ninian in the eighth century had been practised by St. Ninian himself in the fourth. Nor will the fact that St. Ninian dedicated his church to St. Martin on hearing of that holy bishop's death in 397 weigh with them as it should, accustomed as they are to the modern meaningless dedication of Protestant churches.

Fortunately we have a document which throws a vivid light on the meaning of that dedication. St. Ninian is said to have visited St. Martin at Tours when returning from Rome. St. Martin had another friend, named Victricius, who was archbishop of Rouen.

Victricius is thought by many to have been a Briton. After serving in the Roman army like St. Martin, like St. Martin he became a Christian, and subsequently a most zealous bishop, and is himself venerated as a saint. Now in the year 396, when St. Ninian was

---

[1] Eddi, ch. 51. See also Haddan and Stubbs, iii. 140, and ii. 5.
[2] Eddi, ch. 21.   [3] Bede, iii. 24.   [4] Ib. 26.
[5] Labbe, vi. 1458; Haddan and Stubbs, ii. 7.
[6] The one point of dissension—the Easter cycle—will be discussed in Chapter VII.

building his cathedral and considering to whom it should be dedicated, St. Victricius was invited over into Britain to help the British bishops to quell a disturbance arising from Arianism or Pelagianism or some other cause. On his return to Rouen he took part in a solemn translation of the relics of the Apostles and many other martyrs and virgins to his cathedral. He embodied the discourse he made on that occasion in a treatise 'De Laude Sanctorum.' I take from it the following passage, in which he addresses the saints whose relics he was honouring: 'O holy and venerable martyrs, you will pardon, I trust, my delay in coming to this solemnity, since it was in obedience to your precepts that I passed over into Britain, and was there detained. My fellow priests and bishops invited me to help in promoting peace. Since I was your soldier, I could not refuse a work like this. I knew that by the merit of your power you are everywhere, for heavenly glory is shut out from no spot of earth. Forgive me then if I have only tardily come to meet you at the fortieth mile of your journey. I was serving you in Britain, and was detained beyond the ocean by your honour. I attribute all (my success) to your majesty, since you are the body of Christ, and the spirit that dwells in you is divine. . . . I have then been executing in Britain the command of the Lord Jesus and yours, not indeed as I should have done, but as far as I could. In those who were wise I infused the love of peace, I taught it to the ignorant, and forced it on the reluctant—according to the Apostle being urgent in season and out of season—and by teaching and persuasion I found an entrance into their minds. But when either the place or my own weakness became a cause of temptation to me, I implored the help of your spirit. I did what those do in a great storm who navigate the sea: they implore the mercy of the Divine Majesty, rather than the skill of the pilot. For that Jesus who lives in you is able to calm the waves and restrain the winds, while human art is of no avail.'[1]

If, then, it was by the help and invocation of the saints that one friend of St. Martin was contending against heresy in the south of Britain, there is nothing more probable than that another friend of the same saint should be fighting against paganism with the same arms at the same time in the north of Britain. Thus St. Ninian's dedication of his church to St. Martin implied his urgent desire to secure for his people the constant intercession of that great saint, whose reputation had been so great even during his lifetime. And

---

[1] The treatise of St. Victricius is to be found in Gallandus viii., and in Migne's *Patrologia*, tom. xx. Victricius was a friend of St. Paulinus of Nola, who has related his virtues in some of his letters.

there was therefore nothing contrary to St. Ninian's own practice in Alcuin's imploring the prayers of a saint.

Of the Southern Picts, after the death of St. Ninian, we have no detailed history. St. Palladius, St. Serf, and St. Ternan are commemorated as their apostles in the fifth century; but there is one word of evil omen occurring in a letter of St. Patrick which hints at a falling back into paganism, or at least into pagan immorality. In his letter to Coroticus, written before 493, St. Patrick complains that that British prince had made a hostile incursion into Ireland, and had cruelly slain many Christian neophytes, while still wearing the white robes of their baptism, and had sold Christian women and children into slavery to the still heathen Scots or Irish and (these are his words) 'to the most wicked, detestable, and apostate Picts.'[1]

This expression does not of course imply that the whole nation had apostatised from Christ, but merely that there were some amongst them who by their cruelty, lust, and contempt of baptism, acted as apostates. About a hundred years after the date of St. Patrick's letter, St. Kentigern or Mungo, a Briton from South Wales, laboured with great success in rekindling the faith of the Britons of Strathclyde and reforming their life. He fixed his episcopal see at Glasgow, and his diocese is thought to have extended from the Clyde to the Mersey, and from the Western to the Eastern sea. It has been already mentioned how in the next century the Angles of Northumbria encroached on this district and established an English bishopric at Whithern in 730. During the ninth, tenth, and eleventh centuries, our information about the history of the south of Scotland, whether civil or religious, is exceedingly scanty, and there is nothing whatever to record regarding the Blessed Sacrament, its celebration or reception. It will be easier for the reader to picture in his own imagination the details which are unwritten, when he has perused what I am about to relate of the first celebrations of holy mass in the western islands and in the north.

II. THE NORTHERN PICTS.

Happily the life of St. Columba, the apostle of the Northern Picts—or at least an account of his graces, visions, miracles, and

---

[1] The whole letter is very touching, and breathes throughout in its boldness and tenderness the spirit of St. Paul. Some have thought that Coroticus was Ceredig, prince of Ceredigian or Cardigan. Mr. Skene considers that he was prince of Strathclyde. If St. Patrick was also a native of Strathclyde, his words in this letter are easily explained: 'To you who do such things I cannot give the title of *fellow-citizens of mine or of the holy Romans*, but rather of fellow-citizens of demons.'

prophecies—has been written by one who, if not an eye-witness, yet conversed with eye-witnesses, and, as being of the saint's own family and his successor as abbot of Iona, had every means of acquiring authentic information. This writer is St. Adamnan, and from his biography [1] I shall quote, word for word, those passages which allude to the Holy Eucharist. Before doing this I will relate just so much of the external facts of St. Columba's life as may be necessary to render the quotations intelligible.

He was born in Ireland in 520, of a royal family, and early embraced the ecclesiastical state, and became abbot and founder of several monasteries. At the age of forty-two he left Ireland and settled among his fellow-countrymen, the Scots of Dalraida (Argyle and the Isles), the king of which was his relative. His principal monastery was in the little island of Hy. But his zeal was not confined within the cloister, nor to the Christian nation of the Scots. As St. Mungo was at that very time evangelising the Britons of Strathclyde and the Southern Picts, St. Columba turned his steps to the north and north-east—Aberdeen, Banff, Inverness, Ross, and the Orkneys; and the faith was spread throughout the whole of this region, either by the saint himself or his disciples. He died in Hy—called after him Hycolumcille—at the age of seventy-seven in the year 597, the very year that St. Augustine landed in Kent for the conversion of the Anglo-Saxons.

Adamnan relates an incident of the youth of St. Columba which gives us a picture of the worship in which he was brought up. 'When the venerable man was still a youth in Ireland, with St. Findbar the bishop, learning the wisdom of the Holy Scriptures, on a certain solemnity there happened to be no wine for the sacrificial mystery. When the youth noticed the ministers of the altar lamenting to one another about the want, he took a cruet and went to the fountain, as if to draw water as a deacon for the ministry of the Holy Eucharist; for at that time he ministered in deacon's orders. Having drawn the water he blessed it, calling on the name of our Lord Jesus Christ, who in Cana of Galilee changed water into wine; and by His Divine operation the inferior nature of water was now changed into the better nature of wine by the hands of this venerable man. Returning then from the fountain and entering the church, he placed the vessel containing this liquor near the altar, and said to the ministers: "You have now wine which the Lord Jesus has sent you for the perform-

---

[1] Adamnan's *Life of St. Columba* has been often published. The edition prepared for the Irish Archæological and Celtic Society in 1857, by the Rev. Dr. Reeves, is a marvel of erudition well applied. The life of St. Columba is perhaps the most perfect part of Montalembert's *Monks of the West*.

ance of His mysteries."[1] This miracle is supposed to have taken place about the year 542, when the saint was about twenty years old.

In this one anecdote a whole system of religious faith, discipline, and worship is revealed. We have the various orders of bishop, deacon, and other ministers, and of course that of priesthood is implied There is an altar; there is a celebration to be performed (*ad peragenda mysteria*) which is called not merely 'the ministry of the Eucharist,' but 'the sacrificial mystery' (*sacrificale mysterium*). Though nothing is here said of the Real Presence or of Transubstantiation, yet every candid Protestant will admit that men who could believe in the change of water into wine, not only by Jesus Christ himself, but by His servants at the invocation of His name, would not have much difficulty in believing the change of the substance of bread and wine into our Lord's Flesh and Blood. Now no species of miracle is of more frequent occurrence in the lives of Welsh and Irish saints. Dr. Reeves refers to examples in the lives of St. David, St. Fursa, St. Aidus, St. Finnian, St. Kieran, St. Mochoemhog, St. Gildas, St. Sizinus, St. Hymelinus, St. Kiaran. I am not bringing these miracles as a proof of the Real Presence, nor even of the faith of the Welsh and Irish in the Blessed Sacrament. But they may fairly be adduced as evidence of a state of mind, either arising from an habitual sense of God's omnipotence engendered by their belief in transubstantiation, or at least as a proof that such a doctrine could have met with little resistance on account of its intrinsic difficulties, if for other reasons it was proposed for acceptance.[2]

That it was thus proposed cannot be absolutely proved from the life of St. Columba, which does not treat of matters of doctrine, but it is expressed sufficiently and presupposed throughout, as I will show presently. I may, however, here give one document belonging to the Irish Church to show in what doctrines and practices St. Columba had been brought up. One of his contemporaries was another Columba, more commonly called Columbanus, who left Ireland and passed to the continent and became the founder of Anegray, Luxeuil, and Fontenay in Burgundy. The Regula Cœnobialis of St. Columbanus has been preserved. The fifteenth chapter is as follows:[3]

---

[1] *Life of Adamnan*, lib. i. cap. 1.

[2] In the Gotho-Gallic Missal of the 6th century, published by Mabillon, when the changing of water into wine is commemorated on the feast of the Epiphany, the people are taught to pray that 'He, who then changed water into wine, may now change the wine of the oblations into His own Blood.' (*De Liturg. Gal.* lib. i. cap. 1.)

[3] *Opera S. Columbani*, in Bib. Max. Lugd. tom. xii. p. 8.

'Whoever loses the Sacrifice and knows not where it is, let him do penance for a year.' For negligence in renewing the sacred Host various penances are imposed according to the degree of neglect. The sacred species, if entirely corrupted, is to be burnt, and the ashes are to be placed in the earth near the altar. If anyone fell into the water when carrying the Blessed Sacrament, as from a boat, bridge, or horse, he was to drink the water from the chrismal or pyx and to consume the particle. If this was a mere accident, one day's penance was prescribed ; but if in wading through a river he had not taken care sufficient (*non consideravit de periculo sacrificii*), then he was to do forty days' penance.

These prescriptions were made for the clergy travelling as missionaries on foot or on horseback in the rugged passes of the Vosges, and they reveal to us what were the precautions adopted, or the penance to be done for neglect of caution, by the monks who travelled in the wilds of Drumalban, or who rowed their osier boats in the lochs and rivers of the highlands. They carried with them the Holy Eucharist, already consecrated, and (as it seems evident from the above rules) only under the species of bread. They were to take more precautions with regard to it than of their own limbs and life. To have been upset in a boat in passing down the rapids, or for a horse to have slipped with his rider into the river in passing over the trunks of trees laid across a stream, was not considered penance enough for the sufferer. He is not blamed for not taking sufficient care of his own neck, but ' because he did not consider the danger to which he exposed the consecrated Host,' the Sacrificium or Victim confided to his custody. Even if he is conscious of no fault, he must perform a rigid fast for one day as an act of humiliation and reparation. But if he has been foolhardy or too attentive to himself, when in danger, to think of taking his pyx from his bosom and lifting it high above his head as he waded through the torrent, a fast of a whole Lent must expiate the sin ; while to have lost the sacred Particle will involve a year's penance and a year's absence from the altar.

All this, without asserting our Lord's Presence in so many express words, most unmistakably implies it. And it is also evident that that Presence was independent of the act of communion or the faith of the recipient. It was the result of consecration.[1] On this point there is abundant evidence in the life of St. Columba, as the

---

[1] Canons, just like those of St. Columbanus, were made by the British Church (see *supra*, ch. i.), by St. Bede and by St. Theodore, and by St. Egbert, for the Anglo-Saxons (see *infra*, ch. xvii.).

following passages will show. Adamnan relates that when the saint was at Trevet (near Skreen, in County Meath) he went to a small monastery on a Sunday. 'There he heard a certain priest consecrating the sacred mysteries of the Eucharist, whom the brethren had chosen to perform the solemnities of mass (*ad missarum peragenda solemnia*) because they esteemed him a very religious man.' St. Columba during the mass exclaimed : 'Clean and unclean are now mixed together : that is, the clean mysteries of the sacred oblation are ministered by an impure man.' The priest, says Adamnan, confessed his sin thus supernaturally detected, as well as his hypocrisy.[1]

The same truth of the effect of consecration is taught in a more pleasing anecdote, also related by Adamnan. 'A stranger from Munster, named Cronan, came to the saint. Out of humility he concealed himself as much as he could, that no one should know that he was a bishop. But the fact could not be hidden from the saint. For on a Sunday, having been invited by Columba to consecrate as usual the Body of Christ (*Christi corpus ex more conficere*) he calls the saint to him, in order that together as two presbyters (*presbyteri*) they might break the Lord's Bread. The saint therefore going up to the altar, suddenly looking into his face, thus addresses him : 'May Christ bless thee, brother; do you alone break this bread after the episcopal rite. Now we know that you are a bishop. Why have you endeavoured till now to conceal yourself, that the veneration which is due to you might not be paid by us?'[2]

To understand this anecdote it must be remembered that St. Columba was not himself a bishop. Bishops sometimes lived in monastic obedience subject to an abbot, but their episcopal character was never lost sight of, and at the altar they were treated with special reverence. In some countries at that time a bishop used to consecrate the Blessed Sacrament surrounded by his clergy, who were co-celebrants, as now in the mass of ordination. But this discipline was never adopted in the British, Irish, or English Church; at least I am not aware of an instance of it. But it appears to have been the custom in Ireland, that when a simple priest celebrated mass in the presence of his abbot, he should invite him at the time of communion to come and break from the consecrated Host a particle with which to communicate himself. If a bishop celebrated, this honour was not paid to the abbot. The bishop consecrated and communicated alone, and then administered communion to the rest.

Adamnan relates a miracle which shows St. Columba not as an assistant or communicant merely, but as a celebrant. Some abbots

[1] Lib. i. cap. 40.   [2] Lib. i. cap. 44.

visit him, 'and request that in their presence he will celebrate the sacred mysteries of the Eucharist. On the Sunday, according to custom, he enters the church after the reading of the Gospel; then, while the solemnities of mass are being celebrated, St. Brendan sees a fiery globe burning as it were from the head of St. Columba, as he stood before the altar and consecrated the sacred oblation, and this continued to burn till the sacred mysteries were ended.'[1]

It does not appear from this life whether there was more than one altar in the church; but as we know that when the Irish monks, who had been brought up under the Columbian discipline, carried the faith into Northumbria in the next century, they constructed many altars in the churches, it is probable that this may have been the case in St. Columba's own monastic churches. We know at least from one event recorded that there were side chapels or oratories.[2]

Nor can we gather from this life what was the frequency of celebration; though it would seem to have been confined to Sundays and festivals, unless when some special reason, as the news of a death, caused an extraordinary mass to be offered. 'One day,' says Adamnan, 'St. Columba bade a monk quickly prepare for the celebration of the Eucharist; for to-day, he added, is the birthday of holy Brendan. The monk replied: "Why do you order the solemnities of the mass to be prepared to-day, since no news has come from Ireland of the death of that holy man?" St. Columba answered that he had seen his soul during the past night carried by the angels to heaven.'[3] At another time, 'just as the monks were putting on their shoes to go out to their daily tasks, Columba ordered a holiday to be kept, and he said that he would say mass. Now, when in the chanting of the service that prayer was being sung in which the name of St. Martin is commemorated, suddenly the saint said to the singers who were coming to the mention of that name: "To-day you must sing for Bishop Colman."'[4]

This is the only reference to the nature of the liturgy, and it is somewhat obscure. Dr. Reeves seeks to explain it by means of the Gallican liturgy. He shows that in a list of names recited from the diptychs after the offertory in the Church of Arles, St. Martin's was the last mentioned. He thinks therefore that the Irish Church had borrowed this liturgy, and that at this point of the mass St. Columba bade the chanters add the name of St. Colman. But the recent

---

[1] Lib. iii. cap. 17. It is an incidental proof of identity of faith that an exactly similar fact is recorded of St. Martin in Gaul.
[2] Lib. iii. 19. [3] Lib. iii. 11. [4] Lib. iii. 12.

publication of the 'Canon of the Stowe Missal,'[1] an Irish MS. belonging to the seventh century, suggests to me another interpretation. In the Memento for the Dead, after the commemoration of patriarchs, prophets, apostles, martyrs, and hermits, comes the list of holy bishops. Among these the very first was St. Martin. After him came Gregory, Maximus, Felix, Patrick, &c. This was in all probability the liturgy used in St. Columba's churches; and if so, Adamnan's allusion would mean that when the singers or reciters came to the order of bishops (*i.e.* came to St. Martin's name), Columba informed them of the death of his friend, and of his rank and name, and that he should be therefore commemorated at the end of the series.[2]

[1] In 1879 the Rev. F. E. Warren published the MS. Irish Missal, belonging to Corpus Christi College, Oxford, of the 12th century. In the beginning of the book he gives in parallel columns the canon of the Sarum Missal, that of the Stowe Missal (7th and 9th centuries), the Drummond M. of the 11th, and the Corpus M. of the 12th, and the Rosslyn M. of the 14th. The last four are the only ancient Irish Missals in existence. None of them differs much from the Sarum except the Stowe Missal.

[2] On the same supposition that the Stowe Missal represents, with few variations, the use of St. Columba's monks, I may here add a few details from this most precious and unique relic. In the prayer beginning *Te igitur*, at the commencement of the canon, there was a commemoration of the Roman Pontiff— 'una cum N. papa nostro, episcopo sedis apostolicæ.' Before the *Communicantes* there is another evidence of Catholic communion. The celebrant prays 'pro domino papa, episcopo, et omnibus episcopis et presbyteris et omni ecclesiastico ordine.' The next words, ' pro imperio Romano et omnibus regibus Christianis,' were probably added in the ninth century, when the Roman Empire had been re-established in Charlemagne. In the same prayer the dead are thus mentioned :—' pro fratribus quos de caliginosis mundi hujus tenebris Dominus arcessere dignatus est, uti eos in æterna summæ lucis quiete pietas divina suscipiat.'

In the *Communicantes* (which is in the 7th century hand), the same apostles and martyrs are commemorated as in the Sarum and in the ancient and modern Roman uses. The first words, however, differ, and our Lady and St. Peter are specially honoured :—'Communicantes et memoriam venerantes imprimis gloriosæ virginis Mariæ, genetricis Dei et Domini nostri Jesu Christi. M. tuorum Petri, sed et beatorum apostolorum ac martyrum Pauli, Andreæ, Jacobi.'

After the words, 'Per Quem . . . sæcula sæculorum, Amen,' instead of going on at once to the Pater Noster, this Missal has, in the 7th century hand, the following words :—' Let Thy mercy, O Lord, be upon us, as we have hoped in Thee. They knew the Lord, Alleluia, in the breaking of bread, Alleluia. The bread which we break is the Body of our Lord Jesus Christ, Alleluia. The chalice which we bless, Alleluia, is the blood of our Lord Jesus Christ, Alleluia, for the remission of our sins, Alleluia.' Then, in the 9th century hand, it continues :— ' We believe, O Lord, we believe, that in this breaking of (Thy) Body and pouring out of (Thy) Blood we are redeemed, and we trust by the reception of this sacrament to be protected, that what here we possess in hope, we may enjoy for ever in heaven in its true fruits. Through our Lord Jesus Christ.'

RITUAL AND LITURGY.

There is one fragment of Scoto-Celtic liturgy, of which the date is considered to be not much later than A.D. 800. It is a visitation of the sick, or at least that part of it which belongs to Holy Communion. It begins with the following prayer said by the priest:

'Creator of all natures and Father of all in heaven and on earth, receive from Thy throne in the inaccessible light the pious prayers of Thy trembling people, and though Thou art surrounded by the unceasing praises of the cherubim and seraphim, yet deign to listen to the supplications of our unwavering hope.' The Pater Noster was then said or chanted, and the priest continued: 'Deliver us, O Lord, from evil, O Lord Jesus Christ, keep us always in every good work. O God, Fount and Author of all good, empty our souls of their vices, and fill them with virtue, through Thee, O Jesus Christ, who' &c.

Rubric in Gaelic: 'Hisund dubar sacorfaice dan,' *i.e.* 'Here give the sacrifice to him.' The words of administration were these: 'Corpus cum sanguine Domini nostri Jesu Christi sanitas sit tibi in vitam perpetuam et salutem,' *i.e.* 'The Body with the Blood of our Lord Jesus Christ be health to thee to life eternal and to salvation.' The priest then recited with the clerks:—

'V. Fed on the Body and Blood of Christ, let us ever say to Thee O Lord, Alleluia, Alleluia.

'R. He hath filled the empty soul and satisfied the hungry soul with good things, Alleluia, Alleluia.

'V. Let them sacrifice the sacrifice of praise, and exult for ever, Alleluia, Alleluia.

'R. I will receive the chalice of salvation, and call upon the name of the Lord, Alleluia, Alleluia.

'V. Fed on the Body &c. (as above).

'V. Laudate Dominum &c. (Ps. cxvi.).

'R. Quoniam &c.

'V. Gloria Patri &c.

'R. Fed on the Body &c.

'V. Sicut erat &c.

'R. Fed on the Body &c.

'V. Sacrifice the sacrifice of justice and hope in the Lord.

'Let us pray.

'We give thanks to Thee, O Lord, through whom we have celebrated these holy mysteries, and of Thee we ask the gifts of holiness; have mercy on us, O Lord Saviour of the world, who reignest for ever and ever.'[1]

---

[1] From the *Book of Deer* (a town in Aberdeenshire). An account is given of this MS. in *Home and Foreign Review*, Oct. 1862, p. 484. The fragment is

With regard to this remnant of Celtic Scotland it must be remarked that it is in Latin, but in Gaelic characters. The whole document is written on a leaf in the middle of a copy of the Gospels, or rather of fragments of them. As the Gospels were frequently carried to the sick to be read to them or over them, it was found convenient to have the form for the administration of communion in the same book. But as the mass is not given, it is evident that the Blessed Sacrament was not consecrated in the sick man's chamber. It is very improbable that it was carried from the church in both species, and the form 'Corpus cum Sanguine,' *i.e.* the Body with the Blood, testifies to the faith that both are present under one species.[1]

In this volume are some very rude and quaint illuminations, or rather rough pen-and-ink sketches which are only slightly coloured with pale yellow and brownish-red paint. Some of the figures are apparently intended to represent priests; and as Professor Paley, the writer of the article in the 'Home and Foreign Review,' remarks, 'considerable interest must attach to a representation, however rude, of the vestments worn by a Gaelic priest in the ninth century. Two figures in the frontispiece seem to be attired in a chasuble, the ends of which are folded over the knees in a circular form. Over the breast is a rather large square apparel, or *rationale*, suspended from the neck by three strings. The collar, or rather the neck folds, seem to be most ample, and quite unlike any fashion that we are acquainted with in the middle ages.'

To return now to the life of St. Columba, I will mention one other point in which it confirms what has been already said of the unity of faith and devotion in the Celtic, Saxon, and continental Churches—viz. in the Invocation of Saints. Adamnan relates [2] how he

---

also printed by Haddan and Stubbs, vol. ii. part i. p. 275, and by Dr. Forbes, *Arbuthnot Missal*, preface, p. xiv.

[1] Two very similar liturgical forms exist in the books of Moling and of Dimma, both Irish. They also are copies of the Gospels, with the form for communion copied into them. In the book of Moling, the form of administering is the same as in that of the book of Deer, except that the word *salutem* is omitted. The book of Dimma has 'Corpus et Sanguis Domini nostri Jesu Christi, Filii Dei vivi, conservat animam tuam in vitam perpetuam.' Dr. Forbes tries to show that these three documents belong to the Ephesine family of liturgies through a Gallican origin, and not to the Roman. He notices that in the Gelasian, Ambrosian, and Gregorian liturgies, the Pater Noster is always introduced with the words 'Præceptis salutaribus,' &c., whereas here, as in the Ephesine, occasionally at least, it is without such preface. I confess that I do not see the force of the argument, since these forms are not part of a mass.

[2] Lib. ii. 45.

himself, wishing to obtain a favourable wind for the transport of some trees, for the rebuilding of the monastery, 'placed upon the altar the vestments and books of the blessed man' (*i.e.* of St. Columba) 'with psalms and fasting and the invocation of his name.' And in recording instances of graces obtained by Columba's intercession, he gives the very words with which he had adjured his heavenly patron. Being detained by contrary winds, he cried out: 'Is then, O Saint, this delay pleasing to you? Hitherto we have trusted that we should receive through you, from God's mercy, some consolation and assistance in our labours, esteeming that you have great interest with God (*alicujus esse grandis apud Deum honoris*).' Immediately, says Adamnan, the wind changed, and that gentle accusation of the saint greatly helped us.

Another time, wishing to celebrate St. Columba's feast at Iona, and being at a considerable distance on the vigil, and the wind contrary, Adamnan prayed as follows: 'Must we then, O Saint, keep your feast to-morrow among the people and not in your own church? It is an easy thing for you to obtain from God that at the beginning of so great a day the wind should change, that we may celebrate the solemnity of the mass (*missarum solemnia*) of thy festival (*natalis*) in thy church.' On this occasion also the prayer was heard. They reached Iona next day, after tierce (*i.e.* between nine and twelve o'clock), and having washed their hands and feet, entering the church with the brethren, at noon they celebrated together the solemn mass.[1]

There is nothing known to us regarding the frequency of communion in the Scottish or Pictish Churches, either in monasteries or among the laity. One incident preserved by Adamnan shows us the working of the penitential system. An Irishman named Libranus had slain a man and afterwards violated a solemn oath. He came over to Iona and made a full confession to St. Columba, and swore he was willing to fulfil any penance. The saint required him to live in exile but in monastic service for seven years, and at the end of his penance to return to him during Lent, that he might receive communion at Easter.[2]

If Holy Communion was the reward of the sincere penitent, it was also the strength of the patriots ready to die in defence of their homes and altars.

One little glimpse of Scotland which has been preserved in the Irish Annals shows the devotion which was retained towards

---

[1] Lib. ii. 45.
[2] 'Ut in Paschali solemnitate ad altarium accedas et Eucharistiam sumas.'

St. Columba long after his death, and at the same time reveals the practice of communion immediately before battle. In the year 909, say the Annals, 'the men of Fortrenn (Scotch) and the Lochlanns (*i.e.* Norwegians) fought a battle. Vigorously indeed did the men of Alban fight this battle, for Columcille was assisting them, for they prayed to him fervently, because he was their apostle, and it was through him they had received the faith. On a former occasion, when Imhar Conung was a young man, he came to plunder Alban with three large battalions. What the men of Alban, both laity and clergy, did, was to remain until morning fasting and praying to God and to Columcille, and they cried aloud to the Lord, and gave many alms of food and clothes to the churches and to the poor, and to take the Body of the Lord from the hands of the priests, and to promise to do every good as their clergy would order them. And they would have as their standard at the head of every battle the crosier of Columcille, for which reason it is called the Cathhuaidh (*i.e.* battle-victory) from that time forth.'[1]

Equally beautiful with this story of brave men strengthened by the Body of Jesus Christ to fight against the heathen, is another which shows us holy men waiting their death by the same cruel heathen at the foot of the altar. The Irish Annals write at the date A.D. 825 'Martyrium Blaithmaci filii Flainn a gentilibus in Hy Coluimcille.' Such short entries as this constitute in most cases all that we know of the men of those days, their deeds and sufferings. But in this case it is otherwise. The word Blaithmac means 'Son of the Flower,' and the martyr is sometimes called Florigenius or Florus, in English Florence. The history of his martyrdom has been written by Walafrid Strabo. Walafrid's monastery, Reichenau or Augia Dives (Rich Meadow), was of Irish foundation. It was on an island in the Lake of Constance. Of this Walafrid was abbot from 842-849, and he himself mentions how many Irish were travelling at the beginning of the ninth century, owing to the incursions of the Danes, and how some had come to Reichenau. It was from these that Walafrid learned the details of the recent martyrdom of Blaithmac. He says that Blaithmac was of royal blood, and even heir to his father, an Irish king, but he became a monk; and at last, to escape the importunities of his father and the nobles, fled to Iona, where he was made president or prior. He had sought Iona in hopes of martyrdom, for the Danes had already devastated it in 802. Knowing supernaturally

---

[1] Skene, *Chronicles of Picts and Scots*, p. 405. As the Imhar Conung, *i.e.* Ivor the King, was slain in 904, and the event here related happened when he was a young man, it must have occurred in the latter half of the 9th century.

of their return and of his own death, he counselled such of the monks as did not feel a desire or strength for the coming conflict to save themselves by flight. Some did so, others remained with him and shared his fate. He had hidden the shrine of St. Columba in the earth, and refused to make known to the plunderers where it was concealed. He and his companions were slain while he was in the act of saying mass. 'The holy doctor,' says Walafrid, 'was celebrating the holy rites of mass, and stood himself as a spotless victim before the sacred altar, to be immolated to God by the cruel sword of the heathen; his monks lay prostrate around, with tears and prayers commending their souls to God.'[1]

Nor was this a solitary example. On the contrary, all accounts agree in representing the Danes, wherever they went, in England, Scotland, or Ireland, as pouring out their heathen fury on the defenceless clergy. And these seem generally to have prepared for martyrdom by holy mass and communion, or to have found a last consolation in breathing out their souls before the altars at which they had so often prayed. The anonymous author of the history of the translation of St. Cuthbert's body, writing of the very period of the martyrdom of Blaithmac, and of the north of Britain, says: 'Then might be seen noble and illustrious priests butchered around the very altars on which they had consecrated the holy mysteries of the Body and Blood of the Lord.'[2]

We must now take leave of the north of Britain, and return to the British Church of the south. When we have considered its desolation by the heathen Angles and Saxons, we shall pass to the conversion of the latter, and then once more we shall meet the disciples of St. Columba as the Apostles of the English.

[1] *Bib. Max. Lugd.* tom. xv. p. 209; *Acta SS.* ii. 236; Dr. Reeves's notes to Adamnan, preface, p. xxii. and p. 389.
[2] In Dr. Giles's ed. of Bede, vol. vi. p. 383.

CHAPTER IV.

DEVASTATION.

HENRY BRADSHAW, a monk of St. Werburge's, Chester, in a metrical life of his patroness which he composed at the beginning of the sixteenth century, pronounces the following eulogy on the good city in which he dwelt :—

> Certainly since baptism came to Chester city,
> Soon after King Lucius and afore King Arthur,
> By the grace of God and their humility
> The faith of Holy Church did ever there endure,
> Without recidivation and infection, sure.
> Wherefore it is worthy a singular commendation
> Above all the cities and towns of this nation.
>
> So after that the Angles, Jutes, and Saxons,
> By fortune of battle, power and policy,
> Had clearly subdued all the old Britons,
> And them expelled to Wales and wild country,
> The faith of Holy Church remained at Chester city;
> In the said church truly, by singular grace, alone,
> Like as the faith of Peter never failed at Rome.[1]

Bradshaw was mistaken in his history, for Chester shared the fate of most of the other great cities built by the Romans, and lay in almost utter desolation for more than a century;[2] but his verses may serve to bring before our minds a very startling fact which we might easily fail to realise in reading of times so remote as the fifth and sixth centuries of Christianity. The fact is this : that, though it is probable that, from the day that the Blessed Eucharist was first consecrated in Great Britain to the present hour, the sacramental Presence of Emmanuel has never ceased day or night to ennoble and to plead for the land, yet not only after the rise of Protestantism, but also at an earlier period, an interval of centuries occurred during which it

---

[1] *The Holy Lyfe and History of Saint Werburge*, by Henry Bradshaw (Chetham Society, vol. xiii.).

[2] It was taken by Ethelfrid the Fierce in 613, and probably burnt.

was swept away from by far the greater part of what we now call England. How long to us the interval seems between the accession of Elizabeth, followed by the abolition of the Holy Sacrifice from every parochial church throughout the country, to the timid and scanty reconstruction of Catholic chapels in the middle of the eighteenth century! A similar period elapsed between the first desolation of Christian churches in Kent in the fifth century so pathetically described by Gildas, and the conversion of the South Saxons by St. Wilfrid towards the close of the seventh, by which paganism was once more banished from the island. During those two hundred and fifty years the conquest of Christian Britain by the Teutonic invaders was going on, and simultaneously during the latter part of that period the conversion to the faith of the invaders themselves. Churches were being burnt and priests murdered by the pagan Saxons in one part of the land, while churches were being built and priests ordained by the converted Saxons in another. In the meantime, districts where the daily sacrifice had been offered under Roman and British rule were forsaken by their Christian inhabitants, or these were as utterly deprived of the ministrations of religion by their new Saxon masters as were the persecuted Catholics in the days of Elizabeth and James. In some instances for a hundred, in others for nearly two hundred years, the old church lay in blackened ruins, and a heathen temple was built near to it, and heathenish rites were performed, where once the Christian people, filling the air with psalmody, had crowded round St. Lupus or St. Germanus. What strange vicissitudes! Writing in A.D. 547, Gildas tells us that in his day were still standing some of the old heathen temples erected by the Romans, with idols mouldering in them. At that time the whole island north of the Thames and south of the Firth of Forth was British. But in a few years the fate of the heathen temples had befallen Christian churches. They remained here and there, sad monuments that the land had once been Christian.[1] And then another century passes, and the question has to be discussed as to what shall be done with the now deserted Saxon temples, and it is decided that, when purified, they may be used for the Christian sacrifice.[2]

If it is hard to realise in our minds the length of time filled by this heathen desolation, it is impossible now to ascertain its precise extent. There is every probability that the Britons who were conquered by the Saxons were all, or nearly all, nominally Christians. They had

---

[1] The heathen Saxon seem to have built on other sites, and not to have used Christian churches. See Kemble, *Saxons in England*, book ii. ch. 7.
[2] St. Gregory's letter to St. Augustine, about A.D. 600.

bishops, and though some of these may have been without diocesan jurisdiction, yet we know that the country had to some extent been divided into dioceses, and perhaps these again gathered into provinces.[1] Of their numbers we have no historical evidence. Gibbon, judging by analogy, computes them at thirty or forty.[2] That they had lands is proved by the fact that St. Wilfrid afterwards demanded that these church lands, having once been consecrated to God, should be restored to the Church by their Saxon occupants.[3] When St. Augustine landed in 597, the eastern half of Britain was already conquered and pagan, the western half was British and Christian.[4] But in the next half-century the range of heathendom was greatly extended through the central and west central parts, owing to the foundation of the kingdom of Mercia by the pagan Penda, while its limits were being diminished in the east and north by the conversion of Ethelbert and Edwin, with their kingdoms of Kent and Northumbria.

The pagan conquerors massacred multitudes of the Britons, sometimes, as at Anderida (Pevensey), exterminating even women and children. Multitudes also retired before the invaders 'to Wales and wild country,' as Bradshaw sings. Many crossed the sea to Ireland and to Armorica. Of those that remained some would be reduced to slavery, and many of the British women would be taken in marriage by the Saxon warriors. In Dorsetshire and Wiltshire, and still more in Somersetshire and Devonshire, the number of British who maintained themselves among the Saxon settlers is known to have been very great. Nor were all who remained reduced to slavery. Lappenberg remarks that 'we find no considerable difference with regard to the *wergild*, the capability of bearing witness, and other rights, between the Britons and the Saxons, mentioned in the laws of Ine,' whence he justly concludes that such as were not prisoners of war remained in peaceable possession of their property and rights.[5]

What was the condition of these as regards religion? We can only answer by conjecture. Lappenberg speaks more than once of

---

[1] Haddan and Stubbs, *Councils*, vol. i. p. 142.

[2] Gibbon, *Decline*, ch. 31. He refers to Bingham, vol. i. book ix. ch. 6, but the calculation is only conjectural.

[3] Eddius, *Vita S. Wilfridi*, 17 : ' Ea loca sancta in diversis regionibus quæ clerus Britannus aciem gladii hostilis manu gentis nostræ fugiens deseruit.' This must mean at least churches and churchyards.

[4] A strip of land had, however, been conquered by Wessex to the mouth of the Avon, thus cutting the Britons of the West from those of the South-west.

[5] *History of England under the Anglo-Saxon Kings*, p. 125.

the 'extinction and oblivion of Christianity.'[1] He does not refer to Wales, since he affirms in another place[2] that in Cambria and Cumbria no apostasy from the Christian faith had taken place. He therefore must be understood to speak of those parts of Britain occupied by the Anglo-Saxons. Yet, in relating the conversion of Ethelbert, he somewhat inconsistently speaks of the king as having before St. Augustine's arrival 'paid little attention to the faith professed by the great number of his subjects forming the oppressed British population.'[3] If we may judge by analogy of what is known of other nations in similar circumstances, these words must more correctly represent what is likely to have taken place than those which allude to total extinction of the Christian faith. When Catholic countries have been thoroughly overrun and reduced to subjection by heathens or heretics, we find, as a rule, that many yield an outward compliance to the religion of their conquerors, and their children fall away altogether from the faith, while the few, taught by misfortune, cling to their religion more firmly than before, and even succeed in handing it down as a sacred inheritance to their children and children's children. We may suppose this to have been the case with the conquered Britons. No conclusive argument against the existence of a large Christian population of Britons in the midst of heathenism can be drawn from the silence of Bede. On such matters as would be familiar to his first readers he is often silent. He says almost nothing about the nature of the worship of his own heathen countrymen. On one occasion only does he mention a heathen priest.[4] He does not inform us what became of the ministers of the temples when idolatrous worship was suppressed. Yet from the legislation of councils we know how long idolatry lingered in England after the nominal conversion of the country; and we cannot be mistaken in supposing that the relapses into idolatry which he does record were promoted by the heathen priests who had been deprived of their trade. It is not then rash to suppose, though we have no historical testimony of the fact, that there remained many faithful Christians, many half Christian, amid the heathen population. Were these then never visited and consoled by a priest, such as St. Amphibalus who in the persecution of Diocletian found admission in disguise to the house of Alban and converted his host to the faith, or such as

---

[1] *History of England under the Anglo-Saxon Kings*, pp. 54, 64.

[2] *Ib.* p. 132.

[3] *Ib.* p. 138. On the probability that many Britons survived and mingled with the Saxons, see Kemble, *Saxons in England*, i. 19–21.

[4] 'Primus pontificum Coifi,' *Hist.* ii. 13. This priest favoured Christianity. Eddi mentions one who opposed St. Wilfrid's landing in Sussex.

the good priests who, when deprived of their benefices by Queen
Elizabeth, remained hidden yet were ever moving amongst the faithful Catholics? Bede has not indeed told of any such, but quite incidentally he has recorded a fact which was probably not a solitary
one. The South Saxons were among the first invaders. In 447 they
conquered that part of Britain to which they have left the name of
Sussex. Yet they were almost the last to become Christians, only
yielding to the zeal of St. Wilfrid in 681. In relating St. Wilfrid's
success, Bede mentions that previous to his coming there was an
Irish monk named Dicul or Dichuil, who had established in Sussex,
at a place called Bosenham, a very small monastery, where he
served God with only five or six monks. 'But of the surrounding
people (*provincialium*) no one cared either to imitate their life or
to listen to their preaching.'[1] Surely, if merit is not measured by
success—and, according to St. Bernard, to labour in a stony and ungrateful soil has often more merit with God than to cultivate a rich
and fertile field—then the name of Dicul ought not to be forgotten
among the Augustines, Wilfrids, Chads, and Aidans who are the glory
of those days. He had travelled far, in his zeal for souls, for certainly no other motive could have made him fix his home among
those pagan and obstinate men. In saying that no one cared to
listen to their preaching, Bede intimates that Dichuil and his companions did raise their voices in the wilderness. What then remained
for them? They spoke to Him who always hears, though He grants
in His own good time. One at least in the monastery was a priest,
probably even two or three, and they had therefore in their hands a
means divinely provided for propitiating God's mercy, and thereby
softening the hearts of stubborn men. They had a Victim whom they
could daily offer on the altar for the heedless or scoffing heathen
around. Lest I should seem to write from mere conjecture, I will
here set down what Bede has recorded of two other missionaries, not
to the Saxons in Britain, but to their kinsmen the Saxons in Frisia;
and though in this case the missionaries were Angles by birth, yet
they had dwelt long in Ireland, and brought thence the same faith
and zeal and the same religious customs which belonged to Dichuil
and his monks. 'Two priests of the English nation,' writes Bede,[2]
'who had long lived exiles in Ireland, for the sake of the eternal home
went into the province of the Old Saxons, to try whether they could
there gain any to Christ by preaching. They both bore the same
name, as they were of the same devotion, Hewald being the name of
both, with this distinction, that, on account of the difference of their

---

[1] Bede, *History*, iv. 13. [2] *Ib.* v. 10.

hair, the one was called Black Hewald and the other White Hewald. They were both piously religious, but Black Hewald was the more learned of the two in the science of the Holy Scriptures. On entering that province, these men took up their lodging in a certain steward's house, and requested that he would conduct them to his lord, for that they had a message and something to his advantage to communicate to him. The steward received and entertained them in his house some days, promising to send them to his lord, as they desired.

'But the barbarians, finding them to be of another religion, by their continual prayer and singing of psalms and hymns, and because they daily offered to God the sacrifice of the saving Victim [1]—for they had with them sacred vessels and a consecrated table for an altar—began to be suspicious of them, lest, if they should come into the presence of their chief and converse with him, they should turn his heart from their gods, and convert him to the new religion of the Christian faith, and thus by degrees all their province should be compelled to change its old worship for a new. Hereupon they, on a sudden, laid hold of them and put them to death. The White Hewald they slew immediately with the sword; but the Black they put to tedious torture and tore limb from limb; and their dead bodies they cast into the Rhine.' This tragedy took place on October 3, 695.

The conduct of the South Saxons towards Dichuil was very different from that of the Old Saxons to the Hewalds. They looked on them with contempt and indifference.[2] But it is not rash to suppose that St. Dichuil—for the Irish Church honours him as a saint—the companion of the great St. Fursey, took the same means of asking God's blessing on his missionary labours as the martyrs of Frisia. And as these, though they converted none themselves, yet by their masses and their bloodshedding prepared the soil for St. Willibrord, so did the masses and prayers offered day by day in the monastery of Bosenham by that little band of Irish priests prepare the way for the success which a few years later was granted to

---

[1] 'Quotidie sacrificium Deo victimæ salutaris offerebant.'

[2] It is most strange, considering the great cruelties of the Anglo-Saxons to the Britons, especially to the priests, that they never inflicted any bodily injury on any missionary sent to themselves, whether Italian, Irish, Frank, or Saxon. Kings never went further in persecution than exile. The people are said (but by a late and doubtful authority) to have tied fish-tails to the clothes of St. Augustine's companions. St. Wilfrid was imprisoned in a dungeon; but this was by a Christian prince. The martyrs were among the kings, as St. Oswald; not among the clergy.

St. Wilfrid. The Hewalds had no congregation, but served each other's mass at a temporary altar set up in the house of a heathen. In the oratory of St. Dichuil's monastery there were but three or four lay brethren. Of the men and women around none, or almost none, cared to see or hear. But the Divine Victim pleaded for mercy for the obstinate and ungrateful people. Dichuil came over from Ireland in 633,[1] and, after spending some years with St. Fursey in East Anglia, is said to have settled in Sussex about 645. Nearly forty years had to come and go before the harvest of those labours and tears and masses would be gathered in by Wilfrid, and by that time Dichuil and some of his companions must have passed away without seeing any answer to their prayers. Let us recall the words of our Divine Redeemer: 'It is one man that soweth, and it is another that reapeth . . . that both he that soweth and he that reapeth may rejoice together.'[2] St. Dichuil and St. Wilfrid are rejoicing together in heaven; and I have dwelt on Dichuil's apparent failure, because we at the present day must learn to study the disappointments of the saints as well as their triumphs, and to gather encouragement from both. In how many places in England has a Catholic priest to offer the daily sacrifice with no assistants but his server and one or two faithful worshippers; or to preach for years to his scanty congregation of Catholics, though hundreds and thousands of redeemed men pass within hearing of his voice, and in their indifference or prejudice will not pause to listen. Let him faithfully persevere, and especially let him faithfully plead for the ignorant and misguided at the holy altar. In eloquence or learning he may be surpassed by the ministers of heresy or of infidelity. But his Breviary and his Missal are his own, and the power to offer sacrifice can never be usurped by others. Let him make faithful use of this. A Wilfrid may some day come and gather in the fruit of those solitary masses and despised exhortations. And though, when that day comes, the obscure Dichuil may be dead and forgotten upon earth, He whom he faithfully served will give him the joy of the 'harvest-home' in heaven.

I have dwelt long on this little incident, not only for its lessons to ourselves, but also because it shows that missionaries were sometimes openly tolerated by the pagans, though despised by them. We may suppose, then, without improbability, that Christian priests would not have been always forbidden to minister to Christian Britons, whether enslaved or free. And as Bertha prepared the mind of

---

[1] See Bede, iii. 19. On St. Dichuil, see Dr. Moran, in *Transactions of the Ossory Archæological Society*, part iv. p. 525.
[2] John iv. 37, 36.

Ethelbert to accept the preaching of St. Augustine, so we may be sure did many a Christian wife of British origin dispose her heathen husband to listen with docility when at last 'the day of visitation' came.[1]

Before relating how churches and altars were built and masses celebrated where idolatry had prevailed, let me once more remind the reader that the worship of the true God had never ceased in many parts of Britain from the time of its first introduction. Scotland beyond the Firths, and its south-west portions and all the west of modern England from Cumberland to Cornwall, were undefiled by heathenism. Into all this region, as we have seen, the faith had penetrated long before the arrival of St. Augustine; and if parts of these districts were invaded and subjugated by the Anglo-Saxons, it was not until after their own conversion to the faith. When this was the case, the inhabitants may have been reduced to slavery, but their religious worship was as free to them as before. The churches changed owners, but tombs and altars were respected by their Christian conquerors. Thus we have seen an English episcopate substituted in Whithern for a British one, while the shrine of St. Ninian was only made more splendid by being more widely known. In the year 658 Kenwalch, the West Saxon king, extended his conquests as far as the river Parret in Somersetshire, and thus the famous British sanctuary of Glastonbury came under Saxon rule, not however to be profaned or demolished, as that of St. Alban had been by the pagans, for at that period the West Saxons were already Christians, and they vied with and surpassed the British in their reverence and generosity towards the holy place.[2] But this is said by anticipation. Let us now turn to the mission of St. Augustine. We shall first consider his repulse by the Britons of Wales, and then the successes or reverses which he and his fellow-labourers met among the Anglo-Saxons.

---

[1] 1 Pet. i. 12, iii. 1.

[2] The ancient wattled church of the Isle of Avalon, or Glastonbury, was covered with wood and lead by St. Paulinus, according to Malmesbury. It is the earliest church known to have been dedicated in Britain to the Blessed Virgin. When the British were driven from it, it was served by Saxon monks, and endowed by Heddi, the West Saxon bishop, in 680. A stone church was built by the Saxon monks, and it is said to have been munificently decorated by King Ine about A.D. 704. The wooden church was preserved at least to the Conquest. See Freeman, *Old English History*, p. 239.

CHAPTER V.

BRITISH ISOLATION.

We have seen the British Church, after occupying the whole or nearly the whole of South Britain or modern England, driven further and further towards the West. They thus lost most of their old seaports and means of travelling to the continent and to Rome. The invasion of Gaul by the Franks and of Italy by the Ostrogoths made communication with Rome still more difficult. Yet Gildas, writing about the middle of the sixth century, instead of complaining of the isolation of his Church from the rest of Christendom, deplores that the intercourse was abused by ambitious men. Of certain bishops he says that if they meet with resistance at home in obtaining the coveted prize of a diocese, they send before them messengers, and do not grudge, but rather delight, to traverse seas and great tracts of land, that they may sell all and buy the precious pearl whose beauty by a diabolical delusion so enchants them. Then returning home with head erect they force themselves in, and stretch out their hands over the most holy sacrifice of Christ—hands worthy rather of the flames of hell than of the venerable altars.[1]

Shortly after this was written the pagan conquests were renewed, and neither princes nor ecclesiastics had heart or leisure for ambition. If they went abroad, it was to fly to the nearest coast for safety and with little hope of return. Episcopal sees ceased to be objects of cupidity. Driven as the Britons were from cities[2] built with all

---

[1] *Epist.* i.; Haddan and Stubbs, i. 76. These words are very puzzling to us, though no doubt clear to those for whom they were written. There was simony enough in those days in the appointment of bishops by Frankish kings, but those kings could have no influence in Britain. The Gothic kings of Italy were usurping the appointment of the popes, but of course they had even less power in Britain than the Franks. The British clergy can have sued to none but to the popes; yet in the fearful wars and sackings of Rome in the first half of the sixth century, one would have thought they had little leisure to attend to our distant isle. That their appointments were respected shows how great was the reverence for the See of Peter.

[2] Bath, Cirencester, and Gloucester had been conquered in 577.

the elegance of Roman architecture, filled with baths and libraries, and being obliged to construct rude dwellings in rugged and uncultivated mountains, and to leave behind them not only luxury but learning, they of course soon fell back into a comparative state of barbarism, and were in a great measure forgotten by the rest of the Christian world. Procopius and Stephanus, two Constantinopolitan writers of the sixth century, give the most ridiculous descriptions of Britain.[1]

They were, of course, not forgotten at Rome, and St. Gregory in sending St. Augustine seems to have been anxious not only for the welfare of the heathen invaders of Britain, but also for that of its older Christian inhabitants. St. Augustine, acting according to his instructions, as soon as he had gained a solid footing in the country, turned his thoughts to his Christian brethren in the west of the island. He sought them out, not, as many modern histories pretend, to impose on them Roman fetters hitherto unknown, nor even to subject them to his own metropolitan jurisdiction, but to invite them to join in the spiritual conquest of the conquerors of their country. It is well known that his efforts were unsuccessful, that the Britons took no part in the evangelisation of the Anglo-Saxons, and remained for centuries in hostility. It is important for the history of the Sacrament of peace and union that we should get as full and clear a knowledge as possible of the nature, causes, and results of this failure of St. Augustine.

I cannot but attribute it to spiritual pride and national resentment working subtly together and giving birth to uncharitableness and a Pharisaic spirit of isolation tending towards schism. This view is derived from Gildas no less than from Bede. It will require some development. There are good reasons for thinking that during the sixth century a vigorous movement of reform passed over the Welsh Church, and thence into Ireland and Brittany. The monastic life especially took a new development, and austerer forms of ascetic discipline arose as a protest against the corruption and disorder of the world. There is a second epistle of Gildas which has only come down to us in fragments. If the first was directed against the license of worldly men, whether nobles or ecclesiastics, the second is an earnest warning against the spiritual dangers which accompany a profession of austerity. These fragments are very interesting, because they are the only memorial now remaining of the kind of teaching which was addressed by the saintly abbots like St. David and St. Gildas to the multitude of earnest but often rude and ignorant men whom their fame had attracted to the cloisters. 'Abstinence from bodily food,'

[1] See Skene, *Celtic Scotland*, i. 115.

says Gildas, 'without charity is useless. Better therefore are those who without great labour fast, and abstain from God's creatures within bounds, keeping their heart carefully clean within before God, from whom they expect their reward, than those who eat no flesh, enjoy no worldly food, and use neither chariots nor horses, and on that account think themselves better than others; for to them " death enters through the windows " of pride. . . .

'It is better not to judge our fellow bishops and fellow abbots, and those who are not our subjects. But if any of them should have an evil reputation we should not rebuke and denounce them at once, but gently admonish them with patience. Those who are suspected may in conscience be avoided as far as possible; but we should not excommunicate them as convicted criminals, and exclude them from our table and company, if any reason of necessity require us to meet or speak with them. We should let them know that they are not acting rightly, but not condemn them. Suppose that they communicate unworthily, yet let us beware lest by our rash suspicions and evil thoughts we communicate with demons. But if we know of any who are impure beyond all doubt, then indeed we must exclude them from our table and society, whatever may be their canonical order, unless in canonical order they do penance. For this we have the apostolic decree: "If any man that is named a brother be a fornicator &c.;"[1] "and on account of the greater crimes evidently proved, but for no other reason, ought we to put away our brethren from the communion of the altar and the table, at the fitting times."'

'It is good that bishops and abbots should judge their own subjects, "whose blood God will require at their hands," if they do not rule them well.'

'Let those who are disobedient to their fathers be like the heathen and the publicans; and let the maxim of the Apostle, that each should esteem other men better than themselves,[2] be our rule in thinking of all, both good and bad, unless they are our subjects. That maxim is applicable (even to the bad) because of the uncertain result of life, since we read in Scripture that an apostle was lost by avarice, and a robber received into Paradise on account of his confession. . . . See how, when Aaron took part with Mary in blaming Moses for his Ethiopian wife, Mary was condemned to leprosy; whence we have reason to fear who speak evil of good princes for trifling faults.'

'As to those monks who come from a lower to a more perfect place, when their abbot has so degenerated from the service of God

---

[1] 1 Cor. v. 11. [2] Phil. ii. 3.

as to deserve not to be received to the table of the saints, and is burdened with the crime of an impure life, not in suspicion merely but by evident proof, receive such monks without any scruple, and without consulting their abbot, since they are flying to you as from the flames of hell. But we ought not to receive them against the will of the abbot, when he is one whom we do not, on account of infamy, exclude from the holy table (*de mensa sanctorum*). How much less should we receive those who desert holy abbots, against whom there is no graver suspicion or charge than that they have horses and carriages,[1] either because such is the custom of their country, or on account of their weakness; for such things do less harm to those who use them, if they do it with humility and patience, than is suffered by those who themselves drag the plough, and themselves dig the furrows, but do it with pride and presumption. Whatever is superfluous in worldly things ought to be counted as luxury and riches for a monk; but what he has, not by cupidity but by need, in order not to succumb to want, is not to be imputed to him as evil.'

'The inferior members ought not to despise the head which is the principal ornament of the body, and the head ought not to look down with contempt on the daily but useful labour of the hands. Neither one nor the other can say "We have no need of you," since both belong to the common good of the body. We have said this, that the higher priests may know, that as the inferior clergy may not despise their superiors, so also neither may they despise their clergy, just as the head may not scorn the other members.'[2]

These striking admonitions of St. Gildas are the more interesting, that they reveal the defects which proved the stumbling-block of the British Church. These were spiritual pride, and a want of discernment between the essence and the external form of humility. The British bishops who met St. Augustine in conference judged him to be proud and arrogant because of the omission of an arbitrary and accidental form of courtesy; while they proved themselves obstinately attached to their own judgments, indocile to their lawful superior, and unforgiving to their enemies. As this conference forms an epoch

---

[1] 'Pecora et vehicula' may of course mean cattle and wagons, but I have translated it horses and carriages, because the context seems to imply that these were for the personal service of the abbot, and because of the corresponding phrase before, 'neque vehiculis equisque vehuntur.'

[2] Part of the above epistle was printed by D'Achery and by Martene and Durand, and a part by Wilkins. But it is given in all the extant fragments by Haddan and Stubbs, i. 108–113. I am not aware that it is to be found in any English translation.

VOL. I.   G

in the history of the British Church, and decided its fortunes for centuries, I will here give its history as related by Venerable Bede.

The conference, or rather two conferences, took place in the year 602 or 603, five or six years after St. Augustine's landing in Kent. Ethelbert, who was not only king of Kent, but overlord of all the Teutonic kingdoms, had arranged the meeting, and obtained for St. Augustine and his companions a safe-conduct to the place afterwards known as St. Augustine's Oak, probably Aust near the mouth of the Avon and the passage of the Severn. The purpose of this journey of Augustine was to induce the Britons—who of course had a promise of safety for themselves from Ethelbert—'that, preserving Catholic unity with him, they should undertake the common labour of preaching the Gospel to the Gentiles.' For this purpose it was necessary that they should reform their Easter cycle, which was astronomically incorrect, lest the discrepancy of their religious observances should impede united action, and cause perplexity to their converts.[1] The saint also wished them to abandon some other peculiarities of discipline or ritual in which they differed from the rest of the Catholic world. His exhortations, though enforced by a miracle, were to no purpose, and the conference was prorogued. To the second meeting 'there came, as is asserted '—and now I will give the very words of Bede—'seven bishops of the Britons, and many most learned men, particularly from their most noble monastery, which in the English tongue is called Bancornaburg, over which the abbot Dinoth is said to have presided at that time. They that were to go to the aforesaid council repaired first to a certain holy and discreet man, who was wont to lead an eremitical life among them, advising with him whether they ought, at the preaching of Augustine, to forsake their traditions. He answered : " If he is a man of God, follow him." " How shall we know that?" said they. He replied : " Our Lord saith, 'Take My yoke upon you, and learn of Me, for I am meek and lowly of heart;' if, therefore, Augustine is meek and lowly of heart, it is to be believed that he has taken upon him the yoke of Christ, and offers the same to you to take upon you. But if he is stern and haughty, it appears that he is not of God, nor are we to regard his words." They insisted again : " And how shall we discern even this?" "Do you contrive," said he, "that he may first arrive with his company at the place where the synod is to be held ; and if at your approach he shall rise up to you, hear him submissively, being assured that he is the servant of

---

[1] The necessity for this change will be explained in Chapter VII., where the origin of the discrepancy will be related.

Christ ; but if he shall despise you, and not rise up to you, whereas you are more in number, let him also be despised by you."'[1]

Certainly respect for piety and austerity is good, and God is wont to converse with the simple, yet it must be allowed that the bishops and doctors of the Britons did not find a very wise counsellor in the hermit. Humility is indeed a mark of a true servant of Christ, but the validity of a superior's authority cannot depend on its possession ; and had St. Augustine been as haughty as he was really meek, his authority to teach and admonish and command would not have been forfeited thereby. One of the fragments of the epistle of Gildas, from which I have already quoted, says : 'Truth is fair in the eyes of the wise, by whosoever mouth it is spoken.' The hermit might more profitably have recommended humility to his hearers than bidden them search for it so narrowly in St. Augustine. The wisdom of the British doctors ought also to have taught them that the test of Augustine's humility proposed by the solitary was very fallacious. A humble man occupying a position of authority may remain seated, and an ambitious man, like Absalom, may rise up and salute and take by the hand and kiss, in order to flatter and carry his own projects. The result, therefore, was what might have been expected. Augustine did not appear humble as tried by this test, and the Britons seized on the pretext to fortify their own pride. 'They did as the hermit directed,' continues Bede ; 'and it happened that when they came Augustine was sitting on a chair, which they observing were in a passion, and charging him with pride endeavoured to contradict all he said. He said to them : "You act in many particulars contrary to our custom, or rather the custom of the universal Church, and yet if you will comply with me in these three points—viz. to keep Easter at the due time ; to complete the administration of baptism (*compleatis*) by which we are born again to God, according to the custom of the Roman Apostolic Church ; and jointly with us to preach the word of God to the English nation—we will readily tolerate all the other things you do, though contrary to our customs." They answered that they would do none of those things, nor receive him as their archbishop ; for they alleged among themselves : "If he would not now rise up to us, how much more will he contemn us, as of no worth, if we shall begin to be under his subjection !"[2] To whom

[1] Bede, *Eccl. Hist.* ii. 2.
[2] Dr. Lingard remarks that it is incredible that if the Britons had been hitherto independent of the Holy See, and the question had been about the surrender of that independence, they could have risked it on so uncertain a contingency as the behaviour of St. Augustine ; but if it was a personal question about

the man of God, Augustine, is said in a threatening manner to have foretold, that since they would not join in unity with their brethren, they should be warred upon by their enemies; and, if they would not preach the way of life to the English nation, they should at their hands undergo the vengeance of death. All which, through the dispensation of divine judgment, fell out exactly as he had predicted.'

There is, perhaps, no fact in history which has been so much distorted as that of the conference between St. Augustine and the Britons. Bede has been accused of suppression of truth, St. Augustine of pride, duplicity, and even of wicked vengeance in bringing about the fulfilment of his own prophecy, although he probably died the following year, long before the event happened to which Bede refers, *i.e.* the slaughter of the monks of Bangor, which was effected by the fierce pagan, Ethelfrith the Wild, with whom, as Professor Stubbs says, 'Christian influence had little enough at any time to do.' And again imaginary speeches have been put into the mouth of Dinoth the abbot. And even by those who reject all these legendary accretions conclusions have been drawn from the simple narrative of Bede regarding Papal supremacy which would astonish Augustine and the Britons alike. I shall have to return to this history and discuss some of these matters in a future chapter; in the meantime we must sorrowfully leave the Britons in their selfish isolation, instead of welcoming them as fellow missionaries with St. Augustine in the conversion of the Saxons. Happily there were other Celtic Churches in the island which showed a very different spirit; and the glory of converting Anglo-Saxon England falls to the Scotch, that is, the Irish missionaries, no less than to the Italians.

It will be better to take a review of the conversion of the barbarians and establishment of the Anglo-Saxon Church before discussing the nature of the controversies which disturbed the relations of the different Churches in the island. The British Church of the West and the Celtic Churches of the North are both claimed by Protestants as precursors of themselves in their alienation from Rome and from Catholic Christendom. But their position and conduct were so different, that it is only when we have studied this contrast that we shall be able to understand the real nature of the divisions.

accepting Augustine himself as leader in a missionary work and archbishop, then indeed their conduct, though foolish, is intelligible.

CHAPTER VI.

ANGLO-SAXON CONVERSION.

THERE is an event in the earthly life of our Divine Redeemer, in which we may see a type of God's providence over His Church. The birth of the Son of God was surrounded by prodigies. The angels inviting the shepherds to His crib, and the star guiding the magians with their gifts, might appear to betoken a life to be passed amidst the love and adoration of men. But no sooner had these things taken place than terror seemed to seize on the heavenly host, and an angel was sent on a swift message to Joseph : 'Arise, and take the Child and His Mother, and fly into Egypt, and be there till I shall tell thee. For it will come to pass that Herod will seek the Child to destroy Him.'[1] What is the meaning, ask the holy doctors,[2] of this apparent weakness? They reply that it is the first lesson of 'The Economy'—that it is a sign that God has become man in very truth, and not a phantom, and is subject to the conditions of human life. God will now show His power and providence, not by destroying kings, as Pharaoh and Sennacherib, but by baffling them, by seeming to let them triumph, and yet working out His own ends by their means. And by the life of His Incarnate Son, God will teach His servants what they are to expect in every age. 'You see at His birth,' says St. Chrysostom, 'first a tyrant raging, then flight ensuing, and departure beyond the border ; and for no crime His mother is exiled into the land of the barbarians. And this is done that thou, hearing these things—shouldst thou have been appointed to any spiritual charge and then see thyself suffering incurable ills and enduring countless dangers—shouldst not be greatly troubled, nor say : " What can this be ? Surely I ought to be crowned and celebrated for fulfilling the Lord's commandment ? "'

The lessons of the Flight—that kings seem to do all things at their will, and are nevertheless controlled by God's hand—that God's

---

[1] Mat. ii. 13.

[2] St. John Chrysost. *Hom.* 8 *in Mat.* ; St. Peter Chrysologus, *Serm.* 151, ' De fuga Christi.'

designs appear to be frustrated, and His work overthrown, just when He is carrying out some deep plan of His wisdom and love—that God's friends may fly before the face of His enemies, and yet be in His company—that they appear to be saving or protecting Him, while He all the time is shielding them—that the times are placed by God in His own power, and that we must wait with uncertainty, but with patient trust, till His angels summon us—these lessons must be well pondered by us if we would not take scandal from the history of the Most Holy Eucharist. They are exemplified in every age, and certainly not least in that on which we are now entering. The reader of Bede's history of the early days of the Anglo-Saxon Church will be charmed by many a noble or pathetic tale; but when he ponders on the whole story of England's second conversion, he will be lost in wonder at the strange and secret ways of God's providence. All seems to depend on kings and rulers. When they protect religion, it flourishes; when they withdraw their protection, it fails. What triumphs for the Church under good kings, the Ethelberts, Edwins, Oswalds, Oswins, Sigeberts, and so many more! But what reverses under the Eadbalds, Cadwallons, Pendas, and the rest! And what sudden misfortunes come to disappoint the brightest and best-founded hopes! What irregularity in the progress of the faith! How it advances and retires, and follows no apparent plan and seems the sport of circumstances! Yet, all the time, faith in God's providence, and the analogy of our Lord's own life, and the inspired record of the Acts of the Apostles, assure us that, though Herod and Pontius Pilate combine their powers, it is only 'to do what God's hand and God's counsel decreed to be done.'[1]

The history of the conversion of the heathen races who had overrun Christian Britain is not to be written here; nor is it any part of the plan of this work to sketch even an outline of the course of religion in general. Nothing will be related but what bears immediately or proximately on the Holy Eucharist; and I must suppose my reader's acquaintance with the main facts of English history, whether civil or ecclesiastical. In the present chapter, following the narrative of Bede,[2] I will set down the principal matters at least, which regard the gradual erection of churches and altars for the ce-

---

[1] Acts iv. 28.

[2] I cannot too warmly urge the reading of Bede's History in his own words. Canon Bright has given an admirable summing-up of Bede's merits in his *Chapters of Early English Church History*, pp. 326-329, and has interpreted and elucidated Bede's narrative in a masterly and most impartial manner. His views, however, about Papal supremacy are not those of Bede.

lebration of the Sacred Rite, from the landing of St. Augustine to the final closing of heathen temples and the cessation of all public idolatry.

When St. Augustine landed in Kent, there was a Frankish bishop named Liudhard attached to the court of Ethelbert's Christian queen, Bertha, the daughter of King Charibert of Paris. He appears to have held in the palace of the heathen king much the same position as the bishop-chaplain of Henrietta Maria in the court of Charles I. He was allowed to celebrate the holy rites in the church assigned to him—an old British church dedicated to St. Martin—but it seems he was not permitted to make converts. The Roman missionaries, however, obtained permission, not only to say mass (*missas facere* [1]), but also to preach, baptise, and propagate the faith, which they did most successfully. In the very first year the king, whose heart had been prepared by the prayers and example of his saintly wife, set the example of conversion to his subjects. And here let me remark that in saying that the success of the Gospel among the Anglo-Saxons depended in great measure on the encouragement or opposition of kings, I am not underrating its power; for surely to convert kings and make so many of them zealous apostles of the faith was a triumph of the Gospel no less wonderful than to have converted a bigoted Pharisee and made him 'a chosen vessel to carry the name of Christ before kings and peoples.'[2] What Bede says of Ethelbert is true of St. Edwin, St. Oswald, and the other saintly kings: 'The king so far encouraged his people's conversion, as that he compelled none to embrace Christianity, but only showed more affection to the believers, as his fellow-citizens in the heavenly kingdom.'[3] The conversions, therefore, were due, not to fear or interest, but to the grace of God, and the means employed were perfectly legitimate.

We learn from a letter of St. Gregory that on the first Christmas Day as many as ten thousand Kentish men were baptised. Some of the old British churches were restored for Christian worship, and new churches were built.

The grievous disappointment which St. Augustine experienced from the refusal of the British bishops to co-operate with him in preaching the Gospel was somewhat compensated the year after by the conversion of Sabert, king of the East Saxons, and the erection of a church dedicated to St. Paul in London. St. Augustine also saw a bishopric established at Rochester, and a church built in honour of St. Andrew. But as the glories of our Lord's birth had been quickly followed by the flight into Egypt, so were the first triumphs of grace in England followed by reverses and humiliations.

[1] Bede, i. 26.   [2] Acts ix. 15.   [3] Bede, i. 26.

Bede gives us a glimpse of St. Mellitus, the first bishop of London, offering mass in the church of St. Paul's and distributing communion to the faithful,[1] but it is only to show a sad contrast in the background of the picture. The three sons of Sabert had remained idolaters at their father's death in 616. They did not at first persecute the missionaries, but, drawn by curiosity to the church, they fancied that a slight was put on them by the Italian bishop because he would not admit them to the privileges of Christians, which they neither cared for nor understood. 'Why do you not give us also that white bread which you used to give to our father Saba, and which you still give to the people in the church?' Then, because St. Mellitus refused to be guilty of such a sacrilege, they banished him from their kingdom.

London was even then a great commercial city, 'the mart of many nations who thronged to it by sea and land,' says Bede. For twelve years the holy sacrifice was offered in its cathedral, many were baptised, many communicated. St. Gregory had marked it out as the metropolitan church of the south of England. But from the expulsion of Mellitus the church remained desolate and profaned for seven-and-thirty years. Many of the Christians who had 'once been illuminated, had tasted also the heavenly gift, and were made partakers of the Holy Ghost,'[2] fell away altogether from the faith. 'The people,' says Bede, 'having been once turned to wickedness, even when the authors of it were destroyed, would not be corrected, nor return to the unity of faith and charity which is in Christ.'[3] The impious princes who were the first to insult the Blessed Sacrament in England were soon slain in battle. The king of Kent, Eadbald, the son of Ethelbert, recalled Mellitus, and would have sent him back to his diocese, but 'the Londoners would not receive him, choosing rather to be under their idolatrous priests, nor did Eadbald's power enable him to reinstate Mellitus against the will and in spite of the refusal of the pagans.'[4] A new generation grew up, and the church of St. Paul's was doubtless pointed out to them with scorn by some—we should hope with remorse and regret by others—as the place where once the Christian sacrifice had been offered. We are reminded of the Gospel history when Jesus had driven out the evil spirits from the man, called Legion, and 'all the multitude of the country besought Jesus to depart from them; and He going up into the ship returned back again.'[5]

---

[1] Bede, ii. 5: 'Cum viderent pontificem, celebratis in ecclesia missarum solenniis, eucharistiam populo dare.'

[2] Heb. vi. 4.   [3] Bede, ii. 5.   [4] *Ib.* ii. 6.   [5] Luke viii. 37.

St. Augustine's own churches at Canterbury were spared this profanation. Bede has told us how St. Laurence, St. Augustine's successor, was preparing to abandon his work on account of the unworthy conduct of Eadbald, the son and successor of Ethelbert, and how the night before his departure he kept a tearful vigil in the church of SS. Peter and Paul :

> On his knees
> Meantime that aged priest was creeping slow
> From stone to stone, as when on battle-plain,
> The battle lost, some warrior wounded sore,
> By all forsaken, or some war-horse maimed
> Drags a blind bulk along the field in search
> Of thirst-assuaging spring. Glittered serene
> That light before the Sacrament of Love :
> Thither he bent his way, and long time prayed.[1]

St. Peter appeared to him that night in vision, warned and scourged him. Eadbald was converted, and showed himself henceforth no unworthy son of Ethelbert.[2]

In the north there was a similar vicissitude : a bright beginning, a terrible reverse, and a glorious restoration. In 627 the heathen priest Coifi profaned the temple in which he had served his gods, and became a convert to Christianity. For six years St. Paulinus preached with great success, and baptised multitudes in the Bowent, the Swale, and the Trent. King Edwin had been baptised in his royal city of York, in a little wooden chapel which was long carefully preserved within the stone cathedral afterwards erected.

But this picture is marred by a still darker shadow than that of London ; for now we have Cadwallon the Briton, a nominally Christian king, in whom national hatred triumphed over any feeling of religion he may have had, joining the heathen Penda in an attack on the newly converted Edwin. And God, who had granted Edwin a victory over his enemies in 626, to secure his conversion from idolatry, now in 633 by defeat and death admits him to His heavenly kingdom. Paulinus, like Mellitus, saw all his work of love and patience overthrown. The Britons, says Bede, paid no regard to the Christianity of their Teuton invaders, and treated them as pagans. They and their heathen allies, after the death of Edwin, ravaged the country and spared neither helpless women nor innocent children.[3] St. Paulinus had been too busy travelling from place to place over a vast region, preaching, catechising, and baptising, to build many churches. But 'he had erected a basilica at Campodunum'[4] (per-

[1] Aubrey de Vere, *Legends of the Saxon Saints*, p. 53.
[2] Bede, ii. 6.   [3] *Ib.* ii. 20.   [4] *Ib.* ii. 14.

haps Almondbury or Tanfield in Yorkshire), 'where was then the royal villa, and this was burnt down by the pagans, by whom Edwin was slain.' An altar, that was of stone, escaped destruction by the fire, and was still kept in Bede's time, *i.e.* a century later, in a monastery in the forest of Elmete,[1] probably on the site of the existing parish church of Leeds.

St. Paulinus, on this overthrow of his work, retired to Kent, conducting with him Edwin's widow, Ethelburga, the daughter of Ethelbert, and, the see of Rochester being then vacant, Honorius, the Archbishop of Canterbury, committed it to his care. Two relics of St. Paulinus's mission to Northumbria were long kept in Canterbury, 'a large golden cross and a golden chalice, dedicated to the use of the altar,' which had been presents of Edwin, and which St. Paulinus carried with him in his flight.[2] He left behind him, however, something far more precious, his deacon James, a man of God, who survived to a great old age, and never ceased to carry on the work of preaching and baptising, though as a deacon he could not offer the holy sacrifice.

After the defeat of Edwin, the two great provinces of which Northumbria was composed, Deira and Bernicia, were divided between two kings, the former falling to Osric, a convert of St. Paulinus, and the northern province, Bernicia, to Eanfrid, who had also been baptised while living in exile among the Scots. Both these princes apostatised, in order, as they hoped, to secure the support of their heathen subjects; but both fell beneath the sword of Cadwallon in the first year of their reign—a year, says Bede, that was afterwards called 'the hateful year,' because of these apostasies and of the ravages of the British king.[3]

God had prepared for the rebuilding of the Church of Northumbria a man after His own heart—'vir Deo dilectus,' says Bede, and who must be loved as well as admired by everyone who reads his history. This was the King St. Oswald; and it was by his means that the Irish Church of Dalraida, which had already spread the faith northwards, to Caithness and the Orkneys, was to find a new field of labour in South Britain, and from its new home in Lindisfarne to send bishops not only throughout Northumbria, but to Lichfield and even to London.

St. Oswald during his exile in Scotland had received the faith and the grace of baptism from the monks of St. Columba. Far from imitating the miserable Eanfrid and seeking by apostasy to win earthly favour and strength, he gathered together 'an army, small

[1] Bede, ii. 14. [2] *Ib.* ii. 20. [3] *Ib.* iii. 1.

indeed in number, but strengthened with the faith of Christ.'[1] The night before the battle, in which he was to meet a much larger army of Britons under Cadwallon, at a place already by good omen called Heavenfield, near Hexham, St. Columba appeared to him and promised him victory.[2] The victory was a glorious one for St. Oswald, and happy in its results on the Church of Northumbria; but it is nevertheless sad to think that it was a victory of Christians over Christians, of men only recently converted from paganism over men whose fathers and forefathers had been Christians. Cadwallon had been so elated with his victory over Edwin, that he hoped to recover the ancient British territory and exterminate its invaders. We can but admire his bravery and his patriotism; but his mode of warfare had been cruel, and the policy of extermination, which the Britons preferred to that of conversion, had no blessing from God. The same St. Columba who three centuries later assisted the Scotch to repel the heathen Norwegians,[3] now assisted the pious Oswald and his faithful band of followers in their battle against the Christian but cruel Britons. They were defeated with great slaughter, and Cadwallon himself perished.

St. Oswald's first care was to continue the work begun by St. Paulinus. But he did not send to Canterbury for missionaries, nor could he of course look to the Britons in the West, whose fellow-countrymen he had just defeated. He naturally turned to the Church in which he had himself received baptism, and whose founder St. Columba had encouraged him in vision. The abbots of Iona, though usually only presbyters themselves, had bishops in their community, and a monk named Corman was consecrated and sent to the work of evangelising the English, and when he returned disheartened St. Aidan took his place. Though St. Aidan so far clung to his early habits as to fix his dwelling in a remote and barren island, and he and his successors were monks as well as bishops, yet the Columban anomalous discipline of placing bishops under the jurisdiction of presbyters was never transferred to England, nor did the abbot of Iona claim any authority over the new colony.

Into the history of the work of St. Aidan, and of Finan and Colman his successors, I need not enter. Bede says that when St. Oswald erected his cross before the battle of Heavenfield there had been no church, no altar, no external sign whatever of the Christian

---

[1] Bede, iii. 1.

[2] He told this vision or dream himself to Seghine, abbot of Iona, from whom Adamnán learned it. (*Vita Col.* i. 1.)

[3] See *antea*, ch. iii. p. 68.

faith, hitherto erected throughout all the nation of the Bernicians.[1] By the labours of St. Aidan and the faithful priests whom he trained the faith was spread, monasteries were founded, churches were built in that province, which extended from the Tees to the Firth of Forth. 'The religion which he taught,' says Professor Bright, 'was essentially identical with that which prevailed at Canterbury or Dunwich, where his name was held in honour' (by Archbishop Honorius and Bishop Felix). 'Mass was celebrated at Lindisfarne on Sundays and holy days, certainly with no splendour of visible surroundings, and probably with rites differing in some measure (not, of course, as to the essentials of the service) from those of the Gregorian Liturgy which Augustine had brought into Kent, and cognate to the Gallican use which Felix, perhaps, had introduced into East Anglia; but the usual language about "the mysteries of the sacred Eucharist" was as familiar to a disciple of Hy or of Lindisfarne as to the churchmen of Gaul or Italy.'[2]

In this passage reference is made to the see of Dunwich in East Anglia. This comprised Norfolk and Suffolk. Redwald, their king, had been baptised in Kent, probably in the time of Ethelbert. On returning home, he had sought, with a policy common enough to kings, to unite two things incompatible, the worship of Christ and the worship of the devil. Bede says that in the same temple he constructed 'altare ad sacrificium Christi et arulam ad victimas dæmoniorum'—an altar for the Christian sacrifice (or perhaps for a sacrifice to Christ), and another on which to offer victims to his demons.[3] Bede does not say whether he found a Christian priest willing to offer the holy mass in this temple, and it seems more probable that he was contented with getting one of his heathen priests to imitate the Christian mysteries, offering sacrifice to Christ as to a new god received into the pagan Walhalla.

His son Earpwald, and Sigbert his stepson, were better advised; and Felix, a Burgundian bishop, succeeded in gaining the people to the faith, and establishing churches and even a seminary for priests. The conversion of the East Anglians was begun about A.D. 628.

The West Saxons were the next converted. Their conversion was due to St. Birinus. He was sent to England by Pope Honorius in 634. Of the great devotion of this saintly missionary and bishop to the Blessed Sacrament an incidental proof has been recorded by William of Malmesbury. Pope Honorius, among other things, 'had

---
[1] Bede, iii. 2.
[2] *Chapters on Early English Church History*, p. 145.
[3] Bede, ii. 15.

given him a pall or corporal on which he was accustomed to consecrate the Body of Christ, and in which also he used to wrap the Lord's Body and carry it with him hanging from his neck. But when he was consecrating the sacred mysteries he placed it on the altar.'[1]

Bede gives no details of the labours of St. Birinus, except that he placed his episcopal see at Dorchester (near Oxford), that 'by his labours he called many to the Lord,' and that 'he built and consecrated churches,' among which was one at Winchester, dedicated to St. Peter and St. Paul.[2] Beneath the cathedral church of Winchester his sacred relics now repose.

Mercia and Mid-Anglia or South Mercia were brought to the faith by English and Scottish missionaries, 653–655. They did not swerve under political changes. St. Chad, though not the first in order of time, is the most famous of the early bishops who spread and ruled the Church in the central district of England. His little church of St. Mary stood near the site of the present cathedral of Lichfield. In an oratory near this church he received a visit of angels announcing his approaching death, and 'after he had secured the safety of his departure (*munivit obitum suum*) by the reception of the Body and Blood of the Lord, his soul being delivered from the prison of the body—the angels, as may justly be believed, attending him—he departed to the joys which never end.'[3] This was on March 2, 672.

It was St. Chad's brother, St. Cedd, who was God's instrument for reconverting the East Saxons. Thirty-seven years after the banishment of St. Mellitus, A.D. 653, King Sigebert III., surnamed the Good, had been persuaded to renounce idolatry by the Northumbrian king Oswy. Having been baptised he was filled with zeal for the salvation of his subjects, and St. Cedd with another priest was sent to preach the faith. These East Saxons seem to have verified our Lord's words of the rocky soil. 'They received the word of God with joy,' just as they had done fifty years before; but 'having no roots, they believed for a while, but in the time of temptation fell away.'

---

[1] This history is in perfect harmony with the customs of the early ages, when men were sometimes allowed, in times of persecution or on long journeys, to carry the Holy Eucharist with them. The chronicler of the abbey of Hyde, in Winchester, writing in the fourteenth century, though using old documents, adds some story about Birinus walking on the sea to fetch his treasure which he had left behind. (*Book of Hyde*, p. 12, Rolls Series.) This is probably a legendary growth derived from what St. Ambrose says about his brother committing himself to the sea and coming safe to land, trusting in the Blessed Sacrament, which he carried from his neck.

[2] Bede, iii. 7.   [3] *Ib.* iv. 3.

St. Cedd converted great numbers, and, having been consecrated bishop by Finan at Lindisfarne, he returned to Essex, and 'built churches in various places, and ordained priests and deacons.' Bede does not mention his work in London. Indeed, by naming Ithancæster and Tilbury as the centres of his labours, he rather implies that the Londoners did not give him a cordial reception. When the bishop was carried off by the great plague in the year 664, some of his converts 'clung with great devotion to the creed they had received,' being animated by the example and persuasions of their sub-king Sebbi; whereas another part of the kingdom under Sighere 'forsook the mysteries of the Christian faith and turned apostate.' They attributed the pestilence to the vengeance of their false gods, and at once 'began to restore the temples that had been abandoned and to adore idols.' Happily for them the overlord, Wulfhere, King of Mercia, was a zealous Christian. 'Understanding therefore that the faith of the province was partly profaned, he sent Bishop Jaruman' to recall them. 'He proceeded,' says Bede, 'with much discretion, as I was informed by a priest who bore him company in that journey, for he was a religious and good man, and travelling through all the country, far and wide, reduced both king and people to the way of righteousness, so that, either forsaking or destroying the temples and altars they had erected, they opened the churches and rejoiced in confessing the name of Christ.'[1]

The South Saxons were the last to be converted. They were a fierce and ignorant people. We have seen the sullen indifference with which they received the preaching of St. Dichuil. At last, however, in 681 the time of God's visitation came for them. St. Wilfrid, then an exile from his own diocese of York, won their hearts by helping them in the time of famine. Ethelwald, their king, had been lately baptised in Mercia. His example was as usual powerful, and was followed by his principal soldiers and nobles. St. Wilfrid himself baptised them, and the priests he brought with him soon found abundant work in instructing and baptising the rest of the nation. The king gave him the promontory of Selsey, with its inhabitants. He founded a monastery, which became the seat of a bishopric, afterwards removed to Chichester. 'Wilfrid instructed the people of this territory in the faith of Christ, and baptised them all. Among these were 250 men and women slaves, all of whom he, by baptism, not only rescued from the servitude of the devil, but he gave them their bodily liberty also, and exempted them from the yoke of human servitude.'[2]

---

[1] Bede, iii. 30. [2] *Ib.* iv. 13.

There is a very interesting story related by St. Bede, with regard to St. Wilfrid's monastery in Selsey, which well illustrates the history of the Holy Eucharist.[1] St. Wilfrid committed the monastery, during his absence, to 'the most religious priest of Christ, Eappa.' Not long after the events above related a grievous mortality ravaged the province. 'The brethren in consequence thought fit to keep a fast of three days, and to implore the Divine goodness that it would vouchsafe to extend mercy to them, either by delivering those that were in danger by the distemper from death, or by delivering those who were snatched out of this world from the perpetual damnation of their souls. There was at that time in the monastery a little boy of the Saxon nation, lately called to the faith, who had been seized with the same distemper, and had long kept his bed. On the second day of the fasting and supplications it happened that the same boy was, about seven o'clock in the morning, left alone in the place where he lay sick, and through God's appointment the most blessed Princes of the Apostles vouchsafed to appear to him; for he was a child of an extraordinarily mild and innocent disposition, and with a sincere devotion kept the mysteries of the faith which he had received. The Apostles therefore, saluting him in a most affectionate manner, said : " Do not, dear child, fear death about which you are so uneasy, for we will this day conduct you to the heavenly kingdom. But you are first to stay till the masses are said, that, having received the viaticum of the Body and Blood of the Lord, and delivered from sickness and death, you may be carried up to the everlasting joys of heaven. Call therefore to you the priest Eappa, and tell him that the Lord has heard the prayers of the community, and accepted their devotion and their fast, and that not one more shall die of this plague, either in the monastery or its adjacent possessions. But all your people who anywhere labour under this distemper shall be eased of their pain and restored to their former health, except you alone, who are this day to be delivered by death, and to be carried into heaven, to the vision of our Lord Christ, whom you have faithfully served. This favour the Divine mercy has vouchsafed to grant you through the intercession of the religious and God-beloved King Oswald, who formerly ruled over the nation of the Northumbrians; for this very day that king was killed in war by the infidels, and taken up to the everlasting joys of souls in heaven, and associated among the number of the elect. Let them look in their books, wherein the departure of the dead is set down, and they will find that he was this day taken out of this world. Let them therefore celebrate masses in all the

[1] Bede, iv. 14.

oratories of this house, either in thanksgiving for their prayers being heard, or else in memory of the aforesaid King Oswald. It was because he formerly governed their nation that he has prayed humbly to the Lord for them, as for exiles from his nation. Let then all the brethren assemble in the church and communicate in the heavenly sacrifices, and then, ceasing to fast, refresh their bodies also with food."

'The boy called the priest and repeated all these words to him. The priest particularly inquired after the habit and form of the men that had appeared to him. He answered: "Their habit was noble, and their countenance most pleasant and beautiful, such as I had never seen before, nor did I think there could be any men so graceful and comely. One of them was tonsured like a clerk, the other had a long beard ; and they said that one of them was called Peter, the other Paul ; both of them were the servants of our Lord and Saviour, Jesus Christ, sent by Him from heaven to protect our monastery." The priest believed what the boy said, and, going thence immediately, looked in his Calendar and found that King Oswald had been killed on that very day. He then called the brethren, ordered dinner to be prepared, masses to be said, and all of them to communicate in the usual way (*more solito*). At the same time he ordered a particle of the Lord's oblation from the same sacrifice to be carried to the sick boy.

'Soon after this the boy died on that same day, and by his death proved that what he had heard from the Apostles of God was true. A further testimony of the truth was that no person died but himself at that time of that monastery. By which vision, many that heard of it were wonderfully excited to implore the Divine mercy in adversity and to adopt the wholesome remedy of fasting. From that time the day of the nativity (martyrdom) of that king and soldier of Christ began to be yearly honoured with the celebration of masses, not only in that monastery, but in many other places.'

This history Bede received from Acca, bishop of Hexham, who affirmed that it had been told him by most faithful brethren of that same monastery. It is full of interest from every point of view ; it shows St. Oswald watching over and praying for the Church of the South Saxons, as he had himself been watched over and prayed for by St. Columba, the Apostle of the Northern Picts, and so binds together the whole of Great Britain, from the Orkneys to the Isle of Wight,[1]

---

[1] The Isle of Wight, once Christian, had been utterly pagan for two centuries, when St. Wilfrid sent thither the priest, Hiddila, and mass was once more offered. (Bede, iv. 16.)

in one communion of prayer and sacred rites and of heavenly patronage. But, even should anyone doubt the truth of the child's vision, the testimony of Bede would still remain to the faith and practices of piety which he relates, and which were of course matters with which he was familiar. We see many oratories even in a newly constructed monastery, with altars where many priests can say mass at the same time. We see a church in which the high or public mass is said, and at which the lay brethren communicate as usual. We see the viaticum administered under one species (*particulam*) to the dying boy; and though he is a child (*puerulus*) and only recently baptised, it is evidently not his first communion, and he is well instructed in the faith. We notice the hour at which masses were usually offered—about nine o'clock—and we see some of the intentions of the sacrifice. These are matters on which much will have to be said. Let us first make a general survey of the work thus happily begun and of the obstacles to its completion.

At the beginning of the seventh century the greater part of England was covered with the dark clouds of paganism. On the land occupied by the Teutonic invaders one bright star alone is seen shining at Canterbury, the altar where Bishop Liudhard says mass and Queen Bertha communicates. But as, when the wind rises, the clouds disperse, and for a time there are clear spaces in the heavens filled with stars, and then again these are hidden by the clouds, and afterwards other and larger spaces are opened, until at last the clouds are cleared away and the whole heavens are one brilliant field of light, so was it with England. Churches were built and heathen temples closed; then the temples were reopened, and churches were shut or burnt. But at last the Spirit of God moving in the hearts of men triumphed over the demons of idolatry, and at the end of the century there was no longer a heathen temple standing unpurified or unsanctified.

Still the work was not complete. The closing of heathen temples had to be followed by the removal of ignorance and vice from heathen hearts. They had to be regenerated by the sacrament of baptism, and, according to our Lord's commission, taught 'to observe all things whatsoever He had commanded.' One of the first steps towards this work was to send priests everywhere among the people. But before this could be done the priests themselves had to be found. The number of those who came from Italy and Gaul was small, and though the Irish from North Britain gave zealous and efficient help, yet a native clergy was a first necessity. Hence St. Cedd at once ordained priests and deacons, and St. Aidan even ransomed slaves and gave them the instruction necessary for the priesthood, that they might help in the conversion of their fellow-countrymen; and Bede urged Egbert to ordain priests to preach in the villages. Of course neither the Italian nor the Irish priests were familiar with the Saxon tongue, and had sometimes to preach by the help of an interpreter. King Edwin gladly performed this office for St. Paulinus, and King Oswald for St. Aidan. The advantage of having priests who could speak the language of the people was so great that the bishops seem at first to have been satisfied with the absolutely indispensable amount of ecclesiastical learning. Though the liturgy of the mass was invariably in Latin, and no other tongue was ever used for the divine office or for the administration of sacraments, yet Bede tells us there were in his time, in the north, many *sacerdotes idiotæ*, priests who might be able to read Latin, but who knew little of it, and were only familiar with their own language. Perhaps in the south the discipline was more severe, since in St. Theodore's genuine Penitential we read that 'Holy Communion (*Sacrificium*) is not to be received from a priest who cannot properly (*secundum ritum*) recite the prayers and lessons.'[1]

At a very early period resident priests, whether monastic or secular, were attached to country churches.[2] Possibly the south was for a time better supplied with such churches than the north. In 734, Venerable Bede wrote to Egbert, archbishop of York, complaining that in mountainous and remote regions, for years together, the bishop was never seen; and that not only no bishop went to confirm the baptised, but that no preacher was there to teach the faith and the difference between right and wrong, though care was taken that everyone paid his tribute to the bishop; and he exhorts Egbert to ordain priests, who might give themselves to preaching the word of God in every village, to the consecration of the heavenly mysteries (*consecrandis mysteriis cælestibus*), and especially to administering baptism. It was probably partly owing to this letter, which was the saintly historian's last legacy to the Church, that measures were taken more strenuously to supply the want, as we see to have been the case from the legislation of councils held after his death. Yet long before this time, though resident pastors had not been appointed, many zealous priests had been found to go about among the country folk; St.

---

[1] Haddan and Stubbs, vol. iii. p. 192.

[2] There can be no doubt that St. Willibrord copied in Frisia the system in which he had been brought up. Now Alcuin says in his life that many laymen were moved by their newly acquired faith to offer him land (*patrimonia sua*). He ordered churches to be built on these lands, and appointed priests in each of them (*statuitque per eas* [*sc.* ecclesias] *singulos presbyteros*). (*Opera* Alc. tom. ii. 188.)

Boniface, who was himself an assiduous missionary in England before he went to convert the heathen on the continent, remembered that when he was a child five years old (A.D. 685) 'it was the custom in England for priests and clerks to go about preaching to the people, stopping for a time in the houses of laymen.'[1] And in these missionary labours, that the poorest serfs or bondmen were not forgotten or excluded from the holy sacraments and holy mass, is made known incidentally—for it was quite unnecessary to state it explicitly—in what is said of St. Boniface, 'that he neither flattered the rich nor was too severe with slaves.'[2]

Bede complained of the want of priests settled in remote districts, and also perhaps of a falling off in missionary zeal, yet he has recorded many beautiful examples which show how the knowledge of the faith, and with it the possession of the most holy sacrifice, was gradually propagated throughout the land.

In the early years of St. Cuthbert, before he entered the monastery of Melrose, about 650, an occurrence is related which shows that in spite of their baptism the hearts of the rustics were sometimes infected with their ancient paganism. For, seeing some monks being driven out to sea and in danger of being lost at the mouth of the Tyne, the people 'began to deride their manner of life, as if they had deserved their fate by abandoning the usual life of men and framing new rules for themselves. When Cuthbert rebuked them and bade them pray, they replied angrily: "Let none pray for them, and may God spare none of them, for they have taken away from men the ancient rites and customs, and how the new ones are to be attended to nobody knows."'[3]

Some years later when Cuthbert, who had witnessed this outburst of heathen petulance, was a monk and a priest, his zeal was stirred to instruct these ignorant men. 'He used often,' says Bede,[4] 'to go out from his monastery (of Melrose), sometimes on horseback, sometimes on foot, to preach the way of truth to the neighbouring villages, as Boisil, his predecessor, had done before him. It was at this time customary for the English people to flock together when a clerk or priest entered a village, and listen to what he said, that so they might learn something from him and amend their lives.

'Now Cuthbert was so skilful in teaching, so affectionate in his persuasions, and had so angelic a light beaming from his countenance, that none dared conceal from him the secrets of their hearts, but they confessed openly what they had done, for they were convinced that

---

[1] See Life by St. Willibald, apud Migne, *Patrol.* tom. lxxxix. p. 605.
[2] *Ib.* p. 609.   [3] Beda, *Vita S. Cuthb.* cap. 3.   [4] *Ib.* cap. 9.

nothing could be concealed from him, and they expiated the faults they had confessed by worthy fruits of penance, according as he imposed them.

'He was also wont to seek out and preach in those remote villages which were situated far from the world in wild mountain places and fearful to behold, and which, as well by their poverty as by their distance up the country, prevented intercourse between them and such as could instruct their inhabitants. He often remained a week, sometimes two or three, or even a whole month, without returning to his monastery, but dwelling in the mountains called the people to heavenly things both by his preaching and his holy life.'[1]

This account given by Venerable Bede of North Britain in the seventh century is exactly similar to the records of the 'missions' given by St. Francis Regis in the mountains of Switzerland in the seventeenth century, of St. Leonard in Corsica or St. Alphonsus in Calabria in the eighteenth. St. Cuthbert, though not charged with the cure of souls, leaves the retirement of the cloister to catechise, to exhort, to hear confessions, for a week, a fortnight, or a month; and though Bede does not here mention it, from similar histories we know that he said mass daily, and gave communion to all whom he could prepare, according to the canonical discipline then in force. Authors of Jansenistical tendencies complain [2] that it was the missions of itinerant preachers and confessors of the orders of St. Dominic and St. Francis in the thirteenth century that made the observance of canonical penance previous to communion impossible, and thus changed the Church's discipline. But it would seem that they should have gone back at least six centuries earlier. They would have

---

[1] It is curious that, in giving this extract from Bede, Mr. Skene (*Celtic Scotland*, vol. ii. p. 208) omits the whole passage about the administration of the sacrament of penance, so that for his readers the identity between the missions of St. Cuthbert in the seventh century and those of Catholic priests in the nineteenth is lost. The saint merely appears as a preacher, not as a confessor. Dr. Giles, too, though he gives the Latin—'et confessa dignis, ut imperabat, pœnitentiæ fructibus abstergerent'—translates it thus: 'they hoped to merit forgiveness by an honest confession.' I do not for a moment suspect either writer of a wish to conceal or to mislead. I suppose the circumstance of confession did not interest Mr. Skene, and that Dr. Giles missed the force of the words, which show that the confession was sacramental. Yet Catholics will see in this example the necessity of consulting original documents. Bede repeats the same thing in almost the same words in his *History*, iv. 27, and there Dr. Giles translates correctly, or rather prints the correct translation of another.

[2] Chardon, *Histoire des Sacrements*, 'Pénitence,' sect. iii. pt. 4, ch. 1. Fleury, 6ᵉ discours: 'Ces missionnaires passagers ne pouvaient suivre pendant un long temps la conduite des pénitents pour examiner le progrès et la solidité de leur conversion,' &c.

found similar facts, and an author like Venerable Bede, not lamenting over, but rejoicing in, the results.

The words of Bede supply also a refutation of an error of a contrary character. One of the latest Protestant authorities—Dr. Smith's 'Dictionary of Christian Antiquities'—states, as if it were a proved fact, that to a period considerably later than that of St. Cuthbert or St. Bede, confession, though a common practice, was not considered of strict obligation. Most certainly neither the simple mountaineers of Bernicia, nor their saintly missionary, nor his learned biographer had heard of this view of the subject. St. Cuthbert had evidently taught them that confession must be made for grievous sins committed after baptism, and penance performed as imposed by the confessor. On this supposition only can we explain Bede's remark, that, however shame might have tempted them to keep back their sins or confess them imperfectly, yet they confessed clearly and openly, no one *daring* to keep the most secret thing hidden (*nullus latebras ei sui cordis*[1] *celare præsumeret, omnes palam, quæ gesserant, confitendo proferrent*).

I have purposely dwelt on this incident, because we thus learn the character of the teaching of the great missionaries of those days—the Aidans, Kentigerns, Columbas, and the rest, whose biographers generally dwell on the personal incidents of their lives, their miracles, or the details of their virtues, rather than on their doctrine and discipline, which were of course those of the whole Catholic Church, and therefore well known to the readers whom alone those biographers or historians could foresee.

[1] This is the very expression used by the Council of Trent.

CHAPTER VII.

THE EASTER CONTROVERSY.

WE have studied the doctrine and discipline of the Holy Eucharist in the ancient British Church in her own native documents, and we have found a perfect unity, not only with the Catholic Church of other lands at that period, but also with the Catholic Church of our own time. The distinction between ancient and modern Catholicity is, of course, unmeaning to those who believe in ' One, Holy, Catholic, and Apostolic Church ; ' yet the reiterated proof of this marvellous identity will not be thought superfluous in the presence of modern controversies. A recent Protestant historian contrasts ' the advance of corruption in government, in faith, in doctrine, which was being made under papal leadership' throughout the rest of Europe, with the steadfast adherence to primitive truth and discipline which distinguished the isolated British Church. And he points to the Conference of St. Augustine with the British bishops in 603 as 'one of the tidemarks of time, as the meeting of the Christianity of the year 400 with that of 600.'[1] Now it has been shown that this isolated Church held the same faith with ourselves on one of the central Mysteries of Christianity. We have thus one more proof of the apostolicity of the Church.

The same result has followed from the study of the Church of the Scots and Picts. We found it in communion with the Britons, with the Irish of Hibernia, with the churches of the Continent, and especially with that of Rome ; and in this case also, from the intrinsic evidence of native documents, we have seen that these Christians on the remotest confines of Christendom, in those far-off ages, were as familiar as ourselves with the Christian priesthood, the ' sacrificial

---

[1] Rev. Dr. Boultbee, *History of the Church of England* (1879), pp. 33, 37. It is almost needless to say that the writer gives no proof of corruption, or of change, or of disagreement. He supposes, indeed, that the British Church knew nothing of papal supremacy, which would apparently fall under ' government.' But he does not say what question of ' faith ' or of ' doctrine ' was raised, nor does he explain how faith and doctrine differ.

mystery of the Eucharist,' the permanent and objective Presence of our Lord's Body and Blood, and all else that regards the essence of the great Commemorative Rite.

In confirmation of this unity of faith and worship we have seen, in the last chapter, missionaries from Rome meeting and mingling with missionaries from Iona, and the work of Anglo-Saxon conversion accomplished by these two agencies with one harmonious result. When we shall have studied in detail, from the fuller documents which we possess, the faith and practice of the Anglo-Saxons, the light thus obtained may be reflected back on the Scottish Church, and indirectly on that also of the Britons.

But before proceeding to this study I must examine a matter which, while it testifies to the unity of faith, somewhat mars the unity of love in the seventh and eighth centuries among the Christians of Great Britain. I refer first to the Easter controversy, and secondly to its results in engendering a real or supposed schism.

In the first place, then, the disputes which we are about to investigate bring out, in the most incontrovertible and convincing way, how absolute was the unanimity of belief between the Roman missionaries and the Christians whom they found in these islands, not only as to the Eucharist, but also as to every other point of faith. There were antagonisms, jealousies, and disputes on points of discipline, and in the zeal of controversy every difference, even in the shape of a tonsure, was magnified and sometimes made a byword of reproach; yet not once did there escape from the lips of either party a reproach implying defect in faith or error in worship. Discrepancies had arisen in the celebration of the Easter festival, from different reckoning of time, not from diversity of principle. As to the Mystery which was commemorated at Easter, or the Rite of commemoration, there was no discrepancy. St. Bede does indeed affirm that, besides their error in computing the time of Easter, the Britons 'did also very many other things contrary to ecclesiastical unity.'[1] It is, however, certain that, whatever was the nature of these things, they in no way affected faith, morals, or worship; for St. Augustine was content to tolerate the diversity, provided only they would reform their Easter cycle, and complete[2] the ceremonies of baptism. As regards the nature of British peculiarities in other matters we are left to conjecture. They cannot have been of great importance, since almost the only one that became a topic of contention was the shape of the

---

[1] *History*, ii. 2.

[2] It is not certain in what the defect consisted. Some think it was in not confirming after baptism, others in the omission of certain unctions.

ecclesiastical and monastic tonsure. An old document, attributed to St. Gildas, though probably of a somewhat later date, but in any case emanating not from a Roman or Saxon adversary, but from a British zealot for Roman unity and reform, makes what seems at first a formidable charge against the Welsh. 'The Britons,' it says, 'are contrary to the whole world, enemies to Roman customs, not only in the mass, but also in the tonsure.'[1] These words cannot have been written after the eighth century, for by that time the Britons in every part of the island had conformed to the Roman fashion of wearing the corona instead of the old British tonsure, made by shaving the front part of the head. With the tonsure we are not concerned. Were the peculiarities of the mass of a more serious nature? Was it a question of ceremonial or of what is essential in the sacred rite? There can be no hesitation in answering these questions. No question of doctrine was involved, nothing that regarded the Real Presence, or the nature of the sacrifice, or the intentions for which it should be offered. As to such matters no breath of accusation was ever heard on either side. Again, there was nothing regarding the validity of the sacred rite, the time or place of sacrifice, or the dispositions of the celebrant. St. Gregory had been asked by St. Augustine: 'Since the faith is one and the same, how is it that there are different customs in different churches, and that one custom of masses is held in the Holy Roman Church, and another in those of Gaul?' St. Gregory had replied: 'Your fraternity knows the custom of the Roman Church, in which you have been brought up. I consent, however (*mihi placet*), that if you have found anything, whethe in the Roman, or the Gallic, or in any other Church, which may be more pleasing to God' [than other rites], 'you should carefully select it; and so in the English Church, which is new as regards the faith, you should introduce in its first foundation whatever you have thus been able to gather together from the different Churches. For things are not to be loved for the sake of places, but places for the sake of good things.'[2]

St. Augustine made a sparing use of this permission as regarded the English Church. He found nothing preferable to the Roman rite; he therefore introduced it with only one or two modifications borrowed from Gaul.[3] The rule of St. Gregory, however, served as his guide in dealing with the Britons. He made no complaint as to their peculiarities of prayer or ceremonial. Though he did not see how the Italians and the Britons could co-operate as missionaries to

---

[1] Haddan and Stubbs, i. 112.   [2] Bede, i. 27.
[3] On this subject see Chapter XIII.

the heathen, if their catechumens were to be bewildered by different rites of baptism, or if the great Christian festival was celebrated at different seasons by men living in the same place and engaged in the same work, he had no objection that the Italian and British priests should celebrate at the same altar with only slightly varying rites. There was nothing in such a spectacle of a nature to scandalise the heathen or to perplex the neophytes.

All ecclesiastics were not as tolerant as St. Gregory and St. Augustine. Hence the bitter tone of the complaint quoted above. It may be added that when, in the year 624, an accusation was made at the Council of Mâcon against the Scottish liturgy—which was probably the British or closely akin to the British—nothing more serious was alleged than the multiplicity of collects.[1] As the question of baptism, whatever it may have been, was never again alluded to, so far as we know, and other discrepancies were judged to be quite secondary, we may confine our attention to the Easter dispute.

To those unfamiliar with astronomical calculations and computations of time it is not easy to explain the nature of this controversy; nor is it necessary for my purpose to enter into detail. It is enough to say that from the first centuries, and indeed from the days of the Apostles, a great festival had been instituted to commemorate our Lord's Resurrection. This was not fixed on a certain day of the month, but was moveable. On Easter depended the feast of the Ascension, that of Pentecost, and of course the time for beginning the fast of the forty days of Lent. The recurrence of this festival was regulated to some extent by that of the Jewish Passover, which had typified our Lord's Redemption; and it was therefore called the Paschal day.[2] The Jews killed their lamb on the fourteenth day of the moon after the vernal equinox; and it was agreed that Christians should take the Sunday after the fourteenth day for their Paschal day. Some Eastern Christians who observed the fourteenth day with the Jews were condemned as Quartodecimans. The Nicene Council decreed not only that the festival should always be kept on a Sunday, but also that if the fourteenth day fell on a Sunday the Pasch should be deferred to the Sunday after. There were no real Quartodecimans at any time in Britain. Since, however, the Celtic Churches neglected from ignorance part of this decree of the Council and kept the festival

---

[1] Haddan and Stubbs, i. 154.

[2] The English word *Easter* is derived from the name of a Saxon goddess whose feast fell about that season, just as Saxon deities have their names embodied in our days of the week. *Lent* merely signifies Spring, and has been transferred to the spring.

on the fourteenth, when that day was a Sunday, though not otherwise, their opponents applied to them uncharitably the nickname of Quartodecimans.

There is in fact nothing in the Paschal disputes with which we are here engaged to connect the British Church with the East or to confirm the theory of its original independence of Rome. Such a theory was maintained by several of the older Protestant controversialists. It is now universally abandoned by candid and learned men 'The facts of the case,' says Mr. Haddan, 'prove the Western, not the Eastern, origin of the British Church. And the difference arose in that Church, as Bede testifies of the Scots of Hii, "from having none to bring them the synodal decrees for the observance of Easter, by reason of their being so far away from the rest of the world."'[1]

The same learned author writes: 'Up to the Council of Nice (A.D. 312) the practice of the British harmonised with that of the entire Western Church, *i.e.* with the Roman. From the Council of Nice up to the middle of the fifth century, the Britons followed the Western Church in its gradual divergence from that of Alexandria and the East, arising mainly from the use of different lunar cycles. But when St. Augustine and the Saxon Church came in contact with them in the sixth century, it appeared that the Britons still acted upon the cycle which the Church of Rome had used with some changes up to 458, but had then changed, and still retained what had (it would seem) been the original Roman rule, of keeping the fourteenth day of the moon (so determined) if a Sunday.'[2]

To have been dispossessed of a great part of their country, to have been isolated from the rest of Christendom, and in their sufferings and isolation to have clung to their ancient faith, and to the rules received from Rome, these were certainly not crimes in the Britons. To have fallen behind Rome in the progress of astronomical calculations, and so to have got out of harmony with the more enlightened part of Christendom, was merely their misfortune. How far they were to blame in clinging to a rule which had become antiquated is a further and a difficult question. They well knew that if faith is in-

---

[1] Haddan and Stubbs, *Councils*, i. 153. See Bright, p. 79.
[2] *Ib.* p. 152. We have seen in Chapter I. that the British bishops had agreed at Arles that the Bishop of Rome should announce to them the time for keeping Easter. And, in fact, so late as A.D. 455, in a case wherein Rome and Alexandria temporarily differed, the Britons followed the directions of Pope St. Leo the Great, as their own annals testify. 'Pasca commutatur super diem Dominicum cum papa Leone episcopo Romæ.'

variable, discipline may change. Yet they certainly refused reform, and seemed obstinate in their isolation, and, as it were, proud of it, for a time. After a long study of all the documents on this question I can see in this no formal rebellion against the Holy See, nor positive schism with the rest of Christendom; but rather a national pride which made them unwilling to acknowledge themselves in the wrong, and especially to learn what was right from a nation which had been their deadly enemy, and had been only recently converted to the faith.

But why, it may be asked, did St. Augustine insist so strongly that the Britons should conform on this point?

By some Protestants, who have little experience of festivals (in the spiritual sense of the word), and none whatever of fasts, he has been blamed for exacting uniformity in a trivial matter as a condition of co-operation. It has been said that he forgot the wise rules given him by St. Gregory. It is quite evident, however, by his toleration of ritual diversity, that he had in no wise lost sight of those rules. The application of them had been left to his own discretion. He foresaw that so great a discrepancy as that of keeping Lent and Easter in different weeks would have engendered quarrels among Christians, or at least would have been an almost insuperable obstacle to united prayer and action, while it would have utterly scandalised the heathen or bewildered the converts. What he foresaw did indeed actually take place. For though the Britons refused to yield or to co-operate in preaching to their heathen invaders, the two ecclesiastical systems at last met and came into collision in the north of Britain. Bede has related the nature and the results of this collision. 'At this time' (*i.e.* about A.D. 652) 'a great and frequent controversy happened about the observance of Easter; those who came from Kent or France affirming that the Scots kept Easter Sunday contrary to the custom of the Universal Church. . . . James, formerly the deacon of the venerable archbishop Paulinus, kept the true and Catholic Easter with all those whom he could instruct in the more correct way. Queen Eanfleda (the daughter of Ethelbert, St. Augustine's first convert) and her followers also observed the same, as she had seen practised in Kent, having with her a Kentish priest who followed the Catholic mode, whose name was Romanus. Thus it is said to have happened in those times that Easter was twice kept in one year, and that when the king, having ended the time of fasting, kept his Easter, the queen and her followers were still fasting and celebrating Palm Sunday.' This difference, continues Bede, was borne patiently out of personal respect for St. Aidan and St. Finan until their deaths. 'But after the death of Finan, who succeeded Aidan, when Colman, who was also sent out of Scotland (A.D. 661), came to be bishop, a greater controversy arose. Whereupon this dispute began naturally to influence the thoughts and hearts of many, who feared "lest, having received the name of Christians, they might happen to run, or to have run, in vain."[1] He then relates how the matter was discussed and settled at the synod of Whitby, and how, when Colman and some of his followers would not abandon their customs, they were obliged to withdraw from the country, since it had been found impossible for the two systems to work together.[2]

Nor must it be thought that this was one of those matters which was only drawn to be a cause of strife by the excesses of religious or ecclesiastical zeal. If we can for a moment put aside our modern prepossessions and think what was the significance of Lent and Easter in those days, it will not be difficult to understand why St. Augustine insisted on unity of ecclesiastical computation before there could be unity of action. Ash Wednesday and Easter Sunday, to most modern Protestants, are mere names of bygone things. Though this is not the case with modern Catholics, yet the secular life takes such precedence of the devotional life, and the Church has for various reasons been compelled to modify her discipline of fast and abstinence to such a degree, that we cannot judge of the importance of ecclesiastical observances in the seventh century from anything with which we are ourselves familiar.

Let it then be remembered that to taste meat even once during Lent was a thing unheard of, and that for adults the fast from all food was not broken till near sunset ; that, on the other hand, the celebration of the Easter festival absorbed the whole attention of the people, to the complete interruption of every secular pursuit. On the computation of Easter depended of course that of Ascension and Whit Sunday; while at Easter and Whitsuntide the catechumens were solemnly admitted to baptism and communion. Lastly, it must be kept in mind that the divergence in the computation might amount sometimes to a week, sometimes to a whole month.[3] If these things are taken into account, he must be singularly dull or prejudiced who does not or will not see that this was not, as Hume affirms, 'a frivolous controversy in theology,' nor 'a dispute of the most ridiculous kind and entirely worthy of those ignorant and barbarous ages.'

Whether the other disputes recorded in history, or those for which

---

[1] Gal. ii. 2.   [2] *Eccl. Hist.* book iii. ch. 25.
[3] See Reeves's *Adamnan*, p. 347 ; also pp. 26-28. For an example see St. Gregory of Tours, v. 17.

nations now go to war, are of a more important nature, or whether the disputes of philosophers are more calmly conducted or of a nobler character than those of theologians, are questions which might perhaps admit of discussion. Supposing, however, that the God who created men did really love them so as to die for their sake, and then rise victorious from the tomb—supposing that it is worth while for men to keep a vivid memory of such facts—supposing that God is propitiated by faith, prayer, fasting, and penance, and that He has given men, as channels of His grace, sacraments which must be worthily received—supposing that, to keep alive in all times and countries the memory of His earthly sufferings and to convey the fulness of His divine benefits, He has given power to men to consecrate His own Body and Blood, to offer them in sacrifice to His Eternal Father, and has promised that those who feed on them worthily shall live in Him and He in them—let us make such suppositions as these, and it will probably appear to us that no more important matter could occupy men's minds than the due celebration of Lent and Easter, and no more perplexing and serious controversy could divide their minds than such as would arise from uncertainty as to the time at which those seasons should annually recur. No doubt, if Christianity is a gigantic falsehood or delusion, as Hume and his school teach, then the human race must find other matters to agree in or to dispute about. That they will find anything more worthy or more beneficial to happiness and civilisation than what seemed vital to Celts and Saxons in the seventh century, has not yet been made evident.

Hume continues his sneer as follows : 'The dispute lasted more than a century, and was at last finished, not by men discovering the folly of it, which would have been too great an effort for human reason to accomplish, but by the entire prevalence of the Romish ritual over the Scotch and British.' What human reason, aided by grace, did discover, was, not merely the importance of the Easter celebration—of that men had been always convinced—but the importance of uniformity in its celebration, if it was to be a bond of union and not a source of division between men ; and the impossibility of attaining to this uniformity by any other means than by submission to the central and divine authority of Rome.

The disputes lasted long, and produced in some cases disastrous results. Many influences were at work to retard uniformity. Some were kept for a time in erroneous discipline merely by attachment to old ways and the difficulty which is found everywhere and in all times, but especially in times of civil disturbance, of introducing ecclesiastical reforms. This cause alone seems to have operated in the south of Ireland, where the necessary changes were earliest introduced. 'The Southern Irish,' says Professor Bright, 'gave up their Paschal reckonings in deference to Papal exhortations, to the opinion of some of their own leading men, *e.g.* St. Cummian, and to evidence obtained as to the prevalence of the "Catholic Easter," not only at Rome, but in other leading Churches—about A.D. 634.'[1] In the north of Ireland the obstacle was greater; for the authority of St. Columba's example was alleged in favour of the old system, and could Columba have been mistaken? It was, however, by the influence of St. Adamnan, St. Columba's successor at Hy, that the north of Ireland yielded in 704. He was less successful with his own community of monks, whose attachment to St. Columba was stronger. 'Returning to his island,' says Bede, 'after having celebrated the canonical Easter in Ireland, he most earnestly inculcated the observance of the Catholic time of Easter in his monastery, yet without being able to prevail; and it so happened that he departed this life before the next year came round, the Divine goodness so ordaining it, that, as he was a great lover of peace and unity, he should be taken away to everlasting life before he should be obliged, on the return of the time of Easter, to quarrel still more seriously with those that would not follow him in the truth.'[2]

The Picts were not merely the spiritual children of St. Columba, but were under the ecclesiastical government of Iona. Yet they did not think themselves bound to wait for their monks' example or permission before obeying the holy Roman Church. In 710 Naitan, the British king, sent messengers to Ceolfrid, abbot of Jarrow, where Bede then resided, 'desiring that he would write him a letter, by the help of which he might the better refute those that presumed to keep Easter out of the due time. He also prayed to have architects sent him to build a church in his nation after the Roman manner, promising to dedicate the same in honour of St. Peter, the prince of the apostles, and that he and all his people would always follow the custom of the Holy Roman and Apostolic Church, as far at least as their remoteness from the Roman language and nation would allow them to become acquainted with it.' Ceolfrid did as the king desired, and concludes a very long letter with these words: 'But I now admonish your wisdom, O king, that you endeavour to make the nation, over which the King of kings and Lord of lords has placed you, observe in all points those things which appertain to the unity of the Catholic and Apostolic Church; for thus it will come to pass

---

[1] *Chapters of Early English Church History*, p. 98.   [2] Bede, v. 21.

that, after your temporal kingdom has passed away, the most blessed prince of the apostles will open to you and yours the entrance into the heavenly kingdom, where you will rest for ever with the elect.' The king obeyed this exhortation, says Bede, ' and the nation thus reformed rejoiced as being newly put under the discipline of Peter, the most blessed prince of the apostles, and secure under his protection.' [1]

It is not a little strange that where St. Adamnan, the abbot of Iona, and the relative and successor of St. Columba, had failed, an English priest should have succeeded. But God had reserved the work of pacification to Egbert, a man of God, of whom Bede often speaks in terms of almost unbounded admiration. He was a native of Northumbria, but had spent many years in Ireland in penance, prayer, and study. He had planned an apostolic journey to the continent for the conversion of his pagan kinsmen in Frisia and Old Saxony. While he was making preparations for this journey he twice received an intimation from one of his companions that this was not the will of God; that Boisil, formerly abbot of Melrose (a Columban foundation), had appeared to him in vision, and told him that Egbert's zeal should rather be extended to the Columban monks at Iona, since 'their ploughs did not go straight.' Though Egbert treated these visions as delusions, yet when the ship in which he set sail with his companions for Saxony was wrecked on the coast of Ireland, he desisted from his enterprise, and resolved to attempt the work in which Adamnan had failed. 'He was joyfully and honourably received,' says Bede. Being a most agreeable teacher, and devout in practising those things which he taught, and being willingly heard by all, he, by his pious and frequent exhortations, converted them from that inveterate tradition of their ancestors, of whom may be said those words of the Apostle, 'that they had the zeal of God, but not according to knowledge.' His success is attributed by Bede to a singular grace given to these monks as a reward for their charity towards the English, just as he attributes the greater obstinacy of the Britons to their want of this charity. 'The monks of Hy adopted the Catholic rites under Abbot Dunchad, in A.D. 716, about eighty years after they had sent Aidan to preach to the English nation. The man of God, Egbert, remained thirteen years in the island of Iona. In the year 729, in which the Paschal feast was observed on April 24, after he had celebrated the solemnities of mass in honour of our Lord's resurrection, he passed away to the Lord; and thus he completed in heaven, with our Lord and His apostles, that high festival

---

[1] Bede, v. 21.

which he had begun on earth with the brethren whom he had converted, or rather he did not complete it, but will continue it for ever.'[1]

The Britons yielded more reluctantly than the Irish. The spirit of resentment against their conquerors, which had prompted their ungracious answer to St. Augustine, had been intensified by the spiritual isolation that they had imposed upon themselves. He who refuses contemptuously to do a good work seldom rejoices when he sees it done by another; he criticises and depreciates it. If we may believe the testimonies of St. Bede and St. Aldhelm, and we have nothing whatever to set against them, the Britons were so far from rejoicing in the success of the Roman and Irish missionaries that they counted their work as nothing. When, therefore, they had refused to make any concession of national customs at the invitation of St. Augustine, they were likely to be much more obstinate when they saw the discipline that they had rejected adopted by their hated enemies, and when they heard this discipline lauded by them as the Orthodox, the Catholic, the Roman, they fell back with pride on the antiquity of their own, and associated it with the illustrious names of St. David, St. Cadoc, St. Gildas and St. Terlo, St. Dubricius, and St. Illtyd, who had flourished before St. Augustine's landing. Their obstinacy was blamed not only by Anglo-Saxons, but also by the Irish.

An Irish canon of the latter part of the seventh century says: 'Britones omnibus contrarii sunt, et a Romano more et ab unitate Ecclesiæ se abscidunt.'[2] But before their obstinacy could degenerate into formal schism, Elrod, Bishop of Bangor, whom the Welsh annals call 'a man of God,' set the example of adopting the Roman Easter in his own diocese in 755, and, after some opposition arising from local jealousies, Catholic discipline was restored throughout Wales.[3]

This long-protracted and acrimonious strife had, under the providence of God, at least one good effect. It brought home, to Celts and Saxons alike, the importance of unity and the divinely appointed means of attaining it. Heresy had early been suppressed among the Britons. In Ireland it had not found a footing. St. Columbanus wrote to Pope Boniface IV. about A.D. 610:—'We Irish who inhabit the extremities of the world are the disciples of St. Peter and St. Paul, and of the other apostles who have written under dictation of the Holy Spirit. We receive nothing more than the apostolic and

---

[1] Bede, v. 9, 22.   [2] Haddan and Stubbs, *Councils*, i. 126.
[3] *Ib.* pp. 203, 204.

evangelical doctrine. There has never been either a heretic, a Jew, or a schismatic among us.' In the period which we have been studying, both Churches, the British and the Irish, gloried in their orthodoxy. But orthodoxy cannot be safely entrusted to the keeping of mere nationalism, however conservative and tenacious of ancient ways. And an unyielding orthodoxy of this inherited sort may be easily allied with narrowness and obstinacy in matters wherein change is lawful and sometimes a duty. Thus it seems to have been with St. Columbanus, who brought trouble upon himself and gave trouble to others by his obstinate perseverance when in Gaul in celebrating Easter according to the Irish usage.[1] Thus it certainly was with the Britons, and in a less degree with the Irish in Britain. And had not Britons and Irish admitted the authority of the see of St. Peter in Rome, the dissensions to which nationalism gave rise, instead of being healed, would have grown more and more bitter, and would have led to open schism, and ultimately to heresy. But Celts as well as Saxons did acknowledge the supremacy of Rome, and though the obedience yielded was somewhat slow, it was the fruit of profound conviction. The Holy See was very tolerant and very patient. In the words of Venerable Bede, of St. Wilfrid, and St. Aldhelm, vindicating the rights of Roman usage against the Celts, there is some asperity, and, as regards the Britons, an apparent forgetfulness of the reasons they might have for declining to listen to Saxon advocacy even of a good cause. But Rome did not doubt the loyalty of her Celtic children, and waited gently for their submission. It was only when a few of them took upon themselves to propagate their national usages and to set them up where already the Catholic discipline was in possession, that they were treated as schismatics and subjected to censure.[2]

The consequence of this forbearance was, that when the children, who had been wilful rather than rebellious, submitted to their mother's wishes, there was no sullenness, no soreness from a sense of humiliation, not even a remembrance of alienation. Welsh documents of every class will be searched in vain for even one expression

---

[1] 'This peculiarity,' says Montalembert, 'at once trifling and oppressive, disturbed his whole life and weakened his authority.' (*Monks of the West*, vol. ii. p. 406, Eng. Tr.) Yet Montalembert has vindicated St. Columbanus's sentiments with regard to the supremacy of the Holy See.

[2] St. Theodore condemned as schismatic the Britons and Scots who, *being in England*, refused to adopt the established and Catholic usages ; and Pope Gregory III., in 739, warned the Bavarian bishops against British missionaries. (Haddan and Stubbs, i. 203, and iii. 197.) These authors seem to me greatly to exaggerate the disputes, which never attained to 'formal schism,' except in the case just mentioned.

betokening disaffection to Rome, or the record of past disaffection. Political causes kept up jealousies and bitterness between the sister Churches of Wales and England, long after every ecclesiastical difference had ceased, yet the Welsh Church even vied with the English in affectionate loyalty to the see of Peter. If Saxon kings went on pilgrimage to Rome, so did Welsh. If Alfred the Great was devout to the Holy See, Howel the Good was still more so. Howel Dda became king of South Wales in 909, and of North Wales in 915. Being desirous, like Alfred, to make good laws for his people, he took with him three bishops, and made a journey to Rome to learn what were the laws in other Christian countries, and what had been formerly the laws in Britain in the time of the Roman emperors. He then returned to Wales, and with the assistance of his wise men drew up a code which he took himself to Rome for confirmation. The preface of the Venedotian copy of this code charmingly says : 'And after they had constituted the laws as they considered to be fitting, Howel the Good, and the Bishop of Menevia, the Bishop of St. Asaph, and the Bishop of Bangor, together with others, making thirteen in number, of teachers and of other wise men of the laity, went to Rome to obtain the authority of the Pope of Rome for the laws of Howel. And there were read the laws of Howel, in the presence of the Pope of Rome, and the Pope was satisfied with them and gave them his authority ; and Howel, with his companions, returned home. And from that time until the present day the laws of Howel the Good are in force.' [1]

This, then, had been the result of the three centuries which had passed since the conference between St. Augustine and the British bishops. The British certainly owed little or nothing to the Saxon Church during that period. According to Protestant writers, they owed nothing, either then or formerly, to Rome. Not only so, but after living in isolation from Rome for two centuries, so we are told, they were thrown by the ambition of Rome into a state of violent antagonism. Yet we find them emerging, at the end of three centuries more of isolation, not, as we should expect from the laws of human nature, with feelings of hatred to Rome intensified, with love of independence grown into a passion, with the pride of ecclesiastical purity, and with national traditions telling of the battle for liberty bravely fought—no ! but with national traditions filled with stories of uninterrupted communication with Rome, with a pride in having known no other mistress than Rome, and in having been, from the earliest times, her cherished daughter. 'It will be a great honour to

[1] Haddan and Stubbs, i. 219.

the Roman Church,' wrote Giraldus the Welshman to Innocent III. in the year 1200, 'if the Church of Wales is subject immediately to her (and not to Canterbury), as is the Scotch Church, *and as she herself formerly was* and ought to be.'[1] On Protestant theories all this is inexplicable. There is some plausibility, perhaps, in their attempts to explain the intense loyalty of the Anglo-Saxons to Rome. The Anglo-Saxon Church, they say, never knew independence; it was founded by Rome when ultramontane ideas were becoming dominant, and the daughter would not criticise too closely the claims of its mother.[2] But the very necessity of such theories to explain Anglo-Saxon sentiments is a *reductio ad absurdum* of the theories of the former independence and antagonism of the Celtic Churches which came to the same result under other influences.

Prejudices have here placed Protestants in a curious dilemma. If they maintain the original independence and the long separation of the British Church from Rome, they must grant the apostolic origin of many doctrines and practices which they usually attribute to the corrupting influence of Rome, and which are yet found equally developed in the British Church. If they prefer to attribute the presence of these doctrines to Romish corruption, they must renounce their theory of British independence and opposition. But it is idle, as some do, to hold both these theories at once. Dr. Boultbee in one place speaks of 'corruption in government, in faith, in doctrine, which under papal leadership affected the whole Church.' But in another place, anxious to underrate the debt which England owes to Rome, he says: 'The British Church which survived at the end of the sixth century in the west of the island, and the Celtic Christianity of Scotland which spread so rapidly southward, owed nothing to Rome as far as authentic history can acknowledge. The Christianising work of the Roman mission has been shown to have been very limited in its effective results.'[3] So, then, according to this historian, Rome did very little good to England, because its range of influence was very restricted; but it did a great deal of harm, since its power of influence was very great. It could not subdue the pagan Anglo-Saxons. That was the work of a purer Church which knew not Rome. Yet it ultimately seduced both Celts and Saxons!

I may conclude this long and somewhat tedious discussion with some words of the late Mr. Brewer, who, as editor of the works of Giraldus, had given much attention to the state of Wales. In his

---

[1] *Opera* Giraldi, iii. 176 (Rolls Series).
[2] See Bright, *Chapters of Early English Church History*, pp. 61, 63.
[3] *Church History*, p. 59.

preface to the 'Gemma Ecclesiastica' of that author, Mr. Brewer writes:[1] 'As I have stated already, the Romish discipline and ecclesiastical system had never prevailed in Wales. The Welsh owed no debt to Rome, as did their Saxon and Norman neighbours; and they were inclined to yield no submission. And though, from the absence of the necessary documents, it may be difficult to arrive at positive conclusions on this subject, we are warranted in believing, by the feeble light which has come down to us, that the Welsh Church presented the rare spectacle of an ecclesiastical society which had undergone little, if any, change during ten centuries of unexampled strife and convulsion throughout the continent of Europe. We hear, indeed, of Pelagians disseminating their views among the British Churches in the beginning of the fifth century, of saints and bishops sent over from the continent to preach and counteract the growing evil; but what heresies sprang up in Wales from that century until the thirteenth, when Giraldus flourished, what controversies raged, what synods were held, whether its Church throve under persecution or languished in prosperity, it is not given us to know. Heresies are at least a proof of intellectual activity and vitality; controversies denote something better than somnolence and mere indifference; but we have not even those indications, unsatisfactory as they appear, for guessing at the condition of the Welsh Church during this long and dismal period. So far as conjecture can pierce, it continued much in the same state as the Anglo-Saxons had found it centuries before; a needy and unlettered clergy, a laity intractable and uncivilised, yielding a precarious submission and still more precarious subsistence to their pastors and instructors, who in most respects differed little from their flocks, and eked out a scanty livelihood by breeding cows and feeding swine.'

This is not a flattering picture, nor can we accept every statement in it. It is not true that the Welsh owed nothing to Rome, since even if their first apostles did not come to them directly from Rome —which is uncertain—they were, in the earlier centuries, in intimate communion with Rome according to the admission of all. Whenever a gleam of light falls on the intervening centuries, it shows this communion still subsisting, as in the case of Howel the Good; and when at last the works of Giraldus, written at the end of the twelfth and beginning of the thirteenth century, give us a full view of the Welsh Church, we find it not refusing submission to Rome, but appealing to her with filial confidence against the encroachments of the English

---

[1] *Giraldi Cambrensis Opera*, edited for the Master of the Rolls by the Rev. J. S. Brewer, vol. ii. p. xli.

power. In one thing, however, Mr. Brewer's account is most accurate. The Welsh were singularly conservative by character, by position, and by the absence of any elements of change whether from within or from without. How then does this Church emerge upon our view at the end of the twelfth century, after 'undergoing little, if any, change during the ten centuries' of its existence? It is in every respect, as regards doctrine and essential discipline, like the churches of York and Canterbury, of France and Italy. Giraldus, a Welshman by his mother's side, near of kin to the princes of South Wales, and brought up there in his youth, studies in Paris, and on his return is made Archdeacon of Brecknock. Both in the vigorous execution of this office and as visitor of the diocese of St. David's, and later as companion of Archbishop Baldwin in his itinerary through Wales to preach the crusade, Giraldus has the most ample opportunities to learn the state of the whole country. No one is more plain-spoken or less careful to hide abuses. He exposes them unsparingly, but among them there is no hint of difference in faith from the rest of the Church, while every page of his writings gives overpowering proofs that wherever Protestants differ from Catholics, the Welsh had inherited from their forefathers Catholic tenets and practices, and had never even heard of modern negations. In the book to which Mr. Brewer's words are a preface—the 'Gemma Ecclesiastica,' 'intended exclusively for my own country of Wales,' as Giraldus says—the supremacy of the Holy See, the canon law binding all parts of the Church, devotion to the saints, invocation especially of the Blessed Mother of God, transubstantiation, mass for the living and the dead, confirmation, extreme unction, excommunication, indulgences, and whatever else may be considered by Protestants as special emanations from mediæval Rome, are found to have permeated every valley and mountain in Wales, and to be familiar to every parish priest and cleric just as they are to-day to every priest in communion with the See of Peter. Neither Gerald nor those for whom he writes have heard that these things are foreign importations unknown to their forefathers. Yet his book was written in 1197, nearly a century before the final subjugation of Wales, and while the Welsh were still contending for their ancient rights and liberties. Who can conceive that, had their religion been revolutionised or even considerably modified by the influence of the Saxons or Normans, no memory of the change would have survived? Protestants must therefore choose between the horns of this dilemma. If the isolation and independence of the Welsh were as great as they pretend, then their state in the twelfth century is a new proof of the apostolicity of those doctrines and practices which Protestants call mediæval corruptions. If, on the contrary, the Welsh are supposed to have been gradually infected with those doctrines and practices, then it could only have been from their intimate union with Rome. The truth, however, will be found in neither of these hypotheses. The faith of the Welsh was indeed the primitive faith, but in form and expression it had been somewhat modified by centuries of intercourse with Ireland, with France, and with Rome. Their isolation as regards England was great; but Welsh and English were united in their common mother, the Roman Church. In nothing is the unity, the apostolicity of the Church more wonderful, than in this power of holding together and gradually assimilating nations, whom every human influence tended to isolate and pervert.

CHAPTER VIII.

ANGLO-SAXON FAITH.

It will not be an inappropriate introduction to the question whether the faith received by the Anglo-Saxon Church from Rome was the same as that which Rome now holds, if I state what was held among the Anglo-Saxons as to the unchangeableness of faith and the indefectibility of the Church. And no better spokesman of the Anglo-Saxon Church could be chosen than Venerable Bede, the historian of her first beginnings and the teacher of her later days. These are his words in his commentary on the last chapter of the book of Proverbs :—

'" *Who shall find a valiant woman?*" It is the Catholic Church which is thus designated. She is a woman bearing spiritual children to God conceived of water and the Holy Ghost : she is valiant, for she despises for the faith of her Maker both the prosperity and adversity of this world. When, indeed, He who made her appeared in the flesh, He found her weak, but by his very finding of her He made her valiant.

'Solomon then, seeing the human race ensnared in innumerable errors, and that no patriarch, no prophet, no saint was able to save it, but only the Mediator between God and man, exclaimed : " *Who shall find a valiant woman? far and from the uttermost coasts is the price of her.*" As if, in open admiration of the future grace of our Lord, he had said : Who is this of such power and merit as to be able to gather out of so many incredulous and wicked nations of the world the one Church of His elect, and to make her by His grace valiant and invincible by all adversity ? Most surely He who can do this is not like us, nor likely to come in our time, but at the end of the ages, when God descending from heaven shall become man and redeem men by His passion and death. So that indeed "*far and from the uttermost coasts is the price of her.*" . . .

' But because the Lord has not only redeemed His Church, and taught her to receive the word of salvation, but has also endowed her that she might constantly strive for it and preach it to the world, therefore Solomon adds : "*The heart of her husband trusteth in her.*" By the husband of the holy Church he means her Lord and Redeemer, who also deigned to become her "Price." Hence the Apostle says, "I have espoused you to one husband, that I may present you as a chaste virgin to Christ."[1] Therefore the words, "The heart of her husband trusteth in her," are derived from what occurs amongst men. For as a husband, who has a brave, faithful, and chaste wife, most confidently trusts her, knowing that she will do nothing against his will, nor be faithless to him even in thought, and that she will willingly endure any adversity for his love, and will desire to make him as many friends as possible, so also does our Lord and Redeemer trust in His Church. He knows the spirit of grace which He Himself has given her. He knows the power of charity which He Himself has poured into her heart. And therefore He is sure, not only that she never can be drawn from the integrity of His faith, but also that she will perseveringly labour to bring many to the unity of the same faith.

'He adds : "*He shall have no lack of spoils.*" For the Church despoils the devil when by her preachers she recalls to the way of truth those whom he had deceived. And it is well said : "He shall have no lack of spoils," for never shall the Church cease to restore to the faith of Christ souls whom she delivers from the deceit of the devil, until she has made up the appointed number of her members, and the world thereby completes its course.'[2]

To those who share the conviction of Venerable Bede that the Catholic Church has never erred and never can err, because she is the Spouse of Christ and has received the Holy Ghost for her dowry, there is no need to prove that the early Church was one in faith regarding the Blessed Sacrament of the Altar with the Church of to-day, and for them it will be enough to know that the Scots and Picts were in communion of worship with the Anglo-Saxons, and both with the Church of Rome, to be sure that, when St. Gregory planned a new hierarchy for Great Britain in the sixth century, the same faith was preached, the same sacrifice offered, as when Pius IX. and Leo XIII. divided the island in the present century. Nor ought it to be difficult to convince any unprejudiced mind of this identity of faith by the identity of language on the subject of the Eucharist. A modern Catholic reading the life of St. Columba, written by Adamnan in 696, or the 'Ecclesiastical History of England,' written by Bede in 736, will find every formula familiar to himself, and expressing his faith exactly as well as adequately. Protestants, on the

---

[1] 2 Cor. xi. 2.   [2] Ven. Beda, *Super Parab. Salom.* lib. iii. cap. 31.

contrary, whether Calvinists, Zuinglians, Lutherans, or High Church Anglicans, are uneasy at such language, carefully avoid it themselves, and sometimes even distort or evade it when making quotations. To give one example. Bede relates that King Ethelbert gave St. Augustine the old church of St. Martin, and that 'in this they began to meet, to chant psalms, to offer prayers, to celebrate masses (*missas facere*), to preach, and to baptise.'[1] In relating this Carte says they preached and performed 'other acts of devotion ;' Collier that they 'preached, baptised, and performed all the solemn offices of religion ;' Churton that they 'administered the sacraments.'

Such vague expressions show well enough a want of sympathy with Bede even as regards so simple and venerable an expression as Mass. How much less then would Protestants use or understand the various periphrases so familiar to Bede and to all our early writers : as the celebration of the most sacred mysteries, the celestial and mysterious sacrifice, the offering of the Victim of salvation, the sacrifice of the Mediator, the sacrifice of the Body and Blood of Christ, the memorial of Christ's great passion, the renewal of the passion and death of the Lamb! All these expressions are used by Bede ;[2] and for the Blessed Sacrament itself (as distinct from the rite of offering it to God)—besides the more common designations Hostia and Sacrificium (in the vernacular Housel)—they would speak of the saving Victim of the Lord's Body and Blood, the Victim without an equal, a particle of the sacrifice of the Lord's offering. These expressions are also found in Bede. Adamnan the Scot speaks of the sacrifice of mass, the sacrificial mystery, the mysteries of the most holy sacrifice ; and he tells us of the priest at the altar who performs the mysteries of Christ, consecrates the mysteries of the Eucharist, celebrates the solemnities of masses.[3]

If we turn to the writings of Eddi, or St. Boniface, or St. Egbert, or to the decrees of early councils, we find the same or similar phrases, varied in every possible way to express a mystery, the sublimity of

---

[1] Bede, i. 26.

[2] See Lingard, *Anglo-Saxon Church*, i. ch. 7. The expressions will be found in his history and homilies : 'celebratis missarum solemniis' (ii. 5), ' victimam pro eo (defuncto) sacræ oblationis offerre ' (iii. 2), ' particula de sacrificio Dominicæ oblationis ' (iv. 14), ' oblatio hostiæ salutaris, sacrificium salutare ' (iv. 22), ' sacrificium Deo victimæ salutaris offerre ' (iv. 28), ' corpus sacrosanctum et pretiosum agni sanguinem quo a peccatis redempti sumus denuo Deo in profectum nostræ salutis immolamus ' (*Hom. in Vig. Pasch.*).

[3] 'Sacrificale mysterium,' 'sacrosancti sacrificii mysteria,' 'munda mysteria,' 'sacra Eucharistiæ celebrare mysteria,' 'missarum solemnia peragere,' ' mysteria conficere,' &c. (*Vita S. Col.* ii. 1, i. 40, 44, iii. 17.)

which was beyond human utterance. A multitude of verbs were in common use to designate the action of the priest at the altar. 'Missam cantare' or 'canere' might designate the whole action, though with special allusion to the vocal prayers. 'Missam facere,' 'offerre,' 'celebrare,' 'agere,' would also refer to the whole divine action; 'conficere,' 'immolare,' 'libare,' regarded the Hostia, or Victim, which was our Lord's Body and Blood, or our Divine Lord Himself; and the secret operation by which the bread and wine were changed into our Lord's Body and Blood was indicated by every word by which transubstantiation can be expressed, among which we find 'transferre,' 'commutare,' 'transcribere,' 'transformare,' 'convertere.'

In spite of all this evidence, which exists in abundance, and lies, so to say, on the very surface of Anglo-Saxon religious literature, there are still Protestants who affirm that transubstantiation was unknown to the Anglo-Saxon Church. It will in all probability be useless to offer further proofs on this subject to those whose minds are prejudiced. Yet it may be of service to some to remind them that with equal plausibility it might be denied that Catholics hold the doctrine of transubstantiation at the present day. How, it may be asked, do Catholics now succeed in expressing their belief not only to themselves but even to their opponents? Whatever answer is given to this question, it is easy to show that the very same tests, when applied to the Anglo-Saxon Church, will give the same result. Perhaps it would be said that modern Catholics hold the Real Presence of our Lord not in some vague and undefined mode, as many Anglicans do, but that they make formal and explicit declaration of their belief in a change of substance; or that they not only call the sacrament our Lord's Flesh and Blood, but speak of it as containing Christ Himself; or again that, among them, reports are current of miracles and visions attesting the Real Presence of Him who died on the cross. Let us then take these three tests and see how they apply to the faith of the disciples of St. Augustine, St. Paulinus, or St. Aidan.

I. First, then, Catholics are very explicit in saying what they mean by speaking of the Body and Blood of Christ. They use expressions that do not admit of being taken vaguely and metaphorically. They imply change of substance. Would anyone, for instance, mistake the meaning of the following letter addressed to a Catholic priest? 'I beg you will not forget your friend's name in your holy prayer. Store it up in one of the caskets of your memory, and bring it out in fitting time when you have consecrated bread and wine into the substance of the Body and Blood of Christ.' Are not these words explicit? Well, they were indeed used in writing to a Catholic priest, but it was more than a thousand years ago, and he who used them was Alcuin,[1] the disciple of Bede. And Alcuin's scholar, Aimo, writing in A.D. 841, says :[2] 'That the substance of the bread and wine, which are placed upon the altar, is made the Body and Blood of Christ, by the mysterious action of the priest and thanksgiving, God effecting this by His divine grace and secret power, it would be the most monstrous madness to doubt. We believe then, and faithfully confess and hold, that the substance of bread and wine, by the operation of divine power—the nature, I say, of bread and wine is substantially converted into another substance, that is, into Flesh and Blood. Surely it is not impossible to the omnipotence of Divine Wisdom to change natures once created into whatever it may choose, since when it pleased it created them from nothing. He who could make something out of nothing can find no difficulty in changing one thing to another. It is then the invisible Priest who converts visible creatures into the substance of His own Flesh and Blood by His secret power. In this which we call the Body and Blood of Christ, the taste and appearance of bread and wine remain, to remove all horror from those who receive, but the nature of the substances is altogether changed into the Body and Blood of Christ. The senses tell us one thing, faith tells us another. The senses can only tell what they perceive, but the intelligence tells us of the true Flesh and Blood of Christ, and faith confesses it.'

I would observe that Aimo does not say that the senses are deceived ; on the contrary, he says that they convey true messages to the mind—' sensus carnis nihil aliud renuntiare possunt quam sentiunt '—but that the mind would be deceived if it formed its usual judgment on their testimony. The senses tell us nothing about substance, the existence of which is known by reason. And reason judges rightly, as a general rule, that where the accidents of bread and wine appear, there is also the substance. But reason does not tell us that this is necessarily so. There is always this tacit exception— unless by God's omnipotence it is otherwise. And God's revelation tells us that in the case of the consecrated bread and wine *it is* otherwise ; that the natural substance is not there, but is converted into (*transubstantiatur*) the substance of our Lord's Flesh and Blood.

[1] Alcuin, *Ep.* 36, *ad Paulinum Patriarcham Aquilensem.*
[2] Tractatus Aimonis, apud D'Achery. *Spicileg.* t. i. p. 42, ed. 1723. The full Latin text is given by Dr. Rock, *Church of our Fathers*, vol. i. p. 21, to whom I am indebted for this passage.

St. Thomas of Aquin says: 'The accidents subsist in this sacrament without a subject, that faith may find room, when a visible thing is received invisibly, being hidden under a foreign appearance; and *yet the senses are kept free from deception*, since they judge about the accidents which are known to them.' When the same great doctor writes:

> Visus, tactus, gustus in Te fallitur,
> Sed auditu solo tuto creditur,

he does not contradict himself. He means that the senses are deceived, not in the things of which they are proper judges, viz. the accidents, but in Christ's Presence (*in Te*), for this they cannot detect and have no means of reaching.[1]

It seemed good to make this commentary on Aimo's words, that it may be seen that these old writers did not speak at random; and also to meet the ordinary Protestant objection, that the God of truth could not deceive us by subjecting our senses to illusion. But, putting aside the question of the change of substance being imperceptible to the senses, was not Aimo right, it may be asked, in believing in God's power to make the change? To those who deny creation such a doctrine as transubstantiation has of course no significance; but surely in itself, and to those who reflect on what they believe, it is much harder to say: 'I believe that God called into being things that were not,' than to say: 'I believe that God, after becoming man, has instituted, for most wise and loving reasons, the change of our bodies' food into His own substantial Presence, who is the Bread of life.' His divine power changed man from senseless clay into a living being of flesh and blood, yet imposed on him at the same time the law that he should support that flesh and blood on the fruits of the earth whence he was taken; is it then not conceivable that, having redeemed that fallen creature, He should find a means in harmony with his double nature, to make him feed on his true life? Thus the outward forms of bread and wine remind him of the dust from which he was taken, while the hidden Presence reminds him of the end for which he was created, and of the redemption by which that end is again placed within his reach. The words, 'I am the Way, the Truth, and the Life,' have never more fulness of meaning to the soul of a Catholic than in the act of assisting at mass or receiving holy communion. The doctrine of Transubstantiation is also in perfect harmony with the history of God's prodigies both in the Old and New Testaments. He converted a dry rod into a living

---

[1] On the other theory of *species intentionales* see Theol. Wirceburgensis *De Sac. Euch.* n. 284. In this system also there is no deception.

serpent, and the living serpent He changed back again into a dry rod; is it then incredible to believers in Scripture that bread and wine should be transformed into the living and life-giving Flesh and Blood of Christ, and that, when the outward species are corrupted, the flesh and blood should cease to be present, and the former substances, as some think, be again restored?[1] The Son of God Himself took flesh at the word of a woman by the operation of the Holy Ghost; is it incredible to Christians that by the power of the same Holy Ghost, at the consecration of the priest, using Christ's own words and doing so by His own command, He should be again as it were incarnate? He changed water into wine to grace an earthly nuptial feast; is it contrary to analogy that He should change wine into His Blood in celebrating the perpetual banquet with the souls of men? During the days of His mortality He showed His Body at one time walking on the waves of the sea, at another lifted up from the earth and all-glorious at His Transfiguration; is it to be thought so strange that, now it is glorified above the heavens, He should for our sakes reduce it to conditions which exceed our experience and baffle our comprehension? He appeared and disappeared suddenly and mysteriously during the forty days He spent on earth after His resurrection, passing through the closed sepulchre and penetrating the closed doors; was it not to accustom us to modes of being remote from ordinary laws? And lastly, He multiplied visibly yet incomprehensibly the loaves of bread, distributing them by His Apostles' hands, till, after feeding thousands, the fragments that remained far surpassed in bulk the loaves unbroken; shall we then murmur when He promises to feed the millions of His Church on 'His Flesh which is meat indeed,' and 'His Blood which is drink indeed,' and shall we say: 'This saying is hard, who can hear it?' &c. 'How can this man give us His flesh to eat?'

II. To proceed now to our second test. Modern Catholics speak of the Holy Eucharist as containing Christ Himself. This follows necessarily from our belief in the presence of His Flesh and Blood, for these can now neither be really separated one from the other, nor from our Lord's soul, much less from His Divinity. Yet at the present day there are Anglican writers who admit with us that Christ's Flesh and Blood are present beneath the veils of bread and wine,

---

[1] 'Speciebus corruptis desinit præsentia Domini, et sub nova forma producitur materia, probabiliter pristina, quæ in consecratione esse desierat.' (Schouppe *Theol. Dog.* Tr. xiii. n. 173.) There have, however, been various opinions in the Catholic schools on this matter. See Harper's *Peace through the Truth*, 1st series, pp. 206-9.

yet deny that He Himself is there to receive our adoration.[1] They seem to have meditated little on our Lord's words : 'He that eateth my Flesh and drinketh my Blood *abideth in Me, and I in him*. As the living Father hath sent Me and I live by the Father, so he *that eateth Me*, the same also shall live by Me.'[2] But our forefathers pondered more deeply on divine things. The very earliest document of the faith of the Anglo-Saxon Church is the letter written by St. Gregory to St. Augustine. In this he contrasts the angel who appeared on Sinai with the Lord of the angels who is contained in the Blessed Sacrament. 'If so much purity,' he says, 'was then required, where God spoke to the people by the means of a subject creature, how much ought those to be purer who receive the *Body of Almighty God*, lest they be burdened with the greatness of that unutterable mystery!' The same great doctor of the Church, and of the English in particular, says in his Book of Dialogues : 'This sacrifice of His Body and Blood saveth the soul from everlasting destruction, which reneweth to us through the mystery the death of the only begotten Son of God, who truly arose from the dead, and after that dieth no more, nor hath death any more dominion over Him; yet though He be living in Himself immortal and incorruptible, *He is again sacrificed for us* in the mystery of the holy oblation.'

Since St. Gregory believed that the God of the angels is present in the Holy Eucharist, no wonder that he teaches that the angels also are present around the altar to adore Him. 'Who then of believing men,' he asks, 'can have any doubt that during the time of oblation the heavens are opened at the prayer and voice of the priest? Who doubteth of this, that troops of angels are present during the mystery of Jesus Christ?'

All the above words of St. Gregory were familiar to the Anglo-Saxons, and they often make them their own.[3]

The following prayer for the blessing of the altar canopy or ciborium gives another clear proof of the faith of the Anglo-Saxon Church :

'Almighty and everlasting God, we beseech Thy ineffable cle-

---

[1] *Ex. gr.* the Rev. Philip Freeman in his *Principles of Divine Service* (1862), part ii. pp. 278, 479. The late Mr. Keble well showed the Nestorianism of this view in his answer to the Pastoral letter of six bishops of the Scotch Episcopal Church of May 27, 1858. I shall return to the subject in the second volume.

[2] John vi. 57, 58.

[3] Bede quotes the letter, and has a passage exactly similar about the angels. Werfrith of Worcester, one of the literary assistants of King Alfred, translated the *Dialogues* into Anglo-Saxon, and it is from this translation that Dr. Lingard has made the version in the text.

mency, that Thou wouldst deign to pour Thy heavenly blessing upon this covering of Thy venerable altar, on which Thy only begotten Son, our Lord Jesus Christ, who is the propitiation for our sins, is constantly immolated by the hands of the faithful, and under which the bodies of Thy saints are placed which were truly the ark of the covenant.'[1] Here the bodies of the saints are mere relics, for their souls are absent, but the Body of Jesus Christ is Jesus Christ Himself, who is rightly surrounded by the relics of those whom He redeemed, and who have honoured His Redemption by their lives and deaths.

III. The third test which I proposed of Anglo-Saxon faith was this. There are many stories current amongst modern Catholics regarding visions, apparitions, and miracles, by which the Real Presence of Jesus Christ beneath the sacramental veils has been attested. Protestants may consider these to be either delusions or impostures, yet they do accept them as evidence of our belief. Why, then, if similar stories were current among the Anglo-Saxons, should not the same conclusion be drawn? Now there were many such, and a few may be here related in the very words of those who first recorded them. The first is the vision of St. Edward. It is thus related by the Abbot St. Ælred, who was born about forty years after St. Edward's death.

'In the monastery of St. Peter, which he had rebuilt or enlarged, before the altar of the Blessed Trinity the most Christian King was assisting at the mysteries of our redemption. Count Leofric, whose memory is in benediction, and who can never be named without reverence and spiritual joy, was present together with his wife Godgiva.

'The holy count was standing at a little distance from the king. The holy mystery was being celebrated at the altar, and the divine sacraments were in the priest's hands, when behold He who is beauteous beyond the sons of men, Christ Jesus, appeared standing on the altar visible to the bodily eyes of both, and with His right hand stretched over the king He blessed him with the sign of the cross. The king, bowing his head, adored the presence of the divine Majesty, and with humble posture paid honour to so great a blessing.

'But the count, not knowing what was passing in the mind of the king, and wishing him to share in so great a vision, began to draw near to him. But the king, knowing his thoughts, said: "Stop, Leofric, stop; I see what you see." They both give themselves up to prayers and tears, and are inebriated with the fulness of God's

[1] Anglo-Saxon Pontifical in British Museum (Tiberius, c. 1, fol. 106); Rock, i. 17.

house and drink of the torrent of His delights.[1] When mass is over, they converse on the heavenly vision.

'The king forbids the count to mention it to anyone during his life. In this he imitates our Lord after the Transfiguration. The count merely tells it to a religious at Worcester in confession, binding him also to secrecy, but begging him to write it that it may be revealed later on. This was done, and so it became known after the king's death.'[2]

Another history is that of St. Odo, Archbishop of Canterbury, who died in 959.

'About this time some clerks, seduced by a malignant error, tried to assert that the bread and wine which are placed on the altar, after consecration remain in their first substance, and are only the figure of the Body and Blood of Christ, and not His true Body and Blood. The blessed Odo, wishing to destroy this enormous perfidy, one day, while devoutly offering the sacred rites of the mass in the presence of the whole people, with tears besought the clemency of God Almighty to favour his ministry so as to destroy their error and show the substantial nature of the divine mysteries. When he had come to the breaking of the life-giving bread—O ineffable mercy of God! O evident presence of the Divine Majesty!—blood immediately began to drip from the fragments of the Body of Christ which the pontiff held in his hands. He shed tears of joy, and called to the assistant ministers, that those especially should draw near who had lately staggered in faith. They came quickly; and, stupefied at the contemplation of such wonders, they cried out with trembling voice: 'O most happy of men, to whom the Son of God thus reveals Himself in the flesh!" and again: "Pray, O Father, the Divine Majesty, that this Blood be changed back into its first form, that the divine vengeance overtake us not for our incredulity." The priest prayed, and after his prayer looked at the altar, and where he had placed the Blood he found the accustomed species of wine. When he had partaken of the heavenly sacraments, to the joy of all who were present at this great spectacle, the bishop commanded the poor to be gathered from every side, and a solemn feast to be prepared for them, for a memorial of this miracle.'

I have given this history as it is recorded by Eadmer,[3] the friend

---

[1] Ps. xxx. 8.

[2] St. Ælred's *Life of St. Edward* has been printed by Migne in his *Patrol. Lat.* tom. cxcv. col. 760.

[3] It is attributed to Osbern by the Bollandists, but was written by Eadmer, as is shown by Sir T. D. Hardy. It is printed also by Wharton in the *Anglia Sacra*, tom. ii.

of St. Anselm, and himself brought up in Canterbury. There is certainly no improbability of the event having been accurately handed down in Odo's own church for a hundred years. But Canon Stubbs, in his learned and candid 'Introduction to the Lives of St. Dunstan,' seems to consider that it gives proof of a development of doctrine, and that Eadmer is attributing to the Saxon Church a fulness of belief in the Real Presence which was of a later period, being the result of the controversies with Berengarius.[1] I call attention to this, not so much for the purpose of discussing the credibility of the particular miracle as for the admission contained in the learned Professor's criticism. It implies that belief in such visions or miracles could be current only where there coexists a fully developed and explicit belief in transubstantiation, such as is not denied to have been the doctrine of Lanfranc and the Norman Church. Now such histories as have just been related have been current among Catholics from the earliest periods in East and West. They are related by St. Gregory of Tours in the sixth century, by St. Arsenius in the fifth, by Palladius in the fourth, by St. Cyprian in the third.[2] But to keep to this country, John the Deacon expressly declares that in his time (he wrote about A.D. 875) a history was wont to be read in the English Churches about the miracles of St. Gregory the Great—how that at his prayers on one occasion the sacred host took the form of a finger dropping with blood, to convict the incredulity of a lady. So also Paschasius Radbert, writing in the middle of the ninth century, tells us a very similar vision granted at the prayers of a priest named Plecgils in the church of St. Ninian at Whitherne in Galloway, and he says that this was read in the acts of the English (*in gestis Anglorum*).

But to return to the vision of St. Odo. When Professor Stubbs published his 'Memorials of St. Dunstan' in 1874, there existed a unique MS. of the life of St. Oswald of York, to which the learned Professor had himself called attention as 'an invaluable and almost

---

[1] *Memorials of St. Dunstan* (Rolls Series, 1874), p. lxiii. Canon Stubbs does not state in what point the teaching of the Saxon saints was 'behind the developed dogma of Lanfranc and St. Anselm,' but I conceive that he can speak of nothing but the Eucharist. Indeed, when asserting that 'Eadmer, like Anselm, is zealous of doctrine,' he explains in a note that 'the most important passages in proof of this will be found in Eadmer's *Life of Odo*, on the subject of the Eucharist.' (*Ib.* p. lxvii.)

[2] After quoting the words of Palladius, who died in 431, a critic in the *Spectator* (Nov. 15, 1879, p. 1447) says: 'The sooner the attempt to find a Protestant theology in patristic literature is given up, the better;' though he characteristically adds: 'But Protestant theology need not be one whit weaker for that.'

unknown evidence for the reign of Edgar and Ethelred.' It had been written during the episcopate of Archbishop Ælfric (A.D. 995–1005), and therefore half a century before the Norman conquest and a century before Eadmer's 'Life of St. Odo.' In 1879 this MS. was published for the first time by Canon Raine,[1] and it is found to contain not a Norman but a Saxon account of the vision of St. Odo. The substance of the history is identical with that of Eadmer, while the differences in detail are very instructive. The anonymous writer, a monk of Ramsey, who had been intimate with St. Oswald, Odo's nephew, and had probably learnt from him what he relates, writes as follows: 'On a certain day when he (*i.e.* Archbishop Odo) was offering pontifically to the Great King (*i.e.* to God) the worthy ministry of the divine Sacrament, and was celebrating apart with his (household) the paschal feast of the glorious Lamb (of God), that heavenly Lamb deigned to console him by the following miracle. After the recitation of the Gospel and the offering of the Divine Gift, and when his soul was full of compunction and his eyes flowing with tears, such as are often shed by the faithful and happy worshippers of God, amidst these holy mysteries this trusted friend of the Redeemer began to touch with chaste hands the species of His Body (*Ejusdem effigiem corporis*). While he was doing this, he beheld an ancient miracle renewed in our times. For a drop of Blood flowed from the true Flesh of Christ's Body (*fluxit gutta sanguinis ex vera carne Christi corporis*). On beholding this most clearly with his eyes he marvelled; his mind was filled with fear, and he was troubled in spirit. He calls immediately a faithful attendant who was near at hand, and secretly shows him the miracle. To whom the priest replied: "Rejoice, most reverend father, since Christ the Son of God has to-day so honoured thee, that thou hast been worthy to see with thy bodily eyes Him who is over all, God blessed for ever. Pray,[2] I beseech you, the power of the ineffable God, to make His Body return to its first form." And when he had prayed, he arose, and found It as It was before, and received It with exultation of soul. On that day he ordered all the poor, the pilgrims, the orphans and widows to be assembled, to whom, in honour of so great a miracle, he commanded that a solemn feast should be given. Thus it came to pass that while the head of the Kentish city was feeding on a heavenly banquet, the members were feasted on earthly food.'

[1] *The Historians of the Church of York and its Archbishops,* vol. i. (Rolls Series, 1879).

[2] 'Exoro, quæso' (Raine, p. 407), probably by a slip of the writer of the MS. for 'exora, quæso.'

The fact of the great banquet given to the poor by St. Odo in honour of some great prodigy at the altar can scarcely be called in question, related as it is both by Eadmer and by this contemporary writer. That the prodigy consisted in the truth of transubstantiation being made visible is also related by both; and let him deny or explain away the miracle who will, at least this is evident—that the Saxon writer of the tenth century held exactly the same faith in this regard as the Norman writer of the eleventh century. In one respect the story has grown and somewhat changed in Eadmer's narrative. Eadmer, perhaps preoccupied with the thought of Lanfranc's contest with Berengarius, declares that there were some among the clergy of Canterbury who doubted the Real Presence, and that Odo asked the miracle for these and showed it to them. The Saxon writer, on the contrary, mentions no doubters; he supposes the miracle granted as a simple grace to the saintly celebrant, and to be witnessed by only one other, a faithful priest. Not a word indicates that the Saxon writer has any controversial or dogmatic purpose in relating the miracle. His only remark is that in his own day God had once more granted a prodigy which had often been witnessed in the early Church (*antiquum miraculum nostris temporibus renovatum*). Thus then, about fifty years before Berengarius began to sow doubts in France, this monk of Ramsey testifies not only to the faith, but to the antiquity of the faith, of the Anglo-Saxon Church in transubstantiation.

Nor should the words in which this is related be passed over inattentively. The narrator makes St. Odo's attendant priest say to him: 'Christ the Son of God has so honoured you, that you have seen with your bodily eyes Him who is over all, the blessed God.' (*Sic hodie te Christus, Filius Dei, honoravit, ut Eum, qui est super omnia benedictus Deus, carnalibus perspicere dignus fuisti obtutibus.*) Now, what had he seen? Some drops of blood flowing from flesh. He had seen (such at least was the belief of the Saxon monk) with bodily eyes what was always present in the consecrated Host, though only visible to faith. The expression here used is a bold one, yet dogmatically correct. 'He had seen God.' This implies that the Flesh and Blood are ever united with the Divinity, and are therefore worthy of supreme adoration. The Saxon Church was therefore one with us in saying: 'Blessed and praised every moment be the most holy and divine Sacrament.' But we say this, not because an unknown monk of the tenth century said it also, but because that Church which has received from her Divine Spouse the Spirit of Truth as her dower, declares now, as in every former age, that she is in possession of these stupendous Mysteries. If He who founded the Church has kept the promise that He made to be with her all days, even to the consummation of the world, by His Spirit, then must He also be present all days in His Flesh, because this is her belief and teaching, and her perpetual song of joy and thanksgiving.

When Œcolampadius, after being a priest and religious of the order of St. Bridget, became first a disciple of Luther and afterwards with Zuingle founder of the sacramentarian heresy, he attempted to defend his new views and give them a ground in antiquity by explaining away the language used by the holy fathers about the Real Presence. His opponent, Cardinal Fisher, was so indignant at the impudent perversions to which Œcolampadius resorted, that he exclaimed: 'Why, by such means you might as easily prove that you yourself never held the Real Presence, and might explain away the sermon which you published a few years back in its defence; for certainly you said then nothing stronger or clearer than had been said by the fathers whom you now distort.' Fisher was quite right. He who undertakes to prove that St. John Chrysostom did not hold the doctrine of transubstantiation might as successfully maintain the same thing of Bossuet. And he who would deny that the Anglo-Saxon Church held on the subject of the Eucharist the doctrines afterwards defined by the Council of Trent, might also deny that the Council of Trent defined the doctrines now held by Roman Catholics.

CHAPTER IX.

AN HISTORICAL CONTROVERSY: ÆLFRIC.

THAT modern Protestants should have tried sometimes to claim the ancient Britons as their own forerunners is not hard to understand. The information that has come down to us regarding them is in many points scanty and obscure, and lends itself therefore to theories and glosses. The Britons were for a time isolated from the rest of Christendom. Hence there was a certain plausibility in the notion that they had preserved in purity the doctrines and practices to which the rest of Christendom had been unfaithful. But that the Anglo-Saxon Church, that derived its dogmas and institutions directly from Rome and continued always in the most intimate communion with Rome, should be thought to have developed a system peculiar to itself, and yet in harmony with modern Anglicanism, and with primitive Christianity as distinguished from mediæval corruption—this is an historical view with as little of *a priori* likelihood as of basis in facts. Yet it is held, and held pertinaciously. As lately as 1878, Mr. Kington Oliphant went out of his way in a philological treatise [1] to speak of an English tenth-century writer named Ælfric as 'upholding the old Teutonic idea of the Eucharist, and overturning the new-fangled Transubstantiation.' Now we can understand what is meant by authors who extol Wycliffe as the author of 'Teutonic Christianity.' The schism of the northern nations in these latter centuries is an undisputed fact, and with all their variations in doctrine there is a certain unity of negation among them, especially as regards the Holy Eucharist, which, though it is not Christianity, may yet by courtesy be called 'Teutonic Christianity.' But to throw back these negations into the tenth century, and to glory in them as the peculiar appendage of one's own nation or race, is surely anti-Catholicity gone crazy. Were not the great defenders of transubstantiation in the ninth century, Paschasius Radbert and his disciples, Teutons? [2] As to

---

[1] *The Old and Middle English*, p. 155 (ed. 1878).
[2] Dr. Boultbee, an ardent nationalist and stickler for English claims to heresy,

England, Professor Lechler, a German writer willing enough to find predecessors of Wycliffe in his spirit of reform, and writing on this very subject, candidly confesses [1] that 'up to a period later than the middle of the thirteenth century no sects or divisions had ever arisen in the national Church, nor any departure of any sort from the characteristic form of the Church of the West.' And again the same author declares: 'In all the writings of Wycliffe which I have searched through in manuscript I have never come upon a single trace to indicate that either in his own time or in earlier centuries heretics of any kind had made their appearance in England.' William of Newborough, an author of the twelfth century, well acquainted with history, and living near enough to the Norman Conquest to know what was then thought in England of the belief and practice which had prevailed in England among the Anglo-Saxons, testifies to the complete identity of their faith with that of his own age. Having related how thirty poor peasants of the sect called Publicani had crossed over from France into England in the time of Henry II., he thus continues: 'England has been always free from this and other heretical pestilence, while there are so many heresies in other parts of the world. The Britons, indeed, produced Pelagius, and were corrupted by his doctrine. But since Britain has been called England no contagion of heresy has ever infected it, nor ever, until the time of Henry II., did any heretic enter it to spread his errors. And even then the attempt (just alluded to) was met in such a way that for the future they will be afraid to enter our island.' [2] William was no prophet, as we know too well; but he was a good historian, and had there been any divergency between the faith of the Anglo-Saxons and the Normans regarding the Eucharist, the collision would have been so immediate, sharp, and universal, that it would have left a record in the traditions of the people in the next century scarcely less vivid than that of the invasion itself. Yet it was reserved to the sixteenth century to make the discovery that transubstantiation had been only introduced into England by the Norman Conquest, and that, by the influence especially of Lanfranc and St. Anselm, the two Italo-Norman primates, it had supplanted the ancient and pure Protestant or quasi-Protestant doctrine which had till then prevailed.

---

allows that 'Paschasius Radbertis, about 831, unreservedly propounded the doctrine of transubstantiation in the absolute sense.' (*A History of the Church of England*, by T. P. Boultbee, LL.D. (1879) p. 134.)

[1] *John Wiclif and his English Precursors*, by Professor Lechler, D.D., translated by Peter Lorimer, D.D. (2 vols. 1878), vol. i. pp. 72, 73.

[2] Guliel. Newbridg. *De Rebus Anglicis*, ii. 13.

This discovery is attributed to Archbishop Parker. It is paraded in the pages of Foxe the martyrologist, and thenceforth repeated over and over again. There is, however, but one name cited in support of this theory. This is a homilist of the tenth century named Ælfric. I have perused very carefully the translation of his writings made by Mr. Thorpe, and I confess freely that there are in them many phrases of evil sound, though capable of an orthodox interpretation. He uses language different in tone from that of other writers of an earlier as well as of a later age. His homilies, however, are merely translations or compilations, and in those on the Eucharist he seems to have borrowed from Ratram or Bertram, the opponent of Paschasius. Yet, as Ælfric's language is capable of being understood in a Catholic sense, it is but fair that he should have the benefit of his reputation, which was unassailed until he was patronised by the heretics of the sixteenth century. I will give presently some reasons for this judgment.

But let it be clearly stated that the question of Ælfric's faith or orthodoxy has nothing to do with that of the Anglo-Saxon Church, unless it can be proved that he was her representative. Now this he was not either by position [1] or reputation. If Ælfric were shown to be Protestant in his doctrine, it would only follow that his doctrine was singular and his opinions erroneous. There is no man better entitled to speak on this subject than Dr. Lingard, who gave to Anglo-Saxon literature and institutions a lifelong attention. His judgment is as follows: 'If Ælfric indeed taught Protestant doctrine, he must have been the first who taught it, for it was not the doctrine of those who wrote before him. Of it, or of anything like to it, not a trace is to be found in any document connected with the ancient English Church; not in the acts of her councils, not in the liturgical and euchological forms of her worship, not in the correspondence or biography or works of her writers. And I make this assertion with the greater confidence, not only because I have made the enquiry myself, but also because it is now almost three hundred years since Archbishop Parker and his followers were challenged to produce the testimony of any other native writer in support of this supposed doctrine of Ælfric; and yet, as far as I can learn, no man to the present day has responded to the call. Undoubtedly they would have done so, had it been in their power.'

What Dr. Lingard stated is still true. In 1879 appeared a new 'History of the Church of England.' The author, Dr. Boultbee, as

---

[1] Dr. Lingard, in his *Anglo-Saxon Church*, vol. ii. note S, has shown that Ælfric was neither archbishop of Canterbury nor of York.

usual maintains that the Saxon Church did not hold transubstantiation, yet still the only authority quoted is Ælfric. He admits indeed that 'language was often heard which might seem to imply a very absolute and literal corporal presence, and that undoubtedly here and there transubstantiation itself was beginning to be heard of. Still,' he says, 'when the leading Church teachers were pressed on the subject, and the question could be fairly raised—"Setting aside typical, symbolical, sacramental presence, what do you believe the elements in the Lord's Supper to be?" the answer was still for the most part that which had been in like manner given by the earlier divines. The elements are still simply and truly bread and wine. They can no more be transubstantiated into the substance of the Lord's body than His human nature can be converted into the divine essence.'[1] Here is a bold and categorical assertion. We ask then: Who were the leading teachers who for the most part denied transubstantiation? On what occasion was the supposed question thus answered? Who were the earlier divines who declared a change of substance impossible? Dr. Boultbee gives no names, nor could he give any. He quotes Ælfric only, and thus concludes: 'Whatsoever else may be obscure in Ælfric's homily, it is clear that he repudiates transubstantiation.'

Although Ælfric is the only author who can be quoted with any plausibility in support of this view of the doctrine of the Anglo-Saxons, yet it is the custom to multiply him into a legion. Mr. Soames quotes Ælfric's words and none but his, yet he at once begins to speak of the 'unyielding array of testimony against Lanfranc's new divinity which echoes from the whole theological school of ancient England.'[2]

If I am asked how I explain the confident and reiterated assertions of so many writers on the other side, I reply that while some of them are the result of ignorance and prejudice, others may be accounted for without any impeachment of sincerity or learning.

In the first place it must be remembered that ever since Protestant controversy adopted a metaphorical interpretation of Scripture and of the ancient Fathers regarding the Eucharist, Protestant ears have become habituated to the use of what to Catholics seems forced and unnatural metaphor. When a Protestant hears the Communion called, in a popular hymn,

<blockquote>Rich banquet of His flesh and blood,</blockquote>

while he knows for certain that neither minister nor people believe in

---

[1] *History of the Church of England*, by Dr. Boultbee, p. 134.
[2] Soames, *Anglo-Saxon Church*, pp. 225, 226.

the Real Presence, he not only gets to use such language without any sense of incongruity, but, when he meets with it in ancient Catholic writers, he is easily persuaded that they meant no more than himself. So 'I believe in the Holy Catholic Church' has come to be an empty phrase in the mouths of many, and therefore sounds as empty to their ears when used by true Catholics or when quoted from ancient writers. In proportion, then, as we deplore the mischief done to men's minds by this use of empty formulas, strained interpretations, and unnatural metaphors, must we in fairness excuse those whose minds have been warped by being placed under such influences.

In the second place, just as it is a fundamental principle with Catholics that the Church's faith never varies, so it is a fundamental principle with Protestants that it is ever varying, that it never was steadfast and never will be. As with Catholics there is a presumption that an ancient writer who lived and died in the Church's communion intended at least to say what the Church now says, and every effort is made to interpret his words in a Catholic sense, so, on the other hand, there is a presumption in the minds of many Protestants that an ancient writer could not have intended to say what Catholics now say. He may use the same language, but every ambiguity or omission is seized on as a reason for attributing to him another meaning.

In the third place, the mystery of the Eucharist is very profound. Those who have a perfectly correct faith may easily err in theological statement; and the most correct theological statements may be easily misunderstood by those whose faith is erroneous or whose minds are not trained in theological questions. Hence Catholic writers have been quoted as unorthodox, sometimes from their own deficiency in expressing their meaning, and still oftener from the inability of their readers to apprehend it. Besides this, the Catholic doctrine has been rendered so monstrous to the imagination of many Protestants, that when they meet with its rigid theological expression they do not recognise the figment of their own brains, and conclude that such language is incompatible with the Catholic faith.[1]

I have selected a few examples of the working of these sources of

---

[1] Perhaps Dr. Pusey is the most notable example of erudite blundering. The Protestant or Anglican reader, who wishes to know what Catholic theology really means by transubstantiation, will do well to read Father Harper's treatise on this subject in the first series of his *Peace through the Truth*, where he will find also abundant instances of Dr. Pusey's amazing mistakes. Mr. Cobb also, in his *Kiss of Peace*, and its Sequel, shows how Protestants fight against their own fictions.

error in order to make my meaning clearer and at the same time to pave the way for a direct examination of the solitary difficulty which arises from the language of Ælfric.

The illustrious Colet, Dean of St. Paul's, London, who died in 1519, wrote in his catechism for the scholars of St. Paul's school: 'By gracious Eucharisty, where is the very presence of the Person of Christ under form of bread, we be nourished spiritually in God.' These words, so far as they go, exactly express the Catholic doctrine now held. Yet an Anglican scholar calls attention to this formula as 'much nearer to the language of our own Church than it is to that of the Council of Trent.'[1] One would have thought that the faith of Colet, the friend of More and Fisher, might go unchallenged, at least on such grounds as this.

Let me take another example. In the fifteenth century the unfortunate Bishop Pecock wrote as follows in a work intended for the laity, called 'The Poor Men's Mirror.' It is in the form of a dialogue.

'(*Son.*) Father, to what purpose, intent, and end, ordained God the Eucharist to be received and haunted? (*Father.*) Soothly, son, for that the receiver in the Eucharist, receiving, should oft remember himself thereby upon Christ's holy life and passion, and upon His benefits and His law, and followingly should take and make a sad (serious) purpose to God (though without new bond and covenant) that he will be one to God, and to his neighbour in charity and in keeping virtues and the life which Christ kept and taught on earth. Right as thilk (those) signs which he eateth and drinketh be made, or seem to be made, one to him, or joined to him in his bodily substance. And for to make oft this remembrance and oft this purpose, was ordained the Eucharist oft to be eaten and drunk, as to be oft of this purpose a remembrancing-token or sign-of-witness thereof.'

Now there is not a single word here that is not to be found in innumerable Catholic ascetical treatises on the Holy Eucharist. Pecock does but expose a very first principle of theology, viz. that our Lord has given us his Flesh and Blood under the species of bread and wine to teach us that He is our food. And what Catholic ever dreamt that we feed on Him with our mouths only and not with our minds and hearts? Yet against this passage of Pecock in the

---

[1] *A Treatise on the Sacraments of the Church*, by John Colet, D.D., edited with Introduction by J. H. Lupton, M.A., 1867, Introd. p. 23. Mr. Lupton proves his desire to be thoroughly fair by giving on the same page a prayer of Colet to the Blessed Virgin. How would he interpret Colet's words given by Knight in the Appendix to his life? 'When I shall die I shall call for the sacraments and rites of Christ's Church betimes, and be confessed, *and receive my Lord and Redeemer Jesus Christ.*' (Rules for his School.)

original manuscript a Protestant possessor of the sixteenth century has written the words : '*Transubstantiation not knowne.*'[1] 'As if,' says Bossuet to similar logicians, 'because we are commanded to eat Christ's Body, and commanded to eat it with faith, therefore it is only by faith that we eat it.'

Though Pecock is not treating of the Real Presence in the above passage, but of the object and purpose of the Real Presence, yet he carefully guards his words. He does not say that bread and wine are made one with the communicant, but that 'the signs are made, or seem to be made, one with him.' But a curious style of reasoning is adopted in regard to the Eucharist by many Protestants, that, whenever an old author does not explicitly say a thing, he is supposed to have denied it. To show that I am not speaking too strongly, and merely on account of an anonymous marginal note, I will give another specimen of this method.

The Rev. Mr. Morton has edited for the Camden Society a work of the thirteenth century, called the 'Ancren Riwle,' or 'Rule for Recluses.' In his Preface, he admits, indeed, that 'we find the doctrine of transubstantiation' in the book. But he is so anxiously on the look-out for some token or indication of Protestantism, that he adds 'Transubstantiation is distinctly disavowed by Ælfric, and there is a prayer in the present work, from which, if it stood alone, we might reasonably infer that the same doctrine formed no part of the creed of the learned and pious author. But, as the doctrine in question appears, from other passages, to have been received and professed by him, we may conclude that this prayer is a relic transmitted from primitive times, and not yet expunged from the liturgical services of the Church.'[2]

It would be reasonable to ask Mr. Morton for proofs that the Catholic Church ever adopted the practice of *expunging* ancient liturgical forms, under the disingenuous consciousness that they contained another doctrine from her present one. But, to say no more of this insinuation, I would ask the reader to take careful note of Mr. Morton's acknowledged rule of procedure. Had the prayer, he says, *stood alone,* then he would have considered it reasonable to infer—what? why, something now disproved by evidence—that his author did not hold transubstantiation. But a method of inference which can thus lead to false conclusions is surely not a reasonable

---

[1] See Mr. Babington's Introduction to Pecock's *Repressor* (Rolls Series), vol. i. p. lxxii. Mr. Babington, in giving the Protestant gloss, adds candidly : 'This can hardly perhaps be deduced.'

[2] P. xvi. The prayer is p. 34.

one. Had the prayer stood alone, he would have suspended his judgment, unless he had other grounds for forming it. But Protestant controversy is crowded with these 'reasonable inferences' drawn from negative premises, and which are as false as would have been Mr. Morton's. It may be added, however, that the prayer which this writer thinks so Protestant is perfectly Catholic. It is as follows: 'Grant, we beseech Thee, Almighty God, that Him whom we see darkly and under a different form, on whom we feed sacramentally on earth, we may see face to face, and may be thought worthy to enjoy Him truly and really as He is in heaven.' Mr. Morton will find plenty of prayers like this still remaining in our Missal.

Let us now turn to the Anglo-Saxons. If writers of the sixteenth, fifteenth, and thirteenth centuries are thus dealt with, what may we expect as regards those of the ninth and tenth? Mr. Sharon Turner says boldly:[1] 'It is certain that the transubstantiation of the Eucharist was not the established or universal belief of the Anglo-Saxons.' What now are the grounds of Mr. Turner's certainty? This alone, that in some Saxon Ecclesiastical Constitutions of about the date of the Conquest it is declared 'the housel is Christ's body, not bodily, but spiritually; not the body in which He suffered, but the body about which He spoke when He blessed the loaf and wine.' But Mr. Turner ought to have understood that although these words do not assert transubstantiation, neither do they deny it. They would leave it *uncertain*, if we had no other grounds for judgment, whether their writer held it or not. For surely Catholics teach that our Lord's body is spiritually present. 'Not in a bodily and passible, but in a spiritual way,' are the words of an eminent doctor of the Sorbonne in the seventeenth century, in a work in which he aims at the most exact definitions of the Catholic faith.[2]

'The mode of our Lord's Presence,' writes a great modern theologian, Cardinal Franzelin, 'is altogether analogous to the mode of presence of spirits, nor can it be conceived or explained by us except according to this analogy.' Then, after showing that the Fathers call our Lord's sacramental Body sometimes incorporeal, and sometimes spiritual, he warns us that this mode of presence is neither to be perceived by the senses nor pictured by the imagination, and that we might as well try to hear colours and see sounds as to *imagine* our

---

[1] *History of the Anglo-Saxons*, vol. iii. p. 499, 6th ed.
[2] 'Summa doctrinæ nostræ in eo sita est, ut verum et reale corpus Christi profiteamur esse in hoc sacramento, non more corporali et passibili, sed spirituali et invisibili nobis omnino incognito.'—Holden, *Analysis Fidei*. Holden was an Englishman, though a doctor of the Sorbonne.

Lord's bodily Presence. We can only rise by certain steps towards an understanding of this Presence by considering what wonders are related of the bodies of saints even in this life, what we are told of the 'spiritual body'[1] after the resurrection, and above all what faith tells us of the state of our Lord's Body, formerly on earth and now in heaven.[2]

The above is one sense of the word 'spiritual' as applied to the Blessed Sacrament, but it is not the only one. Sometimes, by a still further extension of meaning, the word 'spiritual' is opposed to 'gross' or 'carnal.' And very frequently among the Anglo-Saxons it means holy or consecrated, as contrasted with what is profane or common.

The words of the Anglo-Saxon writer quoted by Mr. Turner appear to be taken from St. Augustine of Hippo: 'Spiritualiter intelligite quod locutus sum: non hoc corpus quod videtis manducaturi estis, et bibituri illum sanguinem quem fusuri sunt qui me crucifigent.' But St. Augustine had, just before using these words, explained his meaning. He had said that the men of Capharnaum had understood foolishly our Lord's promise that He would give them His Flesh to eat; they had thought carnally that He would cut off particles of His Flesh to give to them, and they had said: 'This word is hard,' whereas they themselves were hard, &c.[3] The same saint explains our Lord's words, 'It is the spirit which quickeneth, the flesh profiteth nothing,'[4] by the words of St. Paul: 'Knowledge puffeth up, but charity edifieth.' 'As science alone is valueless and even hurtful,' says the saint,[5] 'so flesh alone, even our Lord's Flesh, is useless. But, as science joined to charity is very useful, so is our Lord's Flesh when vivified by His Spirit and united to His divinity.' This may explain what the Saxon author meant by his assertion that our Lord's Body is a spiritual one, and present, though not in a bodily way.

A third and still more common use of the word 'spiritual' or

---

[1] 1 Cor. xv. 44.

[2] Franzelin adds that analogy implies both similitude and diversity. The mode of our Lord's presence beneath the sacred species is similar to that of a spirit in this, that as our soul is not by parts (for it has no parts) but entire in each part of the body and entire (without diffusion) throughout the whole body, so is our Lord's body present throughout the whole Host and in every particle, and yet present wholly everywhere. The difference is that the soul is wholly present in one place by its essential simplicity, and diffused as it were throughout by its connatural and intrinsic power; whereas a body has essentially distinct parts, and these connaturally require to exist in different parts of space, one outside the other. It is therefore a stupendous and altogether singular miracle that it is otherwise in the Eucharist. See Franzelin, *De Euch.* Thesis xi. p. 151; Lessius, *De Perf. Div.* xii. 16.

[3] S. Aug. *in Ps.* xcviii.   [4] John vi. 64.   [5] *Tract* 27 *in Joan.* n. 5.

ghostly among Anglo-Saxon writers of that age by no means implies the absence of body, but its fitness or consecration for spiritual purposes. This may be clearly seen from the 35th canon of Ælfric's collection, which is thus translated by Mr. Thorpe : 'Christian men should attend church frequently, and no one may discourse or conversation hold within God's church, because it is a prayer-house hallowed to God for *ghostly* discourses. Nor may one drink nor thoughtlessly eat within God's house, which to that is hallowed, that God's Body be with faith there eaten. Yet men now do too often foolishly, so that they will watch and madly drink within God's house, and play shamefully, and with idle speeches God's house defile. But for them 'twere better that they in their beds lay, than that they God angered in that *ghostly* house.'[1] Here a ghostly discourse is not one without spoken words, but one made up of words all tending to the edification of the soul. And the ghostly house is not a metaphorical house, but one hallowed for God's worship. So too, when our Lord's Body is said to be ghostly, not natural, not mortal, not visible, not such as He suffered in on earth, it is not intended to deny its reality or essential identity with His mortal body, but a mystery is indicated, a spiritual state and a spiritual purpose. Writers who used such expressions were combating gross and carnal ways of thinking ; and, since Protestants attribute such ways of thinking to modern Catholics, it is almost inevitable that they should misconstrue such language into the repudiation of Catholic doctrine. Thus one error begets another, and they criticise like men stumbling in the dark.[2]

[1] *Laws and Institutes of England*, vol. ii. p. 356.

[2] I may illustrate what has been said by the language of a well-known modern writer. Mr. Keble, in his *Christian Year*, in his lines on Holy Communion, wrote as follows :—

> 'Fresh from th' atoning sacrifice
> The world's Creator bleeding lies,
> That man, His foe, by whom He bled,
> May take Him for his daily bread.'

In a Catholic writer such words would have had but one meaning. They would have been held to express Catholic doctrine. What was Mr. Keble's meaning? This might have seemed doubtful, for in some verses on Gunpowder Treason in the same volume, he wrote :—

> 'If with thy heart the strains accord,
> That on His altar-throne
> Highest exalt thy glorious Lord,
> Yet leave Him most thine own ;
> O come to our Communion Feast :
> There present in the heart,
> Not in the hands, th' eternal Priest
> Will His true self impart.'

As regards Ælfric I have admitted that he uses language both unusual and ill-sounding. He keeps insisting that the Body of Christ as received in the Eucharist is not the same body that hung on the cross. Now these words might have a true sense or a false one. According to the Catholic faith it is essentially the same, yet it is not the same according to its mode of existence. Our Lord said of St. John the Baptist that he was Elias, John himself said that he was not. They spoke in different senses. The ancient Fathers who wrote against the Manichees insisted on free will as if to the neglect of grace; those who wrote against the Pelagians insisted on grace as it were to the disparagement of free will. There was no real contradiction, but the opponents or objections required different language. So has it been with regard to the Eucharist. Against those who would adopt figurative interpretation of our Lord's words Catholic writers will insist upon the reality of His Flesh and Blood. Against men whose minds are gross and sensual the same Catholic writers would insist on the presence being spiritual. In fact, from

The context shows that Mr. Keble intends by these words to set forth a special Anglican doctrine as an antidote to the seductions of the 'fallen elder sister,' *i.e.* the Roman Church. And certainly many readers understood Mr. Keble to advocate nothing more than the virtual Presence taught by Calvin. Here would have been a knot for commentators to untie, and matter for fruitful controversy: Did Mr. Keble hold, or did he reject, a real objective Presence? Mr. Keble, however, has been his own commentator. In a treatise on *Eucharistical Adoration*, written many years later, he says: 'As partakers of the altar we are permitted to eat of the sacrifice; which sacrifice in this case is that Man who is the Most High God. That, therefore, of which we eat, the same we are most humbly to worship. . . . If we really believe that that which He declares to be His own Flesh and Blood is Jesus Christ giving Himself to us under the form of bread and wine, how can we help thanking, and therefore adoring (for to thank God is to adore), the unspeakable gift as well as the most bountiful Giver, seeing that in this case both are one?' (Ch. ii. sect. 46.)

There can be apparently no doubt that Mr. Keble, in spite of his expression 'not in the hands,' really held an objective presence, and not Calvin's virtual presence but real absence. His book teems with proofs that he rejected Zuinglianism and Calvinism. Had he then changed his views? In the preface to the second edition of the work just quoted, he seems to say that he had never intended to deny the objective presence; for after asserting that some early Anglican writers, who were quoted as denying the Real Presence, perhaps only meant to deny 'the notion of a gross carnal presence,' he adds in a note: 'I may perhaps be excused for exemplifying this by the expression sometimes quoted from the *Christian Year*, "present in the heart, not in the hands."' I do not pretend to understand Mr. Keble's theology, or to know how transubstantiation is carnal, or how 'not in the hands' denies transubstantiation without denying all objective presence. But the explanation given by Mr. Keble ought to make Protestant writers less positive in interpreting Ælfric.

the very nature of the question, there will be the same double meaning and consequent ambiguity which is attached to the word 'flesh' in Holy Scripture. St. John speaks of the sons of God 'who are born not of the flesh;' and then immediately adds, 'and the Word was made flesh.' The eternal Son of God was made flesh that the adopted sons of God might not be carnal.

If we knew the state of mind of those for whom Ælfric was writing, we could judge better about his meaning. When it is said that heresy was unknown in England, it is meant that there were no teachers of formal heresy, not that none doubted or denied articles of the faith. Now if these men entertained gross views of what was meant by the Real Presence, and were therefore tempted to doubt its reality, then the language of Ælfric is quite intelligible and Catholic. He is combating disbelief by proving that belief requires no such rude conceptions as they stumbled at.

I am confirmed in this view of Ælfric by the conduct and language of Lanfranc. How was it that the great champion of the doctrine of transubstantiation against Berengarius never denounced the writings of Ælfric, and never accused the Anglo-Saxon Church of heterodoxy with regard to the Eucharist? My own answer is that Lanfranc saw in such teaching not an adverse theology, but a different phase of controversy. In his treatise against Berengarius, written before he came to England, are the following words: 'It may be truly said that we receive the very Body which was born of a Virgin, yet not that very Body. It is that very Body, if you consider its essence and the propriety and efficacy of its true nature. It is not the same, if you consider the appearance and the other qualities of bread and wine. This faith has been held from the beginning, and is still held by that Church which is called Catholic, because it is spread throughout the world.'

But Ælfric's words are not merely capable of a Catholic interpretation; there are some of them that seem to admit of no other. He narrates several miraculous apparitions of our Lord in the Blessed Sacrament. This is what Lanfranc writes on the subject of such histories: 'No one even slightly versed in ecclesiastical history and the lives of the holy Fathers is ignorant of these miracles. And although the writings in which they are recorded have not that supreme authority which belongs to those of the prophets and apostles, yet at least they prove this—that all the faithful before us from the earliest times had the same faith that we have.'

The canon of criticism here laid down by Lanfranc would have sufficed for the vindication of the orthodoxy of Ælfric had any accusation been brought against him. It would have been held that the clear and undoubting way in which Ælfric urged his hearers to hold the true faith in the Eucharist, by recording miraculous apparitions of our Lord's Flesh and Blood, proved that he had nothing whatever in common with Berengarius. Assuredly, if he intended to deny the Real Presence in the Catholic sense, or was an opponent of transubstantiation, he concluded his homily in a way very unusual to those who hold the 'Teutonic' views of Mr. Oliphant or Mr. Soames. 'We read,' he says,[1] 'in the "Vitæ Patrum," that two monks prayed to God for some manifestation respecting the Holy Eucharist, and after their prayer attended at mass. There they saw a child lying on the altar at which the priest said mass, and God's angel stood with a sword waiting till the priest brake the housel, when the angel divided the child in twain upon the dish, and poured the blood in the chalice. But afterwards, when they went to receive, it was changed again to bread and wine; and they received it thanking God for His manifestation.'

Now, if Eadmer's story about St. Odo, quoted in the last chapter, proves that the narrator at least held the doctrine of transubstantiation, Ælfric's story must in fairness be held to prove the same. Why then are his ambiguous sentences about receiving the Body of Christ, 'not in a bodily but a ghostly manner,' to be taken in a Calvinistic sense, as if he had never recorded this and similar miracles? And why, on the contrary, are not the miraculous apparitions which he does record taken as the key to his ambiguity, since, as has been already said, his language is capable of Catholic interpretation? When, therefore, he says, 'not bodily but spiritually,' he does *not* mean what is implied by Protestants when they say 'not really but figuratively;' but he means as St. Augustine meant, and explained his meaning to be, 'not in a gross sensible manner, but in a hidden and mysterious manner.' Certainly such an illustration as that of Ælfric could not be used by a Calvinist, since it clearly implies that in whatever way our Lord's Body is present, it is present objectively on the altar by virtue of consecration, and not subjectively in the recipient by virtue of faith.

To Dr. Boultbee's assertion that, 'whatsoever else may be obscure in Ælfric's homily on the Eucharist, it is clear that he repudiates transubstantiation,' I reply that, whatsoever else is obscure in his homily, at least his histories of the miraculous apparitions are not obscure. Let Dr. Boultbee, therefore, judge by his own standard; for in writing of Paschasius Radbert he says that he 'unreservedly

[1] Ælfric's *Homilies*, vol. ii. p. 273 (Thorpe's translation).

propounded the doctrine of transubstantiation in the absolute sense, confirming it by stories of persons to whom had been vouchsafed the vision of the sacred Body perceptible in the elements.'[1]

This is true, and Paschasius is himself a witness to English faith. In his fourteenth chapter he writes as follows : ' No one, who has read the lives and examples of the saints, can be ignorant that often these mystic sacraments of the body and blood have, either in favour of doubters or of ardent lovers of Christ, been shown in visible appearance in the form of a lamb, or in the colour of flesh and blood.' But the only example which he relates is an English one ; and, as Paschasius takes care to point out, it was a vision granted to an Englishman who did *not* doubt, but had been brought up in piety from his childhood, and desired out of love to behold that in which he already firmly believed. The name of the priest was Plecgils, and the vision was granted to him when saying mass over the body of St. Ninian at Whithern. Let anyone believe in Plecgil's vision or not, as he may choose, one thing at least he cannot reasonably call in question, viz. that in the ninth century Paschasius Radbert knew of no peculiar and Teutonic views of the English on the subject of the sacrament of the altar ; whereas he did know that they were reported to hold ' the doctrine of transubstantation in the absolute sense,' to use Dr. Boultbee's idiom, and that they confirmed it by stories of miraculous apparitions.[2]

[1] *History of the English Church*, p. 134.
[2] The book of Paschasius Radbert, abbot of Corby, has been often published. It was edited more correctly by Martene after collating twenty MSS., in all of which this history occurs. Paschasius refers to the *Gesta Anglorum* as his authority. Dr. Rock conjectures, with much probability, that this history was one of those miracles which the scholars of York related in verse in their letter to Alcuin concerning the glories of St. Ninian. (See *antea*, p. 54.) The history is given in full in Latin and English by Dr. Rock, *Church of our Fathers*, i. 44 *sq.*

CHAPTER X.

THE MASS-PRIEST.

THE Catholic clergy as a body has conferred upon it by the great High Priest His own threefold powers called Magisterium, Ministerium, and Imperium, the power to teach, to minister, and to rule. The power of Ministerium is alone considered here, and no other Ministry than that of the Holy Eucharist, the most sublime and distinctive of all the functions of the priesthood. The power to change bread and wine into our Lord's Body and Blood, and to offer the holy sacrifice, was believed by the Anglo-Saxons to be conferred by ordination on the priesthood, and it belonged to no lower grade amongst the clergy.[1] We find the ambition of deacons suppressed by councils when they sought to usurp other functions of the priesthood, such as imposing penance and even hearing confessions, but I remember no example in England of a deacon claiming to say mass. They were allowed, however, in the absence of a priest, to distribute Holy Communion which a priest had consecrated.

The name by which the priest was known was sometimes *sacerd* (a mere adaptation of the Latin *sacerdos*) and sometimes *preost* (which is also generally taken to be an adaptation of the Latin *presbyter*). But *preost* was a name given also to the minor clergy, and was a generic designation like our clergy or clergyman.[2] When

---

[1] Dr. Rock (vol. i. p. 131) notices a curious instance of mistranslation. Mr. Sharon Turner, in describing the death of the holy widow, Æthelflida, makes her say to St. Dunstan : 'Do thou early in the morning cause the baths to be hastened, and the funeral vestments to be prepared, which I am about to wear ; and after the washing of my body *I will celebrate the mass*, and receive the sacrament ; and in that manner I will die.' We are accustomed to Protestant mistakes about Catholic matters, but this one is certainly startling—a lady saying mass, and that too in her funeral shroud ! It need scarcely be said that according to the Latin it was St. Dunstan who was to say the mass. Æthelflida, already prepared for burial, was to receive the viaticum.

[2] From forgetting that *preost* does not necessarily mean a priest, Protestants have come upon mare's nests of married priests, whereas they were married clergy of lower grades. Ælfric says : 'To priests of common order it is allowed that they may chastely enjoy wedlock. But to others who serve at God's altar, that

the grade of priesthood was specially designated, the clergyman was called *mæsse-preost* (mass-priest), or *mæsse-thegn* (mass-thane), or even altar-thane.

The priest represented our Lord Jesus Christ, the 'Priest for ever after the order of Melchisedech.' It is interesting to read in the pontifical of Egbert, Archbishop of York in the eighth century, how the various orders of the clergy were understood to participate in our Lord's priesthood. I translate literally, omitting only a few unimportant phrases: 'Christ was a Porter (*ostiarius*) when He shut and opened the ark of Noe, and opened the gates of hell. Wherefore now those who are called porters have charge of the doors of the church and sacristy, and ring the bell to call all men to the church. Christ was a Reader (*lector*) when He opened the book of Isaias the prophet; He was an Exorcist when He cast the seven devils out of Mary Magdalen; He was a Subdeacon when He blessed water at Cana and changed it into wine. The subdeacon must read the epistle, clothe and decorate the altars, and minister to the deacon. Christ was a Deacon when He broke the loaves to feed the multitudes, and washed the feet of His disciples; for the deacon must minister at the altar, read the gospel in the church, baptize and give communion in the absence of the priest, wash the feet of pilgrims (or strangers), and bury the dead. Christ was a Priest (presbyter) when He took bread and the chalice into His sacred hands, and, looking up to heaven to God the Father, blessed them, giving thanks. Now a presbyter (or elder) is thus called not on account of age, but of merit and wisdom. It is the duty of the priest to bless, to offer (sacrifice), to preside well, to preach, to baptize, and to give communion, for he is above the other degrees and holds the place of the bishop in the Church. Christ was a Bishop when, raising His hands, He blessed His apostles before His ascension. A bishop must judge and interpret (the law), consecrate and perfect, ordain, offer, and baptize. The word bishop means overseer, because he ought to see over and set in order everything.'[1]

In this enumeration the grade of acolyte, the highest of the four minor orders, is omitted, but this is probably a mistake of the copyist, for the form is given for his ordination. The cruet was given to him 'to pour out wine for the Eucharist of the Body of Christ.' The bishop gave the subdeacon the empty chalice and paten and maniple.

---

is to mass-priests and deacons, all such intercourse is wholly forbidden.' (Vol. ii. p. 95.) (*Gemánes hádes preostum.*) Similar mistakes have been often made about the word *clericus* in later times.

[1] Egbert's *Pontifical* has been published by the Surtees Society, vol. xxvii. (1853).

To the deacon he gave chasuble, poderis, alb, stole, girdle, and amice; a stole over his left shoulder, and the book of the gospels. He also imposed hands on him, and anointed his hands with holy oil and chrism. The priest had the stole placed over both shoulders, and both the bishop and all the assisting priests held their hands over him. He prayed that God would pour His blessing on him, that he might keep pure and immaculate the gift of His ministry and, for the service of God's people, transform (*i.e.* consecrate by transforming) bread and wine into the Body and Blood of His immaculate Son. When the bishop placed the chasuble on the priest, he prayed the Father, Son, and Holy Ghost to bless him, 'that he might be blessed in his priestly order, and offer atoning sacrifices for the people's sins.' When his hands were anointed the bishop again prayed that the hands might 'be sanctified to consecrate the sacrifices (*hostias*) which are offered for the sins and negligences of the people.' His head also was anointed with holy oil, but not with chrism.

Thus it appears that the offering of Holy Mass was considered the characteristic and highest function of the priesthood. And as this power could only be received by valid ordination, great care was always taken that no doubtfully ordained priest should be permitted to celebrate at the altar. In the 'Dialogue' of St. Egbert, Archbishop of York,[1] written between 732 and 766, it is said that 'wandering priests or those ordained doubtfully,[2] without commendatory letters, and passing from province to province, are nowhere to be allowed to minister or to give sacraments, without the knowledge of the bishop of the place. Necessary sustenance may be given them, but they must not be admitted to the ministry of sacred things without the greatest discretion.' And in the Province of Canterbury a similar precaution was adopted in 816 by the Council of Celchyth. 'No Scot' (*i.e.* Irish priest, whether coming from Ireland or from North Britain) 'was to be allowed to administer sacraments or to say mass;' and this, not because there was any hostility between the nations, much less any discord or schism between the churches, but, as it is immediately stated, 'because it is unknown to us where they have been ordained, or if they have been ordained at all.'[3]

[1] Haddan and Stubbs, *Councils*, iii. 407.

[2] 'Absolute ordinatos.' The adverb seems a misreading, but from the context it may have been 'abroad,' or 'illegally,' or 'uncertainly.'

[3] Haddan and Stubbs, iii. 581: 'Quia incertum est nobis unde vel an ab aliquo ordinentur.' That this canon indicates neither national nor ecclesiastical antipathy, is evident from the fact that an exactly similar decree had been made against the Scoti at Chalons, in France, three years before. (Labbe, vii. 1281.) We do not know the circumstances which set them roving.

The mass-priest might be either a monk, a canon regular, or a secular. Until the invasion of the Danes at the beginning of the ninth century, probably the greater number of the priests were monks. Monks became missionaries through the country parts, and often it was one of their number who was made the permanent and local pastor of a country church, remaining, however, subject to his abbot.[1] Yet secular priests, *i.e.* priests not under monastic vows, had also the care of districts allotted to them. These districts were called priestshires, shriftshires, or kirkshires.[2]

Such secular priests seem to be alluded to in the eighth and ninth canons of the council of Clovesho, celebrated by all the bishops of the Province of Canterbury, under Archbishop Cuthbert, in 747. The priests are commanded 'to watch over their oratory (*oratorii domum*) and everything belonging to its service or decoration, and to pay great attention to the celebration of masses and the singing of psalms,' *i.e.* the two great divisions of the worship of God. For it may here be said once for all, since the subject does not belong to the present treatise, that the Divine Office, as well as the Mass, was performed publicly in every parish church from the arrival of St. Augustine until the Reformation, unless when some extraordinary circumstances made it impossible. That the above canon relates rather to secular than monastic pastors seems probable from the next canon, which orders 'that priests, throughout the places and regions of the laity, which have been assigned to them by the bishops of the province, shall endeavour to fulfil their evangelical and apostolical ministry in baptizing, instructing, and visiting the people, uniting zeal for souls with obedience to ritual' (*sub legitimo ritu ac diligenti cura*).[3] Forty years after this, in 786, two legates, George, Bishop of Ostia, and Theophylact, Bishop of Todi, were sent from Pope Adrian I. to make a visitation of England. From the court of Offa, king of Mercia, George proceeded to Northumbria and held a council, and afterwards returning to the south held another council, but the same canons were promulgated in both; so that we may gather from them the discipline then prevailing throughout all those parts of the island belonging to the English. In these councils we have the first mention (in England) of canons living in community, as distinct from monks. The sixth decree is as follows : 'No priest or deacon is to be ordained, unless of approved life and properly

---

[1] See Lingard, *Anglo-Saxon Church*, vol. i. p. 146.
[2] *Parochia* is used by Gregory of Tours for a country *parish*, but in most early writers it means a *diocese*.
[3] Haddan and Stubbs, iii. 365.

instructed, and they must remain in the title to which they are ordained, so that no one presume to receive a priest or deacon from another title [1] without a reasonable cause and commendatory letters.' All the churches were to have performed in them publicly and reverently the divine office (*cursum*) at the canonical hours. Regulations were also made about mass, which will be noticed elsewhere.[2]

It would be a most interesting and instructive study to gather from history, especially from the lives of the saints, whatever might throw light on the subject of the priesthood—to consider the numbers of the clergy at different periods, the motives that influenced candidates, the means taken to test those motives—the studies and moral preparation previous to ordination, the question of celibacy, the worthiness or unworthiness of the ministers of the altar, their influence, their secular position, and the rest. No subject has been more misrepresented, none better deserves careful and candid attention. But though the state of the priests is a subject closely connected with the Blessed Sacrament, it is a wide and distinct field of research, into which it is impossible here to enter fully, and which it is better to pass over altogether than to treat inadequately. That there were many unworthy priests is most certain, that there were many zealous and saintly priests is abundantly proved. We shall meet as we proceed with examples both of the good and of the bad. One only caution will I add. Neither the value of the sacrifice as offered to God, nor the efficacy of the sacrament as ministered to man, depends on the sanctity of the minister of the altar, but on the institution of God, and on Jesus Christ who is both High Priest and Victim, and whose power cannot be lessened nor His purity soiled by any unworthiness on the part of His visible representative. In saying this I in no way detract from the importance of sanctity in the priest both for his own sake and for the sake of others.

[1] The 'title' here mentioned indicates a fixed means of sustenance approved by the canons (such as is still required on admission to holy orders), and it appears that the title could be that of poverty, as we call it, for those who led a monastic life, or else it might be founded on a benefice; while the benefice might be held either by a priest living in community and following a canonical rule, or by a priest serving a country church.

[2] See Haddan and Stubbs, iii. 450, 461.

CHAPTER XI.

CHURCHES AND ALTARS.

It has always been the rule in the Catholic Church that the holy sacrifice of the Mass should be celebrated on a consecrated altar and within a consecrated building. Only in very exceptional circumstances has it been permitted to dispense with the altar, as in the prisons of the primitive martyrs, when the altar was the hands or even the breast of the sufferers for Christ. To celebrate on an altar, but outside a consecrated building, has been often permitted for less urgent reasons, though it has always been an exception or a privilege.

I have not found any instances of mass having been said without an altar in England. Among the decisions given by Archbishop Theodore, in answer to certain questions proposed to him, decisions which are rather solutions of cases of conscience belonging to the seventh century than canonical decrees for future times, occurs the following: 'Licet in campo . . . presbitero missas agere si diaconus vel presbiter ipse calicem et oblationem manibus tenuerit.'[1] Here at first sight it might seem that no altar is required; but does it not rather mean that mass may be celebrated in the open air if the priest or deacon holds the chalice and the host *with*, and not in, his hands (*manibus tenuerit*), to prevent them from being moved by gusts of wind?

No doubt, before the building of churches, the first missionaries often said mass beneath a tent or in a tabernacle of boughs, like St. Germanus, or in the houses of their hosts when preaching in a village, but on these occasions they used a portable altar. We read too of masses being offered on certain spots of holy or mournful memory. Thus Venerable Bede tells us how St. Oswald, when seeking to win back the kingdom of Northumbria from Cadwallon the Briton, erected a wooden cross at Heavenfield, near Hexham, before which he and all his army knelt in prayer. To this prayer a victory was granted, which led to the establishment of the faith throughout that

[1] Haddan and Stubbs, iii. 191.

province. Oswald was slain in battle some years later, fighting against the pagan Penda, but the monks of Hexham used to go to Heavenfield on the vigil of the anniversary of his death and sing the office of the dead (*vigiliæ mortuorum*) for the repose of his soul, and the following morning the holy sacrifice was offered for the same end (*victimam pro eo mane sacræ oblationis offerre*). There was a peculiar propriety in this, since St. Oswald was said to have fallen on the field of battle uttering the words 'God have mercy on the souls of my soldiers!'[1]

A somewhat similar act of piety is related by Ingulf. During the devastations of the Danes in the ninth century, Theodore abbot of Croyland, and his aged monks, and the children of the monastery, had been all fearfully butchered at the very altar and during the celebration of the holy mysteries. The impious pagans had then gone to Medeshamstede, now Peterborough, where Hubba the Danish king, after besieging and taking the monastery, slaughtered with his own hand the abbot and eighty-three monks. Godric, the successor of Theodore at Croyland, not only reverently paid the debt of piety to his own abbot and former brethren, but also carefully buried the mangled bodies of the monks of Medeshamstede. The rest of the history may be given in the words of Dr. Lingard, which are a free translation of Ingulf. 'To perpetuate their memory, Godric placed over their grave a small pyramid of stone, on which was rudely engraved the history of this bloody catastrophe; and opposite to the pyramid he raised a cross, on which was engraved the image of Christ. The public road lay between them, and the pious abbot hoped that the presence of the crucifix would prevent travellers from profaning so sacred a spot, and that the figures on the monument would induce them to offer a prayer for those whose ashes reposed beneath it. During the rest of his life these victims of Danish barbarity were seldom absent from his recollection. Yearly, on the anniversary of the massacre, he visited the cemetery, pitched his tent over the grave, and spent two days in celebrating masses and performing other devotions to which Catholic charity has attributed the power of benefiting the souls of the departed.'[2]

---

[1] Bede, iii. 2. Alban Butler places Maserfield, the scene of his last battle, at Winwick, near St. Helen's, in Lancashire. Others are in favour of Oswestry, in Shropshire. But in neither case could the monks of Hexham pray at his grave.

[2] *History of Anglo-Saxons*, ii. 214. Though the history which goes under the name of Ingulf is now generally admitted to be the work of a later writer, and in some respects a forgery, yet, as Mr. Freeman remarks, ' whoever did write

It was allowed then, under circumstances like the above, to celebrate the holy rites outside a consecrated building; and indeed there is, in a Pontifical of Archbishop Egbert preserved in Paris, a special mass called *Missa in Cimiterio*, which seems to show that on certain anniversaries mass could be said even in a churchyard.[1]

Another exception was also authorised. Mass could be celebrated in the apartment of a dying person. The thirtieth of the canons called Dunstan's or Edgar's, of the year 967, says: 'We declare that no priest may celebrate in any house which is not a consecrated church, except on account of some one's grievous sickness;' and in 970 the twenty-fifth of the canons of Ælfric decrees that 'mass must not be said except in consecrated places, unless under a great necessity or in a last sickness.'[2] The reasons of such a prohibition are evident enough. That it was sometimes evaded or disregarded is proved from the testimony of William of Malmesbury, an unprejudiced writer, who lived near enough to the times that he described to be well informed on this subject. In his description of the decline of piety and luxury of manners which preceded the Norman Conquest, he tells us that the English nobles, instead of going to the church, would have a hurried mass said in their chamber by their chaplains, before they rose from bed.[3] We must remember, however, that a few examples of such things get easily exaggerated, as if they were a common custom, especially by a painter of morals who is in search of dark colours for his picture.

Let us now consider the nature of these churches and altars, and of their consecration to God. When Pope St. Gregory first heard of the success of St. Augustine's preaching, he wrote to King Ethelbert to destroy the temples of his gods.[4] Afterwards in a letter to St. Mellitus he says that the temples must not be destroyed, but only the idols, and that when the temples have been sprinkled with holy water, and altars built in them and relics brought, they may then be used for Christian rites.[5] But as such temples probably were not numerous, and for their construction or associations were not considered desirable by the missionaries, great efforts were made, as we have seen, to erect oratories and churches throughout the land. Into the history of the structure and endowment of these I need not enter,

it may have worked in some stories from the old traditions and records of the Abbey.' (*Old Eng. Hist.* p. 111.)

[1] It is printed by Dr. Rock, vol. iii. p. 14.
[2] These canons are printed by Spelman and Wilkins.
[3] Guil. Mal. *De Gestis reg. Angl.*; Mat. Paris, *Hist.* p. 5 (ed. Wats.)
[4] S. Greg. *Epist.* xi. 66.   [5] *Ib.* xi. 76.

for it has been well investigated by Dr. Lingard and other writers.[1] Many were at first mere log huts, and timber churches remained here and there in remote country places until the Norman Conquest and even later. Yet Bede shows us that in more important places stone churches were constructed at the very outset. Blæcca, the prefect of Lincoln, built a stone church of great beauty (*egregii operis*).[2] St. Bennet Biscop is renowned for bringing workmen from Gaul skilled in building, decoration, and working in glass and metal. St. Aldhelm, St. Egwin, St. Wilfrid, in the seventh century, vied with one another in erecting handsome churches at Malmesbury, Worcester, Hexham, York, and Ripon. No art or expense was spared in making the interiors of the greater churches as splendid as possible; and did we not remember the immense plunder which must have been taken from the conquered Britons by the ancestors of these new Christians, we should be utterly at a loss to know whence came all the gold and silver and precious stones which their piety poured out upon the altars. Chalices, patens, crosses of pure gold and of silver gilt, vestments and hangings of the most costly texture were given by kings and queens and nobles.[3] As evidence of the faith and piety of the donors some of these gifts will be hereafter recorded; but I will confine myself at present to the rites and prayers by which the churches, whether rich or poor in material construction, were set apart for the service of God.

Substantially these were the same throughout Europe in the seventh and eighth centuries as they are now in the nineteenth. Raban Maur, Archbishop of Rheims and a disciple of our Alcuin, at the beginning of the ninth century, describes minutely the consecration of a church. The substance of his description is as follows. The preceding night relics of saints were brought to a tent in the churchyard, and solemn vigils were kept around them with psalms and prayers. The next morning they were carried by priests processionally to the church, the procession first making on the outside of the church three circuits of the building. Twelve lights were placed inside around the walls; the altars were sprinkled with holy water and anointed with chrism, and on them incense was burnt; relics

---

[1] On the structure of Anglo-Saxon churches see Lingard, *A. S.* ii. note C; on their endowment, i. ch. 6 and note I. On their interior arrangement consult Dr. Rock, i. 190 *sq.*

[2] Bede, ii. 16.

[3] Innumerable examples will be found in the pages of Dr. Rock. I may say that his four volumes are almost a catalogue of the riches and splendours of ancient churches, from the days of Ethelbert to those of Henry VIII.

were placed under the altar slabs; and lastly solemn mass was sung.'[1] We have still in existence the Office used in England in this sacred ceremony as early as the time of Venerable Bede, viz. in the Pontifical of Egbert. It abounds with the most exquisite prayers. After the procession of relics and the singing of the Litany of the Saints, the consecrating bishop chanted the following invocation: 'O blessed and holy Trinity, who purifiest, cleansest, and adornest all things; O blessed Majesty of God, who fillest, governest, and disposest all things; O blessed and holy hand of God, who sanctifiest, blessest, and enrichest all things; O God, the Holy of holies, we humbly implore Thy clemency, that by our ministry Thou wouldst purify, bless, and consecrate this church to the honour of the holy and victorious Cross and the memory of Thy blessed servant N. Here may Thy priests offer to Thee sacrifices of praise; here may Thy faithful people perform their vows; here may the burden of sins be lightened, and those who have fallen be restored to grace. Grant that all who shall enter this temple to pray may obtain the effect of their petition, and rejoice for ever in the bounty of Thy mercy. Amen.'[2] The baptistery, often a separate building, had a special blessing. At the same time many objects belonging to the church were set apart to the service of God by prayer, but especially the altar with its furniture.

The altar was considered by the Saxons, as by the Britons before them, as 'the seat of the heavenly sacrifice,' that for which and by which the church was sanctified. In his description of the consecration of Ripon by St. Wilfrid, Eddi gives special prominence to the high altar—'altare cum basibus suis Domino dedicantes, purpuráque auro textâ induentes'[3]—'the altar together with its supports was consecrated to the Lord, and then decked with a purple covering interwoven with gold,' before the holy mass was offered. Here Eddi distinguishes between the altar-table itself and the substructure on which it was laid. The latter could be a solid mass of stone or wood, or the altar-slab might be made to rest on one or more pillars, or on brackets. The side altars, built against pillars or in oratories and recesses, were often very small. The shape was sometimes square, but more generally an oblong parallelogram, as at the present day. Superaltars, *i.e.* the step or steps at the

---

[1] *De Clericorum Instit.* ii. 45.

[2] *Pont. Egbert* (Surtees Society). In the first vol. of the *Historians of York* (Rolls Series, 1879) there is an account of the consecration of Ripon by St. Wilfrid at p. 25, and of Ramsey by St. Oswald at p. 464.

[3] Eddi, *Vita S. Wilfridi*, cap. 16.

back of the altar (*gradini*), were not in use; and the name superaltar in mediæval documents is to be understood of a portable altar-stone.[1] Whether moveable or fixed, the altar-slab, or altar properly so called, was regularly of stone, and, unless it were such, it was forbidden to consecrate it with holy chrism. 'Altaria nisi lapidea chrismatis unguine non consecrentur.'[2] But these words show that wooden or metal altars at that period were still occasionally used.

The altar was called in Anglo-Saxon *weofod*, in old English *weuede* or *weved*. 'Godes table is the woyeued,' says Dan Michel in the 'Ayenbite of Inwyt.' The altar is also sometimes called God's board, and this phrase is especially (though not exclusively) used when reference is made to Holy Communion. 'I charge you in God's name,' says the homilist in the Festival, 'that none of you come thus to God's board, but if ye be in perfect love and charity, and be clean shriven and in full purpose to leave your sin.' 'He used of God's board,' *i.e.* he communicated from the Lord's table, is an expression in an old poem, and another, referring to both mass and communion, says, 'Richard at God's board his mass had and his rights.'[3] But the much more usual designation of the place of sacrifice was the altar, or, as it was formerly written and pronounced, auter.

The substructure of the altar was plain, not carved or decorated, and it was covered with a frontal. Hence, when stripped on Good Friday, it did not by its splendour contrast with the mournful appearance of the church, but well symbolised our Lord's Body as It hung naked on the cross.[4] As the frontals could be changed, the altar was capable of great adornment on the festivals; and not only rich stuffs, but also embossed plates of gold and silver, were hung around it. According to St. Theodore there were to be no steps before the altar.[5] This prohibition was derived from the Old Testament, and, as it had in reality no reference to the circumstances of the Christian sacrifice, was in course of time disregarded.

There were often many altars in a church. A poem, written about the year 725, mentions fourteen,[6] and another of the same

---

[1] A ledge or shelf was sometimes made on the high altar at a later period. It is called a form, a kalpas, or a desk, in documents of the 16th century. See *Archæol. Journal*, vol. xxxv. p. 384.

[2] *Excerptiones Egberti*, apud Thorpe, p. 104. Though not Egbert's, these are ancient canons.

[3] See these and other examples given by Canon Simmons in the *Lay Folk's Mass Book*, p. 359. 'La sainte table' is constantly used in this sense in French, as well as 'sacra mensa,' or 'mensa Domini,' in Latin.

[4] Rock, i. 233 *sq*.   [5] Haddan and Stubbs, iii. 191.

[6] Among the works of St. Aldhelm; Migne, tom. lxxxix., col. 289.

century by Alcuin tells us there were thirty in the cathedral church of York—

Quæ triginta tenet variis ornatibus aras.[1]

Beneath the present church of Ripon are still to be seen chambers and passages which once formed part of the crypt of St. Wilfrid's abbey church, and which illustrate what is said by an old writer in describing the ancient cathedral of Hexham, that many priests and separate groups of worshippers could offer and assist at mass without being visible to each other.[2]

'Besides the undercroft, the triforium or gallery running all around the church over the aisles or "porticus" had many small chapels with an altar in each of them, built in the upper part of the church.'[3]

There was, however, always one principal or high altar standing towards the east end of the church, and this was distinguished not only by size, position, and splendour, but also by two other peculiarities. It stood in a part of the church reserved for the clergy and separated from the body of the building by a low rail, called cancelli; and it was surmounted by a ciborium, or dome resting on pillars. It appears that in the early Saxon monastery of Abingdon the monks, twelve in number, had each his own chapel, and only on Sundays and festivals was the mass celebrated at the high altar.[4]

Dr. Rock seems to say that the altars were always so built that the priest celebrating turned eastward;[5] and certainly this is true of the high altar, for the church itself was almost invariably built so that the presbytery was at its eastern extremity. Yet Walafrid Strabo expressly states that the altar might be built towards any point of the compass, though the more common or fitting position was towards the east.[6] Still, whatever was the position of the priest, he was in no case supposed to be reading prayers to the people, but addressing them to God. He had, therefore, his back turned towards most of the worshippers gathered round his altar, and taking part with him in the sacrifice.

---

[1] *De Pontif. Eccl. Ebor.* l. 1513. Alcuin gives here a detailed account of the church built in York by Archbishop Albert, and its altars, candelabra, and crosses of gold and silver.

[2] Describing the church built by St. Acca in 710. In Bolland, *Acta SS.* tom. lvi., p. 969.

[3] Rock, i. 231.   [4] *Historia de Abingdon*, i. 273 (Rolls Series).

[5] Rock, i. 220. In Christ Church, Canterbury, there was an apse at the west as well as at the east end, and in each apse an altar. In the western apse, while the people knelt looking westward, the priest celebrated so as to look east and face the people. But this was peculiar.

[6] Walafridus Strabo, *De rebus eccl.*, Migne, tom. cxiv. p. 92.

The altar received a special and most solemn consecration, and this rite was reserved to the bishop. On the altar-slab five or sometimes even nine crosses were cut, one of which was in the centre. These crosses were anointed with holy oil, and on them incense was burnt. The prayers used in these ceremonies expressed in the strongest language belief in the Real Presence of our Lord and in the holy sacrifice, as well as the dispositions which should belong to the celebrant and the worshippers.[1] I select one for translation : 'O holy Lord, O clement Father, in whom neither beginning nor end is found, who art as great as is Thy will to be, holy and wonderful God, whom the universe cannot contain :—we bless Thee, and suppliantly implore that this altar may be to Thee like that which Abel, in figure of the mystery of our salvation, being slain by his own brother and so Thy precursor in his passion, sprinkled and consecrated with his own blood. Let this altar be to Thee, O Lord, like that which Abraham our father raised, when it was given him to see Thee in vision, and like that on which Melchisedech expressed in figure the sacrifice of triumph. Let this altar be to Thee, O Lord, like that on which Abraham, the pattern of our faith, laid his son Isaac, believing in Thee with his whole heart, and on which the mystery of salvation in the passion of our Lord was shown forth, when a son was offered and a lamb was slain. Let this altar be to Thee, O Lord, like that which Isaac, having found a well of deep clear water to which he gave the name of Abundance, dedicated to Thy Majesty.[2] Let this altar be to Thee, O Lord, like that stone which Jacob had placed beneath his head, when in his dream he saw angels ascending and descending on the mysterious ladder. Let this altar be to Thee, O Lord, like that which Moses, when he had received Thy law, built up of twelve stones in type of the Apostles. Let this altar be to Thee, O Lord, like that which Moses cleansed with a purification of seven days and dedicated to Thy heavenly invocation (*alloquio*), as Thou Thyself didst say to him : "If anyone touch this altar, let him be sanctified." On this altar, then, let luxury be slain, let all lust cease, and instead of pigeons let there be offered the sacrifice of chastity, and for the young of doves a sacrifice of innocence. Through our Lord Jesus Christ,' &c.[3]

'There was one custom in the consecration of altars which is no

---

[1] See Gage, *Ordo ad dedicandam Eccl.*, published in *Archæologia*, vol. xv. Other prayers, though not that which I have translated, are given by Rock, i. 104 ; Lingard, ii. 34.

[2] Gen. xxvi. 25, 33.

[3] From Egbert's *Pontifical*, published by Surtees Society.

longer observed, and has given rise to foolish, and worse than foolish, remarks on the part of some Protestant controversialists. A council of all the bishops of the province of Canterbury, held under Archbishop Wulfred in 816 at Celchyth, in its second canon decrees as follows: 'When a church is built, it must be consecrated by the bishop of the diocese. The water must be blessed by him and sprinkled, and the other ceremonies completed, as contained in the book' (the Pontifical). 'Afterward the Eucharist, which is consecrated by the bishop at the time (or for that purpose, *per idem ministerium*), together with other relics, is enclosed in a box, and will be kept in the basilica. And if he cannot obtain other relics, nevertheless this alone will be of the greatest advantage, since it is the Body and Blood of our Lord Jesus Christ.'[1]

It may be thought from the above words that the Holy Eucharist, thus enclosed in a box with relics, was to be kept for use in the church. But from other sources,[2] and especially from the very Pontifical of Egbert[3] referred to by the fathers at Celchyth, it is certain that the box was placed beneath the altar-table, there to remain permanently.

The reason of this canon is thus given by Dr. Rock: 'Living, as they did, on the uttermost bounds of Christendom, far away from the land of the martyrs, though, whenever they went beyond the sea to Italy or the East, they always strove to bring home some relics of the saints, yet it was not at all times easy for the Anglo-Saxon bishops to find at hand such hallowed treasures to deposit under the newly raised altar, or within the church just built, as ecclesiastical usage directed. In this dearth of relics at a period when they were young as a Christian nation, and therefore could not boast of many home-born saints, what were the Anglo-Saxons to do? Their unhalting faith soon taught them to seek in the Eucharist—what was far above the holiest saint's body or the boldest martyr's blood—the body of the Saint of saints, of their Redeemer and their God Himself, Christ Jesus.' Dr. Rock, who rightly considers this practice as a proof of the belief of the Anglo-Saxons in transubstantiation, was probably not aware of the language used on this subject by certain Protestants. One of them, who is often quoted as 'the learned Johnson' because of his edition of the canons of the Anglican Church,

---

[1] Haddan and Stubbs, iii. 580. 'Tamen hoc maxime proficere potest, quia corpus et sanguis est Domini nostri Jesu Christi.'

[2] See Rock, i. 40; also Chaignon, *Histoire des Sacrements*.

[3] 'Deinde ponit tres portiones corporis Domini intus in confessione, et tres de incenso, et recluduntur intus reliquiæ.'

makes the following commentary on the decree of the fathers of Celchyth : ' Here the Eucharistic symbols are set upon a level with the relics of saints, and *scarce that neither*. For if relics could be found, they were necessary for the consecration of the church, and they that could not find them *could make them* ' ! [1] The extraordinary impudence of this remark, as well as its flippant and blasphemous form, may well surprise us, since Archbishop Wulfred and his brother bishops had distinctly said, when giving leave for the use of the Eucharist : ' And this may especially avail, since it is the Body and Blood of our Lord Jesus Christ.' And that their meaning was that the living Body of the Son of God was more than a substitute for the dead bodies of His martyrs, Mr. Johnson might have convinced himself, had he only looked into the book referred to in that very canon. The bishop prayed to God that He would ' accept the adorable Victim that would lie there, and would grant life to all who should partake of that Victim' (*ut super illud altare adorandam Filii sui hostiam Ipse benedicat impositam, Ipse suscipiat consecrandam*) ; and again that He ' would transmute by His invisible power the elements selected for the sacrifice into the Body and Blood of the Redeemer, and cause the nature of the offering to pass into the substance of the Word ;' besides much more to the same purpose. And yet dishonest controversialists who have all this under their eyes, or ought to have, before they express an opinion, tell us that these ancient bishops considered the 'Eucharistic symbols' as beneath the level of the relics of saints, and then joke about their making them if they cannot find them! Assuredly the pagan sons of King Saba, who asked St. Mellitus to give them his white bread, had as much knowledge and as much reverence for Christian mysteries as some who pass for High Church Anglicans. To complete this part of the subject I will add that St. Anselm having been consulted as to whether, when an altar is moved, it has to be consecrated again, replied that ' all are agreed that if the principal altar is violated, the whole church, together with the altars, must be reconsecrated, and that a church cannot be consecrated unless either the high altar or some other altar is consecrated with it. But if the altar remain unmoved and a part of the church be destroyed or added, the new part has only to be sprinkled with water blessed by the bishop. And the reason of this is that the *altar is not for the*

---

[1] These remarks of Johnson have been repeated again and again in different forms by Protestant controversialists. I may say that they have become one of the *loci communes* on this subject.

church, but the church for the altar.'[1] St. Boniface also taught that a priest must not erect a second altar in a consecrated church without getting it consecrated by the bishop.[2] Not only was every church dedicated to Almighty God under the invocation of a saint, but each altar was called by the name of a saint, whose memory it served to recall. On or near the altar was inscribed the name of the saint to whom it was dedicated.[3]

It may perhaps amuse the reader in the midst of these details if I here record, in connection with the subject of the dedication of churches, an example of the way in which some persons study archæology, as we have just had a specimen of the study of canon law. It seems that the Rev. J. Corbel Anderson conceived the praiseworthy idea of looking into the history of the old Catholic Church of Croydon, of which he was appointed the Protestant vicar. He naturally had recourse to the Domesday Book drawn up at the Conquest. In Surrey, he tells us, he finds sixty churches mentioned. Of these sixteen are dedicated to the Blessed Virgin, eight to St. Peter, four to St. Nicolas, and so on. Then comes his own reflection, which is as follows : ' This list is useful, inasmuch as it implies the corrupt state into which the Church of Christ had fallen at the period when these structures were named. With such a list beside us, no need is there to turn to books of ecclesiastical history to ascertain whether or not during the Middle Ages the bright light of the Gospel was obscured, for here we have sermons in stones. Instead of seeking pardon through the atonement and intercession of the sole Mediator between God and man, the sinner, ill informed of the way of salvation, placed himself under the tutelary guardianship of the Virgin Mary, St. Peter, and All Saints. *Amid this series of appellations the sacred name of Christ does not appear.*'[4] If the writer of this new homily on the peril of idolatry had consulted the service for the dedication of churches used by their Anglo-Saxon founders, which was quite as accessible to him as the Domesday Book, he might have read the prayer, given a few pages back, which was used by the bishop when the church was named. He would have seen in what beautiful language the ever-blessed Trinity was implored ' to bless and consecrate the church, to *the honour of the holy and victorious cross*, and the memory of thy blessed servant N.' He would have found also that the very purpose for which the church was consecrated was to

---

[1] S. Anselm, *Op.* tom. ii. p. 135 ; *Ep.* l. iii. n. 161.
[2] *Opera* apud Migne, tom. lxxxix., p. 821.
[3] Council of Celchyth. Haddan and Stubbs, iii. 580 ; Rock, i. 228.
[4] *Croydon Church, Past and Present,* by J. C. Anderson, p. 17.

make the perpetual bloodless commemoration, commanded by our Lord Jesus Christ Himself, of His sacred Passion ; and then, looking more narrowly into the history of his church, he might have found that before the pictures of the saints were whitewashed over by Elizabeth, there stretched across the church a rood screen with an image of our Lord, that all might remember and love their Redeemer. And he would have learnt how all the roods throughout England were pulled down and burnt by the first bishops of his own reformed church, while the lion and unicorn were set up instead. In a word, he would soon have discovered unmistakeable evidence that in the Middle Ages the doctrine of the atonement by our Lord Jesus Christ was known from the king to the bondsman with a familiarity to which the majority of the English poor are, alas ! now utter strangers.[1]

But the two passages which have been quoted in this chapter from Anglican writers are instructive, inasmuch as they show the hateful mania by which so many are possessed to calumniate their forefathers, or to find, by some means or other, evidences of impiety, folly, or stupidity, which are far more conspicuous in their own pages. How much more beautiful was the spirit of William of Malmesbury, who, writing in the century after the Norman conquest and making a review of Anglo-Saxon history, delights to record evidences of piety, though he has no care to hide faults ! Amongst other passages there is one bearing on the present subject of the dedication of churches. It is as follows : 'At their first coming into Britain they (the Angles and Saxons) were barbarians in appearance and reality, given up to war and fanatical rites. But afterwards when they had received the faith of Christ, by degrees, as time went on, they relegated warlike exercises to the second place, and gave all their attention to religion. I refer to their kings, who might have indulged in pleasure uncontrolled, yet some of them in their own country, and some in Rome, put aside their royal robes for the dress of monks, and by a blessed exchange gained a heavenly kingdom. Many others, in outward

---

[1] There may still be seen round the nave of Almonbury Church, in Yorkshire, some English verses (date 1522) which, though rude, are devout :—

> 'Thou man unkind, Have in thy mind
> My bloody face,
> My wounds wide, On every side
> For thy trespass.
> Thou sinner hard, Turn hitherward,
> Behold thy Saviour free (*i.e.* bountiful) ;
> Unkind thou art From me to depart,
> And mercy I would grant thee.'

appearance only belonging to the world, poured out their wealth for the relief of the poor and the foundation of monasteries. And what shall I say of so many bishops, hermits, abbots? Did not the whole island shine with so many relics of its own native inhabitants, that you can scarcely pass through any considerable village without hearing the name of some new saint? And of how many more has the memory perished from lack of historians?'[1]

But to continue and conclude this subject, since a church was a building solemnly set apart for the celebration of the most holy mysteries, placed under the invocation of a saint, and believed, as St. Gregory and St. Bede often say, to be the resort of holy angels, who come to worship their hidden God, it was but natural that it should be kept free not only from what was sinful, but also from what was out of harmony with the worship of God. 'It cannot be doubted,' writes Venerable Bede, 'that where the mysteries of our Lord's Body and Blood are enacted (*geruntur*) there are assemblies of the heavenly citizens, since they guarded with such watchful vigils the tomb where once His venerable Body had been placed, though He had risen from it and departed.' Let these words of this great doctor of the English of the seventh century be noted by those who would persuade themselves that the Anglo-Saxons placed the Holy Eucharist on the same level as the relics of saints. Bede argues that if angels guarded the tomb where the Body of our Lord had once lain but was no longer present, much more must they honour and guard the church where that Body is present. Surely, if words have any meaning, he is speaking of the same Body that lay in the tomb, and not of 'Eucharistic symbols.' 'Therefore,' continues the venerable writer, 'we must, brethren, be very careful, when we enter a church either to pay our debt of praise to God, or to offer holy mass' (*ad agenda missarum solemnia*), 'always to remember the presence of the angels, and so to perform our heavenly duties with fear and reverence in imitation of those devout women who, when the angels showed themselves at the tomb, are related to have feared and cast down their eyes to the earth.'[2]

To maintain due reverence in and about the house of God, in spite of the little faith or rude manners of the people, was the frequent solicitude of the bishops in council. One of the canons of St. Dunstan in 967 says: 'Let priests keep their churches with all honourable care for their divine ministry and for the pure service of God

---

[1] *De gestis reg. Angl.* iii.
[2] S. Bede, *Homil.* apud Martene, *Thesaurus Anec.* t. v. p. 360.

and nothing else. Let them allow nothing unbefitting (*quid superflui*) either inside or near them. Let there be no vain talking or unbecoming act. This is no place for disorderly drinking, nor for any kind of vanity. Dogs must be kept out of the churchyard, and no more swine allowed to feed there than their keeper can control.'[1]

From a story related by Reginald of Durham we may gather with what ceremonies people were then accustomed to enter a consecrated church. He tells us how St. Cuthbert, appearing in vision to a young nobleman, instructed him not to go into the church with pomp and head erect, but, '*as is the custom of Christians*, when you come to the door of the church kneel down, kiss the threshold, the doorposts and doors, and then make the sign of the cross with three fingers of the right hand.'[2]

In order to impress the people with reverence for our Lord, a certain regard was had even to materials which had once belonged to a consecrated church. The penitential of Archbishop Theodore of the seventh century says:[3] 'Wood which has been part of a church may be used only in building another church or a monastery, or it must be burned. It may be used to bake bread, but not for other lay works.'

Having spoken in this chapter of churches and the altars within them, I must here add that portable altars or moveable altar-stones were not unknown in early times. An example was mentioned in a former chapter in relating the martyrdom of the two Hewalds, who daily offered the saving Victim, using 'a consecrated board' as an altar-slab. These portable altars were called *altaria gestatoria* and also *superaltaria*, because they were occasionally used even in a church, being placed on an unconsecrated wooden altar structure. By no other means could mass, as we have seen was sometimes the custom, be said outside a consecrated building, since it was forbidden to say mass without a consecrated altar. Perhaps it was only of those to be used inside a church that St. Anselm spoke when he said that, though he knew such altars were consecrated by bishops in Normandy, he would neither blame them nor imitate them.[4] These portable altars were sometimes made of precious materials, as jet or jasper, and were covered with plates of gold or silver. They were also set in a frame

---

[1] Spelman, i. 447; Wilkins, i. 225.
[2] *Libellus de virtutibus B. Cuthberti*, p. 258 (Surtees Society, 1835).
[3] Haddan and Stubbs, iii. 190.
[4] 'Quod ego non damno, nec tamen facere volo.'—*Epist.* iii. 159.

for greater security.¹ When the altar, whether portable or fixed, was used for the holy sacrifice, it was covered with at least three altar-cloths of linen. But of the rites of mass I shall speak in another chapter.

---

[1] For further information on this subject see Rock, i. 250. There is also an article going over much the same ground in the *Archæological Journal*, vol. iv. pp. 243-248. Such a portable altar is called, in the Decretals, *Viaticum*. See Bened. XIV. *De Sacrif. Missæ*, l. i. 2.

CHAPTER XII.

REQUISITES FOR MASS.

IF so great attention was paid to the place of celebration, it is clear that no care would be deemed superfluous when bestowed upon the materials to be used in the holy rite which our Lord Himself had chosen for conversion into His own Flesh and Blood. He had selected things easily to be procured throughout the world—bread made of the flour of wheat, wine pressed from the grape and mixed with water. These elements were simple enough to be looked on as the very staff of life and normal sustenance of men, yet rich enough not to be excluded from the most luxurious banquet. Unlike most of the victims used on Jewish altars, they are essentially *clean* in their character and use, and such as to cause loathing or disgust to none. And lastly, though easily consumed, they are capable of being kept incorrupt for a considerable time.

The thirty-ninth of St. Dunstan's canons is as follows: 'We decree that no priest shall ever be so rash as to celebrate mass unless he have ready all things necessary for the Eucharist; viz., a pure oflete or oblation, pure wine and pure water. Woe to him who begins mass when any of these is wanting, and woe to him who adds anything which may adulterate them. He would be like those Jews who mixed vinegar and gall and scoffingly offered them to Christ.'[1]

A few words about each of these elements will be sufficient.

The bread used at mass was not common bread, mixed with barm or salt. It was made of the finest wheaten flour that could be procured. Hence Bede makes the pagan sons of Saba say to St. Mellitus, 'Give us that fine white bread' (*panem nitidum*). Alcuin teaches that 'the bread which is consecrated into the Body of Christ should be the very cleanest and without the leaven of any other infection.'[2] In the edition of Theodore's penitential published by Thorpe it is said: 'No priest may offer in sacrifice anything but what our Lord taught should be offered, that is to say, bread without

---

[1] Spelman, i. 447; Wilkins, i. 225; Thorpe, ii. 252.
[2] Alcuini *Epist.* 75.

leaven, and wine mixed with water, for out of the side of our Lord issued blood and water.'[1] A decree of Theodulf, Bishop of Orleans, in the eighth century, which was translated into Anglo-Saxon for use in England, orders the priest either to bake the altar-breads himself, or at least to superintend the baking of them by his servants.[2] The breads in baking were pressed between two irons as at present; these baking irons were called a bult or singing-irons, or in Latin *ferroni* or *ferramentum*. In monasteries the preparation of the breads was converted into an ecclesiastical rite, the ministers engaged in it wearing surplices and chanting psalms.[3] Gilbert, Bishop of Limerick in the time of St. Anselm, mentions that every priest should have his box of altar-breads and baking-irons (*pixis cum oblatis et ferrum eorum*).[4]

In order not to return again to this subject, a few facts belonging to a later period may be here mentioned. A constitution of William of Bleys, A.D. 1229, says: 'Great care must be taken that the altar-breads (*oblatæ*) be made of pure grains of wheat. The ministers of the Church, wearing surplices, must make the altar-breads in an honourable place. The instrument by which they are baked may be smeared with wax, not with oil or grease; the ofletes must be white and well rounded.'[5] William Russell, Bishop of Sodor, A.D. 1350, after saying that the altar-breads must be round, without any flaw, since the Lamb was without spot and no bone was broken, quotes the following lines :—

> Candida, triticea, tenuis, non magna, rotunda,
> Expers frumenti, non mista sit hostia Christi,
> Inscribatur, aquâ non cocta sed igne sit assa.[6]

William de Waddington, in some verses intended for the people, draws many moralities from the qualities of the altar-bread: 'The uble,'[7] he says, 'is small, so should we be little in will; it is made

---

[1] Thorpe, ii. 58. Mr. Chambers, an Anglican, proves the antiquity of unleavened bread in his *Divine Worship in England*, p. 236.
[2] Wilkins, i. 265; Thorpe, ii. 404.
[3] Lanfranc gives directions, *Op.* pp. 135-9 (ed. Giles).
[4] *De usu ecclesiastico*, Migne, tom. clix. p. 1002. From an incident mentioned in the life of St. Vandrelle in 895, it is clear that nuns made altar-breads at least for the use of their own monasteries. (*Acta Sanctorum*, Julii, t. v.; Rock, i. 152.)
[5] Wilkins, *Concilia*, i. 623. Similarly Bishop Peter Quivil of Exeter, A.D. 1287 (*Ib.* ii. 131). [6] *Ib.* iii. 10.
[7] Mr. Furnivall, in his introduction to the *Handlyng Synne*, translates 'wafer,' but Robert de Brunne gives in English 'uble,' or 'oble,' or 'ubble.' This word came from the French 'oublie' and the low Latin 'oblea.' In later English it was 'obley.' And in Myrk's *Instruction to Parish Priests* we find

of wheat, the loveliest corn that men eat, so should we be meek and lovely; its paste must not be of sour dough, and we should not be envious; as wheat will not prick, as oats and barley do, so we must have no thorn of idleness; as the paste is not of mixed corn, so we must not mix up with avarice; as the uble is not thick, so we must not be gluttons; as it is white, we must not be blackly licherous.'[1]

This kind of moralising, of which our ancestors were so fond, may appear trifling or far-fetched, but surely it was good to take every occasion to denounce the seven capital vices. It was but a development of the apostolic words, 'Let us feast, not with the old leaven, nor with the leaven of malice and wickedness, but with the unleavened bread of sincerity and truth;'[2] and the apostle did but enlarge upon his Master's words, 'Beware of the leaven of the Pharisees.'[3] St. Anselm replied as follows to the questionings of Walram, Bishop of Naumburg, on the subject of the controversy regarding unleavened bread: 'Fermented and unfermented bread are substantially the same, and therefore the Eucharist can be consecrated in either; but it is better to consecrate in unleavened bread, both in imitation of our Lord, and for the signification. We are reminded thereby to be free from the leaven of malice and wickedness. We do not Judaise, as the Greeks pretend. To do what Jews do is not to Judaise when it is done for a different reason. When then we use in sacrifice unleavened bread, not in order that by the absence of leaven we may foreshow that Christ will be pure, but that, by the operation of divine power, we may consecrate pure bread into His Body, as He Himself did, we are not following the antiquities of the Law, but the truths of the Gospel.'[4]

In the great Abbey of Evesham very detailed instructions were given to the sacristan on the preparation of the ofletes or obleys:—
'The corn must, if possible, be selected with great care, grain by grain. When selected let it be placed in a clean bag, made of good cloth and kept for that purpose only, and carried by a servant of good character to the mill. Let some other corn be first ground to clean the millstones. The place where the flour is to be made into dough must be surrounded by a curtain. Then one of the ministers,

---

the consecrated particle called the 'ost.' The word 'wafer' was, however, in use for the unconsecrated breads, thus in 1375: 'Pro iiii. m. wafers emptis pro choro, 7s. 8d.' (York Fabric Rolls.) See note by Canon Simmons in *Lay Folk's Mass Book*, p. 232.

[1] Robert de Brunne's *Handlyng Synne*, ed. Furnivall.
[2] 1 Cor. v. 8.   [3] Mark viii. 15.   [4] S. Anselmi *Op.* t. i. 200.

spreading the flour on a very clean table, will sprinkle it with water and knead it well with his hands. The servant who holds the baking-irons will have his hands covered with gloves. While the hosts are being made and baked all will keep silence, except that he who holds the irons may briefly say what is needful to the servant who makes the fire and carries the wood. This wood ought to be very dry and set apart on purpose several days before.'[1] In this document silence is prescribed, but in some places psalms were sung during the baking; and it has been conjectured[2] that from that circumstance the name of singing-bread came to be given to the altar-breads in later English. The devotion of St. Wenceslas is well known, who sowed and reaped and ground the corn and baked the breads with his own hand. An English nobleman named Walter FitzRobert, who died in 1198, gave to the priory of St. Mary of Charity at Daventry, in Northamptonshire, a right annually to 'twenty-four burdens of firewood for the use of the sacrist in preparing the hosts.'[3]

Among the points enumerated in the verses given above was 'Inscribatur,' 'let it be marked.' According to an authority of the ninth century[4] the hosts had certain marks impressed upon them by the irons, either

$$\overline{\text{XPC}}, \text{ or } \overline{\text{IHC}}, \text{ or } \overline{\text{DS}}, \text{ or } {}^{*}_{\text{A}\omega}.$$

A learned Lutheran named Calvör gives an engraving of ancient figures which were stamped on irons, from which we see that there was a great variety allowed, at least at a somewhat later period. We have the Crucifix with Mary and John; angels carrying the instruments of the Passion; our Lord at the column, or in His agony, or an *Ecce Homo*, or our Lord rising from the tomb; or a bannered Lamb; or our Lady, or a church with our Lady and Divine Child behind; or a resplendent sun.[5]

---

[1] The Latin is given in Tindal's *History of Evesham*, p. 185.

[2] By Rev. J. O'Brien in his *History of the Mass* (New York, 1879), p. 157. Dr. Rock supposes the name to come from the singing of the mass. The name survived the Reformation. In 1569 there is an entry in the accounts of the parish church of Sheffield for 'a box to put the synginge bread in.' (Hunter's *History of Hallamshire*, p. 246.)

[3] Baker's *History of Northamptonshire*, i. 311.

[4] See Dr. Rock, i. 149.

[5] Calvör, *de Ritibus*. This plate is reproduced by Mr. J. D. Chambers, Recorder of Salisbury, in his recent work called *Divine Worship in England in the 13th and 14th Centuries* (Pickering, 1877), from which I shall have occasion to borrow again. As an antiquarian work it is singularly learned and accurate; but as applied to the present Anglican Church most eccentric.

As the people for some centuries made their offering of bread and wine, some of which was consecrated for their own communion, the legates of Pope Adrian I. in 786 decreed that 'the oblations of the faithful should not be like crust, but bread.'[1]

Wine was more difficult to procure in England than bread; hence we find a Council of Winchester in 1076 taking precautions lest any priest through excessive ignorance should attempt to celebrate either with water alone, or with beer as a substitute for wine.[2] Wine, however, has been imported into England at least ever since the Romans invaded it, and has been at all times easy to procure from more southern countries. But until the union of the vine-growing provinces of France with the English crown under Henry II. the vine was much cultivated in England. Some authors, indeed, have thought that the word 'vinea' might mean merely an orchard, but the contrary has been successfully proved. The vine was planted in Britain soon after A.D. 280. Bede expressly says that in his day it was grown in certain places.[3] John Twyne thinks that Winchester (Wintonia) derives its name from the wine grown near it. Pegge, an antiquarian who has discussed this subject, says: 'I think there were few great monasteries but what had vineyards.'[4] There were several in Kent belonging to Canterbury. The Bishop of Rochester had one at Halling, the wine from which was good enough to be offered as a present to Edward II. William of Malmesbury praises the wines grown in Gloucestershire. Vineyards are found even as far north as Darley Abbey in Derbyshire. Now, though there was not much danger of adulteration, except perhaps by water, in imported wines in those days, yet it is probable that wine was cultivated in England rather for its purity than for its excellence. Sour or poor wine could be mixed with honey and spices for table use. Of course no mixture of this sort was allowed in wine destined for the altar, and care is frequently recommended in the canons that it should not be too sour.

The colour of the wine was a matter of indifference. Waddington

---

[1] Haddan and Stubbs, iii. 452.
[2] 'Quod sacrificium de cerevisia vel sola aqua non fiat, sed solummodo aqua vino mixto.' (Wilkins, i. 365.)
[3] Bede, i. 1.
[4] See Dr. Pegge, *Archæologia*, i. 344. Sir H. Ellis, in his introduction to *Domesday Book* (vol. i. p. 116), says that there are at least eight-and-thirty entries of vineyards in the different counties, especially in Berkshire, Wiltshire, Middlesex, Hertfordshire, Worcestershire, and Essex.

says it might be 'vermail ou blanc.'[1] The Bishop of Sodor (1350) says 'the wine must not be acid, and rather red than white, though white is valid, if it is not vinegar.' An entry in the churchwarden's accounts of St. Mary Hill, London, for 1531, mentions 'three gallonds and six pynts of malvesay for a yere, for Lady's masse—3s. 9d.,' and in those of Smarden in Kent, in 1553, several kinds of wine are recorded, malvoisie, bastard, red, white, French,[2] but these entries probably belong to the last year of Edward VI. rather than the first of Mary. The churchwardens appear to have been making experiments as regards the taste of the Protestant parishioners. In Catholic times we find many gifts of wine for the altar. Peter of Falconberg, to quote but one example, gave to the monks of Meaux in Yorkshire an annual revenue of five shillings to buy mass wine,[3] a sum which in the fourteenth century would more than suffice for a daily mass throughout the year.[4]

As to the mingling a few drops of water with the wine, Venerable Bede gives this mystical meaning : ' Because we must abide in Christ, and He in us, the wine of our Lord's chalice is mixed with water, since, according to St. John, the waters are the nations. Hence it is not lawful to offer water alone nor wine alone, just as grains of wheat are not offered alone but mixed with water and so converted into bread. And this is done lest an oblation without this use of water should seem to signify a separation of the Head from the members, as if Christ could have suffered except from love of our redemption, or as if we could be saved or made acceptable to God without the Passion of Christ.'

In order that a priest might be able to offer the holy sacrifice with due reverence, some other things were requisite besides those which have been enumerated. He required a paten and chalice for the bread and wine, he was bound to be clothed in certain sacrificial vestments, and the altar itself on which he was to celebrate mass had to be prepared. On all these things the Church had legislated, prescribing what was decent and becoming, but leaving it to the free

---

[1] ' Donc peut-il le pain muer
En char, et en son cors tres cher
E le vin vermail ou blanc
En sun precius sanc.'—*Manuel des Pichés.*

[2] *Archæologia Cantiana,* vol. ix. p. 228.

[3] *Chronicon de Melsa,* i. 419 (Rolls Series).

[4] Stow tells us that, in the reign of Edward III., Gascoign wines were sold at 4d. the gallon, Rhenish at 6d., and that Malmsey, which was most used at the altar, cost 1½d. per pint.

devotion of the clergy and the laity to supply what was rich and splendid.

Though, in times of persecution and under the pressure of great necessity, the Church has allowed every kind of vessel to be used to hold the wine of the sacrifice, and to become the receptacle of the Precious Blood, yet it has been her practice to forbid in general the use of whatever is brittle, porous, or sordid.[1] Hence we find decrees issued by many Anglo-Saxon synods forbidding the use of wax or glass chalices as being too brittle, wood as too porous, and horn as being unclean. Copper also was objected to as liable to oxidise, but tin and pewter were tolerated in case of poverty. Chalices of gold or silver were preferred ; and the paten was required to be of the same material as the chalice. Both chalice and paten were consecrated by the bishop 'ad conficiendum in eis corpus et sanguinem Domini nostri Jesu Christi.'[2]

Both the priests and clergy in general were bound to wear a distinctive dress, and though on a journey they were allowed to put aside the long garment they habitually wore, yet they were commanded to resume it at the door of the church, and in no case to enter the chancel (*cancelli*) or approach the altar without it. But when the priest offered the Holy Sacrifice, besides his usual clerical garment he put on several others appropriate to the rite.[3] The origin of each of these has exercised the minds of liturgical writers and archæologists from a very early period ; but I shall not enter into any detailed description of the sacerdotal vestments. It is enough to say that, by the time Christianity was introduced among the Anglo-Saxons, the dress for mass consisted of various parts 'with very few and unimportant differences, the same both in number, shape, material, and ornament as those which, to the present day,

---

[1] St. Jerome, speaking of the spiritual riches contained in the Blessed Sacrament, and of the poverty of St. Exuperius, Bishop of Marseilles, who had sold the rich vessels of his church for the relief of the poor, wrote : 'There is no one richer than he is, though he carries the Body of the Lord in a basket of twigs, and His Blood in a vessel of glass.'—*Ad Rusticum de B. Exuperio.* (Ep. 125, n. 120; ed. Villarsi.)

[2] Mr. Chambers gives all the forms used from the 8th to the 15th century. There is little variation, except that the use of chrism is ordered by the later Pontificals. (*Divine Worship,* p. 250.)

[3] 'Docemus ut nec missalis sacerdos nec parochialis aliquis intra ostium ecclesiæ veniat vel intra cancellos absque superiori suo indumento, nec ad altaris unquam ministerium absque vestitu designato.' (Dunstan's 46th ; Spelman, i. 476.) So, also, when the Scotch priests were forbidden to say mass 'nudis cruribus,' the meaning was that they should not wear their national dress under the sacrificial vestments.

the Catholic priesthood in England and throughout Christendom wear at the altar.'[1] The priest, then as now, wore an amice, alb, girdle, maniple, stole, and chasuble. The priest did not then cross the stole on his breast, but wore it hanging free, as bishops do now. A change took place in this respect about the fourteenth century. The maniple was at first carried in the hand, and not hung from the arm or wrist as at present. The deacon wore an alb, girdle, stole, and sometimes the folded chasuble, at others the dalmatic. He wore the stole thrown over the left shoulder and hanging loose, not under but over his other vestments. The subdeacon wore an alb, girdle, maniple, and tunicle. Both chasuble and cope were vestments common to the clergy from the highest to the lowest.

Before approaching the altar to offer the holy sacrifice the priest had to see that it was properly prepared, for he could not lay his chalice and paten on the bare altar-stone. It was covered with a pall made of linen or silk, often of a purple dye. Over the pall three or more linen cloths were laid. The outer one was called the corporal, and was not then small like those which we now use, but much larger than the surface of the altar, so that it could be drawn over the chalice and paten. It was always made of white linen; for it was understood to represent the winding-sheet in which our Blessed Redeemer's body was wrapped when laid in the tomb, as Venerable Bede expressly teaches. The corporals were blessed by the bishop, and the prayer beautifully expresses the belief in the Holy Sacrifice: 'O God, who didst allow Thy whole self to be wrapped by Joseph in a winding-sheet woven of linen, kindly take heed unto our words. We beseech Thee, O Lord, that Thou wouldst vouchsafe to bless and hallow these corporals for the use of Thy altar, to consecrate upon them, or to cover and wrap in them, the Body and Blood of Thy Son our Lord Jesus Christ; and that they may be fitting for their high service, so that whatever shall be immolated according to the sacred rite upon them unto Thee, as Melchisedech offered up to Thee an acceptable holocaust which he had brought, so may our sacrifices become acceptable.'[2]

---

[1] Rock, i. 314. I refer the reader once for all to Dr. Rock's *Hierurgia*, *Church of our Fathers*, and other treatises for information on ecclesiastical vestments.

[2] Egbert's *Pontifical*.

CHAPTER XIII.

LITURGY AND CEREMONIAL.

I. *Liturgy.*

THE following story is related of St. Dunstan: 'King Edgar once went out hunting early on Sunday morning, and asked St. Dunstan, who was then at his court, to put off his mass till he should return from the hunt. When nine o'clock was near, the man of God went to the church, put on the sacred vestments, and waited for the king. He stood before the altar, leaning on it with his elbows, and gave himself up to prayer and tears. Then suddenly he was rapt into ecstasy and carried in spirit into heaven, and into the midst of the choirs of angels. He heard them sing to the praise of the Most Holy Trinity, "Kyrie Eleison, Christe Eleison, Kyrie Eleison." When he returned to himself, he asked his attendants if the king had come, and when they replied that he had not he went back to his prayers, and after a short interval he was again ravished, and heard sung in heaven the "Ite, missa est." And when the answer "Deo gratias" had been given, the king's clerks running in cried out that the king had returned, and that the priest must immediately celebrate mass. But St. Dunstan, turning from the altar, said that his mass was done, and that he would not say another that day. And with these words he put off the sacred vestments. Being asked what this meant, he related what he had seen; and, taking occasion from this to speak to the king, he forbade him in future to hunt on Sunday. He taught his attendants the "Kyrie Eleison" which he had heard in heaven, and to this day it is sung in many places at mass.'[1]

This story proves that, in the estimation of our Saxon ancestors,

---

[1] *Acta SS.* tom. x. pp. 357–8. In reference to this history Professor Stubbs says that a 'Kyrie Rex Splendens' used to be sung on the feast of St. Dunstan. This he has printed, and admits that 'there is nothing in it inconsistent with its alleged antiquity, as having come from St. Dunstan.' These developed Kyrie, called Tropes, were older than the date assigned to them by Cardinal Bona. See Stubbs's *Memorials of St. Dunstan* (Rolls Series), p. cxiv. and 357.

the liturgy of the Church militant is not unworthy of the choirs of the Church triumphant; and most assuredly there is nothing in the compositions of man which can be compared with it for sublimity. It is made up in great part of passages of Holy Scripture, admirably arranged to throw light on one another and to illustrate the seasons and festivals of the year; and though there are portions which cannot lay claim to direct inspiration like that of the Word of God, they are nevertheless the production of that 'spirit of grace and of prayer' with which the Church is endowed by her Divine Spouse.

Our Lord Jesus Christ, in instituting the sacred rite which was destined to hold so prominent a place in His religion, said to His disciples: 'Do this for a commemoration of Me;' and giving the commandment He did not leave His Church ignorant of its meaning or of the fitting method of its fulfilment. Whether He Himself, during the forty days after his Resurrection, when He spoke with His apostles on the kingdom of God, gave them instructions regarding liturgy and ritual, may be only a matter of conjecture; but the best liturgical scholars are agreed, from the comparison of the oldest liturgies of East and West, that their central parts are derived from one or more apostolic exemplars. The Church, however, did not hold herself bound to conform exactly to any primitive type, and in the course of centuries liturgies have grown into different families by the moulding of some of the most learned and saintly of the Church's doctors; though all alike express in the sublimest language the great ends of the Christian sacrifice and sacrament.

A minute study of the history of liturgical variations even in one country requires volumes, and I shall here restrict myself to a few general principles or prominent facts, which may be understood by those who have no further acquaintance with liturgical matters than belongs to almost every educated layman.

It has been said already that the language of the liturgy was Latin. The reasons for which the Church has adopted this language throughout the West have been treated of by many writers. But the very glance into history which we have already made suffices to make some of them evident. We have seen St. Augustine and his companions coming from Italy to a country inhabited by races of whose language they were entirely ignorant. They pass through Gaul, and bring with them interpreters. In the meantime they are able to offer the Holy Sacrifice throughout the whole region they traverse in their journey hither, and in all their missionary travels. They find Latin used in offering the holy rites both among Gauls and Britons; and with the knowledge of a common tongue they have an easy means of intercourse. The Scottish (or Irish) missionaries who come to their help in Northumberland, Mercia, and elsewhere, use also the Latin language. The thought of translating those sacred formulæ and prayers, composed by saints, into the uncultivated and various dialects of Angles, Jutes and Saxons, Britons, Scots and Picts, never seems to have suggested itself to any one. And, indeed, for whose advantage should it have been undertaken? Not for the clergy, for unless they were to remain utterly ignorant and to cut themselves off from all the learning of the past and of other nations, and from all intercourse with the rest of the world, it was of absolute necessity that they should learn Latin. Not for the sake of the laity, for most of those, who could be taught letters at all, learned something of Latin, while those who could not read would have gathered very little more of the sense of those mystic prayers and sublime but obscure psalms, had they heard them in their mother tongue. The missionaries, therefore, wisely confined their efforts to instructing the simple laity in the Creed and Lord's Prayer and making them familiar with the elements of Christian doctrine and the outlines of Gospel history. None but those who are unacquainted practically with Catholic populations will imagine that, for want of knowledge of the language of the liturgy, the people were utterly ignorant of what was done or said, or could take no intelligent part in public worship. To enter further into this subject would be superfluous to those who are Catholics, and perhaps useless to those who are not. I would merely observe that it was owing to the use of Latin that the nations of Europe were welded into one commonwealth of Christendom, and it is also due to the same use that we ourselves have any real knowledge of their literature or worship.

To have said that the language of the liturgy was Latin is not the same thing as to assert that the liturgy itself was Roman, for there were various modifications of the liturgy in the West, though Latin was common to them all. Nevertheless it may be affirmed with certainty that the liturgy followed in the south of England from the days of St. Augustine was the Roman one, with but very few local deviations or additions. As to the fact itself there is no dissension among liturgical students. 'Though St. Gregory allowed St. Augustine to choose or to combine,' says the late Dr. Forbes, 'yet he seems to have introduced the Roman rite only, and adhesion to this was commanded by the Council of Clovesho in A.D. 747.'[1] The object of this decree was, as it explicitly states, to

[1] Introduction to the Arbuthnott Missal, by Dr. Forbes, (Anglican) Bishop of Brechin, p. lvi. Canon Simmons, however, seems to suppose that St. Augustine

bring about uniformity. For the Scottish missionaries in parts of England had introduced a form of liturgy somewhat different from that of the Roman Church. The differences were probably much more in the Office than in the Mass, and were of no intrinsic importance. They had been tolerated for more than half a century out of respect to the holy men who introduced them, but the growth of the Church required a more uniform discipline. In the province of York the Scottish custom still lingered on in certain churches, but by the zealous efforts of Alcuin especially the Roman Order was substituted before the end of the eighth century. He wrote to Eanbald II., Archbishop of York in 796 : 'Let not your clergy disdain to learn the Roman use (*ordines*), so that, imitating as far as in them lies the head of the Churches of Christ, they may deserve to receive the eternal blessing of St. Peter, the prince of the apostles, whom our Lord Jesus Christ appointed the head of His chosen flock.'[1] A similar movement led in France to the substitution of the Roman use for the Gallican under Charlemagne. Walafrid Strabo, who died in 849, writes : ' The Romans were taught their observances by St. Peter, the prince of the apostles, but have added at different times what was judged appropriate. And the reason why so many nations admire their usages in sacred things is partly their apostolic origin and authority, and partly that no Church throughout the world equally with the Roman has remained pure from all contamination of heresy during all past centuries. . . . Wherefore there is no tradition equally to be followed, whether in the rule of faith or in that of ritual.'[2]

Some few peculiarities were, however, adopted from the old Gallican liturgy, the principal of which was that a bishop when celebrating gave a very solemn benediction before communion. For this many sublime prayers were drawn up, varying with the festivals. The Benedictional of St. Ethelwold, belonging to the tenth century, has fortunately been preserved. One specimen of these prayers will be enough to give some idea of their nature, and none will be more appropriate to the subject of this work than that for the Thursday in Holy Week, the day on which the institution of the Blessed Eucha-

---

'compiled a special use for England from those of Rome and Gaul, with, it may be, some British customs.' (*Lay Folk's Mass Book*, p. 352.) This is of course a mere conjecture.

[1] Alcuini *Opera* (ed. Froben), Ep. 50 ; Haddan and Stubbs, iii. 503. Also Ep. 171 : 'Numquid non habes Romano more ordinatos libellos sacratorios abundanter ?'

[2] *De rebus eccles.* cap. 22, Migne, tom. cxliv.

rist is commemorated. The bishop chanted as follows:[1] 'Bless, O Lord, we beseech Thee, this people whom Thou hast called to Thy supper. Amen.

'Protect them with the shield of Thy defence, since for them Thou hast deigned to endure the outrages of Thy Passion. Amen.

'Defend them from the snares of the terrible serpent, and absolve them from all their guilt, since on this day Thou didst humble Thy Majesty to wash the feet of Thy disciples with Thy own hands. Amen.

'May the Almighty God bless you, who on this day at supper with His disciples consecrated, by His blessing, bread into His Body, and the chalice into His Blood. Amen.

'And may He grant you, with a conscience pure from all stain of sin, to celebrate with exultation the approaching festival of Easter, who when at table with His disciples said: "With desire have I desired to eat this Pasch with you." Amen.

'May He sanctify your souls, increase your life, adorn you with chastity, and enlighten your understandings in all good works. Amen.

'May He deign to do this who reigneth for ever and ever. Amen.

'The blessing of God the Father, the Son, and the Holy Ghost, and the peace of our Lord be with you. Amen.'

These solemn benedictions belonged exclusively to the bishop, but in the remainder of the rite the prayers used by a simple priest differed in little or nothing from those of the pontiff.[2]

It may be asked whence the service books were procured; and the answer is that though they were preserved with great care and handed down as precious legacies, yet as a rule the candidates for the priesthood, during the time of their preparation, were expected to write them out with their own hands, and by this means they became thoroughly conversant with them. In the Prologue to his genuine Penitential, Archbishop Egbert (732–766) warns the ordinands as follows: 'Now therefore, brethren, let him who wishes to receive priestly authority think seriously before God and get ready his arms before the hand of the bishop touches his head, *i.e.* his Psalter, his Lectionary, his Antiphonary, his Missal, his Bap-

---

[1] Gage's edition, p. 76.

[2] Another peculiarity of the Anglo-Saxon Liturgy was that, though the canon of the mass was almost, word for word, as it stands to-day in the Roman rite, the names of St. George, St. Benedict, St. Martin, and St. Gregory were inserted. (Lingard's *Anglo-Saxon Church*, ii. 357.)

tismal Book, his Martyrology, for the whole year, for preaching with good works, and his Kalendar (*computum cum cyclo*). This is the law of priests. Afterwards his Penitential, that he may learn how to decide all causes.'[1] The canons of 967 order every priest to have a corrected book, and to always have it with him when he celebrates, not trusting to his memory, but keeping it before his eyes, lest he make mistakes.

To ensure correctness in the liturgy, St. Boniface used to examine his priests during Lent in the Ritual, the Office, the Holy Mass, and Catholic doctrine.[2] And in England once at least, often twice, in the year, each priest was obliged to attend the episcopal synod, taking with him one or two of his clerks, and one or two orderly laymen as servants; bringing at the same time the sacerdotal vestments, and whatever was necessary for the celebration of mass, that his manner of performing the service might be approved.[3]

II. *Ceremonial.*

Without any variation in the prayers of the liturgy, much ceremonial might be added; and the Anglo-Saxons had the same distinctions that are familiar to ourselves between a Low Mass, a High Mass, and a Pontifical Mass.

Of the Low Mass I merely remark that a server was prescribed to minister to the priest and make the responses in the name of the people. Yet Walafrid Strabo remarks that sometimes a priest might celebrate without a server. His words are these: 'Though the mass profits those who assist without communicating, and all who share the faith and devotion of the celebrant and communicants, and a priest may sometimes celebrate quite alone, yet the legitimate mass is that at which the priest and server (*respondens*), offerer, and communicant all assist.'[4] A case in which the server might be dispensed with was that of a hermit priest. The server at a Low Mass was generally a monk or cleric. Under the latter name were included not only those in holy orders, priests, deacons, and subdeacons, but all who had received minor orders or merely the clerical tonsure. Of these there were multitudes throughout the country, and one or two were attached to even the smallest parish church. But to serve mass was one of the first things taught to young scholars. In the

---

[1] Haddan and Stubbs, iii. 417. [2] *Ib.* 385.
[3] Lingard, *A. S.* i. 151. It must be remembered that carriages, inns, and shops were unknown in those days. Hence servants on foot or horse were indispensable in travelling, to carry and prepare food, &c.
[4] *De rebus eccles.*, Migne, tom. cxiv. p. 951.

Injunctions put forth by Queen Mary at the very beginning of her reign, one was that schoolmasters should instruct the children that they might be able to answer the priest at mass, as had been the custom formerly.[1] Chantry foundations sometimes made provision for the support of the minister no less than the celebrant.

In no case was a woman allowed to serve at the altar,[2] and this for reasons of evident propriety, not for any slight of the female sex, for perhaps in no nation were women held in greater esteem than among Anglo-Saxons, as in none did they show themselves more zealous for religion. It was by the help of Queen Bertha that St. Augustine obtained the goodwill of her husband Ethelbert. It was by Bertha's daughter Edilberge that St. Paulinus at last won King Edwin to the faith. It was the refusal of Alcflede, daughter of King Oswin, to marry a pagan, that made the son of the obstinate Penda turn his thoughts to the Christian religion, and thus brought about the conversion of Mercia. Nothing is more strikingly beautiful in Bede than the devotion of those first English princesses, who became foundresses or inmates of monasteries. It was in England also that flourished the great double monasteries, separate indeed, yet both to a certain extent under the government not of an abbot but of an abbess.[3] Yet this pre-eminence given to women by the English entailed no privileges at the altar, and the decisions of Archbishop Theodore continued to be observed which forbade women 'to put the altar-cloths, or the oblations, or the chalice on the altar, or to stand among the clergy in the church.' As a proof how strictly this discipline, introduced with the faith into England, was observed down to the Reformation, I will give an extract from the rule of St. Bridget as observed at the great monastery of Sion at Isleworth until its suppression by Henry VIII. The rule was the composition of the saintly Swedish widow, who had restored, in the fourteenth century, the old institution of the double monasteries. One of the regulations was the following : 'When the sacristan of the brethren's side has washed the corporals once, the nun who has care of the sisters' sacristy, with the help of her sisters shall wash them, dry them, fold them up, and deliver them again to the said brother ; so that no sister wash nor touch any hallowed corporals with her bare hands, without linen gloves thereto ordained, nor starch them but with

---

[1] Injunctio 17, anno 1553-4 ; Wilkins, iv. 90.
[2] 'Docemus ut altari mulier non appropinquet dum missa celebratur.'— Can. 44, anno 967.
[3] On the origin and regulations of these double monasteries see Lingard, *A. S.* i. 194.

starch made of herbs only. If they do the contrary, they be straightly bound to tell it to the said sacristan of the brethren's side, that they be new washed and hallowed again.'[1]

I know how indignantly Milton has denounced such regulations as the above as bringing back Judaism, and an insult to the Christian dignity of the laity and the female sex. But I know also how Milton was an advocate of polygamy, and the Catholic Church does not need to receive lessons from such as he about reverence for the laity or for women. It is to the Catholic Church that women owe their freedom and their dignity. It is she who glorified virginity, yet declared marriage an inviolable sacrament. But in her wisdom knowing how ritual observances serve to hedge round the majesty of sacred things, while pressing her children to feed often upon that which she declared to be the Holy of holies, she subjected them to penance for rashly touching that which only served for its more decent celebration. In such matters it is the motive that gives the interpretation to the act. Therefore, while enforcing such minute attention to her rules as I have just described, the Church knew how to applaud the most daring violation of them all, when it proceeded from reverence and love. Thus in Paris, in 1871, the Blessed Sacrament was carried by some devout ladies to the Fathers of the Society of Jesus who were held as hostages in prison by the impious Commune. This could be done lawfully, since they were awaiting their martyrdom. Many instances are on record of a similar trust under similar circumstances in the great French Revolution.

It need hardly be added that since the prohibitions of the Church do not aim at the repression of any intrinsic irreverence, but at the creating or safeguarding of feelings of piety and awe, the Church is always at liberty to modify her own rules, and of the opportuneness of this she is the only judge. If she withdraws any ritual observance or prohibition, it is under the conviction that a firm faith has so perfectly built up the edifice of love and reverence, that the scaffolding may be safely removed. It behoves each of us, whether of the clergy or laity, to take care that, as regards ourselves, she be not mistaken in her trust.

From this digression regarding the exclusion of women from the service of the altar, if digression it is when discussing the subject of liturgy, let us now turn to the ceremonies of High Mass. In the first ages the bishop often was the only celebrant in a church where many priests were present; it is therefore probable that a mass

---

[1] Rule of St. Saviour, p. 367, printed as an appendix to Aungier's *History of Syon and Isleworth*.

accompanied with impressive ceremonial was rather the rule than the exception, and that the Low Mass, shorn as it is of much of that ceremonial, must yield in antiquity to the High Mass. Rabanus Maurus, after minutely describing these ceremonies as practised at the end of the eighth century, adds: 'The Roman Church keeps this order which she has received from the Apostles and apostolic men, and through almost the whole West all the churches hold the same tradition.'[1] What he describes is almost identical with what is known amongst ourselves as a High Mass. It is unnecessary, therefore, to enter into details.[2]

I will merely mention that music, lights, and incense were then as now made use of to enhance the solemnity of the mass. It has been already observed that the words 'missarum solemnia' by no means necessarily imply any unusual or accidental solemnity in the rites, and were used of a Low Mass as of a High Mass. So also the words 'missam cantare' or 'canere' do not necessarily imply the celebration of a musical or High Mass. The expression 'to sing mass' was constantly used when all the circumstances indicate that a Low or private Mass at a side altar is meant. To *sing* for some one's soul meant merely to celebrate; and thus a foundation even for masses without note was a chantry. An old rubric says: 'Let them so end the service that each *sing* his Pater-noster apart,' which meant that he was to recite it silently to himself.[3] To sing, then, meant merely to recite religiously, or to 'make melody in the heart to God.' Sometimes, however, the word is used more technically of musical modulation. Thus Robert de Brunne writes:

> And that day thou owest and shall
> For to hear thy service all,
> Matins, mass hear, to read or sing.[4]

And another old writer:

> When the priest says, or if he sing,
> To him then give good hearkening.[5]

In many masses then the priest intoned certain parts of the mass

[1] *De Cler. Inst.* i. 33.

[2] As to a Pontifical Mass in an Anglo-Saxon cathedral, those who are curious may consult the enthusiastic description of our great liturgical writer, Dr. Rock, *Church of our Fathers*, vol. iii. part ii. pp. 28-42.

[3] See Rock, iii. pp. 104, 196; Lingard, *A. S.* i. p. 291, note. Ratherius says: 'Nullus solus missam cantet;' on which Cardinal Bona remarks: 'Cantare missam, priscorum phrasi, illi etiam dicebantur, qui sine cantu et privatim celebrant.' (*Rer. Liturg.* lib. i. cap. 13.) *The Mirror of Our Lady*, p. 13, speak 'of song without note,' *i.e.* simple recitation of the office.

[4] *Handlyng Synne*, l. 821. [5] *Lay Folk's Mass Book* p. 4

while the choir sang others as at the present day. Bede tells us how the Gregorian chant was brought from Rome and taught throughout the island. Singing was much cultivated among the Anglo-Saxons, and instrumental accompaniments were not deemed out of place. Organs had been introduced into abbeys and cathedrals long before the Norman Conquest.[1] I do not remember any mention of female voices except in the choirs of nuns. The office of singer was looked on as almost one of the minor orders, and there was a form prescribed for his admission into the choir : 'See that what you sing with your mouth you believe with your heart, and that what you believe with your heart you obey in your works.'

Lights were prescribed at mass, though they were placed not upon but near the altar. The 10th canon of Ælfric says that 'the acolytes light candles at mass, not so much to dispel darkness as in honour of Christ who is our light.'[2] And the 42nd of Dunstan's orders that a light must always burn in the church when mass is sung.[3] As this rubric regarded the church and not the altar itself, it is probable that for some time lights were not placed near each side altar, and that when mass was said on a journey or in houses no candles whatever were necessarily lighted. Sometimes the number of lights at a solemn mass was very great. The candles were invariably made of wax.

In order not to return to this subject I will here say a word as to the rules and customs of a later period. On ordinary days the custom seems to have been that at the principal masses said at the high altar two candles should be lighted, and one at the side altars. Archbishop Walter Reynolds (1313-1328) enjoined that 'at the time when the solemnities of mass are performed two candles should be lighted or at least one.' Myrc, in his Instruction to parish priests, says :

> Loke that thy candel of wax hyt be,
> And set hyre so that thou hyre se
> On the lyfte half of thyn autere
> And loke algate ho brenne clere.

The number of lights, however, was often more than two. King Henry the Eighth's chapel on the Field of the Cloth of Gold had ten candlesticks of gold on the altar. Generally at High Mass on feast days even in smaller churches there stood two candles on the altar and two in larger candlesticks at the side. The number was much greater in abbeys and cathedrals. At Chichester in the thirteenth century the custom was to have on great festivals seven tapers of two

---

[1] That at Winchester was blown by sixty men.
[2] Wilkins, i. 250.
[3] *Ib.* i. 225.

pounds each on the altar, eight on the beam above it, and two on the altar step. On minor festivals there were five lights on the altar and two on the step, and on ordinary days three on the altar and two on the step. A number of smaller tapers were occasionally added, but these were not necessarily of wax.[1]

As to incense, Archbishop Theodore in the seventh century writes: 'Incense must be burnt on saints' days, because like lilies they send forth an odour of sweetness, and perfume the Church of God, as a church is perfumed with incense at first round the altar, *i.e.* at its dedication.' St. Aldhelm in the same century, in his poetical description of a great church recently built, speaks of the 'thurible of elaborately worked metal (*capitellis undique cinctum*) hanging from the roof and sending forth smoke and sweet odours when the priests offered mass '—

Quando sacerdotes missas offerre jubentur.[2]

This line shows that the incense was not merely burnt in the churches to grace the festival days, but especially offered in the solemnity of the Holy Sacrifice.[3] Liturgical commentators of the ninth century tell us that it was burnt during the singing of the gospel by the deacon at the ambo, and that the thuribles were waved round the altar by the subdeacons after the bishop had intoned the Creed. In a word, the principle of the Anglo-Saxon Church was that of the Catholic Church in all ages, to dedicate whatever is costly or beautiful to the worship of God, as far as circumstances will allow, and to symbolise and set forth by every means in her power not merely her faith in the Real Presence of her Spouse, but still more her loving adoration, gratitude, and joy.

[1] See *Archæological Journal*, vol. xxxv. p. 386.

[2] The thurible described by St. Aldhelm is very like one mentioned in the life of Pope Sergius, and which the saint may have seen when he was in Rome during that Pope's pontificate. 'Hic fecit thymiatherium aureum majus cum columnis et cooperculo, quod suspendit ante imagines tres aureas B. Petri Apostoli, in quo incensum et odor suavitatis festis diebus, dum missarum solemnia celebrantur, omnipotenti Deo opulentius mittitur.' (Migne, tom. lxxxix. col. 25.) Cardinal Bona proves the apostolic origin of the use of incense. (*Rerum Liturg.* lib. i. cap. 25.)

[3] Gemmulus, a Roman deacon, sent St. Boniface, when in Germany, some cozumbrum of wonderful fragrance to offer to God, morning and evening, and when he celebrated mass. (Letters of St. Boniface, Migne, tom. lxxxix., p. 755.)

CHAPTER XIV.

ON SAYING AND HEARING MASS.

IN the Council of Clovesho, held by Archbishop Cuthbert and the bishops of the province of Canterbury in 747, priests are admonished, besides their other duties, 'to perform with the greatest diligence the ministry of the altar, and whatever belongs to divine worship; to keep carefully their church (*oratorii domum*) and everything pertaining to its adornment; and to devote themselves to reading, to prayer, to the celebration of masses, and the singing of psalms.'[1]

Of all these duties we have to consider at present only the celebration of mass. We know already how and where it was to be said; but there remain several questions which may be asked concerning it, as—At what hour of the day could it be said? How frequently? And in this respect, what was the law and what the custom? With what intentions was it offered by the celebrant? I shall attempt to answer these questions, intermingling, when possible, some examples of saintly devotion.

And first as regards the time. Nothing is more important in reading old documents than to make sure what is understood by divisions of time, whether as regards the year or the day. The hours of the day were not reckoned by our Saxon forefathers from midnight, but from sunrise.[2] Between sunrise and sunset the day was divided into twelve equal parts or hours; the hours or intervals were of course much longer in summer than in winter. The latinised designations of the principal hours, still in use though in a somewhat modified sense, were as follows. Prime was the first hour, or the hour of sunrise. Sext, or the sixth hour, was midday. Halfway between prime and sext was tierce, or the third hour;[3] halfway between sext and sunset was none, or the ninth hour. Supposing the sun to rise at six, tierce would be nine o'clock, sext midday, none three in the

---

[1] Haddan and Stubbs, iii. 365.

[2] See Lingard, *A. S.* i. 272, note, and 286, note.

[3] Sometimes called *undern*, not only in Anglo-Saxon times, but until the Reformation.

afternoon; and it is most convenient for us, though not quite accurate, to associate in our minds the moveable periods of the Church in earlier times with our fixed hours, adding always six hours to their numbers. Thus prime may be considered as our six in the morning, sext as our noon, and none as three in the afternoon. It was at none on fastdays in Lent that it was lawful to break the fast.[1] Now, wherever making holiday or breaking fast is concerned, there is a popular and almost irresistible tendency to anticipate the hour fixed; and thus the hour of none was continually being drawn back towards midday, until at last in common conversation none (noon) and midday became synonymous.

The whole Divine Office, or offering of prayer and praise to God, which the Church in every age pays to Him by the mouth of her ministers, is divided into parts, appointed to be said—at least when performed solemnly in choir—at fixed hours of the day and night; so that the designations prime, tierce, sext, and none were given to the portions of the day office said at those hours. Here again the exact hour was not always observed, so that it occasionally happens that these words must be taken in an approximate sense.

The hours for mass were regulated by the hours of the Divine Office which served as a preparation for it. In accordance with the words of the Psalmist, 'Septies in die laudem dixi tibi,'[2] it was divided into seven parts. Matins, or that portion to be said during the night, consisted of one long or three shorter nocturns. Strictly it began shortly after midnight, and in great monasteries and cathedrals the rigour of this law was upheld. In many churches it was put off till almost daybreak, and thence called uht-sang, or dawn-song. A secular professor of the University of Paris in the twelfth century, John Belethus, complains, as of a shameful degeneracy, that 'care for the worship of God has now sunk so low, that boys rise (to play) sooner than the Church's ministers rise (to pray), and sparrows sing earlier than priests. To such a degree has the love of God grown cold among men.'[3] What would the indignant professor say of our nineteenth century? But to continue—matins were followed in the early morning by lauds, or lof-sang. This was often joined with the

---

[1] In a metrical version of the Parable of the Labourers, written about A.D. 1300, most of the usual divisions of time occur. 'In *marewe* men he sohte, At *under* mo he brohte, At *mydday* ant at *non*, He sende them thider fol son. At *evesong* euen nch,' &c. (*Specimens of Early English*, by Morris and Skeat, part ii. p. 46, ed. 1879.) Marewe, morwe, or morrow, is Morning. Hence Morrow-mass is the early mass. Under, or Undern, is 9 o'clock, or the period between nine and midday.

[2] Ps. cxviii. 164.   [3] *Rationale Div. Offic.* cap. 20; Migne, tom. ccii.

night-song. In a colloquy written in the tenth century to teach Latin to the boy-monks we find the following account of the monastic hours.

Master. Boy, what have you done to-day?

Pupil. I have done many things. Last night, when I heard the signal, I rose from my bed and went to the church and sang uht-sang (*nocturnam*) with the brethren. Then we sang 'of all saints' and morning lauds (*dægredlice lof-sanges*); afterwards prime and the seven psalms with litanies and the first mass (*primam missam, capitol mæssan*), then tierce (*undertide*), and we performed the mass of the day. Next we sang sext (*middæg*), and we ate and drank and slept and rose again, and sang none; and now here we are before you, ready to hear what you will tell us.

Master. When will you sing vespers (*æfen*) and compline (*niht-sange*)?

Pupil. When the time shall come.

Master. Where do you sleep?

Pupil. In the dormitory with the brethren.

Master. Who calls you to matins?

Pupil. Sometimes I hear the signal, and I rise. Sometimes my master wakes me sternly with a rod, &c.[1]

A Norman writer, who died in 1079, says: 'Mass, according to ancient prescription, is said at the third hour (after sunrise), for at that hour Christ was crucified by the tongues of the Jews; but, according to common custom, rather at the sixth hour (midday), for in that He suffered at the hands of the executioners; on fast days at the ninth hour (*i.e.* between midday and sunset), for then He gave up His soul. But they who, in case of necessity, celebrate before tierce or after none, not as a custom but occasionally, from their desire to offer the sacrifice, are not to be blamed; for we read that Pope Leo said mass at early dawn.'[2] ' In such matters as these there was little or no difference between one part of the Church and another. Another writer at the beginning of the ninth century says that Pope Telesphorus ordered that mass should never be offered before tierce, and the Gloria never said in the afternoon (*post meridiem*) except on the vigils of Easter and Pentecost.[3]

In the solemn fast of Lent the mass was much later. It could

---

[1] Ælfric's *Colloquy*, edited by Mr. Wright in the volume of Vocabularies forming part of the Library of National Antiquities (1857), pp. 12-14.

[2] *Liber de Officiis Eccles.*, by John, brother of Richard, duke of Normandy. He was afterwards archbishop of Rouen. (Migne, tom. cxlvii. p. 37.)

[3] Walafridus, Migne, tom. cxiv. p. 951.

not be said till the eighth or ninth hour, which would then be about two or three o'clock in the afternoon. On Holy Thursday, however, it was said somewhat sooner, but on Holy Saturday considerably later.[1] At whatever hour the celebrant said mass, he was obliged to be fasting. But, in monasteries at least, no one (except in case of necessity) ever broke his fast till after the mass which followed tierce had been said, *i.e.* till nine or ten o'clock. On the fast days throughout the year mass was said after sext, and then the meal could be taken. But in Lent mass was said after none, and by strict rule the fast could not be broken until after the vespers which followed mass. Charlemagne caused mass to be celebrated in his palace during Lent at two in the afternoon; mass was followed by vespers, and then only he proceeded to his meal, which was properly called supper, but was also breakfast.[2] The laws of Theodulf of Orleans, translated by Ælfric in the tenth century, state that if anyone should be prevented by his occupations from being present at mass in Lent, he must still remain fasting till after vespers. But no one will be surprised when he finds from the complaints of some of these old writers that the people were impatient to break their fast, and took the signal for none as a signal to run to eat.

It is probable that what has been said regarded public rather than private masses, though an expression of Venerable Bede (*a tertia hora, quando missæ fieri solebant*[3]) seems to show that even these did not begin, under ordinary circumstances at least, in his time before tierce.

As regards frequency of celebration of the divine mysteries, this is treated of explicitly by Walafrid.[4] He considered it an open question. 'Some priests say that mass should be offered only once a day, others two or three times or as often as the priest may please. By the relation of trustworthy men it has come to my knowledge that Pope Leo,[5] as he himself acknowledged, on one day would

---

[1] *Liber Sacr. S. Gregorii*, Migne, tom. lxxviii. p. 315. See notes of the Benedictine editors. John Belethus, in his *Rationale Div. Off.* cap. 50 and 99, notices that mass was said very late (*valde sero*) on the Ember Saturdays, because of the ordinations, and on the Saturdays before Easter and Whitsunday, and that it might in one sense be considered to belong to the Sunday ; but as the celebrant was to be fasting the mass could begin after vespers at nightfall. On Holy Saturday vespers are sung in the mass. Migne, tom. ccii. pp. 56 and 104. See also Giraldi, *Gemma Ecclesiastica*, p. 24 (Rolls Series).

[2] See Hampson, *Medii Ævi Kalendarium*, i. 87, and Peter Comestor, apud Migne, tom. cxcviii. p. 1753.

[3] Bede, ii. 22. [4] *De reb. eccl.*, Migne, tom. cxiv. p. 943.

[5] This was Leo III., who died in 816.

often celebrate seven or nine times, whereas St. Boniface, archbishop and martyr, said mass only once a day. These were both men in our own time, and both high in rank and in science. Therefore, let each one abound in his own sense.' Walafrid, however, gives it as his own opinion that a priest may celebrate more than once a day when there is some good reason. This liberty seems to have lasted long, since even in 967 the 37th of St. Dunstan's canons only restricts the number to three: 'We command that no priest celebrate mass more than thrice a day at most.' A similar prohibition was made about the same time by St. Oswald, archbishop of York. It is of another matter we must understand an ancient canon ascribed to St. Theodore: 'It is allowed by the Greeks to offer two masses on one altar, by the Romans five.'[1] Here the masses are not supposed to be said by the same priest. A somewhat similar restriction is put upon the altar in a canon of St. Boniface, which forbids a priest to say mass on an altar on which a bishop has said mass the same day.[2]

Gildas complained of certain British priests that they rarely celebrated (*raro sacrificantes*), and we shall hear similar complaints at a later period. But among the Anglo-Saxons the Councils appear to have been rather obliged to use restrictions, and if complaints are made by moral writers it is not of infrequent, but rather of too frequent as well as hasty, celebrations. On such a matter it is rash to affirm anything on the scanty information we possess, yet it would seem that devout priests among the Anglo-Saxons were certainly accustomed to offer holy mass daily if possible, and that they looked on this privilege as so precious that they would not allow themselves to be debarred from it even by the fatigues of a long journey. Venerable Bede thus describes the last days of Abbot Ceolfrid: 'He was seventy four years old when he died; forty seven years he had been in priest's orders, during forty-three he had been abbot. He never relaxed his first rigour from any occasions of old age, illness, or travel. From the day he quitted his monastery (to go to Rome) till the day of his death, *i.e.* June 4 (A.D. 716) till September 25, a space of one hundred and fourteen days, besides the canonical hours of prayer, he never omitted to go twice daily through the Psalter in order; and even when he became so weak that he could not ride on horseback, and was obliged to be carried in a horse-litter, every day he sang mass and offered up the sacred Victim to God, except on one which he passed at sea, and the three days preceding his death.'[3]

---

[1] Haddan and Stubbs, iii. 117. [2] Migne, tom. lxxxix. p. 822.
[3] Beda, *Vitæ Beat. Abbatum*, ed. Giles, vol. iv. p. 400.

Hitherto I have been speaking of the priest, the celebrant of mass. I must now add a few details regarding the assistants.

The Protestant Reformers proclaimed a deadly war against what they called private masses, by which expression they meant a mass in which the priest alone communicates. Denying, as they did, that the rite instituted by Jesus Christ is a sacrifice, they would not allow it to be celebrated except for the sake of the communicants, nor would they allow non-communicants to be present at it. They appealed to the practice of the early centuries of Christianity. Into this controversy I need not enter further than to say that even were it proved that every Christian who was present was a communicant, this would in no way imply that the action was not a sacrifice as well as a sacrament, nor would it derogate from the liberty of the priest to offer the sacrifice, even though no other communicant than himself could be found. The Council of Trent has expressed a wish that men so lived that they could all communicate whenever they assist at mass. But in no age of the Church has a priest been forbidden to perform the divine rite in the absence of communicants, nor have non-communicants ever been forbidden to be present, unless they were unbaptized or excommunicated.[1]

Confining ourselves to the period since the conversion of the Angles and Saxons, we find abundant facts to show that priests said mass constantly at side altars, sometimes with only their server to assist, and sometimes in hermitages without even a server. Again, while it is certain that all Christians were bound to be present at mass on Sundays and festivals at least, it is equally certain that all were not communicants. It is related in the life of St. Aldhelm, bishop of Sherborn, who died in 709, that when a young monk at Malmesbury he showed great zeal in drawing the people to church. That part of England had not been long converted from paganism. His biographer tells us that the people, though acknowledging the faith, did not frequent the churches, nor did they care for the authority of the priests. To win them over gently, Aldhelm would on Sundays take his harp and, seated on a bridge outside the town, sing hymns that he had himself composed, for many traders used on that day to come into the town from a distance. When a number had been gathered around him attracted by the music, he would preach to them, and then lead them to the church to

---

[1] Cardinal Bona proves the antiquity of solitary or private masses by abundant examples. (*Rerum Liturg.* l. i. cap. 13, 14.) See, on this matter, *supra*, pp. 46–49.

be present at the holy offices.¹ Certainly very few of them can have been communicants.

What is here said of the reluctance of the people to frequent the churches must be understood only of this early stage of their Christianity. An Anglican clergyman, who was particularly versed in English antiquities, has truly said, in giving the early history of Leeds and alluding to the peasants in Saxon times : 'Whatever might be their ignorance, all had devotion at least, and would resort to the parish church with an eagerness and regularity not always imitated by those who are more enlightened.'[2]

Indeed, before or about the time when this incident is related of St. Aldhelm in the south, Bede tells us how in the north, with which he was personally best acquainted, priests had so effectually evangelized the people in the villages that 'on Sundays they flocked eagerly to the church.'[3]

The use of bells to call the people to church was introduced from the earliest times, and there was a special form appointed for their blessing. When assembled in church the men occupied the south side, the women the north.[4] Dr. Rock assures us that the latter, both old and young, all wore veils in church. Yet the only proof he brings is a quotation which Venerable Bede makes from St. Paul about the duty of women 'to be veiled because of the angels.'[5] That these words were understood more strictly by the Anglo-Saxons than by ourselves, and implied more than a covering for the head, is to me very doubtful, considering how often even Anglo-Saxon nuns are reprehended for their love of dress. If even these could not be induced by entreaties or admonitions to give up rich or gaudy dresses in the cloister, it is scarcely probable that the lay women of this nation concealed their faces or their finery beneath a veil, when there was an opportunity of attracting attention even before the altar.[6] Bede's words are no doubt intended as a gentle hint of what should have been. St. Theodore also says that 'women may receive the sacrifice under a black veil, according to St. Basil;'

---

[1] *Vita*, Migne, tom. lxxxix. p. 68.

[2] *Loidis and Elmete*, by Rev. T. D. Whitaker, p. 13 (ed. 1816).

[3] Bede, iii. 26.

[4] 'In conventu ecclesiastico seorsum masculi et seorsum fœminæ stant. Quod accepimus a veteri consuetudine: masculi stant in australi parte, et fœminæ in boreali.' (Amalarius, *De Eccl. Off.* iii. 2.)

[5] 1 Cor. xi. 10.

[6] On this national love of dress which infected clergy, monks, and nuns, see Lingard, *Anglo-Saxon History*, vol. ii. ch. v. n. 6. 'Flammea puella' was the name by which Archbishop Lullus designated a fashionable lady.

but the saints advise many things which are never carried into practice.

As regards worship on the Sunday, it must be remembered, as I said before, that a day was counted from sunset to sunset, not from midnight to midnight, as with us. 'A vespera usque ad vesperam dies Dominica servetur,' said St. Theodore; but at a later period what was called the freedom of the Sunday was extended. 'Let men keep every Sunday's freedom from noontide on Saturday to the dawn of light on Monday,' say the decrees of Edgar and of Canute. The law which regulated the duties of laymen as regarded the worship of God on Sunday was as follows: 'It is most right and proper that every Christian man, who has it in his power to do so, should come on Saturday to the church and bring a light with him, and there hear the vesper song, and after midnight the uht-song, and come with his offering in the morning to the solemn mass; and when he is there, let there be no dispute, or quarrel, or discord, but let him with peaceful mind, during the holy office, intercede with his prayers and his alms, both for himself and all the people of God. And after the holy service let him return home and regale himself with his friends and neighbours and strangers, but at the same time be careful that they commit no excess in eating or drinking.' And in another place: 'We command all men, whatever may be their rank, to attend at the high mass, with the exception only of the hallowed maidens whose custom it is not to go out of their minsters; these should continue within the enclosures of their minsters and there hear mass.' Many priests said private masses, and this gave occasion to an abuse— viz. that many laymen, satisfied with having assisted at one of these low masses, did not come to the high mass, and so did not hear the sermon. To prevent this a law was made [1] 'that no one should break his fast or taste any meat before the service of high mass was ended; but that all, both males and females, should assemble at the high mass and in the holy and ghostly church, and there hear the high mass and the preaching of God's word;' and 'we command those mass-priests who, both on Sundays and other mass days, wish to sing before the high mass, that they do so privately, so that they draw off no portion of the people from the high mass.' Those who, through weakness of health or heedlessness of the above law, were not fasting, were not allowed to receive the pax or kiss of peace.

---

[1] The above laws are thus translated by Thorpe (*Institutes*, ii. 420, 440-442). Some of them were really a translation into Saxon of the canons which Theodulf of Orleans had made in the eighth century. (See Wilkins, i. 265-282.) It is not certain that they had canonical force in England.

The same prohibition extended to those who were doing penance and not yet allowed to receive communion. These, not being excommunicated in the proper sense of the word, could be present at mass with the rest of the faithful, but not receive the pax.[1] Infidels, catechumens, and excommunicated persons could not be present during the solemn part of the mass after the sermon.[2]

The Council of Clovesho in 747 bids the priests be very urgent with the people to come to the sermons and to the holy mass.[3] Nothing is said in this canon about their being bound in the same sense to be present at the divine office. This seems to have been a matter of counsel. So also travellers were bound to assist at mass, but not at other services. 'Sunday,' says the law,[4] 'is very solemnly to be reverenced ; therefore we command that no man dare on that holy day to apply to any worldly work unless for the preparing of his food, except it happen that he must of necessity journey. Then he may ride, or row, or journey by such convenience as may be suitable to his way, on the condition that he hear his mass, and neglect not his prayers.'

The Holy Sacrifice of the Mass was indeed, then as now, the great act of worship and religion. It was used to sanctify every solemn occasion of life. It was celebrated at the consecration of a church, and at the ordination of the clergy. It was offered to ask God's blessing upon the nuptial contract no less than on the profession of a monk or a nun, or the installation of an abbot or an abbess.[5] It was with the rites of the holy mass that the body was committed to the grave. It was part of the ceremonial of the coronation of a king, and it preceded the consultations of the Witan or Saxon parliament.[6] But perhaps nothing better proves the supreme importance attached to mass than that provision should have been made for its celebration even in time of war. St. Boniface sends to Archbishop Cuthbert

---

[1] 'Qui non communicat non accedat ad panem (*aliter* pacem) neque ad osculum in missa.' (Theodore's *Penit.* l. ii. 1 ; Haddan and Stubbs, iii. 190.)

[2] The sons of Saba, who witnessed the communion, had probably refused to leave the church, or an exception was made for kings.

[3] Haddan and Stubbs, iii. 367.

[4] Thorpe, ii. 420.

[5] Theodore's Penitential prescribes nuptial mass and blessing at a first marriage. The mass was said by a bishop at an ordination, by an abbot at the profession of a monk, by a priest at the consecration of an abbess, and by a bishop at that of an abbot. 'Nuns and churches,' he says, 'are always consecrated with mass.'

[6] Kemble shows that 'the witena-gemot was opened by the celebration of mass.' (*Saxons in England*, i. 145.) In Egbert's Pontifical is the ceremonial of coronation.

a copy of the canons he had made in 742, which are known as the capitularies of Carloman.¹ One of them is as follows : 'It is forbidden to the servants of God (monks or priests) to bear arms or to fight, or to accompany the army against an enemy, except to those who are selected purposely for the Divine Mystery, that is the celebration of mass, and for carrying the relics of the saints : viz. the prince may have with him one or two bishops, with their chaplains ² and presbyters ; and each prefect may have one priest to judge and give penance to the men who confess their sins.' That similar regulations were carried out in England is evident from several incidental notices of historians. King Æthelred I., at the famous battle of Æscendun or Ashdown, in Berkshire, fought in 871 against the Danes, showed a devotion like that of Sobieski.

The story is thus related by Mr. Freeman from the ' Chronicle ' and Asser's ' Life of Alfred.' ' The heathen men came on against them, but King Æthelred heard mass in his tent, and men said, " Come forth, O King, to the fight, for the heathen men press hard upon us." And King Æthelred said : " I will serve God first and man after, so I will not come forth till all the words of the mass be ended." So King Æthelred abode praying, and the heathen men fought against Alfred the Atheling. And Alfred said : " I cannot abide till the King my brother comes forth ; I must either flee or fight alone with the heathen men." So Alfred the Ætheling and his men fought against the five earls. Now the heathen men stood on the higher ground, and the Christians on the lower. Yet did Alfred go forth trusting in God, and he made his men hold close together with their shields, and they went forth like a wild boar against the hounds. And they fought against the heathen men and smote them, and slew the five earls. Then the mass was over, and King Æthelred came forth and fought against the two kings, and slew Bagsecg the king with his own hand. So the English had the victory, and smote the heathen men with a great slaughter, and chased them even unto Reading.' ³

Perhaps nothing more contributed to the overthrow of all disci-

---

¹ *Opera S. Bonif.*, Migne, tom. lxxxix., p. 807 ; Haddan and Stubbs, iii. 384.

² The Latin word *capella* is derived from the word *capa*, a cope, because the kings of the Franks carried with them to battle the cope of St. Martin as their most precious relic. The tent in which it was kept was the capella, and the priestly guardians the capellani. (Walafrid Strabo, *De Rebus Eccl.* cap. 31.) Hence the modern words, ' chapel ' and ' chaplain.' Yet some sectaries prefer the word ' chapel,' derived from a saint's relic, to ' church,' which means the Lord's house !

³ *Old English History*, by E. A. Freeman, p. 111.

pline and devotion both amongst clergy and laity than the terrible devastations of the Danes, especially in the ninth and tenth centuries. An ancient author who lived when traditions of their last inroads were yet fresh, writes that, 'when the Danes were masters in England, the Saxons in their poverty and sufferings were so depressed that the churches were no longer frequented, nor the day and night office said by monks and nuns.'[1] To the same cause were probably due the terrible disorders among the clergy in the tenth century with which all Protestant historians have taken good care to make us familiar. Among these disorders we find, as we might naturally expect, that neglect of mass went along with luxury and intemperance,[2] just as it had done among the British clergy during the invasions of the Saxons, according to the testimony of St. Gildas.

And so, on the other hand, we find that the great reformers of those days, and holy prelates, such as St. Odo, the two Saints Elphege, St. Oswald, St. Ethelwold, St. Dunstan, drew from the holy mass the strength which enabled them to stem the torrent of iniquity, and found in it the means of reviving piety in others. Professor Stubbs has vindicated the memory of St. Dunstan, and has shown what was the character of his work. 'The true mark of Dunstan's mind,' he says, 'must be looked for in Edgar's legislation, and in the few canons passed at the ecclesiastical assemblies of the reign. The laws that bear Edgar's name must bear the impress of Dunstan's mind.' Then, after proving that these were really passed during St. Dunstan's pontificate, and giving an abridgment of them, he adds : 'If Dunstan's work is here, we have some justification of the praise of his biographers. The ecclesiastical laws of the period are of the same constructive and progressive stamp.'[3]

Whence then did St. Dunstan draw his wisdom and his strength? According to the unanimous testimony of his biographers, two of whom were contemporaries, and one an eye-witness,[4] one of the

[1] Faricius, in *Vita S. Aldhelmi* (Migne, tom. lxxxix. p. 77). Faricius is here writing of times long subsequent to St. Aldhelm. But Bishop Lupus, or Wulfstan, in a sermon preached or written in 1013, draws a fearful picture of the vices and impiety of the English in those days of disorder. The sermon is to be found in Hickes, and also in Langebek's *Rerum Danicarum Scriptores*, tom. ii. 464, in Latin.

[2] 'Male morigerati clerici, elatione et insolentia ac luxuria præventi, adeo ut nonnulli eorum dedignarentur missas suo ordine celebrare, repudiantes uxores quas illicite duxerant, et alias accipientes, gulæ et ebrietati jugiter dediti.' (*Hist. Aben.* ii. 260.)

[3] Introd. to *Memorials of St. Dunstan* (Rolls Series, 1874), p. cv.

[4] Canon Stubbs has published for the first time a life of St. Dunstan, by

characteristics of his life was his devotion to the Blessed Sacrament of the Altar. I have given in a former chapter the history of his vision of the heavenly mass, while in his pontifical robes he leant upon the altar in prayer, waiting for the king's return from hunting, and of the rebuke he then administered to the king for disturbing the Sunday's rest and delaying the divine worship by his eagerness for sport. A more startling history than this, though it contains no vision, is related by Osbern and Eadmer, the saint's later biographers. I say more startling, because at first sight it betokens a love of justice which may seem excessive and even rigorous. It is fair to say, before relating it, that it does not appear in either of the contemporary writers who have recorded St. Dunstan's life. However, Osbern and Eadmer, though they flourished nearly a century after the event they relate, were well acquainted with the traditions handed down in the Church of Canterbury, and had also other sources of information besides the earlier lives which now exist. Osbern, in an apostrophe to St. Dunstan on his elevation to the bishopric of London, says: 'Give judgment against the false coiners, the defrauders of the people, and do not approach the holy altar on the day of Pentecost to offer sacrifice until vengeance has fallen on them and justice has been done to the people of God.'[1] The very obscurity of these words shows that Osbern was alluding to some well-known story. Eadmer tells us what it was; and though in so doing he evidently embellishes a little, and puts words into Dunstan's mouth which are not, strictly speaking, historical, yet his narrative contains not only the well-known fact, but also the traditional estimate of the saint's character. 'At another time,' he says, 'three coiners had been captured with their false money and condemned to the penalty which had been proclaimed throughout the kingdom' (this was to lose the hand). 'The matter was known to St. Dunstan, and on Whitsunday, being about to offer mass, he inquired whether justice to God's people had been executed on these malefactors or not. He was told that, out of reverence for so great a feast, the execution of the penalty was put off to another day. "By no means," he replied; "these coiners are thieves, and thieves of the worst kind. By false money they rob and disturb the whole land. They injure all classes, rich and poor alike, bringing them to shame, to poverty, or to utter ruin. Know then that I will not offer sacrifice to God until the sentence has been carried out. As the matter concerns me, if I neglect to appease God by the

Adelard, written a very few years later than the anonymous one printed in the *Acta Sanctorum*.

[1] *Memorials*, p. 106.

punishment of so great an evil, how can I hope that He will receive sacrifice from my hands? This may be thought cruel, but my intention is known to God. The tears, sighs, and groans of widows and orphans, and the complaints of the whole people, press on me and demand the correction of this evil. If I do not seek as far as in me lies to soothe their affliction, I both offend God who has compassion on their groans, and I embolden others to repeat the crime." Thus he spoke, yet, out of pity for the pain of those who were to lose their hands, he began to shed tears, so that it was easy to see from what source the decree which seemed cruel really proceeded. When he heard that justice had been executed, he rose and washed his face, and went to the church with a more cheerful countenance, saying: "Since I have listened to God to-day by obeying the laws of justice, I trust that He in His mercy will receive sacrifice from my hands."' Eadmer goes on to say that he was not disappointed, since a white dove was seen to hover over him during the mass, which at its conclusion seemed to disappear in the tomb of St. Odo.[1]

It would be a great mistake to gather from this history that sternness was the characteristic of St. Dunstan, as it would be to form such a judgment about our Divine Redeemer, because He pronounced woe to the scandalous, or looked round with anger on the obstinate, or drove the money-changers from the Temple. The great archbishop's tender pity and love for the people, and the love which the people entertained for him, are proved by abundant testimony. Professor Stubbs, who has nobly rebuked some of our leading historians for their utterly baseless accusations against St. Dunstan, thus writes: 'He was only sixty-four when he died, but his public life had begun early and lasted long, and his fame lived, both at home and abroad, in the praises of the strangers whom he had befriended, the churches that he had planted, the scholars whom he had taught, but chiefly in the longing remembrance of the peace and glory which Edgar under his teaching had maintained. Yet Dunstan's memory was worshipped not only from a feeling of regret; his beatification in popular regard scarcely waited for his death.'[2]

To the saint's tender piety we have the following testimony of an eye-witness :—'When he was minded to pay to Christ the Lord the due homage of service and the celebration of Mass, he laboured with such entire devotion in singing that he seemed to be speaking

---

[1] *Memorials of St. Dunstan*, p. 202. Osbern also relates the vision of the dove, but attributes it to his first mass at Canterbury. Adelard, the contemporary writer, alludes to the vision, but without specifying time or place. (*Ib.* p. 62.)   [2] *Memorials*, introd., p. civ.

face to face with the Lord, even if just before he had been vexed with the quarrels of the people. Like St. Martin he constantly kept eye and hand intent on heaven, never letting his spirit rest from prayer. And whenever he performed any act of religion, as in the sacred ordinations of priests, or in the consecration of churches or altars, he shed such abundant tears as showed that his soul was the habitual dwelling-place of the Holy Ghost.'[1]

I conclude this chapter by the beautiful account left by his contemporary, Adelard, of the Saint's last Mass and his death.[2]

'On Ascension Day, 988,' he says, 'Dunstan preached as he had never preached before; and as his Master, when about to suffer, had spoken of peace and charity to His disciples, and had given His Flesh and Blood for their spiritual food, so too did Dunstan commend to God the Church which had been committed to him, raising it to heaven by his words, and absolving it from sin by his apostolic authority. And offering the sacrifice of the Lamb of God, he reconciled it to God. But before the Holy Communion, having given as usual the blessing to the people, he was touched by the Holy Ghost, and pronounced the form of benediction with unusual grace.[3] Then having commended peace and charity to all, while they looked on him as on an angel of God, he exclaimed: "Farewell for ever."

'The people were still listening eagerly to his voice and gazing lovingly on his face, when he returned to the holy altar to feed on his Life; and so, having refreshed himself with the Bread of Life, he completed this day with spiritual joy.

'But in that very day the column of God began to totter, and as his sickness increased he retired to his bed, in which the whole of the Friday and the Friday night, intent on celestial things, he strengthened all who came to visit him. On the morning of the Sabbath (*i.e.* the Saturday), when the matin song was now finished, he bids the holy congregation of the brethren come to him. To whom again commending his soul, he received from the heavenly table the viaticum of the sacraments of Christ, which had been celebrated in his presence, and, giving thanks to God for it, he began to sing: "The merciful and gracious Lord hath made a memorial of His wonders, He hath given meat to them that fear Him." And with these words in his mouth, rendering his spirit into his Maker's hands, he rested in peace. Oh! too happy whom the Lord hath found watching!'

[1] *Memorials*, introd., p. l., from the oldest life by the Saxon Priest B.
[2] *Ib.* p. lxv.
[3] It has been said in the account of the Anglo-Saxon Liturgies, that in pontifical masses a solemn blessing was given before communion.

CHAPTER XV.

INTENTIONS OF THE CELEBRANT.

ONE reason of the great importance attached to the daily celebration of mass was, that it was thoroughly understood that the unbloody commemoration of our Lord's Passion, like our Lord's Passion itself of which it is the perpetual application, not only profits the celebrant, the communicants, and the assistants, but also profits the absent, whether living or dead. The language as well as the practice of our forefathers in this respect is too plain to be misunderstood.

'The bishop and the priest,' says, in the tenth century, the author of the 'Blickling Homilies,' 'if they will rightly serve God, must minister daily to God's people, or at least once a week sing mass for all Christian people and for all who have been born from the beginning of the world. And it is God's will that they should intercede for them. Then shall they receive from God greater reward than they may do by any other gifts, for very dear to God are His people. And those that are in heaven shall intercede for those who are engaged in this song. And they shall be in the prayer of all earthly folk who have been Christians or yet may be; and they shall never die in their sins, and God's mercy and that of all saints shall be upon them.'[1]

In accordance with this doctrine the priest in his very ordination was authorized by the Pontifical 'to offer up oblations for the living and for the dead; and that, for his own weal and the weal of all the people, he was to transform, by an unspotted blessing, the Body and the Blood of the Son of God.'[2]

Part of the liturgy of the mass is invariable, and is therefore called the canon or rule. Other parts vary according to the Sunday, ferial day, or festival. Masses have also been composed for special occasions, and are called votive masses, because said according to the *votum*, *i.e.* the intention or desire of the celebrant, who in this may either satisfy his own needs or devotion or those of others for whom

---

[1] *Blickling Homilies*, p. 44 (Early English Text Society).
[2] *Pontif. Anglo-Saxonicum*, apud Rock, i. 27.

he offers sacrifice. In Leofric's Missal there are masses appointed 'for the living and dead,' 'for friends and relatives,' 'to ask for the suffrages of the angels,' ' in honour of the Holy Cross,' ' in honour of the saints whose relics are in the church,' and the like. Alcuin likewise drew up several masses for special intentions, as in honour of the Most Holy Trinity, for wisdom, for the gift of compunction and perfect charity, for the intercession of saints and angels, and for that of the Blessed Mother of God.[1]

Bede tells how, in memory of a special mercy, mass was to be said 'either in thanksgiving or else in memory of St. Oswald,' to whose intercession the grace was attributed.[2] In this case, as no proper mass of St. Oswald had then been composed, it seems that the interior intention was alone changed, and not the liturgy.

When Bishop Ethelheard deserted his church in time of danger, Alcuin wrote to admonish him of his fault, and advised him in expiation to appoint a fast day, to give alms, and to have masses said to appease God's anger.[3]

In a time of general calamity no means more efficacious was known to bring God's blessing on the remedies employed than to offer the Son of God to His heavenly Father, who had sent Him down to earth out of compassion for men's miseries. About the year 1012 some ecclesiastical laws were made at Haba under King Ethelred II. The times were indeed calamitous. In vain had the weak and ' unready ' king bought off the Danes. They came in still greater numbers, marking their course by pillage, massacre, and conflagration. Canterbury had been taken, the cathedral violated, all the monks but four slain, men, women, and helpless infants butchered. St. Elphege, the archbishop, seeking to intercede for his people, had fallen into the hands of the pagans, and, after seven months of prison and torture, had been brutally massacred at Greenwich.[4] Under these terrible afflictions the whole nation was called to prayer, but especially the priests and monks. The third chapter of the laws enacted at Haba was as follows : 'We command that in every community a mass shall be sung daily and publicly for the king and all his people. It will take the place of the conventual mass, and shall be the votive mass "against the pagans." At each of the canonical hours the whole community, prostrate on the earth, shall recite the

---

[1] Alcuini *Opera*, i. 59, 256, ii. 13 ; Rock, i. 73, iii. 187.
[2] See Chapter VI., p. 96, *antea*.
[3] A.D. 798 ; Haddan and Stubbs, iii. 519.
[4] A most graphic description of the death of St. Elphege is given by Lingard, *A. S.* ii. 293-296.

psalm "Domine, quid multiplicati sunt" (Ps. iii.) and the collect against the heathen. And this shall be done as long as the present necessity lasts. And in every monastery or community of monks each priest shall say thirty masses for the king and people, and every monk thirty psalters.'[1] Nor were these prayers in vain, though they were heard not altogether according to the intention of the suppliants. The Danes triumphed indeed, and became masters of the land, but not as formerly the Angles and Saxons had triumphed over the British. The triumphant Danes yielded to the Christian faith. Canute, who had till then acted as a barbarian, on becoming sole monarch of England and Denmark, Norway, and part of Sweden in 1017, led a life in conformity with his baptism, and sought to atone for his usurpation by a just and wise government. He rebuilt magnificently St. Edmund's Bury in order to make reparation for the outrages of his father Sweyne, and he not only consolidated the faith among his Danish and Saxon subjects in England, but also spread it throughout Denmark. It is almost impossible not to see in this conversion of the Danes a reward for the piety, sufferings, and zeal of the Anglo-Saxons, whose conduct presents a great contrast with that of the British Christians towards their ancestors. The Britons, even at the earnest request of St. Augustine, had refused in any way to help in the conversion of their hated enemies, and even long after their conversion would scarce regard them as Christians. Far different was the conduct of St. Elphege. During the siege of Canterbury he devoted himself to his countrymen and spiritual children by exhortations, by preparing them for Holy Communion, and strengthening them for martyrdom.[2] But when he was in the hands of his cruel enemies his zeal was no less ardent for their conversion. Though he could have raised the large sum asked for his ransom, he refused to take a measure that would impoverish his priests and the poor, and he replied to the Danes that he had no other gold for them than the knowledge of the true God. When they were afflicted with an epidemic, he prayed for them and blessed bread for their recovery, and was successful in baptizing and confirming some of them before his martyrdom. This charity, with the prayers and masses said at the command of his fellow bishops, met this striking reward, that when in 1023, eleven years after his death, his uncorrupted body was solemnly translated from London to Can-

---

[1] Spelman, i. 531 ; Wilkins, i. 295.

[2] 'Episcopali super illos benedictione effusa, pacis communione in osculo sancto libata, dum divini epuli omnes participes efficeret, se illis, illos sibi, utrosque autem omnium Protectori Deo commendavit.' (Osbern.)

terbury, Canute, the Danish king, with his own hand held the tiller of the ship that carried the precious burden while it passed across the Thames.[1]

It was not only in times of calamity that mass was offered for the king. This was an obligation often imposed at the foundation or endowment of a monastery. Thus, in a charter written before the high altar of St. Peter in the city of Winchester, in 855, King Ethelwulf requires, in return for his benefactions, that all the brethren and sisters of Winchester and Shireburn every week, on Wednesday, in each of their churches shall sing fifty psalms, and each priest shall say two masses, one for the king and another for his generals or nobles (*ducibus*), for their good estate and pardon of their sins. After their death one of the masses was still to be offered for the king, the other for his nobles.[2] In 821 King Kenulf granted a charter to Abingdon. Every Sunday the community was to offer seven masses for the king and other prayers. Ethelred II., in a charter to the same monastery, mentions that the monks had already offered for him 1,500 masses and 1,200 psalteries.[3] These things are sneered at by certain Protestant writers, as if the kings were evidently the dupes of designing monks. But assuredly, were there deception in trusting to the efficacy of the Holy Sacrifice, the monks and clergy were its victims as much as kings and nobles. In private correspondence, never meant for the public eye, much less to come down to us, they show as great a faith in the divine commemoration as they could have wished to find among benefactors.

Thus Sigebald, a monk, writes to St. Boniface to ask him to be his bishop, together with his diocesan bishop Daniel, and declares that he mentions the name of Boniface in his mass together with that of Daniel; and promises that if he survives Boniface he will mention his name together with that of his deceased bishop Esenwald.[4] Eadburga, an English nun, writes in 719 to the same saint, then in Germany: 'I beg you to offer the oblations of holy masses for the soul of my relative, and by the same bearer I send you fifty shillings and an altar-cloth.'[5] Again, Ebwald, an abbot, makes an interchange of prayers and masses with St. Boniface. The bishop is to be remembered by name in the masses of Ebwald's

---

[1] See Alban Butler, April 19th; and Osbern in *Anglia Sacra*, ii. 122.

[2] Haddan and Stubbs, iii. 641; Kemble, *Cod. Dip.* t. v. p. 94.

[3] *Historia de Abingdon*, i. 27 and 362. Mr. Kemble thinks the charter of Ethelred a forgery, but without sufficient reason according to Mr. Stevenson. See other examples in Dr. Rock, ii. 326.

[4] Inter *Op. S. Bonif.*, Migne, tom. lxxxix. p. 723. [5] *Ib.* p. 692.

monastery and at the seven hours of prayer. The abbot will also send to St. Boniface, when opportunity serves, the lists of his monks who shall die, that they may be remembered by him.[1] The King of Kent and the Bishop of Rochester write a letter to Lullus, the successor of St. Boniface in the see of Mentz, and thus express themselves :[2] 'It is our earnest wish to recommend ourselves and our dearest relatives to your piety, that by your prayers we may be protected till we come to that life which knows no end. For what have we to do on earth but faithfully to exercise charity towards each other? Let us then agree that when any among us enters the path which leads to another life (may it be a life of happiness!) the survivors shall, by their alms and sacrifices, endeavour to assist him in his journey.' They then send some names of deceased relatives.

Among all the Anglo-Saxon clergy none was more enlightened, none more sincere and earnest, than Venerable Bede. In dedicating his life of St. Cuthbert to the monks of Lindisfarne he begs that 'when he is dead they will pray and offer masses for the release (*redemptione*) of his soul, and place his name among those of their brethren.' He has also in his history related a marvellous event which well illustrates the faith of that age. 'A young soldier named Imma had been made prisoner and put in irons. He had a brother named Tunna, who was a priest and abbot, and who, having heard that Imma had been killed in battle, went to seek for his body, and finding one very like it brought it to his monastery and buried it, and for the release of the soul took care to say many masses. Now it happened that, however fast Imma was chained, his chains were always found to have fallen off. And when the earl, whose prisoner he was, wondering at this, asked him if he had about him any charm, he replied that he knew nothing about charms, but that he had a brother a priest in his province, and " I know," he said, " that he thinks me dead and says masses for me, and now, were I in the next world, my soul through his intercession would be freed from its pains." Now it was at the hour of tierce, when masses are wont to be said, that his chains were loosed. When he gained his liberty and returned to his brother, he found that he had conjectured rightly. And many, hearing from him what had happened, were strengthened in faith and in devotion, to pray and give alms and to offer to the Lord victims of the sacred oblation. For they understood that the saving sacrifice has virtue for the everlasting redemption of soul and body.'[3]

The faith of the Catholic Church is well summed up by

---

[1] Inter *Op. S. Bonif.*, Migne, tom. lxxxix. p. 725.
[2] Ep. 77, inter *Op. S. Bonif.* (Lingard's translation).   [3] *Hist.* iv. 22.

Florus in his treatise on the mass written about 850. He is commenting on the words *Memento etiam, Domine,* &c. 'Remember, O Lord, Thy servants and Thy handmaids, who have gone before us with the sign of faith, and sleep the sleep of peace. To these and to all who rest in Christ mercifully grant, we beseech Thee, a place of refreshment, of light, and of peace.'

'Our pious mother the Church,' he says, 'prays also for her dead, and commends them to God through the intercession of the sacred Oblation, believing most certainly that that precious Blood, "which was shed for many for the remission of sins," is available not only for the welfare of the living, but also for the absolution of the dead, as St. John declares : "The Blood of His Son Jesus Christ cleanses us from *every* sin." Leaving their bodies, the faithful go before us to the Lord ; but they are not cut off from the Church, because they go before with the sign of faith, and sleep the sleep of peace. *With the sign of faith*, because they have been regenerated by water and the Holy Ghost, and are signed with the Cross and Passion of Christ. *They sleep*, because they will truly be aroused from sleep in the resurrection, as our Lord said of the girl whom He was about to raise : "The girl is not dead, but sleeps ;" and again : "Lazarus our friend sleeps, and I go to awake him from his sleep." Hence St. Paul says of the faithful dead : 'We would not have you ignorant, brethren, concerning those who sleep, that you be not sad like those who have no hope." They sleep then *the sleep of peace*, since they were never separated from the unity and society of the Church either by heresies, or by schisms, or by mortal crimes ; or if they were ever involved in these, yet they were restored again and associated to the mystery of Redemption by penance and by the prayer of the Church, to which, in the person of Peter, it was said : "Whatsoever thou shalt loose on earth shall be loosed in heaven ;" and so at least they died in peace through the mercy of Him who desires not the death of the sinner, but that he be converted and live. Nor are the souls of the pious dead separated from the Church ; otherwise the memory of them would not be made at the altar in the communication of the Body of Christ. Nor would it avail anything to run in time of danger to the Church's baptism, lest life should terminate without it, nor to have recourse to her absolution in case one had been separated from the Body of Christ by impenitence or evil conscience. Why are these things done, except that the faithful, even when dead, remain her members?

'Therefore the souls of the dead already reign with Christ, although not yet united to their bodies. Hence in the Apocalypse we read : "Blessed are the dead who die in the Lord ; for even now, saith the Spirit, they may rest from their labours, for their works follow them." The Church, then, even now reigns with Christ, in her living and her dead; for Christ therefore died, says the Apostle, that He might be Lord both of the living and the dead. It is as clear as the light, St. Gregory says, that the souls of the just who are perfect, as soon as they leave the prison of the flesh are received into the heavenly mansions. Therefore St. Paul desired to be dissolved and to be with Christ. He then who does not doubt that Christ is in heaven will not deny that the soul of St. Paul is also in heaven. . . . And so, we must believe, is it with the souls of apostles, martyrs, confessors, and all those of the more perfect life. Yet there are some souls of just men that are detained in certain receptacles away from the kingdom of heaven, though they are in blissful repose. And by this loss of delay it is shown that they had not attained unto perfect justice.

'But there are some preordained, indeed, to the lot of the elect for their good works, but, on account of some bad works with the defilement of which they quitted their bodies, after death endure a severe chastisement, and are committed to the flames of purgatorial fire. These are either, by a long examination even until the day of judgment, cleansed from the defilement of vices; or else, being absolved from their pains sooner by the prayers, alms, fasts, tears, and oblations of the saving Victim on the part of their faithful friends, they also arrive at the rest of the blessed.

'Therefore the holy sacrifice is profitable to those dead, who during their life merited to receive help after death from such good works as are here done for them by others. But we should reflect that the safer way is for each one to do for himself while alive the good that he hopes may be done for him by others. It is more blessed to go forth free than to seek for freedom after enduring chains.

'After the words "who sleep the sleep of peace," it was the ancient custom, as it is still that of the Roman Church, to recite from the diptychs or tables the names of the dead, and then at the end of the list the words were added : " To these and to all who rest in Christ, grant, we beseech Thee, a place of refreshment, light, and peace." The place of *refreshment* is that in which is not felt that burning pain of which the rich man buried in hell complained : " I am tormented in this flame." The place of *light* is that which our Lord promises to His faithful, saying : " I am the light of the world ; he that followeth Me, walketh not in darkness, but shall have the light of life ; " and of which the Psalmist says: "That I may please God in the light of the living!" The place of *peace* is that to which Simeon aspired: "Now Thou lettest Thy servant depart in peace;" and of which the Scripture says that the saints seem to fools to die, but they are in peace.

'This, then, is the pious and religious observance which the Church has without doubt received from Apostolic tradition, and which she keeps uniformly and solemnly throughout the world; and this custom is also commended by the Old Testament Scriptures and the careful observance of the ancient Fathers. For we read in the Books of the Maccabees,' &c.[1]

Let us examine more minutely what rules were made concerning mass for the dead. Archbishop Theodore mentions that, in a mass said especially for the dead, the 'Alleluia' and 'Gloria' were omitted. Though a Greek or Asiatic by birth—he was from Tarsus, the city of St. Paul—yet he had lived long in Rome, and had been sent to England by Pope Vitalian to instruct the English in the customs of the Church. In reply to many questions about the care of the dead he gave the following answers:

'According to the Roman Church it is the custom to carry the bodies of deceased monks or religious men to the church, to anoint their breasts with chrism, to say mass for them there, then with chanting to carry them out to burial. When they are laid in the tomb, prayers are offered, and they are covered with the earth or with a stone. On the first, third, ninth, and thirtieth day, mass is said for them, and an annual commemoration may also be made for them. For a deceased monk mass is offered on the day of his burial, and on the third day after that as many as the abbot appoints. It is the custom also to offer masses for deceased monks and to recite their names every week.

'Masses are said for deceased laymen three times in the year, on the third day, the ninth, and the thirtieth. For a good layman mass is offered. For a penitent' (*i.e.* one who had been put to public penance and died before its full term) 'on the thirtieth day, or on the seventh, after a fast; for his relatives ought to fast seven days and make an oblation at the altar, as the children of Israel fasted for Saul. After that the priest may offer as many as he pleases.

'Many say it is not lawful to offer mass for infants not seven years old. But it is.

'Dionysius the Areopagite says it is blasphemy to offer mass for a wicked man; but Augustine says it may be offered for all Christians,

---

[1] Florus Diaconus, *De actione Missarum* (*Bib. Max. Lugd.* tom. xv. p. 79).

for, if it does not benefit the deceased, it benefits those that offer and those that ask for it.' 'But if a bishop or abbot,' he says in another place, 'command a monk to sing mass for a dead heretic, he must not obey.'[1] A similar rule was observed with regard to those who died excommunicate and impenitent, or for suicides, nor were they buried in consecrated ground.

At subsequent periods special regulations were made as to the suffrages to be offered for certain classes of persons. According to the Regularis Concordia or monastic regulations of St. Dunstan, besides the more solemn mass said at the high altar for thirty days for a deceased monk, each monk in private said thirty masses for his soul.

The Council of Celchyth in 816 decreed that when a bishop died a tenth part of his goods should be given to the poor, and all his English slaves be liberated. His memory was to be kept in all the churches. In each diocese in every church the bell was to be rung to call the people to church to recite thirty psalms for his soul. Thus every bishop and abbot should have celebrated six hundred psalms and one hundred and twenty masses, and free three men and give to each of them three shillings, besides other fasts and alms.[2]

On the principle laid down by the Apostle that 'he who serves the altar should live by the altar,' it was customary to make offerings to the clergy when asking the special application of their intention in the offering of mass. This has been already partly exemplified in what has been said about the foundations of religious houses and cathedrals. I add a few examples of other gifts and legacies. In 796 Charlemagne wrote to Offa, the English king. The letter is interesting as a kind of international treaty of commerce. For first the French monarch promises to let English pilgrims pass to Rome free of tax, though merchants must pay custom ; next he promises to send some black marble which Offa had asked for ; then he complains that the English cloaks which had been sent to France were too long; and lastly he sends presents for all the English bishoprics as alms for the soul of Pope Adrian, who had died in the preceding December, adding 'that he had indeed no doubt but that that blessed soul was already in the enjoyment of rest, but that nevertheless he wished to show his fidelity and love to one who had been his most dear friend.'[3]

---

[1] Haddan and Stubbs, iii. 194, 181.

[2] *Ib.* 584. Bede tells us (*Hist.* ii. 3) that in his time a priest said mass every Saturday, solemnly, at the altar of St. Gregory, in the church of SS. Peter and Paul in Canterbury, for the repose of the souls of the archbishops there buried.

[3] The letter is given by Haddan and Stubbs, iii. 496.

The will of King Alfred has fortunately been preserved.[1] In it he says: 'Also let them distribute for me and for my father, and for the friends that he interceded for, and that I intercede for, two hundred pounds—fifty to mass priests throughout all my kingdom, fifty to poor servants of God, fifty to distressed poor, fifty to the church where I shall rest—and I will that my aldermen and thanes meet together and distribute it.' A very curious will of a bishop of the tenth century has also come down to us. Theodred, bishop of the East Angles, was promoted to the see of London in the time of Edgar or of his son Edmund. He made the following will in Saxon, which I give in Mr. Gale's translation:[2] 'In the name of our Lord Jesus Christ I, Theodred, Bishop of London, will declare my testament of my inheritance that I have obtained, and yet may obtain, by the will of God and His hallows (*i.e.* saints), for my soul, and for my lord under whom I obtained it, and for my ancestors' and for all men's souls that I pray for, and of whom I have received alms, and for whom I ought justly to pray. That is, first, that he (Theodred) gives his lord his heriot, that is two hundred marks of red gold, and two silver cups and four horses, the best I have, and two swords and four shields and four spears, and the land that I have at Ankeswithe, &c. And to St. Paul's Church my two best mass vestments that I have, with all the things that thereto belong, with a chalice and a cup, and my best mass-book, and all my relics, the best that I have, to St. Paul's Church. And I give the land at Tit to St. Paul's Church, towards the bed-land of the convent, with all that therein stands, except the men that are there, who are all to be set free for my soul. And I give the land at Suthereye (*i.e.* Surrey), with all the fishing that thereto belongs, to the convent of St. Paul's Church, and set free the men for the bishop's soul' (*i.e.* his own). And after many other bequests: 'And I give to every bishop's see five pounds to dole out for my soul. And I give to the archbishop five marks of gold. And I grant that ten pounds be doled for my soul at my bishopric within London and without London . . . And I give to Theodred my white mass vestment that I bought at Pavie, and all that thereto belongs, and a feast-chalice, and two mass-books that Gosebricht bequeathed me. And I give Odgar the rich mass vestment that I bought at Pavie and what

---

[1] Mr. Kemble, in the *Codex Diplomaticus*, printed it from an imperfect copy. But it is given in Saxon, Latin, and Early English, in the *Book of Hyde*, where it has also been accurately translated by the editor (Rolls Series, p. 332).

[2] Gale's *History of Suffolk*, 'The Hundred of Thingoe,' p. 273. It is also published in *Codex Diplom.* and in Kemble's notes on the Bishops of East Anglia, in *Proceedings of the Archæological Institute*, 1847.

thereto belongs. And I give Gundwine the other rich mass vestment, that is unornamented, and what thereto belongs. And I give Spratocke the red mass vestment and all that thereto belongs. And whosoever takes from my testament may God take him from the kingdom of heaven, unless he amend it before his death !'

As we have very few Saxon wills, one more specimen may be interesting. It is that of an 'anker' or hermit, who seems to have been a nobleman and to have retained the disposition of his property. Wills were often in old time addressed to the king as to their guardian. 'Mantat, the anker, God's wretch, greeteth Knut the king and Emma the lady most blithely with God's bliss. And I make known to you that our alms I have bestowed on Christ and all His hallows, for the comfort and bliss of our soul, where it longest shall endure ; that is, first the land of Twiwel to Thorney, where our bones shall rest, and the land at Cunnington to priests and deacons who earned it of me in my lifetime. And they have promised to God, and confirmed to me in hand, that they should each year do for us two hundred masses and two hundred psalters, and thereto eke many holy prayers. Now pray I you, for God's love and for our wretched request, that no man pervert this, and that shall be made known of you in the life to come: The King of heaven's angels protect you here in life, and lead you in His light with Him, where without sorrow ye may ever dwell! Amen.'[1]

From some of the preceding documents it appears that there were two principal commemorations on which the Holy Mass was offered for the deceased, viz. the month after the death or burial, and the anniversary. The former was called (as it is still) the month's-mind, the latter the year's-mind, and in later times more frequently the Obit. Almost our very earliest Anglo-Saxon writer, Eddius, in his life of St. Wilfrid tells us how Tatbert, to whom Wilfrid entrusted the government of his monastery at Ripon, ordered a mass to be celebrated and alms to be distributed daily for his soul. On Wilfrid's anniversary during Tatbert's lifetime a tenth part of all the flocks and herds belonging to the monastery was distributed among the poor in addition to the daily alms. Annually also the abbots of all the monasteries founded by Wilfrid came together at Ripon, and, after spending the preceding night in watching and prayer, on the anniversary day assisted at a solemn mass offered for him.[2]

It is evident that special anniversaries could not be kept for every

---

[1] From the Red Book or Cartulary of Thorney Abbey in Cambridgeshire, quoted in *Collectanea Topographica*, vol. iv. p. 58.

[2] Eddius, cap. 64 et 67, in *Historians of York* (Rolls Series, 1879).

monk, or even abbot or benefactor, for as years went on the number became very great. But anniversaries were kept for benefactors in general, and a memento was constantly made for them. For this purpose a register was kept, called the Album, or the Annal, or the Book of Life. A writer who had lived at Durham before the suppression of the monastery writes: 'There did lie on the high altar an excellent fine book, very richly covered with gold and silver, containing the names of all the benefactors towards St. Cuthbert's church from the very original foundation thereof, the very letters of the book being, for the most part, all gilt, as is apparent in the said book to this day. The laying that book on the high altar did show how highly they esteemed their founders and benefactors, and the quotidian remembrance they had of them in the time of mass and divine service, and this did argue not only their gratitude, but also a most divine and charitable affection to the souls of their benefactors, as well dead as living.'[1] By having their names inscribed in such books laymen became brethren of the religious houses, and participants in their good works and suffrages. Venerable Bede, not content with his special brotherhood with his own community at Jarrow, got himself inscribed in the brotherhood of Lindisfarne; and such an interchange of charity became very common, so that at the death of a monk a messenger was sent to have his name inscribed on the mortuary rolls of those religious orders with which there was such a compact.[2]

I give two specimens of entries from the 'Liber Vitæ' of Durham, one of lay benefactors, the other of religious communities.

'This is the agreement which the convent of St. Cuthbert promises to observe for ever towards Malcolm, king of the Scots, and Queen Margaret, and their sons and daughters, viz.: for the king and queen while they live they will daily maintain one poor man, and two poor shall be admitted for them to the mandatum on Holy Thursday, and a collect be recited at the litanies and at mass. And during their life and after death they and their sons and daughters shall share in all that is done for the service of God in the monastery of St. Cuthbert, in masses, psalms, alms, vigils, prayers. And for the king and queen from the day of their decease three full offices of the dead, and every day " Verba mea " (Ps. v.). Each priest will sing thirty masses, and each

---

[1] The *Liber Vitæ*, which lay for six centuries on the high altar, first at Lindisfarne, then at Chester-le-Street, and last at Durham, is still in existence. It has been published by the Surtees Society. The *Antiquities of Durham*, from which the above extract is made, is another of the publications of this Society.

[2] On this subject see Lingard, ii. 58; Rock, ii. 331; also Martene, v. 13.

of the rest ten psalteries. And their anniversary to be celebrated festively every year, like that of King Athelstan.'[1]

'Agreement between the monks of Westminster and the monks of Durham. When a Durham monk dies, seven full offices will be performed for him in Westminster in choir, and each priest sing for him one mass, and the rest of the brethren one psalter; and the lay brethren who do not know the psalter will sing one hundred and fifty Pater Nosters. And the same from the monks of St. Albans.'[2]

Sometimes, when an abbot died, a special messenger, called a Breviator, carrying the bead-roll (*brevia, rotuli*),[3] went round to various monasteries with an account of the death and merits of the deceased, and soliciting spiritual alms. Each monastery entered its promise in the roll. Such an entry was called a *titulus*. Thus, when Vitalis, the abbot of Savigny, died in 1122, the Abbey of Abingdon, in Berkshire, after its promise wrote the following lines:

> Vita brevis, casusque levis, nec spes remanendi;
> Quanta seres, hinc tanta feres, sit cura parandi.
> Plura seras, ut plura feras, ne non seruisse
> Pœniteat, cum nil valeat tibi pœnituisse.

Then, lest the poet should seem by this moralising to be reflecting on the negligence of the deceased abbot, the verses concluded with an address to St. Peter:

> Qui revocas quod in arce locas, Petre, jure potenti
> Huic aperi valvas, superi plaudant venienti.

It was not often, however, that the monks were so ambitious as the poet of Abingdon. The more common formula was

> Vestris nostra damus, pro nostris vestra rogamus;

or,

> Quod dedimus vestris et vos impendite nostris.

But, it may be asked, with all this care for monks, abbots, nobles, and monarchs, was anyone mindful of the souls of the poor? Surely this cannot be doubted, since care of the poor was one of the commonest alms for the souls of the rich. From the nature of the case, the record of masses said for them cannot be gathered from wills and bead-rolls. I find, however, that a case of conscience was laid before Rabanus Maurus: 'Can office and masses be offered for a runaway slave?' He replies that though a bondman may not run away except in case of gross cruelty, yet certainly masses may be lawfully offered

---

[1] *Liber Vitæ*, p. 73.   [2] *Ib.* p. 135.
[3] See paper in the *Proceedings of the Archæological Society* for 1847, by J. G. Nichols, Esq., on 'Precatory or Mortuary Rolls.'

for the repose of his soul.¹ Monastic chronicles and saints' lives are full of touching examples of care for the poor during life and at death. Surely charity accompanied them beyond the tomb. Beautiful things are told of Agelwy, abbot of Evesham. He was elected abbot in the reign of St. Edward, and, contrary to the lot of most Saxon abbots, he enjoyed the favour of William the Conqueror. William even made him governor of several of the midland counties; and he was held in great esteem by all the barons and great men of the time.

Agelwy's devotion and charity were as famous as his prudence. Besides the 'army of poor' whom he fed and clothed, he kept twelve infirm men always with him, and supplied all their wants, and though some of them were lepers he washed their hands and feet every day with warm water. He required them to be present at matins as well as at the day hours, and at both the Solemn Masses. He also gave welcome and hospitality to the great number of pilgrims who then flocked to our Lady of Evesham from Aquitaine and from Ireland. His charity, however, shone out most conspicuously when the fierce Conqueror, in retaliation for some marauding acts committed by the disbanded Saxon soldiers who infested the forests, laid waste the counties of Worcester, Cheshire, Shropshire, Staffordshire, and Derbyshire. The fame of the Abbot of Evesham drew crowds of starving peasants from these counties. He helped them as far as possible, but often his help came too late, and they died of hunger and suffering, seven or eight a day, at the door of the monastery. Agelwy not only provided for their burial, but also took especial care of their orphan children, distributing them among the dependents of his abbey and providing for their education.

This great charity was fed by devotion to the Blessed Sacrament. On the nights of the principal festivals throughout the year, to the honour of God and His saints, he kept a candle burning before each altar in the church. He heard daily as many masses as his duties would permit, and at each of them he would offer, with great compunction, one or more *denarii*. God blessed his abundant alms, and the abbey became rich under his rule. He found but twelve monks, he left thirty-six. He purchased many ornaments, chasubles, copes, altar-cloths, &c., and an altar beautifully worked in gold and silver. He built also a handsome chapel to St. Nicolas, whose charities he imitated.

Agelwy died full of days on the 16th of February 1077, after making true confession and receiving the holy viaticum of the Body and Blood of the Lord, surrounded by his religious brethren and

¹ *Responsa Canonica*, apud Migne, tom. cx. p. 1192.

sons whom he had loved with a father's heart. He was an intimate friend of St. Wulstan, who was his confessor (*pater suarum confessionum*).[1]

The chronicler does not mention that Agelwy had masses said for the souls of the poor peasants; but such a record was certainly needless for those to whom his faith and charity were thus published.

The people above the very lowest state, the small traders of towns and villages, formed themselves into guilds, and many of these supported a chaplain of their own, whose duty it was to say mass for the brethren and sisters, living and dead. They even imposed the obligation of getting masses said as a fine for breaking rules. Thus the rule of an ancient Saxon guild in Exeter, given by Mr. Kemble,[2] says: 'This assembly was collected in Exeter for the love of God and for our soul's need, both in regard to our health here and to the after days which we desire for ourselves by God's doom. Now we have agreed that our meeting shall be thrice in the twelve months, once at St. Michael's Mass, secondly at St. Mary's Mass after midwinter,[3] and thirdly at Allhallows Mass[4] after Easter . . . and let the mass priest at each of our meetings sing two masses, one for our living friends, the other for the dead; and let each brother of common condition sing two psalters of psalms, one for the living and one for the dead. And at the death of a brother each man six masses, or six psalters of psalms. . . . And if any neglect the day, for the first time three masses, for the second five,' &c.

This one example will be sufficient if it is borne in mind that such guilds were widespread associations throughout the land from very early Saxon days to the Reformation. The priests themselves in cities were numerous enough to form themselves into guilds, for we find that Ethelmar, an ealdorman, by his will leaves two pounds to the guild of mass priests in Winchester, and one pound to that of deacons.[5]

Thus, then, no one was excluded from the benefits of the Holy Sacrifice unless he willingly cut himself off from the Church; and even its special application was within the reach of all who were in life careful of their soul's salvation. There will be occasion to return to this subject in speaking of later times, when the doctrine of application of mass for the dead will be explained more fully.

[1] *Chronicon Abbatiæ de Evesham* (Rolls Series), pp. 90-94.
[2] *Saxons in England*, i. App. D, p. 512.
[3] Midwinter is Christmas; St. Mary's Mass is therefore the Purification, Feb. 2.
[4] Probably May 13, *Natalis B. Mariæ ad martyres* (olim).
[5] *Book of Hyde*, p. 364 (Rolls Series).

CHAPTER XVI.

ON RECEIVING COMMUNION.

THE words of Walafrid Strabo have been already quoted, that 'though the mass profits those who assist at it without communicating and all' (whether present or not) 'who share the faith and devotion of the celebrant and communicants, and though a priest may sometimes celebrate quite alone, yet the legitimate (or perfect) mass is that at which priest and server, offerer and communicant all assist.' We have then to devote this chapter to communion among the Anglo-Saxons. We shall consider in what manner they received the Bread of Life, how often, and with what preparation. The history of the communion of the sick and dying will require to be treated apart.

There are many excellent English words, which, through the change of religion in the sixteenth century, have fallen out of modern language. One of these is the term for communion. It is known, however, to most by the famous line in Hamlet,

Unhouseled, disappointed, unaneled,

i.e. without communion, without preparation (by confession), without extreme unction.[1]

---

[1] *Hamlet*, act i. scene 5. The above is, without doubt, the correct reading. 'Unanointed, unanel'd,' as some modern editions print, is mere tautology. An emendation has been proposed, viz. 'unassoiled,' *i.e.* unabsolved, instead of 'disappointed,' but without either authority or necessity. 'A man armed at all points, well equipped, was said to be well *appointed*, and *dis-appointed* in Shakspere appears to be the reverse, *i.e. ill-appointed*, ill-prepared, unprepared.' (Richardson.) So Isabella, telling her brother to prepare for death, says:

'Therefore your best appointment make with speed.'
(Measure for Measure, act iii. scene 1.)

As, therefore, 'appointment' for death might mean the reception of all appropriate sacraments with the right disposition, so 'disappointment,' standing alone, might mean absence of the proper preparation in every or in any point. But in *Hamlet*, from the collocation of the word between two sacraments, it would seem to mean lack of a third sacrament, viz. that of penance. And thus a correct climax is made, for Shakespeare does not mention the sacraments in the order in which they are received, but in the order in which their omission would

Dr. Lingard truly says that 'from the arrival of Augustine till the Reformation, the English name for the Eucharist was the housel.' The Anglo-Saxon word *husel* means offering, oblation, sacrifice. The corresponding word in modern Catholic English is 'host,' from *hostia*, a victim, because communion is participation in the Divine Victim. This word was also used in the fourteenth century:

> Bere thy ost anont thy breste
> In a box that ys honeste

(*i.e.* carry the Host in a decent pyx on thy breast) is the instruction given by John Myrc.[1] But the Host when received is called 'housel.'

> Thou schalt hym soyle
> And geve hym hosul and holy oyle [2]

(*i.e.* thou shalt assoil or absolve him, and give him communion and extreme unction).

In Mr. Morris's 'Specimens of Early English'[3] we have the following passage from 'Havelok the Dane:'—

> Hwan he that wiste, rathe he sende
> After prestes fer and hende,
> Chanounes gode and monkes both,
> Him for to wisse and to rede,
> Him for to hoslon and for to shrive
> Hwil his bodi were on live

(*i.e.* when he knew that, he sent quickly after priests far and near, good canons and monks too, to give him counsel, to housle and shrive him while his body still lived).

The words 'communion' and 'communicating,' from the Latin or French, were beginning to creep into the language just before the

be calamitous. He who is 'houseled' will, as a rule, not only have time to make his confession before communion, but also to be anointed afterwards. But many die without this fulness of the Church's rites. They make their confession and are anointed; but from inability to swallow, or because viaticum is not to be had, they die 'unhouseled.' But should the dying man be speechless and insensible when the priest comes, he may still be anointed, in hopes that he had, before losing consciousness, the due disposition to make the sacrament of extreme unction available. Yet he would then be considered unprepared, or 'disappointed.' The Ghost complains that he had not even this last chance:

> 'Cut off even in the blossoms of my sin,
> Unhouseled, disappointed, unaneled;
> No reckoning made, but sent to my account
> With all my imperfections on my head.'

---

[1] *Instructions for Parish Priests*, l. 1961.
[2] *Ib.* l. 1987.
[3] A p. 40.

Reformation. Bradshaw, a monk of Chester who died in 1513, puts into the mouth of St. Werburgh the following language:

> And I knowledge to Thee with pure intent,
> In Shorpthursday afore Thy Passion,
> Thy most blessed Body in sacrament
> Thou gave to us for our communion.

He also employs the word 'communed' for 'communicated.' The old constitutions of the monks and nuns of Isleworth, which are of a still earlier date, omitting the word 'housel' altogether, frequently speak of 'communing,' though, by the struggles of the writer to spell it, it seems that he had not often seen it in writing before. He writes it 'comenynge,' 'comeynge,' 'comonynge,' and 'comened,' 'comenyd,' 'comyned,' 'comonyd,' with other artificial combinations of y, o, and e, far beyond the usual spelling license of those days.[1] But though the new word 'communion' was not unknown, the old word 'housel' was alone popular before the Reformation, so that the commissioners appointed by Edward VI. to value and seize the chantry foundations, in making their returns of the number of communicants in each place, invariably designate them as 'houseling people.'

During the whole of the period with which we are now concerned it was the general custom of the Church to administer communion during mass to the people under both species. It was, however, often given, under the form of bread only, to the sick, or sometimes of wine only, as to infants; and neither celebrant nor people ever received it under both species on Good Friday, though for many centuries, in some places, it was the custom for the faithful, as well as monks and clergy, to communicate on that day. We shall return to this subject in another place.

The learned editors of the 'Liber Sacramentorum' of St. Gregory the Great say that, although the Eucharist in early times was given into the hands of the communicants, yet before the time of St. Gregory the custom was for the priest to place it in the mouth.[2] An old canon mentioned by Regino in the ninth century, but of an earlier period, says: 'The priest must not place the Eucharist in the hand of any man or woman, but only in the mouth with these words: "The Body and Blood of our Lord profit thee to the remission of sins and life everlasting."'[3] Yet exceptions seem to have been allowed, at least for a time, since Venerable Bede, in describing

---

[1] Rule of St. Saviour, append. to Aungier's *History of Sion and Isleworth*.
[2] See *Liber Sac.* apud Migne, tom. lxxviii. p. 883.
[3] Apud Rock, i. 163, *quem vide*; also Chardon, *Histoire des Sacrements*, 'Eucharistie,' ch. iv. art. 2.

Cædmon's last communion, says that 'while still holding the Blessed Sacrament in his hand, he declared that he died in peace with all men, and so, fortifying himself with the heavenly viaticum, prepared for his entry into another life.'[1] Cædmon, though not a cleric, was a monk, and perhaps on this account a privilege was granted him.[2] It must, however, be admitted that there is no distinct proof that the ancient manner of communicating had ceased to be the general practice in England in the eighth century.

Of course, wherever the custom still subsisted of placing the sacred species in the hand of the communicant, all the precautions were taken that had been prescribed from the earliest times. St. Cyril of Jerusalem, who wrote in 347, thus instructs the people how to communicate : 'Approaching therefore, come not with thy wrists extended, or thy fingers open ; but make thy left hand as if a throne for thy right, which is on the eve of receiving the King. And having hallowed thy palm, receive the Body of Christ, saying after it, Amen. Then, after thou hast with carefulness hallowed thine eyes by the touch of the Holy Body, partake thereof, giving heed lest thou lose any of it, for what thou losest is a loss to thee, as it were from one of thy own members. For tell me, if anyone gave thee gold dust, wouldst thou not with all precaution keep it fast, being on thy guard against losing any of it and suffering loss? How much more cautiously, then, wilt thou observe that not a crumb falls from thee of what is more precious than gold and precious stones ! Then, after having partaken of the Body of Christ, approach also to the cup of His Blood, not stretching forth thine hands, but bending and saying, in the way of worship and reverence, Amen, be thou hallowed by partaking also of the Blood of Christ. And while the moisture is still upon thy lips, touching it with thine hands, hallow both thine eyes and brow and the other senses. Then wait for the prayer, and give thanks unto God, who hath accounted thee worthy of so great mysteries.'[3]

As regards the Precious Blood we have authentic information from many sources about the manner of its distribution. No more than one chalice was consecrated, and, after the celebrant and the clergy assisting him at the altar had communicated from this, what remained of the Precious Blood was poured into a large chalice,[4]

---

[1] *Hist.* iv. 24.

[2] Women, at least in the West, received the Body of our Lord, not, like men, on the hand itself, but on a white linen cloth called *Dominicale*.

[3] St. Cyril's *Catechetical Lectures*, lect. xxiii. (Oxford translation).

[4] The communion chalice was ordinarily a large one with two handles. A

which was gradually filled up with unconsecrated wine, as the number of communicants required—'because wine even not consecrated, yet mixed with the Blood of the Lord, is altogether sanctified,' says the Ordo Romanus. Both the clergy and the people drank from a tube, not from the rim of the chalice. Such tubes were made of gold, silver, ivory, or glass.[1]

If a deacon were assisting, it was the deacon, not the priest, who presented the cup to the laity. The Canons of Ælfric, A.D. 970, say: 'The deacon is a minister who serves the priest, and places the oblations on the altar, and reads the gospel, baptizes infants, and distributes the Holy Eucharist, serving in white vestments and living a chaste life. A priest without a deacon has the name of a priest, but not the ministry.'[2] But though, through the whole period of our Catholic history, there were numerous deacons, subdeacons, and inferior clergy who never aspired to a higher grade, yet there were many of the smaller churches where the priest had none to assist him but his clerk. And in later times a deacon was not allowed to give the Holy Eucharist, except in case of necessity.[3]

As regards the frequency of communion, there were the same and perhaps greater extremes then than now. Walafrid Strabo at the beginning of the ninth century makes a review of past times, and gives the customs prevailing in his own day in the church established by St. Boniface. 'Some,' he says, 'thought that they should prepare a whole year for communion,[4] and these usually received on Thursday in Holy Week. But to others it rightly seemed that men would come all the more unworthily to an annual communion by as much as they esteemed themselves purified of all weaknesses by long delay; and these thought that frequent repetition of a holy act would be better, even though the soul be unworthy, since that spiritual medicine both preserves health and cures diseases. Others received only every Sunday, and only on that day said the Lord's prayer, using the word "supersubstantial" instead of "daily." Gradually the custom came in of receiving daily—at least, some

---

few years ago a two-handled chalice of silver, with gold enrichment of exquisite design and workmanship, was found in a field in Ardagh, County Limerick, and is now in the museum of the Irish Academy in Dublin. A facsimile is in the Mayer Museum in Liverpool.

[1] See these tubes described and represented in Rock, i. 164. On the filling up of the chalice, *ibid.*, and also the notes on the Ordo Romanus, Migne, tom. lxxviii. p. 882.

[2] Wilkins, i. 250. [3] Council of York in 1195, Wilkins, i. 501.

[4] Certainly a euphemistic way of putting it. For 'to prepare for a whole year' would mean, in most cases, 'to unfit themselves for a whole year.'

did so. Gennadius neither dared to praise nor blame them. Among the Greeks he who abstained two or three Sundays was excommunicated.' Walafrid in making this review does not conceal his own opinion that frequent communion is more apostolic. But a little further on in the same treatise he shows that the fervour of some had gone to extremes which the Church has since corrected. 'There are some,' he writes, 'who think it enough to communicate once a day, even though they are present at several masses, while others communicate at as many masses as they hear; Quorum neutros culpandos existimo.'[1]

The Church has not had much difficulty in repressing the indiscretions of too frequent communicants, but she has laboured hard and continually, and often to little purpose, to arouse the zeal or remove the mistaken timidity of the opposite class.

When St. Theodore was consulted, he replied that among the Greeks the rule was to communicate every Sunday, and he who abstained for three Sundays was excommunicated. Among the Romans those communicate who will, those who do not are not excommunicated.[2] But of those who were undergoing (public) penance he says:[3] 'According to the canons, penitents should not communicate before the end of their penance, but out of mercy we permit it after a year or six months.'[4] Such were the decisions of one who was chosen by the Pope and sent to England to instruct the young Church of the Anglo-Saxons in Roman practice, and we see from it that the faithful required to be urged on rather than held back.

About a hundred years after the conversion of Northumbria by St. Aidan and St. Oswald, fervour had so cooled that the practice of frequent communion among seculars was unknown in that part of England. In the year 734 Venerable Bede, feeling that his end was coming, drew up a long and very earnest appeal to St. Egbert, the archbishop of York, on the state of the Church in the north of England, on its wants and their remedies. On the subject of Holy Communion his language is very striking. He begs the bishop to send preachers to instruct the people by what works they may please God, and from what sins those who wish to please Him must abstain, with what sincerity of heart they should believe in God, with what devotion they should invoke His clemency, how diligently they should defend themselves and all belonging to them from the attacks of unclean spirits by the sign of our Lord's cross, ' how profitable (*salutaris*)

---

[1] *De reb. eccl.*, Migne, tom. cxiv. pp. 941, 950.
[2] Haddan and Stubbs, iii. 186. [3] *Ib.* p. 187.
[4] A similar mitigation is found among the judgments of St. Willibrord.

is the daily reception of our Lord's Body and Blood to every class of Christians, according to the practice which you well know the Church to uphold throughout Italy, Gaul, Africa, Greece, and the whole East.' It must not be thought that Venerable Bede was urging the indiscriminate practice of daily communion. He says that the people must be instructed that there is no *class* of Christians to whom it is not profitable, if the individuals of that class would prepare themselves for it. That this is his meaning is clear both from his appeal to the practice of other countries, and from his own words, for he goes on immediately as follows : ' This kind of piety and devout consecration of oneself to God is so alien to the customs of almost all the laity of our province, on account of the negligence of their teachers, and is so perfectly strange to them, that even those among them who appear most religious only venture to communicate in the holy mysteries at Christmas, the Epiphany, and Easter. And yet there are innumerable boys and girls, young men and maidens, old men and women, of most chaste life, who, beyond all doubt or controversy, might be allowed to communicate in the heavenly mysteries every Sunday, and also on the feasts of the apostles and martyrs, as you yourself have seen them do in the Holy Roman and Apostolic Church. Even the married people, if they would observe the ecclesiastical discipline of continence, might be permitted to do the same, and would indeed gladly do it.'[1]

We do not know what fruit this letter produced in the North. In the southern province of Canterbury, three years after its date, a great council assembled at Clovesho, at which, besides the archbishop, were present the bishops of London, Rochester, Leicester, Lichfield, Winchester, Sherborne, Dunwich, Worcester, Lindsey, and Selsey. One of the objects of their solicitude was communion. First the members of monasteries and all ecclesiastics (*i.e.* the clergy, not priests, and the lay monks and nuns) are warned to keep themselves always fit to receive the Holy Communion of our Lord's Flesh and Blood, and the superiors are ordered to see carefully that none of their subjects live so unworthily as to deserve to be deprived of communion, or be indifferent about confession and amendment of life. Should any such be found, they must be sharply corrected. Then, passing to the communion of the laity, the council says : ' Youths of the laity, not yet corrupted by the temptations to which their age is prone,[2] are to be exhorted often to communicate. Even

---

[1] Inter *Op.* Bedæ, vol. vi., ed. Giles ; also Haddan and Stubbs, iii. 314.

[2] 'Laici pueri qui necdum lascivientis ætatis corruptela sint vitiati.' Perhaps : ' Boys too young to have been yet corrupted by the sins of youth.'

those who are older, whether unmarried or married, if they cease to sin, are to be admonished frequently to go to communion, lest they faint for want of that saving food and drink, since our Lord says: "Unless you eat the Flesh of the Son of Man and drink His Blood, you shall have no life remaining in you."[1] On the subject of communion among the Anglo-Saxons a canon is found in Johnson, Wilkins, and Thorpe, and attributed to Archbishop Ælfric in 994. But, as I have observed before, these canons are really by Theodulf of Orleans in the eighth century, and, though translated by Ælfric, there is no proof that they were enacted in England as obligatory. They were perhaps merely put out as a good rule to be followed. However this may be, the 41st Canon enacts that all who are not excommunicated' (*i.e.*, I suppose, deprived of communion while they are performing public penance) 'shall receive communion every Sunday in Lent, and also on the three days before Easter, as well as every day of Easter week.'[2] I do not find any trace of such a practice as this in English history, and, had it been really introduced by Ælfric, the Council of Ænham in 1009 would scarcely have said simply, 'Every Christian must make his confession humbly and diligently; and he must get ready for communion three times a year.'[3] An exactly similar law was enacted under Canute in 1032.[4]

To these general rules a few particulars may be added. And first it must be remembered that during several centuries it was the custom throughout the entire Church to give communion to infants. It was given directly after baptism. St. Paulinus has the following lines:

> Inde parens sacro ducit de fonte sacerdos
> Infantes niveo corpore, corde, habitu;
> Circumdansque rudes sacris altaribus agnos
> Cara salutiferis imbuit ora cibis.

And Raban Maur teaches the same thing in the ninth century.[5] Communion was given to infants in the species of wine alone. The priest dipped his finger into the chalice, and then put it in the mouth of the child. This was done not only on the day of baptism, but also for a whole week: 'Ye shall housel children when they are bap-

---

[1] Haddan and Stubbs, iii. 370.

[2] These last words may be otherwise understood, that the whole of Easter week is to be kept as a holiday like Easter Day itself.

[3] Spelman, i. 511; Wilkins, i. 285.

[4] Spelman, i. 539; Wilkins, i. 299. Dr. Lingard, *A. S.* ii. ch. 10, p. 79, in note, says: 'St. Peter's festival was a day of general communion.' I suppose he must mean in monasteries.

[5] St. Paulin. *Ep.* 12 ad Sever.; Raban, *De Cler. Inst.* i. 29, 30.

tized, and let them be carried to mass, that they be houselled all the seven days, whilst they are unwashed,'[1] *i.e.* till the removal of the chrismal or linen cap put on after the anointing, which was worn for seven days. When it was removed the head was washed with salt and water.

Either immediately after baptism or while still infants they were confirmed by the bishop, and, according to Archbishop Egbert's Pontifical, were then to receive communion (*modo communicandi sunt de sacrificio*).[2] How often in England they continued to receive before attaining the age of reason, or whether they did so at all, I have not been able to discover. That they received when still very little children is proved by a canon of St. Willibrord : 'If any communicate after breaking his fast, let him do penance for seven days on bread and water. But let little children, if they do so, be flogged.'[3]

This canon brings us to the question of preparation for communion and the dispositions for receiving it worthily. One of these was that it should be received before partaking of any natural food ; and the penance for infringing this rule imposed by St. Theodore was the same as St. Willibrord's, viz. a rigid fast of seven days. In renewing this prohibition in the tenth century, the canon mentions an exception, which had, however, always been granted, in favour of those who were in dangerous sickness, *i.e.* a sickness which was thought to be their last. Otherwise the rule regarding fasting admitted no dispensation, however severely it might press on the celebrant or the communicant. It has been said already that the fast of Lent lasted until near sunset. But there was one day on which the fast was still more prolonged, and yet it was the great communion day. Raban Maur, at the beginning of the ninth century, thus describes the ceremonies of Holy Saturday, or the Vigil of Easter. There was no morning mass, but as evening drew on (*die inclinante ad vesperam*) began the blessing of the Paschal candle, the long prayers and baptisms. These could not have taken less than three hours. Then, after baptism and the litanies, followed the celebration of mass and the communion of the Body and Blood of the Lord. 'If anyone abstain from communion this night, I do not know how I can call him a Christian, except those who are excom-

---

[1] Thorpe, ii. 392.

[2] The custom of confirming infants continued to the Reformation, but not that of giving them communion.

[3] 'Parvuli de hoc vapulent.'—*Judicium Clementis* (*i.e.* S. Willibrordi). Haddan and Stubbs, iii. 227.

municated for capital crimes, and are doing penance.'[1] Thus, then, they observed the most rigid fast till perhaps eight or nine o'clock in the evening (according to our computation of time), besides the fatigue of the three or four hours of prayer. But it must be remembered that Easter Day began at sunset, so that this late communion of Holy Saturday was then counted as the Easter communion. The Easter Day masses were not sung till after sunrise, and those communicated again who would. By degrees the late communion of Holy Saturday fell into disuse, and the obligation was transferred to the Sunday morning.[2] It would seem that throughout the whole of this period, as now, the time for beginning the fast was counted from midnight.[3]

With regard to bodily fitness for holy communion, I will merely add that one of the decisions of St. Theodore was: 'Women must receive communion clothed with a black veil, as St. Basil decreed.'[4]

It is far more important to know what was taught regarding spiritual fitness for participation in the spiritual banquet. It is certain that the morality of a Catholic population will depend on the manner in which men approach this sacrament, for on that also will depend the fruits they derive from it. Carelessness on the part of the pastors in instructing the people on this subject may lead to either of two contrary extremes. It may be the cause that the people, as Venerable Bede complained—for he laid the blame on the clergy[5]—while retaining a high reverence for the Blessed Sacrament, will think that frequent communion is only for the clergy or for monks and nuns, and so will approach it rarely, with the necessary result of loss of grace and careless lives. On the other hand, want of proper instruction on its sanctity may lead to careless and indevout frequentation, and even to profanation and sacrilege. We shall find mention of this at a later period, when again the blame was laid on the pastors.

---

[1] *De Cler. Inst.* lib. ii. cap. 38. He says nothing about another communion on Easter morning. So St. Augustine speaks on Easter Day to those who had been baptized the evening before, and after baptism had received communion: 'cujus (i.e. *mensæ Dominicæ sacramenti*) nocte præterita participes facti estis.' (*Serm.* 227.)

[2] I do not find this stated by any liturgical writer, but by this supposition alone can I reconcile the various documents of different dates.

[3] The ceremonies of Holy Week will be described in a subsequent chapter, so far as they regard the Blessed Sacrament.

[4] Haddan and Stubbs, iii. 203. I pass over purposely certain other questions bearing on this point; they would be out of place in a treatise such as this.

[5] 'Per incuriam docentium.'

It was the intention of our Divine Redeemer, in leaving us this sacred feast, to place His children in a kind of holy dilemma. Like St. Peter, at one moment they are tempted to cry out : ' Depart from me, O Lord, for I am a sinful man !' and yet, when asked seriously by our Lord : ' Will you also leave Me ?' they are obliged to answer, ' Lord, to whom shall we go ? Thou hast the words of eternal life.' Thus a holy self-love struggles with a holy fear of self, and a holy love of God's goodness with a holy fear of His sanctity, until the soul, under the Church's teaching, arrives at this solution. It learns that though we have a High Priest ' holy, innocent, undefiled, separated from sinners, and made higher than the heavens,' yet He is also 'the Lamb of God who taketh away the sins of the world ;' and being both Priest and Victim, and offering Himself continually to His eternal Father, 'He is able also to save for ever them that come to God by Him, always living to make intercession for us.'[1] The sinner must then draw near to Him, but does so in order to be cleansed. Being cleansed he must still draw near, and nearer still, for greater purity and in order not to relapse. He draws near to Him as his Redeemer in the sacrament of penance, he draws near again in the sacrament of His Body and Blood. Unless he does this, he has no life in Him. If he does it unworthily, he eats and drinks his own judgment, not discerning the Body of the Lord. ' Let a man then prove himself, and so let him eat of that bread and drink of the chalice.'[2] This is the issue of the dilemma. And when both sides of it are earnestly and prudently pressed upon a Christian population—when the holiness of Christ, which cannot be exaggerated, is so represented as not to deter the timid, and the mercy of God is so stated as not to encourage the presumptuous—then all that there is of faith and hope and love and fear in the hearts of Christians, prompts them to turn from sin, and fly from themselves to Him who is at once their Redeemer and their God, the Way, the Truth, and the Life.

Happily there were not wanting, at any age of the Anglo-Saxon Church, prelates and priests, like Bede and Egbert, Boniface and Dunstan, on whom rested the spirit of St. John Baptist, the 'friend of the Bridegroom.' Their hearts leaped for joy within them when they saw the Bride preparing herself for Him. They were so little and so sinful in their own eyes that they deemed themselves unworthy to stoop down and loose the latchet of His shoe. They thought no purity too great for him who has to perform the least ceremony about the altar. Yet being sent before His face to pre-

[1] Heb. vii. 25, 26.   [2] 1 Cor. xi. 28, 29.

pare a way for Him, like St. John the Baptist, they did not require from the people what they exacted from themselves. Austere to themselves to a degree that fills us with awe when we read of it, they required of the multitude only to flee from the wrath to come, and to bring forth fruits worthy of penance. In proportioning those works they knew the difference between the Publican and the Pharisee, and, like St. John, they had their answer for the soldier as well as for the civilian.[1]

I cannot enter into details regarding the penitential system of those days. It is enough to say that its life and power was faith in the Blessed Sacrament of the Altar, and the necessity of being in the grace and friendship of God before feeding on His Flesh and Blood. Bread that is put in the mouth of a corpse is wasted. When the Bread of Life is given to a soul dead and separated by sin from God, who is its true Life, that Divine Food is profaned, and the soul is burdened with the guilt of sacrilege. On the other hand, Jesus Christ is the Physician of souls, and His Flesh and Blood are the medicine of the feeble and diseased. None of these principles has ever been forgotten in the Church. But as the medical art, though always pursuing the same ends, varies in different ages, according as new diseases appear, or according to the climate and the habits and constitution of the body, so the Church varies her discipline according to the need of souls, often requiring not what is best, but what is possible, and taking heed of the faith and character and circumstances of men. Raban Maur thus states the discipline which St. Boniface had brought from England and left to the German Church : ' Penance must be public for public sins, and last as long as the bishop appoints, according to the variety of sins, and the absolution must be public, by the bishop or priest delegated by him. When the crime has been thus public and scandalized the whole Church, the absolution (*manus impositio*) is given before the high altar. But when the sins have been secret and have been revealed by spontaneous confession to the priest only or to the bishop, then the penance should be secret, according to the judgment of the priest or bishop, lest the weak in the Church be scandalized, seeing punishment, but knowing nothing of the cause. The usual time for absolution is Thursday in Holy Week (*Cœna Domini*), but, in case of sickness and danger, absolution and communion must be given at once. And in general the priest must attend to the confession, penance, and compunction of his penitent, and give him absolution when he has properly satisfied for his sins.'[2]

[1] Luke iii. 10–14.   [2] *De Cler. Inst.* lib. ii. cap. 30.

So, too, St. Theodore declared. 'The Romans reconcile, *i.e.* absolve, the sinner in the apse. The Greeks do not. The absolution of sinners on Holy Thursday is given by the bishop only, and at the completion of the penance. But if the bishop is hindered he can delegate power to the priest. But there is no such public reconciliation in this province, because penance is not public here.'[1] Perhaps public penance was introduced later on, since the form of solemn penance and reconciliation is given in Egbert's Pontifical and elsewhere. But as the bishop could on that day be only in his cathedral, this was an exceptional case, and the ordinary administration of the sacrament of penance was by the parish priest. Indeed, the parish was called the shrift-shire.

To induce the faithful to open their hearts in confession, arguments were made use of exactly similar to those which are common at the present day among Catholics. Thus, to take two passages from the sermons of St. Boniface. At one time he appeals to fear: 'It is better to confess our sins to one man than at the tremendous judgment-day to have them published before the three assemblies of heaven, earth, and hell, and to be put to shame for our sins, and that too not for amendment, but for eternal punishment.'[2]

At another time the appeal is made to hope: 'If anyone falls into any sin, let him quickly rise by confession, and cleanse himself by penance, for the mercy of God is rich in pardon to the penitent if he will turn to the way of justice, as the prophet says: I desire not the death of the sinner, but that he be converted and live.'[3]

So two hundred years later, in 1009, when the Danes were overrunning the land, the Council of Ænham exhorted the people to have recourse to penance and holy communion:[4] 'Let every Christian, as the most necessary exercise of his faith and Christian profession, frequently go to his confessor, and, laying aside shame, confess his sins and diligently accomplish the satisfaction imposed upon him by the priest. Let him also reverently prepare to receive the Holy Eucharist as often as it may seem necessary to him, but at least three times a year.' Such was the language of councils and of saints. But though confession was, then as now, obligatory on all who had been guilty of grievous sin, it was not strictly required before each communion from those who were leading pious lives. Thus the canons translated by Archbishop Ælfric say: 'The people are to be exhorted to prepare themselves for communion by prayer, fasting, alms, and good works. It is very dangerous either to receive

---

[1] Haddan and Stubbs, iii. 187.
[2] S. Bonif. *Sermon* 4, p. 851.
[3] *Id., Sermon* 3, p. 849.
[4] Can. 20; Wilkins, i. 285.

negligently, or, on the other hand, to abstain from receiving too long. No one should receive without the permission of his confessor and after confession and repentance. There are, however, many monks and widows of so holy and religious a life, that they may receive every day when they will.'[1] Raban Maur makes a similar distinction: 'Some say that the Eucharist should be taken every day, unless sin prevents; and they say well, if they receive with devotion and humility and not trusting in their justice and with proud presumption. But if the crimes are such as to remove the soul as of one dead from the altar, penance must be first done.'[2]

I will here add a few words regarding the practice of confessing venial sins in the earlier ages of the Church. It has been ever taught that sins are not only different in kind, according to their object, and varying indefinitely in degrees of malice, but that they differ fundamentally in their effect on the soul, some bringing immediate spiritual death or separation from God, others inflicting wounds more or less severe, but not immediately fatal, and cooling, though not dissolving, the friendship of God. When our Lord compares one sin to a mote of dust settling in the eye, and another to a great beam of wood, He indicates this enormous difference. But still more plainly, when He bade the sinner to 'go and sin no more,' He taught that there are crimes which all men, by the help of the grace offered to them, must and can avoid, whereas it is certain that He never supposed that either those to whom He gave this command, or His own immediate and beloved disciples, were free from all stain of guilt. For such human frailties He provided a daily remedy in His divine prayer: 'Forgive us our trespasses;' and especially in the fulfilment of the condition on which we offer that prayer: 'As we forgive them that trespass against us.' Our Lord is generally understood to allude to the minor defilements contracted in our course through life, when He said to His Apostle St. Peter just before washing His feet: 'He that is washed needeth not but to wash his feet, but is clean wholly. And you are clean, but not all; for He knew who he was that would betray Him.'[3] By this mystical act performed before the institution of the Blessed Sacrament of His Body and Blood, He taught the purity with which we should approach it, not being satisfied with freedom from grievous sins, but seeking even to cleanse ourselves from daily faults.

But the Church has also uniformly taught that whereas the sacrament of Penance is necessary, where it can be had, for the pardon of

---

[1] Canon 44; Wilkins, i. 265.   [2] *De Cler. Inst.* lib. i. 31.
[3] John xiii. 10, 11.

grievous sins committed after baptism, lesser sins obtain pardon more easily, and are, therefore, commonly called venial. They might be submitted to the keys of the Church at the devotion of the penitent, but there was no strict obligation of thus seeking their remission. It need not then surprise any to learn that, as the researches of modern scholars seem to have proved, for some centuries the practice of confession of venial sins was by no means so frequent as it now is, even on the part of those who often approached the altar.

It seems to me that there has been some exaggeration on this subject, and that authors have taken the first mention of a practice, in this as in many cases, as indicating its recent introduction. Yet on the one hand we know that from the ninth to the sixteenth century communion became much less frequent, even among nuns, than it had been previously; and on the other hand we are assured that the practice of confessing venial sins only began to spread, so far as it did spread at all, just about the same period.[1]

It is not meant that all those who approached Holy Communion only two or three times a year had mortal sins on their souls before they went to their confessors. The testimony of Venerable Bede is very different, and he gives, as a reason for granting them more frequent communion, the purity and innocence of their lives. And in the case of such as those it is certain that they were accustomed to make confession, and did not approach the altar without leave of their confessors. These, then, are cases of confession of merely venial sins. When, however, it is stated that the practice was rare, it is meant that those who went frequently and almost daily to communion were not accustomed to make weekly or fortnightly sacramental confessions. I add the word 'sacramental,' because Venerable Bede in the eighth century, and Jonas of Orleans in the ninth, while teaching that mortal sins must be confessed to a priest, recommend all Christians to confess their venial sins one to another. This was then done, and is still done, in religious communities, as regards breaches of the rule, in what is called the Chapter of Faults.

Yet it must not be supposed that the practice of frequent devotional confession, at least in monasteries,[2] was either unknown or little esteemed. The following history would alone prove the contrary.

---

[1] See St. Alphonsus in his *Apology for Frequent Communion* (tom. ii. p. 148, Monza ed.) Mabillon, Martene, Alexander Natalis, are all agreed. See treatise on the subject by Father E. Carpentier, the Bollandist, in *Acta SS.* tom. lvii. p. 720.

[2] In 1340, the author of the *Ayenbite of Inwyt* exhorts both men and women of the world to frequent shrift of their venial sins. He does not treat of communion. (See p. 178, ed. of the E. E. T. Society.)

St. Boniface in a letter gives an account of one who apparently died and was judged and came to life again.[1] For the purpose for which I quote this testimony it matters nothing whether the death or vision really occurred, since a vision, especially if it is an imagination, must be in harmony with the customs of the day. The man then related that, when his soul passed from his body, he heard himself accused of all the sins committed since his youth, which he had either neglected to confess or forgotten, or had not understood to be sins. Some of these are mentioned, as vainglory, boasting, lies, idle words, obstinacy, and disobedience to spiritual superiors, sluggishness in holy studies, wandering thoughts in or out of church, laziness in getting up, needless journeys, and other similar faults, which he had neglected to confess. It is clear, then, that it was understood by St. Boniface, and in general in his time, that such faults were proper matter of confession, and that there was negligence in not confessing them. Besides, on being sent back to life, he is told to confess all those neglected sins to a certain priest. He was also commanded to tell the priest that for many years he had worn an iron circle round his loins for the love of God, and unknown to anyone; by which it is certainly indicated that even to undertake penance, without the approbation of superiors or spiritual directors, was considered to involve an imperfection.

This vision of judgment naturally introduces another phase of our subject, viz. the last communion, made in preparation for death. But I will treat of this in a separate chapter.

[1] *Op. S. Bonif.*, Migne, tom. lxxxix. pp. 713-720.

CHAPTER XVII.

VIATICUM AND RESERVATION.

The communion made in immediate preparation for death was called in Latin *Viaticum*, in Anglo-Saxon *Weg-nest*, both words signifying provision for a journey. In describing the death of the holy widow Elgiva, Osbern says that she begged St. Dunstan to say mass in her room, that she might receive the Body and Blood of Christ, that so, 'being fortified by those life-giving mysteries, she might not be ashamed when she should speak with her enemies in the gate.'[1] These words of the Psalmist thus applied, either by Elgiva or by Osbern, to the holy Viaticum, very happily express the belief of Christians that nothing can better strengthen us for the dread encounter with our spiritual foes than to have just received devoutly the Body and Blood of Him who conquered them and redeemed us from their slavery. So, too, nothing can give us greater confidence to meet our Lord Himself in His Majesty than to have humbly and faithfully welcomed Him in His hidden mystery. It is in these last moments of life that the sincerity and reality of faith are tested, and it often appears, by the unmistakable love then expressed, what hidden treasures of grace have been accumulated during the unrecorded communions of many years.

A few examples of beautiful deaths shall here be related as specimens of the millions which have found no historians and which are reserved for revelation in eternity. To understand these better, we should know what were the regulations of the Church on the subject of Viaticum.

During the Anglo-Saxon period it was allowed to celebrate mass in the chamber of the dying person, and thus to communicate him directly from the altar. St. Dunstan said mass near the bedside of Elgiva, and he also received his last communion when mass was being

---

[1] See Osbern's *Life of St. Dunstan*, *Acta SS.* tom. xvi. 349; also *Memorials of St. Dunstan*, pp. 20 and 88 (Rolls Series). I have alluded to the death of this lady in Ch. X. p. 147, note. The words employed by Osbern are from Ps. cxxvi. 5.

offered by his death-bed.¹ But to offer mass the priest must of necessity be fasting, and he was often called to administer the dying when he had broken his fast, or when for various reasons he could not celebrate the Holy Sacrifice near to the sick person. In such cases the Blessed Sacrament was brought from the church where it was always reserved for this very purpose. Missionaries travelling far from any church were ordered carefully and reverently to carry with them the Blessed Eucharist in readiness for the dying.

The Pontifical, commonly called Leofric's Missal, gives the following directions for administering the Viaticum : 'As soon as they see that the sick person is coming to his end, the holy housel must be administered to him, even if he has eaten that same day ; for communion will be his defence and help in the resurrection of the just, and will itself raise him up. After he has received communion the Passion of our Lord will be read to him by priests or deacons till his death.'

Priests were very strictly commanded by various councils to take care that no one died without the Viaticum of our Lord's Body.² It is called by St. Boniface 'the last and *necessary* viaticum ;' and that great prelate commanded that it should be given to one insensible who might have expressed a desire of it before : 'If a penitent being sick ask penitence, and when the priest arrives has lost his speech or is out of his mind, let those who were present testify to his desire ; and if he is thought very near death, let him be absolved by imposition of hands, and the Eucharist poured into his mouth.' In this case a small particle of the sacred Host was put into some wine, and thus he was made to swallow it, or, if it could be done conveniently, he might be communicated with the species of wine only. But in spite of the great authority of St. Boniface the practice of administering those who were insensible was rightly discountenanced, as somewhat inconsistent with the nature of this sacrament. The thirty-first of Ælfric's canons says : 'They will give the housel to the sick if they are able to swallow, but not to a man who is half dead, for Christ meant that men should *eat it as food*.'

There is reason to fear that, in spite of the protest of the canons in favour of a contrary practice, Viaticum was not usually granted to criminals condemned to death, from an opinion that it would be irreverent to our Lord to hang a man who had just received His sacred Body. And yet the hope was not rejected that one who was by his crimes considered unfit to live longer on earth might by true penance live eternally in heaven. Among the laws of Edward the Elder

---

¹ See Chap. XIV. p. 199. ² 65th Canon of St. Dunstan.

(A.D. 905), one is that criminals condemned to death may always have a confessor,[1] but nothing is said regarding communion. Mere silence would of course be no proof that communion was refused; but Giraldus in the twelfth century complained that by a great abuse the practice was to deny both the Holy Eucharist and ecclesiastical burial to those who had been hanged.[2]

No such prejudice existed against giving holy communion to soldiers about to fight. The Peterborough Chronicler relates how the patriot ealdorman, Algar, during the invasion of Lincolnshire by the northern pirates in 870, gathered a small band of brave men to resist them, and how they spent the night in prayer, confessing and receiving holy communion, which, from their small numbers, they expected would be their viaticum. And so the event too truly proved.[3]

It is only in a case where death is expected from sickness, not when life is in danger from accident or violence, that the sacrament of Extreme Unction can be administered. With regard to that sacrament all that need here be said is that the order of precedence has somewhat varied in different ages. Since about the thirteenth century it has been the rule that the Viaticum should be given before the sacrament of Extreme Unction, unless there is some reason to the contrary. Before that time Extreme Unction was generally given first.[4]

Dr. Rock has, I think, been wanting in his wonted accuracy when he says that 'the sick person received extreme unction once only in every illness, but the Holy Eucharist every day till he died.'[5] He refers to the 'Concordia' of St. Dunstan, which lays down the rule for monks, and it is not improbable that a dying monk often did receive Viaticum daily. But this could not be the case with the majority of Christians. There was no prohibition, however, against repeating the Viaticum.

In monasteries in St. Dunstan's time, the holy Viaticum was brought daily after tierce by the priest who had celebrated the conventual mass. Taking off his chasuble, he carried the Eucharist to the sick. His assistants preceded him with lights and incense, the whole community following, singing psalms, litanies, and prayers. Bede has described many beautiful deaths of monks and nuns, and, though he is not explicit on the subject, it would seem that Viaticum

---

[1] Wilkins, i. 203.
[2] *Gemma Eccl.* dist. i. cap. 40.
[3] Printed in Dugdale, i. 68. 'Sumpto sacro viatico' are the words.
[4] See Mabillon's notes to the *Ordo Romanus*, Migne, tom. lxxviii. p. 928.
[5] *Church of our Fathers*, ii. 454.

was received but once, and generally deferred until the near approach of death.

It is certain that Viaticum might be lawfully administered under either species or under both. The mention by an author of the Body and Blood is no proof that the Eucharist was given under both species, since it was most certainly believed that our Lord's Body and Blood, united to His soul and Divinity, were received by him who participated in either species. St. Cuthbert, a few hours before his death, was carried into the oratory of his hermitage in the island of Farne and placed near the altar. His prose life says 'he prepared for death by the communion of our Lord's Body and Blood;' the metrical life, that 'reclining near the altar he tasted the draught of life and prepared for his journey upwards with the Blood of Christ.' Dr. Bright says : ' It is certain that he received communion in both kinds, and clearly not during mass ... both kinds being kept ready on the altar.' This may have been so, but to me it is quite uncertain. Midnight had just passed, and it is not improbable that the abbot who administered the dying bishop waited till that hour to say mass, since there was an altar. And in any case the words of Bede's metrical life make it probable that he received the precious Blood only, a few drops being poured into his mouth. The expression of the prose life that he received the Body and Blood proves nothing, since Bede distinctly says of a little boy that he received *Viaticum corporis et sanguinis Dominici*, and yet that he only received *Dominicæ oblationis particulam*. Dr. Bright, with his usual candour, admits that 'in certain cases the chalice was not reserved.'[1]

Death comes at all hours, and the Viaticum could be received at all hours. St. Hilda, whose death is described by Bede, received Viaticum about cock-crowing;[2] Cædmon just after midnight.[3] St. Bennet Biscop dies during the night: 'A priest reads the Gospel to him, as had been done on other nights (for he was sleepless); the sacrament of the Body and Blood of the Lord is given to him as Viaticum when his death draws near, and amidst the prayers and psalms of his brethren he breathes out his soul.'[4]

How gladly we should have learned the devotion which he, who wrote these things, himself manifested to the Divine Viaticum when his own hour came ! But though we have one of the most simple

---

[1] *Chapters of Early English Church History*, pp. 344 and 278. The cases tha Dr. Bright refers to are those of Cædmon and of the little boy. See the story of this child's death in Ch. VI. p. 95 of the present work, or in Bede, iv. 14.

[2] iv. 23. [3] iv. 24. [4] Beda, *Vita quinque Abbatum*, lib. ii.

and charming descriptions that has perhaps ever been penned of his last days, the monk, who wrote hurriedly, as he says, for his brother monk, has not mentioned the circumstances of Bede's reception of the sacraments. This is a curious warning how cautious we should be in drawing conclusions by mere negative arguments. Silence like this in earlier centuries would often be taken as conclusive proof that Viaticum and Extreme Unction were then unknown. It would be said that the saint died after long and calm preparation, in full possession of his senses; and that a constant watcher by his bedside has described every minute detail of those days, and yet has said nothing whatever of the sacraments. Could it be then, it would be asked triumphantly, that they were known in his time? But I suppose no one will be bold enough to argue thus about Bede, who has described so many deathbeds, and whose works are so full of proofs of his love and adoration for the Divine Sacrament, and whose most earnest request in dying was that his brother priests 'would celebrate masses and pray diligently for him.' A few passages, however, from this description will show how sweetly they can die, who with a lively faith in the cleansing pains of purgatory—and in this faith Bede has hardly been surpassed—unite an equally lively faith in the power of the Viaticum here and holy masses after death.

'About a fortnight before Easter he was reduced to a state of great weakness, with difficulty of breathing, but without much pain, and in this condition he lasted till the day of our Lord's Ascension, (May 26). This time he passed cheerfully and joyfully, giving thanks to God both by day and by night, or rather at all hours of the day and night.... I can declare with truth that I never saw with my eyes, nor heard with my ears, of any man who was so indefatigable in giving thanks to the living God. He chanted the passage, "It is a dreadful thing to fall into the hands of the living God,"[1] warning us to throw off all torpor of soul, in consideration of our last hour.... He also chanted the antiphon, "O King of glory, Lord of hosts, who on this day didst ascend in triumph above all the heavens, leave us not orphans, but send us the spirit of truth, the promised of the Father, Alleluia." When he came to the words, "leave us not orphans," he burst into tears and wept much; and after a time he resumed where he had broken off, and we who heard him wept with him.' ... (He dictated to his scholars to the last, and sent, as has been said, for the priests, and made them promise to say masses and pray for him after death.) 'When they heard him say that they would see him no more in this world, all burst into tears, but their tears were tempered

[1] Heb. x. 31.

with joy when he said : "It is time that I return to Him who made me out of nothing. I have lived long, and kindly hath my merciful Judge forecast the course of my life for me. The time of my dissolution is at hand. I wish to be released, and to be with Christ." In this way he continued to speak cheerfully till sunset, when the forementioned youth said : "Beloved master, there is still one sentence unwritten." "Then write quickly," said Beda. In a few minutes the youth said, "It is finished." "Thou hast spoken truly," replied Beda; "take my head between thy hands, for it is my delight to sit opposite to that holy place in which I used to pray; let me sit and invoke my Father." Sitting thus on the pavement of his cell, and repeating "Glory be to the Father, and to the Son, and to the Holy Ghost,"—as he finished the word "Ghost," he breathed his last, and took his departure for heaven.'

In spite of this conviction on the part of the narrator, he expresses his great satisfaction at the beginning of his letter at the news his correspondent had sent him, 'that masses and holy prayers are diligently performed for Beda, the beloved of God,' in the monastery where he was dwelling. Confidence in God's mercy made Bede anxious that every means should be taken to implore that mercy for himself, and confidence in Bede's holiness did not prevent his friends from obeying his request.[1]

To these deaths of holy monks I will add one of a pious layman. Æthelwine, ealdorman of the East Angles, is known in history as the 'friend of God.'[2] He was the great protector of the monks after the death of King Edgar. He had been for many years the most intimate friend of St. Oswald, archbishop of York, and had founded the abbey of Ramsey in Huntingdonshire, and watched over its growth in union with that prelate. St. Oswald died at Worcester in 992, in the very act of washing the feet of the poor. When the news reached Ramsey, Æthelwine was there with his two sons, but, after taking part with many tears in the solemn prayers that were offered for the soul of his holy friend, he never smiled again. Nor did he long survive him. One Sunday, feeling, from his sufferings, that his end was drawing near, he made his confession, was anointed and received holy communion from the hands of St. Elphege, bishop of Winchester, and Germanus, abbot of Winchelcombe, in Gloucestershire. Afterwards he begged that the monks who were there might come to his bedside and solace him by singing the Psalms which he knew. He tried

---

[1] Cuthbert's letter is printed with Bede's works by Stevenson, Giles, Migne, and others. I have followed Dr. Lingard's translation.

[2] Freeman's *Old English History*, p. 182.

to join with them; when they sang 'Laudate Dominum in cymbalis,' he added, 'omnis spiritus laudet Dominum' (let every soul praise the Lord), and repeated the words three times; then making the sign of the cross with his right hand, with his left he closed his eyelids and so passed away.[1]

To complete this subject I must say a few words about the reservation of the Blessed Sacrament. From the faith of the Catholic Church that the presence of our Divine Lord is due to the words of consecration, when pronounced by a priest with due intention, and not to the faith of celebrant or recipient, it follows that that Presence is permanent as long as the sacred species remain incorrupt. When, through the action of physical causes, they cease to possess the qualities of bread and wine, and therefore cease to be the signs chosen by our Lord, His substantial Presence ceases also. Hence two duties are imposed on the priests to whom our Lord has committed this sacred Deposit. They must preserve it carefully and reverently, and they must take care not to keep it too long, or in such a manner that the sacred species would corrupt. On these points we have several regulations of Anglo-Saxon prelates.

The Venerable Bede in his genuine Penitential declares that priests, 'when they go among the people far from a church, should take the Holy Eucharist with them.'[2] One of the decrees of St. Boniface was that 'no priest should be on a journey without the holy chrism and blessed oil, and the sacred Eucharist, so that, wherever he may chance to be wanted, he may be found ready at once for his functions.'[3] It is certain that, when the Eucharist was thus carried on journeys, it was under the species of bread alone.

The priest was also commanded to reserve the Blessed Sacrament in his own church, in case it should be wanted suddenly by the dying, since this frequently happened when he was not fasting and therefore could not say mass.[4]

The place and manner of reservation varied in the early ages. Sometimes it was the sacristy, sometimes the high altar, sometimes the baptistery, sometimes the monastic infirmary; and on a journey the priest would carry it suspended round his neck, or deposit it wherever it could be placed with safety and reverence.

It appears from the Ordines Romani that from a very early age the custom was observed of reserving a particle of the sacred Host consecrated by the Pope or by a bishop. This was afterwards carried to the sacristy and there reserved until the next celebration,

---

[1] *Vita S. Oswaldi*, p. 474, in *Historians of York* (Rolls Series, 1879).
[2] Haddan and Stubbs, iii. 329.   [3] *Ubi supra*, p. 821.   [4] Thorpe, ii. 252.

when it was solemnly carried before the Pontiff and placed upon the altar. He consumed this particle at his communion, and replaced it by another. But from the second Ordo we learn that sometimes the place of reservation for this particle was not the sacristy, but the altar.[1] Both these customs appear to have been followed in England. Hence Husel-portic or Sacrament-porch is one of the Anglo-Saxon names for the sacristy. When the place chosen for reservation was the altar, the Blessed Sacrament was generally suspended under the stone canopy or ciborium which was built over the high altar.

On the Continent at least, there are instances of an ark or chest for reception of the Holy Eucharist having been constructed under the altar-table.

We have seen the penalty inflicted on Irish and British priests for carelessness in carrying the Divine Deposit. Similar penalties were appointed by St. Egbert—for allowing a particle to fall to the ground, a day's fast; but for losing it, either forty days, or three forties, or a whole year, according to the degree of negligence.[2] St. Theodore had already made similar decisions. St. Oswald of York[3] imposed a series of fines for this and other negligences, the proceeds of which were applied to pious works.[4]

If the Blessed Sacrament were ever reserved too long so as to corrupt, it was to be burnt, and the ashes placed under the altar; but a penance was imposed of from twenty to forty days on the careless priest.[5]

From an epistle of Abbot Ælfric to Wulfstan, archbishop of York, in 1003, it appears that some priests were accustomed to reserve for the sick, during a whole year, particles consecrated on Easter Day. This custom was reproved as a superstition and an abuse, and they were ordered to renew the sacrament every seven days or fortnight.[6] It is curious that some Protestant writers[7] should be able

---

[1] See Mabillon's notes on the *Liber Sacram*. Migne, tom. lxxviii. p. 933.
[2] Haddan and Stubbs, iii. 417.   [3] Spelman, i. 495.
[4] Concil. Ænham. can. 31; Spelman, i. 511; Wilkins, i. 285. Even when fines were inflicted by secular magistrates for sins against God, in the place of, or in addition to, spiritual penalties, they were left to the disposal of the bishop, who, however, might not apply them to any secular purpose, but, as the canon states, 'for prayers, the relief of the poor, reparation of churches, the instruction of the people, the purchase of books and vestments, and other pious uses.'
[5] St. Theodore's Penit.; St. Egbert's Penit.; St. Dunstan's Canons (the 38th).
[6] Canons of Archbishop Ælfric, Thorpe ii. 361.
[7] Foxe (*Book of Martyrs*, v. 277) quotes Abbot Ælfric's Epistle against these abuses as if it were a proof against the Real Presence. It is hard to see whether he relies on the abuses themselves or on their correction.

to see in such facts as these arguments against the Real Presence, and even against the faith in the Real Presence of the Anglo-Saxons. The very superstition last named came from an unenlightened reverence, as if what was consecrated on Easter Day had a special virtue; but even when abuses proceed from irreverence, surely carelessness and disbelief are two very different things—unless indeed we are prepared to maintain that everyone who forgets God's Presence is an atheist, or everyone who neglects to prepare for death is convinced that he will never die!

The vessel in which the Blessed Sacrament was kept—sometimes called repositorium, sometimes the chrismal, sometimes the eucharistial, sometimes known by other names [1]—had a special blessing, which by its wording expresses the faith of those who used it. It was called 'the new sepulchre of the Body of Christ' (*corporis Christi novum sepulchrum*),[2] and we have already heard Venerable Bede teaching that the sepulchre that contains the living and risen Body of Christ is deserving of more reverence than that which only once contained His dead Body. The Anglo-Saxons gave by word, by sign, and by acts, the highest worship to that which the eucharistial contained. They called it 'adoranda Filii Dei Hostia'—the adorable Host.[3] They gave every sign of outward reverence to the church that contained it, and the altar on which it was offered. Hence, too, they loved to pray in the church and before the altars, not merely during public devotions, but when the church was empty. Of this innumerable examples occur in history and in the lives of saints. Asser tells us of the great King Alfred that not only he used daily to hear mass and to recite the day and night hours, but also in the night-time he would go to the churches secretly to pray (*ecclesias nocturno tempore, orandi causa, clam a suis adire solebat*). The same author tells us how Abbot John was murdered while absorbed in prayer before the altar during the night. The nocturnal visits of St. Wulstan to the altar are also commemorated by his biographer.

The authors who relate these things do not indeed expressly say

---

[1] Alexander Neckam, writing about 1180 a vocabulary for scholars, calls the pyx *filitorium*, if Mr. Wright has read his MS. correctly: 'filitorium in quo conservetur dignissime eucharistia, salus animæ fidelium, quam nisi quisque fideliter firmiterque crediderit, salvus esse non poterit.' (*Library of National Antiquities*, i. 119.) This should probably be *phylacterium*.

[2] Martene, *De Eccl. Rit.* l. ii. c. 13; Gage, *Ordo ad Ded. Eccl.* in *Archæol.* vol. xv. The same prayer is in Leofric's Missal.

[3] 'Super illud (altare) adorandam Filii sui hostiam ipse benedicat impositam.' (English Pontif., date about 800. Martene, *ubi supra*.)

that it was the presence of our Blessed Lord in His Sacrament which thus attracted them. They were not writing for the refutation of sceptics nor for the information of hesitating Protestants. But that with them 'to pray before the altar' meant what the same expression means when used by modern Catholics, results from all that has hitherto been said about their faith, and the innumerable testimonies that remain as to their devotion to our Lord at Holy Mass and in Holy Communion. When Holy Scripture tells us how Anna, the mother of Samuel, prayed before the tabernacle, it is not expressly said that she was thinking of that mysterious Presence between the cherubim, called the Shechinah; yet when we know of that Presence, and know how it was sometimes explicitly invoked, as by Ezechias,[1] it would be utterly unreasonable to doubt that it was the same faith and devotion which moved the heart of Anna. And the same argument holds good of the Christian Shechinah.

[1] 4 Kings xix. 14-16.

CHAPTER XVIII.

A RETROSPECT.

WE may conveniently pause in the history of the Blessed Sacrament in Great Britain at the period of the Norman Conquest. Though that event introduced no change of faith and only slight modifications in worship, it brought a new race into the island and a new civilisation. It is rather more than 800 years since the Norman conquest, and rather less than 900 separated that epoch from the embassy of King Lucius to Rome. We have therefore a convenient halting-place from which to make a review, and to turn our attention upon some of the general results of th Divine Institution which we have been studying.

It requires a mental effort to grasp the magnitude of that space of nine hundred years. It fills but few pages in our ordinary histories. Painted Britons, Roman legions, savage hordes from Saxony, Julius Cæsar, Boadicea, Hengist and Horsa, like the crowned spectres of Banquo's posterity seen by Macbeth, pass across the scene, 'come like shadows, so depart.' How few realise that Roman civilisation lasted in Briton 500 years, and Anglo-Saxon another 500 ! Five hundred years ! If we glance back over the three centuries that separate us from Queen Elizabeth, we see at once how manners and morals may fluctuate for the better or the worse in such a period. Much more was this the case in Anglo-Saxon times, for then the population of the island was more divided. Besides the gradual conversion of the various tribes, there were conquests and reconquests, unions and separations and reunions of these tribes, until at last they formed one kingdom. And scarcely was this accomplished when the invasions of the Northmen brought misery and spiritual destitution where before had been prosperity and peace. In one century the country was covered with religious houses, and they were filled to overflowing. In another century scarcely two or three monasteries remained ; and when Alfred in his zeal tried to recall the religious life, his people disdained to embrace it. What, therefore, was truly said of one age cannot be safely quoted regarding another age. The good or evil we read of in one place did not necessarily extend throughout the land, much less through that long period of five hundred years. Venerable Bede to us may seem to have lived at the very beginning of the Anglo-Saxon Church; whereas he looked back with regret to 'the good old times'[1] of St. Aidan and St. Cuthbert. We think of his times as of the golden age; he, on the contrary, deplored 'his own miserable times,'[2] as if the world were fast hastening to decrepitude. And yet such is the tendency of men to praise the past that Alcuin fifty years later, writing of the days of Egbert, Archbishop of York, *i.e.* of Bede himself, says:

> Tempora tunc hujus fuerant felicia gentis
> Quam rex et præsul concordi jure regebant.[3]

Thus Alcuin praised what Bede deplored, or rather Bede lamented over the evil while Alcuin thought only of the good. Such examples are a warning not to extend to the whole what is said of a part, much less to apply to whole centuries what may have been truly said of one short period.

There are writers who generalise every beautiful act of piety until their readers would be tempted to suppose that Paradise had been on English soil for half a millennium. And there are writers who generalise every instance of ignorance and crime, so that the darkness and the other plagues of Egypt might seem to have settled permanently in the land. With regard to the political and civil state of the country, wiser opinions now prevail, and, without denying their rudeness and violence, men look to those days for the origin of our freest and noblest institutions. So also a loving admiration may be well permitted for a period when the nation was absolutely one in faith, and when saints were seen in courts as well as in monasteries.

But we must not hide from ourselves that the Church on earth is ever militant, not triumphant; and that, however numerous and brilliant may now seem to us to have been her victories, yet, in the heat of the contest, the champions of God saw so much evil on every side, that they were tempted to despair or to grow weary of life.

In a review of these centuries we may find much to admire, much to deplore. We may glorify the power of God's grace or the long-suffering of His patience. There is matter for edification, but not

---

[1] *History*, iii. 26.   [2] *De Tabern.* iii. 14.
[3] *De Sanctis Eccl. Ebor.* l. 1276. The king was Edbert, the archbishop's brother.

for scandal except to the unwise. If anyone reading of brutal violence, shameless lust, or degrading superstition, should enquire how men, who fed on the Flesh and Blood of God Himself, and in whose churches God had chosen for Himself a perpetual dwelling-place, could fall so low, let him remember the complaint made by God of His ancient people: 'Forty years long was I offended with that generation, and I said: These always err in heart.'[1] Yet in those forty years the wondrous cloud, token of God's Presence, was visible both by day and night even to the bodily eyes, whereas the Eucharist is a mystery of faith. Let it be remembered also that all sins in every age and place are committed in the very presence of God, and as 'we live and move and have our being' in Him, so also in Him we commit our sins. The sacramental Presence of the Son of God is not more visible to the bodily eyes than that of His Divinity. Those who walk by faith find in that Presence a perpetual motive of sanctity, while to those in whom a weak faith is held captive by evil passions, too often it is but an occasion of sacrilege and a source of obduracy. Thus, if we read the history of the Christian Church in any land, we shall see the same strange mixture of good and evil which has been recorded by inspired historians of God's people in the older dispensation; but with this difference, that the virtues of Christian saints are more glorious, and the sins of Christians are, if not more grievous in their kind, yet more heinous in their malice. 'The first sons of Aaron,' wrote Venerable Bede, 'after their ordination, for offering strange fire before the Lord, perished by fire from heaven: a foretoken of our miserable times, in which some who have attained the rank of priests and doctors—a sad and fearful thing to tell—preferring the fire of their own cupidity to that of heavenly charity, are consumed by the fire of divine vengeance; and the temporal death of the sons of Aaron is but a figure of their eternal damnation.'[2] If we are shocked at revelations like this, let us turn to some of those beautiful pictures with which the same writer's history is filled, and then bless God both in His justice and in His grace.

Or again we may find Alcuin in 801 writing to Ethelheard, archbishop of Canterbury, that 'the clergy is now for the greater part fallen so low that it vies with the laity in its vanity, and differs from it only by the tonsure. In manners they are both alike, in extravagance of dress, and arrogance of behaviour, and excess of feasting, and in other things which your holy wisdom knows right well.'[3] Here is a miserable picture; but to be just we must put side by side with it another drawn by a contemporary of Alcuin, and himself a saint.

---

[1] Psalm xciv. 10.   [2] *De Tab.* l. iii. cap. 2.   [3] Haddan and Stubbs, iii. 532.

St. Egbert writes in his Dialogues 'that from the time of Pope Vitalian and of Theodore of Canterbury the custom has been in England that not only the clergy in their monasteries, but lay people also, with their wives and families, go to their confessors, and by tears, abstinence, and alms, purify themselves for twelve days to be fit to receive the Holy Communion at Christmas.'[1]

But, on the other hand, if prudence warns us not hastily to generalise facts, we may safely from ascertained facts, widespread and long prevailing, draw some general conclusions.

Though our Lord Jesus Christ is come 'for the fall and for the resurrection of many,'[2] yet the evil which follows from men's malice does not so entirely counterbalance the good intended by God, but that the good distinctly prevails, when viewed in any extended field of history. The Blessed Sacrament is, as the Church sings, 'death to the bad, life to the good.' It is life by its own nature and the purpose of its institution, death only through the malice of men. And men's malice has never so prevailed over God's intentions as to make us forget the words: 'I came that they might have life, and have life more abundantly.'

The earthquake and the hurricane of tropical countries are fierce in their devastations, and the forests are strewed with trunks of mighty trees, lying prostrate for ages to tell of the violence of a few hours. And a witness of that violence might long for the safety of a duller clime amid the slow growth of a more stunted vegetation. Yet if he wanders far and wide and surveys the whole magnificent region, he will see that the fertilising forces of nature are far more active than those of destruction. In a somewhat similar manner we may look upon the history of the Blessed Sacrament of the Altar. There are patches of history made desolate by the hurricane of heresy, there are men great in intellect, but still greater in pride or lust, whom the earthquake of sacrilege has overthrown. Like storms and floods, war and civil strife or worldly prosperity have converted large regions for a time into dismal swamps. Better, we almost say, as we contemplate such things, better the infidel or heretical nations with their lesser virtues and their lesser crimes. Yet if we look more carefully we shall think otherwise. Better indeed for him who falls had he never known the way of justice;[3] and perhaps this may be even applied to nations which apostatise from the faith. But who shall say of a Catholic nation that it would be better for it had it known the truth less fully or less surely, or been deprived of some of the sacraments, or lost the Eucharistic Presence of Jesus Christ? No, while faith

---

[1] Haddan and Stubbs. iii. 413.   [2] Luke ii. 34.   [3] 2 Pet. ii. 20, 21.

survives, while the communion of the saints pervades a people united to the mystic Body of Christ, and while His sacramental Body is offered on its thousands of altars, and is still received with love and adoration by myriads, even though myriads insult or neglect it, grace is more powerful to draw down blessings than sin is to provoke anger.

But I do not of course speak of temporal prosperity, by which so many at the present day are accustomed to measure the favours and benedictions of God. For though holiness would seem of its own nature more propitious to a country's happiness than mere natural virtue united with spiritual ignorance, yet who can know the manner or the times of God's providence? He may try His saints and make them perfect in adversity; He may chastise here the faults of those whose merits will be rewarded eternally; and His chastisements may be themselves a blessing won by the prayers of His servants.

When Tobias was carried with his people captive into Nineveh, many of them, seeing the prosperity of the great heathen city, began to be dazzled and to doubt of God's care for holiness. But Tobias replied: 'We are the children of saints, and look for that life which God will give to those that never change their faith from Him.'[1] 'Thou art just, O Lord'—thus he prayed in his afflictions—'and all Thy judgments are just, and all Thy ways mercy, and truth, and judgment. . . . For we have not obeyed Thy commandments; therefore are we delivered to spoil and to captivity and death, and are made a fable and a reproach to all nations, among which Thou hast scattered us.'[2] Yet when the saint was dying he bade his sons depart from Nineveh, 'for I see,' he said, 'that iniquity will bring it to destruction,'[3] and he foretold the restoration of his own people to the land of their fathers.

When the sacred writer is about to record the cruel martyrdom of the seven young men and their noble mother by Antiochus, he thus introduces the terrible history: 'Now I beseech those who shall read this book, that they be not shocked at these calamities, but that they consider the things that happened, not as being for the destruction, but for the correction of our nation. For it is a token of great goodness when sinners are not suffered to go on in their ways for a long time, but are presently punished. For not as with other nations (whom the Lord patiently expecteth, that, when the day of judgment shall come, He may punish them in the fulness of their sins) doth He also deal with us, so as to suffer our sins to come to their height, and then take vengeance on us. And therefore He never with-

---

[1] Tobias ii. 18.   [2] *Ib.* iii. 2, 4.   [3] *Ib.* xiv. 13

draweth His mercy from us. But though He chastise His people with adversity, He forsaketh them not.'[1]

Lastly, St. Peter utters a most pregnant maxim when he says: 'Dearly beloved, think not strange the burning heat which is to try you, as if some new thing had happened to you. But if you partake of the suffering of Christ, rejoice. . . . For the time is that judgment should begin at the house of God. And if first at us, what shall be the end of them that believe not the gospel of God?'[2]

The glimpse which all these divinely inspired words give us into the ways of God's providence should convince us that the philosophy of history is not one of natural cause and effect. The benefits conferred by our Lord's sacramental Presence and action on a country are not to be measured by its temporal prosperity.

And yet, while saying this, I contend that reverence for this great Sacrament has ever been one of the principal safeguards of national prosperity, and that the rejection of transubstantiation by our own country is a crime undermining morality and dissolving the bonds which knit together a Christian people. In proof of this I propose briefly to pass in review some of the great principles of national prosperity which we have derived from our Celtic or Anglo-Saxon ancestors,[3] and to show how the Holy Eucharist was in every case either their origin or their sanction.

1. The first element of greatness in a nation is freedom. This can never be the state of all its members. A convict working under the eye of his armed gaoler at the present day is reduced to a more abject condition of slavery than was probably ever known in Saxon England. Mr. Thrupp truly remarks that 'the words freemen and slaves, as understood at the present day, are hardly applicable to the state of society under the Anglo-Saxons—the freemen were less free than now, the slaves less slaves.'[4] A nation, however, progresses in proportion as the number of freemen increases, and when none are slaves unless in punishment for their own crimes. Now, in looking into the history of the Anglo-Saxons, we find many causes of slavery. Men lost their

---

[1] 2 Mac. vi. 12–16.   [2] 1 Pet. iv. 12–17.

[3] One can only smile at the eagerness of some recent historians to claim exclusively English ancestry. It might be good to republish Defoe's poetical satire on the *True-born Briton*. To say nothing of Danes, Normans, Dutch, and so many other nations who have been ever mingling their blood with that of the Anglo-Saxon stock, surely a large proportion of the mothers, at least of the early Saxon inhabitants, must have been British women spared in conquest. And are the Picts and Scots and Welsh so insignificant an element in the progenitors of our present mixed population?

[4] Thrupp's *Anglo-Saxon Home*, p. 118.

liberty by war, illegal violence, crime, debt, gambling, or voluntary surrender; and a state of slavery was inherited,[1] and slaves could be bought and sold even out of their native country, as we are reminded by the famous anecdote of St. Gregory. For it was the sight of a fair English boy in the slave market of Rome that first awakened his sympathy for England.

On the other hand, freedom could be regained by purchase or emancipation.

What then was the effect of Christianity on this state of things? At first, indeed, the action of Christianity may have increased the number of slaves. In pagan times the victors slaughtered all the males, and the vanquished nobles even preferred death to slavery. 'But,' says Mr. Thrupp,[2] 'the disregard of life was opposed to the doctrines of Christianity; and the clergy consequently exerted all their influence both to induce the victors to spare the lives of their prisoners and to persuade the conquered nobles to accept the boon of life even at the price of bonds and slavery.' Hence we find from the Domesday Book that in the eleventh century, while in Kent and the South Saxon counties, where war had long ceased, only one-tenth of the registered population was servile, the proportion increased in the Western counties, since war and conquest there had been far more recent. In Cornwall and Devon one-fifth of the population were slaves, and in Gloucestershire on the Welsh border about one-third.[3]

These statistics show that an influence was at work emancipating those first enslaved. This influence was Christianity. Mr. Thrupp has certainly no prejudices in favour of the Catholic religion, yet he writes thus: 'The Christian clergy no sooner obtained power in England than they exerted it to the utmost to put an end to the foreign slave-trade.'[4] And again: 'From the earliest period the Christian clergy used their influence not only to diminish the severity of slavery, but to limit its extent. They constantly freed the slaves who came into their possession, and they exhorted the laity to follow their example. They were eminently successful with men who were on the point of death.'[5]

The example of St. Wilfrid will be recalled, who, after receiving a gift from the king of 250 slaves, instructed them in the Christian

---

[1] The condition did not follow the mother, as among the Romans, according to Mr. Thrupp, though this seems contrary to St. Theodore's *Penitential*, § 14. But Bracton says that the children sprung from union of serf and free were always serf, unless when a free father married a female serf not remaining in villenage. (*De Consuetudinibus Angliæ*, l. i. cap. 6, ed. Twiss, Rolls Series.)
[2] Thrupp, p. 120. [3] *Ib.* p. 139. [4] *Ib.* p. 129. [5] *Ib.* p. 135.

faith, and emancipated them all on the day of their baptism.¹ It will be remembered also how the Council of Celchyth in 816 ordered that when a bishop died all his English slaves should be liberated, and how every bishop and abbot throughout England should give freedom to three men for the good of the deceased bishop's soul.² 'At first,' says Mr. Thrupp, 'about one-third of the population are supposed to have been serfs or servile tenantry. As the nation advanced in civilisation the proportionate number of slaves diminished. The Domesday Book gives only 26,500 slaves to 184,000 villeins and bondsmen. It also mentions 26,000 tenants and socmen, half of whom were free, and half of whom were tributaries or demi-free men. In Yorkshire, Lincolnshire, Huntingdonshire, and Rutland, there is not a single slave registered in Domesday, and in Nottinghamshire the slaves are in proportion of one to two hundred and fifty free men.'³

If, however, this emancipation was in great part due to the action and influence of the clergy, the doctrine which touched them, and gave them power to touch the hearts of others, was that of the dignity conferred on man by his redemption by the blood of Christ and his being made partaker of his Redeemer's Flesh and Blood in the Holy Eucharist. The spiritual equality of men who knelt before the same altars, received the same communion, and were buried side by side in the same churchyards, was so strikingly brought home to the minds and hearts of men, that social inequalities necessarily became less prominent, and whatever there was in them harsh or unjust was gradually removed. As a proof that this was really the influence at work, I may appeal to the testimony of Mr. Kemble. 'Of all forms of emancipation,' he says, 'I imagine this, before the altar of a church, to have been the most frequent, partly because of its convenience, partly because the motives for emancipation were generally of a religious cast, and the sanctions of religion were solemn and awful. Almost all the records which we possess on this subject are taken from the margins of Gospels or other books belonging to religious houses, and the few references in the laws imply emancipation *at the altar*.'⁴

But, again, reverence for the Holy Eucharist, even when it did not procure absolute emancipation, greatly mitigated the perils and misery of slavery. It was a protection to the chastity of female slaves, so that the master who led one into sin was bound to give her

---

¹ See p. 94. ² See p. 208. ³ Thrupp, p. 139.
⁴ Kemble, *History of the Saxons in England*, i. 224.

freedom as well as to do six months' penance.[1] Another limitation to slavery arose from the holidays of the Church. On Sundays the slave could not work either for his master or for himself; on certain other days his master could not compel him to work, yet he was free to work for himself; as, *e.g.*, for twelve days at Christmas, during the week which preceded and that which followed Easter, and the week before the Assumption of the Blessed Virgin. During these and some other times the slave could earn sufficient not only to render his life less miserable, but often to purchase his own freedom from his master. The connection of the Sunday and the great festivals with the Holy Mass, which was the principal act of worship, is evident. So that here also our Lord, in the mystery of love, was exerting His influence for the relief and freedom of His worshippers.

The condition of slavery was mitigated not merely by the hopes of liberty, but of liberty sanctified and elevated by the priesthood. Slavery was indeed an irregularity or a bar to ordination while it subsisted, but it inflicted no stain or moral infamy which would prevent a slave from aspiring to the dignity of the clerical state. Freedom to serve God was all the Church required, and when this was obtained by emancipation no further dispensation was necessary.

By means of celibacy hereditary succession had been effectually prevented in the priesthood, and it could neither degenerate into a low caste, as at the present day in Russia, where priests are generally the sons of priests and marry the daughters of priests; nor could rich benefices be handed down from father to son, as would certainly have been the case under the feudal system, had marriage been possible to the higher clergy. But not only was the Catholic clergy continually recruited from the laity, and therefore bound to the laity by family ties; it was recruited from every class of the laity, from the prince to the bondsman.

The wonderful scene that opens on us in the first page of the Church's history, whether among Britons, Scots, or Saxons, of the highest and the lowest classes meeting in absolute equality in the ranks of the priesthood, continues uninterrupted throughout every age. St. Gildas in Wales, St. Ninian in Cumbria, St. Wilfrid and St. Egbert in Northumbria, St. Columba in Scotland, all belong to royal or noble families; yet they are the companions not only of sons of plebeians, but of slaves. The Brehon Laws of Ireland say: 'The enslaved shall be freed, the plebeians exalted through the orders of the Church and by performing penitential service to God. For the

---

[1] *Penitential of St. Theodore*, § 14; Haddan and Stubbs, iii. 188.

Lord is accessible. He will not refuse any kind of man after belief, among either the free or the plebeian tribes; so likewise is the Church open for every person who goes under her rule.'[1] This was not peculiar to Ireland. Bede tells us how St. Aidan, the apostle of Northumbria, ransomed slaves, instructed them, and even ordained them priests.[2] St. Gregory, even before the expedition which he sent to Britain, had purchased in Gaul British or English boy slaves to be converted and brought up in monasteries;[3] and this was probably with a view to the evangelisation of their own countrymen.

The spirit of the world naturally hated this divine equality, and under our Norman kings several attempts were made to exclude slaves from the priesthood. The Church, however, successfully vindicated her rights and those of the poor and lowly. One of the Constitutions of Clarendon rejected by St. Thomas of Canterbury, as opposed to the rights of the Church, was that no serf's son could be admitted to holy orders. In the time of Richard II. the commons prayed the king 'that no naif or villain shall place his children at school, as has been done, so as to advance their children by means of the clerical state.'[4] Under this influence some of the colleges of the universities at that time closed their gates against bondsmen. But a better spirit triumphed, and down to the period of the Reformation frequent instances occur in bishops' registers and elsewhere of emancipation granted previous to ordination.[5]

[1] See Skene, *Celtic Scotland*, ii. 72.   [2] *History*, iii. 5.
[3] S. Greg. *Ep.* vi. 7.   [4] *Rotuli Parl.* iii. 294.
[5] To give one example : the convent of Ely grants a license to William, son of Thomas Bette, their naif, of Stapilford, to take any kind of sacred orders, his servile condition notwithstanding. This was in the first year of Henry V. (See *Sixth Report of Historical MS. Commission*, part i. p. 300.) It may be useful to mention here some of the principal regulations of the Holy Church on the ordination of slaves. As a rule, emancipation ought to precede ordination, or should at least be formally made by deed immediately before the sacred rite. Pope Gelasius complained that in his day bishops, by abuse of power, ordained slaves without the leave of their lords. He forbade them to do this. (*Decreti* pars i. Dist. 54.) This prohibition was often renewed, as by Alexander III., who wrote to an archbishop : 'Videas ne quemlibet servilis conditionis ad ordines promovere præsumas.' (Tit. xxxiii. cap. 7.) If a slave was ordained without the consent of his lord, then, if he had only received minor orders, he remained a slave, and forfeited his clerical privileges. If he had received holy orders, he became free, but the bishop who thus ordained him knowingly was bound to compensate his lord doubly. If the bishop was deceived, those who deceived him had to make satisfaction. If it was the serf himself who deceived the bishop, he would be bound to make compensation, and if unable to do so otherwise, then, if he were only a deacon, he remained in servitude, and was of course irregular and without clerical privilege. If he was a priest, he was bound to serve as his lord's chaplain, and, if this was not desired,

2. A second great principle of civilisation among our Celtic and Saxon forefathers was the penitential discipline of the Church. This was for ages both the supplement and the support of the civil law, and was the principal means both of preventing crimes and of punishing malefactors. But if you take away the hope of receiving Holy Communion, you take away the keystone from the whole arch of this system, and it would have crumbled to pieces. The necessity of receiving the Body and Blood of the Lord on the one hand, the danger to the soul of doing this without the requisite purity on the other, could alone have induced men to undergo purifications so hard to human nature. And be it remarked that the Church, during this period, dealt not only with sin as an offence to God, but as a crime against society. Her discipline took the place, in a great measure, of civil penalties. While the Church punished crime by penance, the State could leave the matter almost entirely in her hands. When the penitential system became less severe, civil penalties became more rigorous. Or we may perhaps say with equal truth—for in this matter there were mutual action and reaction—when the State, by advance in unity and organisation, became competent to deal with crimes against itself, the Church willingly relaxed her penitential discipline, lest the same crimes should be twice punished. But certainly, during the period now under review, the chief agent in the repression and punishment of crime was the Blessed Sacrament of the Altar, as giving life to the exhortations, admonitions, and maternal corrections of the Church. It was her possession of this great treasure that enabled her to address her children in the language of St. Paul : 'You are the temple of the living God, as God saith, " I will dwell in them and walk among them, and I will be their God, and they shall be my people." Wherefore " go out from among them and be ye separate," saith the Lord, "and touch not the unclean thing ; and I will receive you, and I will be a Father to you, and you shall be my sons and daughters, saith the Lord Almighty." Having

then at least to offer all his masses for him. To prevent serfs acquiring freedom by fraud, the English law declared that, if a cleric or monk once emancipated should return to the secular life, he should be restored to his owner. (Bracton, *De Consuet. Angliæ*, lib. i. cap. vi. p. 32, ed. Twiss, Rolls Series.) The emancipation was not always absolute, as we see from an answer of Innocent III., given in the Decretals, lib. i. tit. xviii. cap. 6. There might be some restriction not inconsistent with the clerical or monastic state, *e.g.* a serf might be freed only to become a monk in the monastery to which he had belonged, not to pass to another. A bishop might give freedom, yet oblige the emancipated cleric to remain in his spiritual service. This will explain some cases mentioned by Mr. Tytler in his *History of Scotland*, ii. 215, of *nativi clerici*. They were the property of the bishop, not of a layman.

therefore these promises, dearly beloved, let us cleanse ourselves from all defilement of the flesh and of the spirit, perfecting sanctification in the fear of God.'[1]

3. There was another safeguard of justice and good order in those times of violence and of undeveloped civilisation. This was the right of sanctuary. However it may have been occasionally abused and however needless when justice came to be well and impartially administered, no one doubts that its influence was most beneficial, both to prevent private vengeance and hasty and violent punishments by public authority. It seems to have prevailed in the Celtic no less than the Saxon Churches, and Giraldus Cambrensis boasts that in no country was there a greater reverence for holy places than in Wales, and that in consequence the churches had greater peace there than elsewhere.

The Welsh annals, called 'Brut y Tywysog,' inform us that the original right of sanctuary was restored in 1150 by Nicolas, Bishop of Llandaff, to several churches in his diocese, and fitting sanctuary was assigned to the new monasteries, 'which occasioned,' says the writer, 'greater quietness in Morganwg than in any other part of Wales. After that, the churches that had been demolished were reconstructed and new ones founded, by which the men of Morganwg and Gwent (Glamorganshire and Monmouthshire) became better agriculturists than soldiers.' It need not be said that sanctuary is intimately connected with devotion to the Blessed Sacrament; for though a church might indeed be venerated simply as a house of prayer, yet the Christian church is sanctified by the altar, and that again by the gift laid upon it.

4. If the material church served as a sanctuary, those who served the sanctuaries exerted an influence around them to which we may trace most of the benefits of both Celtic and Saxon civilisation. If wild marsh and forest land was brought under cultivation it was by the labour of the monks, if towns grew up it was under the protection of the monasteries. The church preceded the town, and was not its supplement, as it is in our days.[2] But if the monastery was the nucleus of the surrounding civilisation the Blessed Sacrament was the nucleus of the monastery itself. The Holy Eucharist alone makes the sacrifices of the monastic life possible. Mass and communion are not only the occupations but the strength of those dedicated to a religious life. And if anyone will consider this matter attentively, weighing well such facts as have been collected by Montalembert in his 'Monks of the West,' he will see that it is no

---

[1] 2 Cor. vi. 16, *sq.*   [2] See on this subject Kemble, book ii. ch. 7.

fantastic dream to trace to the influence going out from the altar and tabernacle, not only the interior emotions of the heart, not only outward acts of devotion, but all or nearly all works of active charity. The Blessed Sacrament cleared the forests, drained the swamps, bridged the rivers, made the roads, built the cottages of the poor, gathered the people into towns and cities, sent out the missionaries, drew together the congregations of worshippers, and penetrated the whole fabric of society, both domestic, social, and political. It was the hidden leaven working through the whole mass of human life and raising it heavenward.

5. Among the free institutions of modern England none is more famous than Parliament. It is well known that this was foreshadowed by the free consultative or legislative assemblies called by the Anglo-Saxons Witenagemot. But it is not so generally known that our forefathers before their deliberations used to ask the light of the Holy Spirit by assisting at holy mass.[1]

6. Even more important than the making of laws is their execution; let us then see what precautions were taken in those days to secure uprightness and impartiality in the courts of justice. In the laws of Howel the Good, king of all Wales, in 928 occur the following words: 'A judge elect is to serve a year's apprenticeship, and then the king's chaplain is to take him to the church, having with him twelve principal officers of the court, to mass. And after mass and an offering by everyone, let the chaplain require him to swear by the relics, and by the altar, *and by the consecrated elements placed upon the altar*, that he will never deliver a wrong judgment knowingly.'[2]

Not only the judge was bound by the sanctity of the oath and reverence for the altar, but witnesses or jurymen also. By the dooms of Ine, king of Wessex in 690, the oath of communicants (*huslgengum*) was of more value than that of others.[3] But, on the other hand, perjury in the church was punished by three years' penance, according to the Penitential of St. Theodore.[4] In the Welsh laws of Howel frequent mention is made of the oath being exacted in the

---

[1] Kemble, i. 145.
[2] Haddan and Stubbs, i. 229. An oath taken by a jury at Cirencester, in the time of Henry I., not only ' tactis sacrosanctis evangeliis,' but ' *super sacramentum sanctum*,' is given in the *Archæological Journal*, vol. xxxvi. p. 206 (1879).
[3] Haddan and Stubbs, iii. 216.
[4] In Haddan and Stubbs (iii. 182) it is eleven. But Bede gives three only (*ib*. p. 330). Probably III. has been changed into XI. by the copyists of Theodore.

church before the altar. So, too, in the Saxon laws of Wihtred of Kent, A.D. 696, it is said : ' Let a priest clear himself by his sooth in his holy garment before the altar, thus saying : " I speak the truth in Christ, I lie not." In like manner a deacon. Let a clerk clear himself with four of his fellows, and he alone with his hand on the altar, let the others stand by ; and so on for the king's thane, the ceorl, and the stranger, and let the oath of all these be incontrovertible.'[1]

Thus in days when there were not the same facilities for detecting crime that now exist, and neither the torture of the rack nor that of the barrister's tongue was yet known, the sanctity of justice rested on faith in the Blessed Sacrament. It is needless to say that that faith was not always lively enough to secure truth or prevent wrong. Gildas had complained indignantly of some miscreants who swore solemnly before the altar, and then went away and broke their oath, ' as if the altar were a heap of dirty stones.'[2] Giraldus at a much later date complained that his countrymen were in this respect still imperfect and required instruction.[3] Perjury was a crime often charged upon the Anglo-Saxons, especially when, the Danes having thrown everything into confusion, preaching was neglected and reverence for holy things decayed.[4] But it may be truly asserted that the seat of justice was really God's altar, and in proportion as that was reverenced did justice thrive.

Certainly no Englishman at the present day should speak lightly of the solemn oaths of Welsh and Saxons. For the last two centuries oaths have been made an idle ceremony, exacted and taken, in ignorance of their meaning or obligation, by the boy matriculating at the university or the clerk passing a bale of goods through the custom house—to say nothing yet of the frightful Test and Corporation oaths. In former days the communicant was presumed to speak the truth ; whereas now no sooner has the witness been hurried indecently through his oath than he is treated by the opposing barrister as if he had come purposely to perjure his soul and to confound justice. Has England or human nature gained by the change ?

7. From what has been said it will have been seen how reverence for the Blessed Sacrament lent a solemn sanction to whatever was most free, most noble, most peaceful, most just, and most beneficial in the institutions of society—in a word, ' to those principles,' to use Mr. Kemble's language in addressing the Queen, ' which have

---

[1] Haddan and Stubbs, iii.
[2] See p. 21 *antea*.
[3] *Gemma Ecclesiastica.*
[4] The *Sermo Lupi.*

given her empire its pre-eminence among the nations of Europe.'
What frenzy then seized on our deluded people when they bound
their kings and queens to repudiate by oath that doctrine of transubstantiation which made England what she was : 'I do solemnly and
sincerely, in the presence of God, profess, testify, and declare, that I
do believe that in the sacrament of the Lord's Supper there is not
any transubstantiation of the elements of bread and wine into the
body and blood of Christ at or after the consecration thereof by any
person whatsoever ; and that the invocation or adoration of the Virgin
Mary or any other saint, and the sacrifice of the mass, as they are
now used in the Church of Rome, are superstitious and idolatrous.'[1]

Compare with these ignominious and sacrilegious words the
noble oath administered by the Saxon Church and people at the
coronation of the king. 'In the name of the Holy Trinity, three
things do I promise to this Christian people, my subjects : First,
that I will hold God's Church and all the Christian people in my
realm in true peace ; second, that I will forbid all rapine and injustice to men of all conditions ; third, that I promise and enjoin
justice and mercy in all judgments ; whereby the just and merciful
God may give us all His eternal favour, who liveth and reigneth world
without end. Amen.' Such is, word for word, the oath administered
by St. Dunstan to Edgar, Edward the Martyr, and Ethelred, and when
it had been pronounced the paper 'was laid upon Christ's altar.'[2]

I cannot forbear giving at least the substance of the account left
by an eye-witness of the coronation of King Edgar, since it has only
lately been made public for the first time in print.[3] It took place at
Bath on Whitsunday, in the year 973. The prelates who performed
the ceremony are both canonised saints, St. Dunstan, archbishop of
Canterbury, and St. Oswald, archbishop of York. No pomp was
wanting. Besides the crowd of nobles there were present not only
abbots with a multitude of the clergy, but abbesses also with their
nuns as attendants on the queen, for the king and queen had founded
many monasteries. The king wearing his crown was led between the
two archbishops to the church, while the choir sang the antiphon:
'Let thy hand be strengthened and thy right hand exalted. Justice
and judgment are the preparation of thy throne. Mercy and truth
shall go before thy face.'[4] Taking off his crown, the king prostrated
himself before the altar, while St. Dunstan intoned the 'Te Deum.'

---

[1] Declaration prescribed by the Act of Settlement, 13th William III.
[2] Kemble, vol. ii. p. 35.
[3] *Historians of York*, 'Life of St. Oswald,' p. 437 (Rolls Series, 1879).
[4] Ps. lxxxviii. 14.

When the hymn was ended, they raised the king, and he took the oath given above. He was then anointed and received the ring, the sword, the crown, and the sceptre. Afterwards St. Dunstan sang the mass. When the religious ceremony was over, two great banquets were given. The king crowned with laurel and roses, accompanied by the archbishops and his nobles, assisted at one, and Queen Elfritha, surrounded by her ladies and the abbots and abbesses, presided at the other.

Very different is the coronation story of another king, Harold Harefoot, the illegitimate son of Canute. A contemporary author informs us that when Harold called on Ethelnoth, the archbishop of Canterbury, to perform the coronation service, the prelate solemnly declared that he would never bless any other as king than one of the sons of Emma, that these had been committed to his trust by Canute, and that he would maintain his fidelity. The regalia were in the charge of the archbishop, and he laid the crown and sceptre on the altar, saying to Harold : 'To you I neither give them nor refuse them ; but by apostolical authority I forbid any other bishop to touch them, to give them to you, or to perform the coronation service (*teve benedicat*). As for you, if you dare to do so, lay your hands on what I have entrusted to God and to His table.' In vain Harold offered bribes ; the archbishop was inflexible. Harold, being unable to obtain this recognition of his claim, not only expressed his contempt for the episcopal benediction, but took an aversion to every act of Christianity. When others entered the church after the Christian custom to hear mass (*missam audire*), he went to hunt in the forest, or occupied himself with low amusements in order to avoid that which he hated.[1] Harold's reign lasted only four years (1035-1040), and the sole event which is associated with his name is the cruel and brutal massacre of Alfred, the brother of St. Edward the Confessor, with 500 of his followers, a deed which, as described by the chroniclers, fully explains, or is explained by, his hatred of the Holy Sacrifice of the Altar.

An oath like that required from Edgar continued to be taken by our sovereigns and placed upon the altar while England remained

---

[1] From the *Encomium Emmæ*, the work of a monk of St. Omer's. It is true that this author is a partisan of Emma, yet he could scarcely either err himself or write what he knew to be incorrect on a matter so public, and which had happened only five or six years before he wrote. It is uncertain whether Harold was crowned afterwards by Archbishop Eadsige, who succeeded Ethelnoth in 1035. Ingulf says the king gave his coronation robe to Croyland, but Ingulf's work is a forgery.

Catholic. Elizabeth herself was crowned according to the Roman pontifical, and promised fidelity, and allegiance, and protection to the Catholic Church ; and as Holy Communion was always administered at the coronation, she sealed her perjury with a sacrilege. From that day she could not bear the name of the holy mass. Not only did she shun it like Harold, but within a year or two she took down and broke to pieces every altar throughout the land ; and then again, following in the footsteps of the king who sought to secure his throne against his own illegitimacy by the murder of Alfred, the perjured queen stained her soul with the blood of Mary.

These things are an awful commentary on the antiphon sung in the old coronation service to remind the sovereign that he held the place of God on earth and should imitate His divine government: ' Justice and judgment are the preparation of Thy throne ; mercy and truth shall go before thy face ;' and it remains for non-Catholic readers to reflect whether the Blessed Mystery of the Altar, which gave sanction and solemnity to the royal oath of former times, deserves to be contumeliously repudiated.

END OF THE FIRST VOLUME.

WORKS BY THE REV. T. E. BRIDGETT.

THE RITUAL OF THE NEW TESTAMENT:
AN ESSAY ON THE PRINCIPLES AND ORIGIN OF CATHOLIC RITUAL.

Second Edition.

Price 5s.

OUR LADY'S DOWRY:
HOW ENGLAND WON AND LOST THAT TITLE.

Second Edition. Illustrated.

Price 9s.

THE DISCIPLINE OF DRINK:
AN ESSAY ON THE USE, ABUSE, AND DISUSE OF ALCOHOLIC DRINKS,

ESPECIALLY IN THE BRITISH ISLES BEFORE THE SIXTEENTH CENTURY.

Price 3s. 6d.

EDITED BY THE REV. T. E. BRIDGETT.

SERMONS ON THE SACRAMENTS.
By THOMAS WATSON,

The last Catholic Bishop of Lincoln.

Price 7s. 6d.

THE SUPPLIANT OF THE HOLY GHOST;
FROM A SEVENTEENTH CENTURY MS.

Price 1s. 6d.

THE ABOVE WORKS ARE PUBLISHED BY
Messrs. BURNS & OATES, 17 Portman Street, London, W.

A LIST OF

C. KEGAN PAUL & CO.'S

PUBLICATIONS.

1 *Paternoster Square,*
London.

A LIST OF
C. KEGAN PAUL & CO.'S PUBLICATIONS.

ADAMS (F. O.) F.R.G.S.—THE HISTORY OF JAPAN. From the Earliest Period to the Present Time. New Edition, revised. 2 volumes. With Maps and Plans. Demy 8vo. price 21*s*. each.

ADAMSON (H. T.) B.D.—THE TRUTH AS IT IS IN JESUS. Crown 8vo. cloth, price 8*s*. 6*d*.

THE THREE SEVENS. Crown 8vo. cloth, price 5*s*. 6*d*.

A. K. H. B.—FROM A QUIET PLACE. A New Volume of Sermons. Crown 8vo. cloth, price 5*s*.

ALBERT (Mary).—HOLLAND AND HER HEROES TO THE YEAR 1585. An Adaptation from 'Motley's Rise of the Dutch Republic.' Small crown 8vo. price 4*s*. 6*d*.

ALLEN (Rev. R.) M.A.—ABRAHAM; HIS LIFE, TIMES, AND TRAVELS, 3,800 years ago. With Map. Second Edition. Post 8vo. price 6*s*.

ALLEN (Grant) B.A.—PHYSIOLOGICAL ÆSTHETICS. Large post 8vo. 9*s*.

ALLIES (T. W.) M.A.—PER CRUCEM AD LUCEM. The Result of a Life. 2 vols. Demy 8vo. cloth, price 25*s*.

A LIFE'S DECISION. Crown 8vo. cloth, price 7*s*. 6*d*.

ANDERSON (R. C.) C.E.—TABLES FOR FACILITATING THE CALCULATION OF EVERY DETAIL IN CONNECTION WITH EARTHEN AND MASONRY DAMS. Royal 8vo. price £2. 2*s*.

ARCHER (Thomas)—ABOUT MY FATHER'S BUSINESS. Work amidst the Sick, the Sad, and the Sorrowing. Cheaper Edition. Crown 8vo. price 2*s*. 6*d*.

ARNOLD (Arthur)—SOCIAL POLITICS. Demy 8vo. cloth, price 14*s*.

FREE LAND. Crown 8vo. cloth, price 6*s*.

BADGER (George Percy) D.C.L.—AN ENGLISH-ARABIC LEXICON. In which the equivalent for English Words and Idiomatic Sentences are rendered into literary and colloquial Arabic. Royal 4to. cloth, price £9. 9*s*.

BAGEHOT (Walter)—THE ENGLISH CONSTITUTION. A New Edition, Revised and Corrected, with an Introductory Dissertation on Recent Changes and Events. Crown 8vo. price 7*s*. 6*d*.

LOMBARD STREET. A Description of the Money Market. Seventh Edition. Crown 8vo. price 7*s*. 6*d*.

SOME ARTICLES ON THE DEPRECIATION OF SILVER, AND TOPICS CONNECTED WITH IT. Demy 8vo. price 5*s*.

BAGOT (Alan)—ACCIDENTS IN MINES: Their Causes and Prevention. Crown 8vo. price 6*s*.

BAKER (Sir Sherston, Bart.)—HALLECK'S INTERNATIONAL LAW; or, Rules Regulating the Intercourse of States in Peace and War. A New Edition, revised, with Notes and Cases. 2 vols. Demy 8vo. price 38*s*.

THE LAWS RELATING TO QUARANTINE. Crown 8vo. cloth, price 12*s*. 6*d*.

BALDWIN (Capt. J. H.) F.Z.S. Bengal Staff Corps.—THE LARGE AND SMALL GAME OF BENGAL AND THE NORTH-WESTERN PROVINCES OF INDIA. 4to. With numerous Illustrations. Second Edition. Price 21*s*.

BARNES (William)—AN OUTLINE OF ENGLISH SPEECHCRAFT. Crown 8vo. price 4*s*.

OUTLINES OF REDECRAFT (LOGIC). With English Wording. Crown 8vo. cloth, price 3*s*.

BARTLEY (G. C. T.)—DOMESTIC ECONOMY: Thrift in Every-Day Life. Taught in Dialogues suitable for children of all ages. Small cr. 8vo. price 2*s*.

BAUR (Ferdinand) Dr. Ph., Professor in Maulbronn.—A PHILOLOGICAL INTRODUCTION TO GREEK AND LATIN FOR STUDENTS. Translated and adapted from the German. By C. KEGAN PAUL, M.A. Oxon., and the Rev. E. D. STONE, M.A., late Fellow of King's College, Cambridge, and Assistant Master at Eton. Crown 8vo. price 6*s*.

BAYNES (Rev. Canon R. H.)—AT THE COMMUNION TIME. A Manual for Holy Communion. With a preface by the Right Rev. the Lord Bishop of Derry and Raphoe. Cloth, price 1*s*. 6*d*.

BELLINGHAM (Henry) M.P., Barrister-at-Law—SOCIAL ASPECTS OF CATHOLICISM AND PROTESTANTISM IN THEIR CIVIL BEARING UPON NATIONS. Translated and adapted from the French of M. le Baron de Haulleville. With a preface by His Eminence Cardinal Manning. Second and Cheaper Edition. Crown 8vo. price 3*s*. 6*d*.

BENT (J. Theodore)—GENOA: How the Republic Rose and Fell. With 18 Illustrations. Demy 8vo. cloth, price 18*s*.

BONWICK (J.) F.R.G.S.—PYRAMID FACTS AND FANCIES. Crown 8vo. price 5*s*.

EGYPTIAN BELIEF AND MODERN THOUGHT. Large Post 8vo. cloth, price 10*s*. 6*d*.

BOWEN (H. C.) M.A., Head Master of the Grocers' Company's Middle Class School at Hackney.

STUDIES IN ENGLISH, for the use of Modern Schools. Small crown 8vo. price 1*s*. 6*d*.

ENGLISH GRAMMAR FOR BEGINNERS. Fcap. 8vo. cloth, price 1*s*.

BOWRING (Sir John).—AUTOBIOGRAPHICAL RECOLLECTIONS OF SIR JOHN BOWRING. With Memoir by LEWIN B. BOWRING. Demy 8vo. price 14*s*.

BRIDGETT (Rev. T. E.)—HISTORY OF THE HOLY EUCHARIST IN GREAT BRITAIN. 2 vols. demy 8vo. cloth, price 18*s*.

BRODRICK (the Hon. G. C.)—POLITICAL STUDIES. Demy 8vo. cloth, price 14*s*.

BROOKE (Rev. S. A.) M.A., Chaplain in Ordinary to Her Majesty the Queen, and Minister of Bedford Chapel, Bloomsbury.

LIFE AND LETTERS OF THE LATE REV. F. W. ROBERTSON, M.A., Edited by.

I. Uniform with the Sermons. 2 vols. With Steel Portrait. Price 7*s*. 6*d*.
II. Library Edition. 8vo. With Portrait. Price 12*s*.
III. A Popular Edition. In 1 vol. 8vo. price 6*s*.

BROOKE (*Rev. S. A.*) *M.A.*—cont.

    THE FIGHT OF FAITH. Sermons preached on various occasions. Third Edition. Crown 8vo. price 7s. 6d.

    THEOLOGY IN THE ENGLISH POETS.—Cowper, Coleridge, Wordsworth, and Burns. Fourth and Cheaper Edition. Post 8vo. price 5s.

    CHRIST IN MODERN LIFE. Fourteenth and Cheaper Edition. Crown 8vo. price 5s.

    SERMONS. First Series. Eleventh Edition. Crown 8vo. price 6s.

    SERMONS. Second Series. Third Edition. Crown 8vo. price 7s.

    FREDERICK DENISON MAURICE: The Life and Work of. A Memorial Sermon. Crown 8vo. sewed, price 1s.

BROOKE (*W. G.*) *M.A.*—THE PUBLIC WORSHIP REGULATION ACT. With a Classified Statement of its Provisions, Notes, and Index. Third Edition, revised and corrected. Crown 8vo. price 3s. 6d.

    SIX PRIVY COUNCIL JUDGMENTS—1850-72. Annotated by. Third Edition. Crown 8vo. price 9s.

BROUN (*J. A.*)—MAGNETIC OBSERVATIONS AT TREVANDRUM AND AUGUSTIA MALLEY. Vol. I. 4to. price 63s.

    The Report from above, separately, sewed, price 21s.

BROWN (*Rev. J. Baldwin*) *B.A.*—THE HIGHER LIFE. Its Reality, Experience, and Destiny. Fifth Edition. Crown 8vo. price 5s.

    DOCTRINE OF ANNIHILATION IN THE LIGHT OF THE GOSPEL OF LOVE. Five Discourses. Third Edition. Crown 8vo. price 2s. 6d.

    THE CHRISTIAN POLICY OF LIFE. A Book for Young Men of Business. New and Cheaper Edition. Crown 8vo. cloth, price, 3s. 6d.

BROWN (*J. Croumbie*) *LL.D.*—REBOISEMENT IN FRANCE; or, Records of the Replanting of the Alps, the Cevennes, and the Pyrenees with Trees, Herbage, and Bush. Demy 8vo. price 12s. 6d.

    THE HYDROLOGY OF SOUTHERN AFRICA. Demy 8vo. price 10s. 6d.

BROWNE (*W. R.*)—THE INSPIRATION OF THE NEW TESTAMENT. With a Preface by the Rev. J. P. NORRIS, D.D. Fcp. 8vo. cloth, 2s. 6d.

BURCKHARDT (*Jacob*)—THE CIVILIZATION OF THE PERIOD OF THE RENAISSANCE IN ITALY. Authorised translation, by S. G. C. Middlemore. 2 vols. Demy 8vo. price 24s.

BURTON (*Mrs. Richard*)—THE INNER LIFE OF SYRIA, PALESTINE, AND THE HOLY LAND. With Maps, Photographs, and Coloured Plates. 2 vols. Second Edition. Demy 8vo. price 24s.

    * Also a Cheaper Edition in one volume. Large post 8vo. cloth, price 10s. 6d.

BURTON (*Capt. Richard F.*)—THE GOLD MINES OF MIDIAN AND THE RUINED MIDIANITE CITIES. A Fortnight's Tour in North Western Arabia. With numerous illustrations. Second Edition. Demy 8vo. price 18s.

    THE LAND OF MIDIAN REVISITED. With numerous Illustrations on Wood and by Chromolithography. 2 vols. Demy 8vo. cloth, price 32s.

BUSBECQ (*Ogier Ghiselin de*)—HIS LIFE AND LETTERS. By CHARLES THORNTON FORSTER, M.A., and F. H. BLACKBURNE DANIELL, M.A. 2 vols. With Frontispieces. Demy 8vo. cloth, price 24s.

CANDLER (H.)—THE GROUNDWORK OF BELIEF. Crown 8vo. cloth, price 7s.

CARPENTER (Dr. Philip P.)—HIS LIFE AND WORK. Edited by his brother, Russell Lant Carpenter. With Portrait and Vignettes. Second Edition. Crown 8vo. cloth, price 7s. 6d.

CARPENTER (W. B.) LL.D., M.D., F.R.S., &c.—THE PRINCIPLES OF MENTAL PHYSIOLOGY. With their Applications to the Training and Discipline of the Mind, and the Study of its Morbid Conditions. Illustrated. Fifth Edition. 8vo. price 12s.

CERVANTES—THE INGENIOUS KNIGHT DON QUIXOTE DE LA MANCHA. A New Translation from the Originals of 1605 and 1608. By A. J. DUFFIELD. With Notes. 3 vols. Demy 8vo. price 42s.

CHEYNE (Rev. T. K.)—THE PROPHECIES OF ISAIAH. Translated with Critical Notes and Dissertations. 2 vols. Demy 8vo. cloth, price 25s.

CLAYDEN (P. W.)—ENGLAND UNDER LORD BEACONSFIELD. The Political History of the Last Six Years, from the end of 1873 to the beginning of 1880. Second Edition, with Index and continuation to March 1880. Demy 8vo. cloth, price 16s.

CLODD (Edward) F.R.A.S.—THE CHILDHOOD OF THE WORLD: a Simple Account of Man in Early Times. Sixth Edition. Crown 8vo. price 3s. A Special Edition for Schools. Price 1s.

THE CHILDHOOD OF RELIGIONS. Including a Simple Account of the Birth and Growth of Myths and Legends. Third Thousand. Crown 8vo. price 5s.
A Special Edition for Schools. Price 1s. 6d.

JESUS OF NAZARETH. With a brief sketch of Jewish History to the Time of His Birth. Small crown 8vo. cloth, price 6s.

COGHLAN (J. Cole) D.D.—THE MODERN PHARISEE AND OTHER SERMONS. Edited by the Very Rev. H. H. DICKINSON, D.D., Dean of Chapel Royal, Dublin. New and Cheaper Edition. Crown 8vo. cloth, 7s. 6d.

COLERIDGE (Sara)—PHANTASMION. A Fairy Tale. With an Introductory Preface by the Right Hon. Lord Coleridge, of Ottery St. Mary. A New Edition. Illustrated. Crown 8vo. price 7s. 6d.

MEMOIR AND LETTERS OF SARA COLERIDGE. Edited by her Daughter. With Index. Cheap Edition. With one Portrait. Price 7s. 6d.

COLLINS (Mortimer)—THE SECRET OF LONG LIFE. Small crown 8vo. cloth, price 3s. 6d.

CONNELL (A. K.)—DISCONTENT AND DANGER IN INDIA. Small crown 8vo. cloth, price 3s. 6d.

COOKE (Prof. J. P.) of the Harvard University.—SCIENTIFIC CULTURE. Crown 8vo. price 1s.

COOPER (H. J.)—THE ART OF FURNISHING ON RATIONAL AND ÆSTHETIC PRINCIPLES. New and Cheaper Edition. Fcap. 8vo. cloth, price 1s. 6d.

CORFIELD (Professor) M.D.—HEALTH. Crown 8vo. cloth, price 6s.

CORY (William)—A GUIDE TO MODERN ENGLISH HISTORY. Part I.—MDCCCXV.–MDCCCXXX. Demy 8vo. cloth, price 9s.

COURTNEY (W. L.)—THE METAPHYSICS OF JOHN STUART MILL. Crown 8vo. cloth, price 5s. 6d.

COX (*Rev. Sir George W.*) *M.A., Bart.*—A HISTORY OF GREECE FROM THE EARLIEST PERIOD TO THE END OF THE PERSIAN WAR. New Edition. 2 vols. Demy 8vo. price 36*s.*

    THE MYTHOLOGY OF THE ARYAN NATIONS. New Edition. 2 vols. Demy 8vo. price 28*s.*

    A GENERAL HISTORY OF GREECE FROM THE EARLIEST PERIOD TO THE DEATH OF ALEXANDER THE GREAT, with a sketch of the subsequent History to the present time. New Edition. Crown 8vo. price 7*s.* 6*d.*

    TALES OF ANCIENT GREECE. New Edition. Small crown 8vo. price 6*s.*

    SCHOOL HISTORY OF GREECE. New Edition. With Maps. Fcp. 8vo. price 3*s.* 6*d.*

    THE GREAT PERSIAN WAR FROM THE HISTORY OF HERODOTUS. New Edition. Fcp. 8vo. price 3*s.* 6*d.*

    A MANUAL OF MYTHOLOGY IN THE FORM OF QUESTION AND ANSWER. New Edition. Fcp. 8vo. price 3*s.*

COX (*Rev. Sir G. W.*) *M.A., Bart., and* **JONES** (*Eustace Hinton*)—POPULAR ROMANCES OF THE MIDDLE AGES. Second Edition, in 1 vol. Crown 8vo. cloth, price 6*s.*

COX (*Rev. Samuel*)—SALVATOR MUNDI; or, Is Christ the Saviour of all Men? Sixth Edition. Crown 8vo. price 5*s.*

    THE GENESIS OF EVIL, AND OTHER SERMONS, mainly expository. Second Edition. Crown 8vo. cloth, price 6*s.*

    A COMMENTARY ON THE BOOK OF JOB. With a Translation. Demy 8vo. cloth, price 15*s.*

CRAUFURD (*A. H.*)—SEEKING FOR LIGHT: Sermons. Crown 8vo. cloth, price 5*s.*

CRAVEN (*Mrs.*)—A YEAR'S MEDITATIONS. Crown 8vo. cloth, price 6*s.*

CRAWFURD (*Oswald*)—PORTUGAL, OLD AND NEW. With Illustrations and Maps. Demy 8vo. cloth, price 16*s.*

CROMPTON (*Henry*) — INDUSTRIAL CONCILIATION. Fcap. 8vo. price 2*s.* 6*d.*

CROZIER (*John Beattie*) *M.B.*—THE RELIGION OF THE FUTURE. Crown 8vo. cloth, price 6*s.*

DALTON (*John Neale*) *M.A., R.N.*—SERMONS TO NAVAL CADETS. Preached on board H.M.S. 'Britannia.' Second Edition. Small crown 8vo. cloth, price 3*s.* 6*d.*

DAVIDSON (*Rev. Samuel*) *D.D., LL.D.* — THE NEW TESTAMENT, TRANSLATED FROM THE LATEST GREEK TEXT OF TISCHENDORF. A New and thoroughly revised Edition. Post 8vo. price 10*s.* 6*d.*

    CANON OF THE BIBLE: Its Formation, History, and Fluctuations. Third and revised Edition. Small crown 8vo. price 5*s.*

DAVIES (*Rev. J. L.*) *M.A.*—THEOLOGY AND MORALITY. Essays on Questions of Belief and Practice. Crown 8vo. price 7*s.* 6*d.*

DAWSON (*Geo.*) *M.A.*—PRAYERS, WITH A DISCOURSE ON PRAYER. Edited by his Wife. Fifth Edition. Crown 8vo. 6*s.*

    SERMONS ON DISPUTED POINTS AND SPECIAL OCCASIONS. Edited by his Wife. Third Edition. Crown 8vo. price 6*s.*

    SERMONS ON DAILY LIFE AND DUTY. Edited by his Wife. Third Edition. Crown 8vo. price 6*s.*

DE REDCLIFFE (Viscount Stratford) P.C., K.G., G.C.B.—WHY AM I A CHRISTIAN? Fifth Edition. Crown 8vo. price 3s.

DESPREZ (Philip S.) B.D.—DANIEL AND JOHN; or, the Apocalypse of the Old and that of the New Testament. Demy 8vo. cloth, price 12s.

DE TOCQUEVILLE (A.)—CORRESPONDENCE AND CONVERSATIONS OF, WITH NASSAU WILLIAM SENIOR, from 1834 to 1859. Edited by M. C. M. SIMPSON. 2 vols. post 8vo. price 21s.

DOWDEN (Edward) LL.D.—SHAKSPERE: a Critical Study of his Mind and Art. Fifth Edition. Post 8vo. price 12s.

STUDIES IN LITERATURE, 1789–1877. Large Post 8vo. price 12s.

DREWRY (G. O.) M.D.—THE COMMON-SENSE MANAGEMENT OF THE STOMACH. Fifth Edition. Fcp. 8vo. price 2s. 6d.

DREWRY (G. O.) M.D., and BARTLETT (H. C.) Ph.D., F.C.S.
CUP AND PLATTER: or, Notes on Food and its Effects. New and Cheaper Edition. Small 8vo. price 1s. 6d.

DU MONCEL (Count)—THE TELEPHONE, THE MICROPHONE, AND THE PHONOGRAPH. With 74 Illustrations. Small crown 8vo. cloth, price 5s.

EDEN (Frederick)—THE NILE WITHOUT A DRAGOMAN. Second Edition. Crown 8vo. price 7s. 6d.

EDGEWORTH (F. Y.).—MATHEMATICAL PSYCHICS. An Essay on the Application of Mathematics to Social Science. Demy 8vo cloth 7s. 6d.

EDIS (Robert W.) F.S.A. &c.—DECORATION AND FURNITURE OF TOWN HOUSES: a Series of Cantor Lectures, delivered before the Society of Arts, 1880. Second Edition, Amplified and Enlarged. With 29 Full-page Illustrations and numerous Sketches. Square 8vo. cloth, price 12s. 6d.

EDUCATIONAL CODE OF THE PRUSSIAN NATION, IN ITS PRESENT FORM. In accordance with the Decisions of the Common Provincial Law, and with those of Recent Legislation. Crown 8vo. cloth, price 2s. 6d.

ELSDALE (Henry)—STUDIES IN TENNYSON'S IDYLLS. Crown 8vo. price 5s.

ELYOT (Sir Thomas)—THE BOKE NAMED THE GOUERNOUR. Edited from the First Edition of 1531 by HENRY HERBERT STEPHEN CROFT, M.A., Barrister-at-Law. With Portraits of Sir Thomas and Lady Elyot, copied by permission of her Majesty from Holbein's Original Drawings at Windsor Castle. 2 vols. fcp. 4to. cloth, price 50s.

EVANS (Mark)—THE STORY OF OUR FATHER'S LOVE, told to Children. Fifth and Cheaper Edition. With Four Illustrations. Fcp. 8vo. price 1s. 6d.

A BOOK OF COMMON PRAYER AND WORSHIP FOR HOUSEHOLD USE, compiled exclusively from the Holy Scriptures. Fcp. 8vo. price 1s.

THE GOSPEL OF HOME LIFE. Crown 8vo. cloth, price 4s. 6d.

THE KING'S STORY-BOOK. In Three Parts. Fcap. 8vo. cloth, price 1s. 6d. each.

⁎⁎ Parts I. and II. with Eight Illustrations and Two Picture Maps, now ready.

EX-CIVILIAN.—LIFE IN THE MOFUSSIL: or Civilian Life in Lower Bengal. 2 vols. Large post 8vo. price 14s.

FIELD (Horace) B.A. Lond.—THE ULTIMATE TRIUMPH OF CHRISTIANITY. Small crown 8vo. cloth, price 3*s.* 6*d*

FINN (The late James) M.R.A.S.—STIRRING TIMES ; or, Records from Jerusalem Consular Chronicles of 1853 to 1856. Edited and Compiled by his Widow ; with a Preface by the Viscountess STRANGFORD. 2 vols. Demy 8vo. price 30*s.*

FOLKESTONE RITUAL CASE : the Arguments, Proceedings, Judgment, and Report. Demy 8vo. price 25*s.*

FORMBY (Rev. Henry)—ANCIENT ROME AND ITS CONNECTION WITH THE CHRISTIAN RELIGION : An Outline of the History of the City from its First Foundation down to the Erection of the Chair of St. Peter, A.D. 42-47. With numerous Illustrations of Ancient Monuments, Sculpture, and Coinage, and of the Antiquities of the Christian Catacombs. Royal '^, cloth extra, £2. 10*s* ; roxburgh half-morocco, £2. 12*s.* 6*d.*

FOWLE (Rev. T. W.) M.A.—THE RECONCILIATION OF RELIGION AND SCIENCE. Being Essays on Immortality, Inspiration, Miracles, and the Being of Christ. Demy 8vo. price 10*s.* 6*d.*

THE DIVINE LEGATION OF CHRIST. Crown 8vo. cloth, price 7*s.*

FRASER (Donald)—EXCHANGE TABLES OF STERLING AND INDIAN RUPEE CURRENCY, upon a new and extended system, embracing Values from One Farthing to One Hundred Thousand Pounds, and at rates progressing, in Sixteenths of a Penny, from 1*s.* 9*d.* to 2*s.* 3*d.* per Rupee. Royal 8vo. price 10*s.* 6*d.*

FRISWELL (J. Hain)—THE BETTER SELF. Essays for Home Life. Crown 8vo. price 6*s.*

GARDNER (J.) M.D.—LONGEVITY : THE MEANS OF PROLONGING LIFE AFTER MIDDLE AGE. Fourth Edition, revised and enlarged. Small crown 8vo. price 4*s.*

GEBLER (Karl Von)—GALILEO GALILEI AND THE ROMAN CURIA, from Authentic Sources. Translated with the sanction of the Author, by Mrs. GEORGE STURGE. Demy 8vo. cloth, price 12*s.*

GEDDES (James)—HISTORY OF THE ADMINISTRATION OF JOHN DE WITT, Grand Pensionary of Holland. Vol. I. 1623—1654. With Portrait. Demy 8vo. cloth, price 15*s.*

GEORGE (Henry)—PROGRESS AND POVERTY : an Inquiry into the Causes of Industrial Depressions, and of Increase of Want with Increase of Wealth. The Remedy. Post 8vo. cloth, price 7*s.* 6*d.*

GILBERT (Mrs.)—AUTOBIOGRAPHY AND OTHER MEMORIALS. Edited by Josiah Gilbert. Third and Cheaper Edition. With Steel Portrait and several Wood Engravings. Crown 8vo. price 7*s.* 6*d.*

GILL (Rev. W. W.) B.A.—MYTHS AND SONGS FROM THE SOUTH PACIFIC. With a Preface by F. Max Müller, M.A., Professor of Comparative Philology at Oxford. Post 8vo. price 9*s.*

GLOVER (F.) M.A.—EXEMPLA LATINA. A First Construing Book with Short Notes, Lexicon, and an Introduction to the Analysis of Sentences. Fcp. 8vo. cloth, price 2*s.*

GODWIN (William)—WILLIAM GODWIN: HIS FRIENDS AND CONTEM-
PORARIES. With Portraits and Facsimiles of the Handwriting of Godwin and his Wife. By C. KEGAN PAUL. 2 vols. Large post 8vo. price 28s.

THE GENIUS OF CHRISTIANITY UNVEILED. Being Essays never before published. Edited, with a Preface, by C. Kegan Paul. Crown 8vo. price 7s. 6d.

GOLDSMID (Sir Francis Henry) Bart., Q.C., M.P.—MEMOIR OF. With Portrait. Crown 8vo. cloth, price 5s.

GOODENOUGH (Commodore J. G.) R.N., C.B., C.M.G.—MEMOIR OF, with Extracts from his Letters and Journals. Edited by his Widow. With Steel Engraved Portrait. Square 8vo. cloth, 5s.

*** Also a Library Edition with Maps, Woodcuts, and Steel Engraved Portrait. Square post 8vo. price 14s.

GOSSE (Edmund W.)—STUDIES IN THE LITERATURE OF NORTHERN EUROPE. With a Frontispiece designed and etched by Alma Tadema. Large post 8vo. cloth, price 12s.

GOULD (Rev. S. Baring) M.A.—THE VICAR OF MORWENSTOW: a Memoir of the Rev. R. S. Hawker. With Portrait. Third Edition, revised. Square post 8vo. 10s. 6d.

GERMANY, PRESENT AND PAST. 2 vols. Large crown 8vo. cloth, price 21s.

GRIFFITH (Thomas) A.M.—THE GOSPEL OF THE DIVINE LIFE: a Study of the Fourth Evangelist. Demy 8vo. cloth, price 14s.

GRIMLEY (Rev. H. N.) M.A.—TREMADOC SERMONS, CHIEFLY ON THE SPIRITUAL BODY, THE UNSEEN WORLD, AND THE DIVINE HUMANITY. Second Edition. Crown 8vo. price 6s.

GRÜNER (M. L.)—STUDIES OF BLAST FURNACE PHENOMENA. Translated by L. D. B. GORDON, F.R.S.E., F.G.S. Demy 8vo. price 7s. 6d.

GURNEY (Rev. Archer)—WORDS OF FAITH AND CHEER. A Mission of Instruction and Suggestion. Crown 8vo. price 6s.

HAECKEL (Prof. Ernst)—THE HISTORY OF CREATION. Translation revised by Professor E. RAY LANKESTER, M.A., F.R.S. With Coloured Plates and Genealogical Trees of the various groups of both plants and animals. 2 vols. Second Edition. Post 8vo. cloth, price 32s.

THE HISTORY OF THE EVOLUTION OF MAN. With numerous Illustrations. 2 vols. Post 8vo. price 32s.

FREEDOM IN SCIENCE AND TEACHING. With a Prefatory Note by T. H. HUXLEY, F.R.S. Crown 8vo. cloth, price 5s.

HAKE (A. Egmont)—PARIS ORIGINALS, with Twenty Etchings, by LÉON RICHETON. Large post 8vo. price 14s.

HALLECK'S INTERNATIONAL LAW; or, Rules Regulating the Intercourse of States in Peace and War. A New Edition, revised, with Notes and Cases, by Sir SHERSTON BAKER, Bart. 2 vols. Demy 8vo. price 38s.

HARTINGTON (The Right Hon. the Marquis of) M.P.—ELECTION SPEECHES IN 1879 AND 1880. With Address to the Electors of North East Lancashire. Crown 8vo. cloth, price 3s. 6d.

HAWEIS (Rev. H. R.) M.A.—CURRENT COIN. Materialism—The Devil — Crime — Drunkenness — Pauperism — Emotion — Recreation — The Sabbath. Third Edition. Crown 8vo. price 6s.

SPEECH IN SEASON. Fourth Edition. Crown 8vo. price 9s.

THOUGHTS FOR THE TIMES. Eleventh Edition. Crown 8vo. price 7s. 6d.

UNSECTARIAN FAMILY PRAYERS. New and Cheaper Edition. Fcp. 8vo. price 1s. 6d.

ARROWS IN THE AIR. Second Edition. Crown 8vo. cloth, price 6s.

HAWKINS (Edwards Comerford)—SPIRIT AND FORM. Sermons preached in the Parish Church of Leatherhead. Crown 8vo. cloth, price 6s.

HAYES (A. H.), Junr.—NEW COLORADO AND THE SANTA FÉ TRAIL. With Map and 60 Illustrations. Crown 8vo. cloth, price 9s.

HEIDENHAIN (Rudolf) M.D.—ANIMAL MAGNETISM : PHYSIOLOGICAL OBSERVATIONS. Translated from the Fourth German Edition by L. C. WOOLDRIDGE, with a Preface by G. R. ROMANES, F.R.S. Crown 8vo. price 2s. 6d.

HELLWALD (Baron F. Von)—THE RUSSIANS IN CENTRAL ASIA. A Critical Examination, down to the Present Time, of the Geography and History of Central Asia. Translated by Lieut.-Col. THEODORE WIRGMAN, LL.B. With Map. Large post 8vo. price 12s.

HINTON (J.)—THE PLACE OF THE PHYSICIAN. To which is added ESSAYS ON THE LAW OF HUMAN LIFE, AND ON THE RELATIONS BETWEEN ORGANIC AND INORGANIC WORLDS. Second Edition. Crown 8vo. price 3s. 6d.

PHYSIOLOGY FOR PRACTICAL USE. By Various Writers. With 50 Illustrations. Third and Cheaper Edition. Crown 8vo. price 5s.

AN ATLAS OF DISEASES OF THE MEMBRANA TYMPANI. With Descriptive Text. Post 8vo. price £6. 6s.

THE QUESTIONS OF AURAL SURGERY. With Illustrations. 2 vols. Post 8vo. price 12s. 6d.

CHAPTERS ON THE ART OF THINKING, AND OTHER ESSAYS. With an Introduction by SHADWORTH HODGSON. Edited by C. H. HINTON. Crown 8vo. cloth, price 8s. 6d.

THE MYSTERY OF PAIN. New Edition. Fcap. 8vo. cloth limp, 1s.

LIFE AND LETTERS. Edited by ELLICE HOPKINS, with an Introduction by Sir W. W. GULL, Bart., and Portrait engraved on Steel by C. H. JEENS. Third Edition. Crown 8vo. price 8s. 6d.

HOOPER (Mary)—LITTLE DINNERS: HOW TO SERVE THEM WITH ELEGANCE AND ECONOMY. Thirteenth Edition. Crown 8vo. price 5s.

COOKERY FOR INVALIDS, PERSONS OF DELICATE DIGESTION, AND CHILDREN. Crown 8vo. price 3s. 6d.

EVERY-DAY MEALS. Being Economical and Wholesome Recipes for Breakfast, Luncheon, and Supper. Second Edition. Crown 8vo. cloth, price 5s.

HOPKINS (Ellice)—LIFE AND LETTERS OF JAMES HINTON, with an Introduction by Sir W. W. GULL, Bart., and Portrait engraved on Steel by C. H. JEENS. Third Edition. Crown 8vo. price 8s. 6d.

HORNER (The Misses)—WALKS IN FLORENCE. A New and thoroughly Revised Edition. 2 vols. Crown 8vo. Cloth limp. With Illustrations.
    VOL. I.—Churches, Streets, and Palaces. Price 10s. 6d.
    VOL. II.—Public Galleries and Museums. Price 5s.

HULL (Edmund C. P.)—THE EUROPEAN IN INDIA. With a Medical Guide for Anglo-Indians. By R. S. MAIR, M.D., F.R.C.S.E. Third Edition, Revised and Corrected. Post 8vo. price 6s.

HUTTON (Arthur) M.A.—THE ANGLICAN MINISTRY: its Nature and Value in relation to the Catholic Priesthood. With a Preface by His Eminence Cardinal Newman. Demy 8vo. cloth, price 14s.

JENKINS (E.) and RAYMOND (J.)—THE ARCHITECT'S LEGAL HANDBOOK. Third Edition, Revised. Crown 8vo. price 6s.

JENKINS (Rev. R. C.) M.A.—THE PRIVILEGE OF PETER and the Claims of the Roman Church confronted with the Scriptures, the Councils, and the Testimony of the Popes themselves. Fcap. 8vo. price 3s. 6d.

JENNINGS (Mrs. Vaughan)—RAHEL: HER LIFE AND LETTERS. With a Portrait from the Painting by Daffinger. Square post 8vo. price 7s. 6d.

JOEL (L.)—A CONSUL'S MANUAL AND SHIPOWNER'S AND SHIPMASTER'S PRACTICAL GUIDE IN THEIR TRANSACTIONS ABROAD. With Definitions of Nautical, Mercantile, and Legal Terms; a Glossary of Mercantile Terms in English, French, German, Italian, and Spanish; Tables of the Money, Weights, and Measures of the Principal Commercial Nations and their Equivalents in British Standards; and Forms of Consular and Notarial Acts. Demy 8vo. cloth, price 12s.

JOHNSTONE (C. F.) M.A.—HISTORICAL ABSTRACTS: being Outlines of the History of some of the less known States of Europe. Crown 8vo. cloth, price 7s. 6d.

JONES (Lucy)— PUDDINGS AND SWEETS; being Three Hundred and Sixty-five Receipts approved by experience. Crown 8vo. price 2s. 6d.

JOYCE (P. W.) LL.D. &c.—OLD CELTIC ROMANCES. Translated from the Gaelic. Crown 8vo. cloth, price 7s. 6d.

KAUFMANN (Rev. M.) B.A.—SOCIALISM: Its Nature, its Dangers, and its Remedies considered. Crown 8vo. price 7s. 6d.

    UTOPIAS; or, Schemes of Social Improvement, from Sir Thomas More to Karl Marx. Crown 8vo. cloth, price 5s.

KAY (Joseph) M.A., Q.C.—FREE TRADE IN LAND. Edited by his Widow. With Preface by the Right Hon. JOHN BRIGHT, M.P. Sixth Edition. Crown 8vo. cloth, price 5s.

KEMPIS (Thomas A)—OF THE IMITATION OF CHRIST. A revised Translation, choicely printed on hand-made paper, with a Miniature Frontispiece on India paper from a design by W. B. RICHMOND. Limp parchment, antique, price 6s.; vellum, 7s. 6d.

KENT (C.)—CORONA CATHOLICA AD PETRI SUCCESSORIS PEDES OBLATA. DE SUMMI PONTIFICIS LEONIS XIII. ASSUMPTIONE EPIGRAMMA. In Quinquaginta Linguis. Fcp. 4to. cloth, price 15s.

KERNER (Dr. A.) Professor of Botany in the University of Innsbruck.—FLOWERS AND THEIR UNBIDDEN GUESTS. Translation edited by W. OGLE, M.A., M.D. With Illustrations. Square 8vo. cloth, price 9s.

KIDD (Joseph) M.D.—THE LAWS OF THERAPEUTICS ; or, the Science and Art of Medicine. Second Edition. Crown 8vo. price 6s.

KINAHAN (G. Henry) M.R.I.A., of H.M.'s Geological Survey.—THE GEOLOGY OF IRELAND, with numerous Illustrations and a Geological Map of Ireland. Square 8vo. cloth.

KINGSLEY (Charles) M.A.—LETTERS AND MEMORIES OF HIS LIFE. Edited by his WIFE. With Two Steel Engraved Portraits, and Illustrations on Wood, and a Facsimile of his Handwriting. Thirteenth Edition. 2 vols. Demy 8vo. price 36s.
  *** Also the Ninth Cabinet Edition, in 2 vols. Crown 8vo. cloth, price 12s.
  ALL SAINTS' DAY, and other Sermons. Edited by the Rev. W. HARRISON. Third Edition. Crown 8vo. price 7s. 6d.
  TRUE WORDS FOR BRAVE MEN. A Book for Soldiers' and Sailors' Libraries. Eighth Edition. Crown 8vo. price 2s. 6d.

KNIGHT (Professor W.)—STUDIES IN PHILOSOPHY AND LITERATURE. Large post 8vo. cloth, price 7s. 6d.

KNOX (Alexander A.)—THE NEW PLAYGROUND; or, Wanderings in Algeria. Large crown 8vo. cloth, price 10s. 6d.

LACORDAIRE (Rev. Père)—LIFE : Conferences delivered at Toulouse. A New and Cheaper Edition. Crown 8vo. price 3s. 6d.

LEE (Rev. F. G.) D.C.L.—THE OTHER WORLD; or, Glimpses of the Supernatural. 2 vols. A New Edition. Crown 8vo. price 15s.

LEWIS (Edward Dillon)—A DRAFT CODE OF CRIMINAL LAW AND PROCEDURE. Demy 8vo. cloth, price 21s.

LIFE IN THE MOFUSSIL ; or, Civilian Life in Lower Bengal. By an Ex-Civilian. Large post 8vo. price 14s.

LINDSAY (W. Lauder) M.D., F.R.S.E., &c.—MIND IN THE LOWER ANIMALS IN HEALTH AND DISEASE. 2 vols. Demy 8vo. cloth, price 32s. Vol. I.—Mind in Health. Vol. II.—Mind in Disease.

LLOYD (Francis), and TEBBITT (Charles)—EXTENSION OF EMPIRE, WEAKNESS? DEFICITS, RUIN? With a Practical Scheme for the Reconstruction of Asiatic Turkey. Small crown 8vo. cloth, price 3s. 6d.

LONSDALE (Margaret)—SISTER DORA : a Biography. With Portrait, engraved on Steel by C. H. Jeens, and one Illustration. Nineteenth Edition. Crown 8vo. cloth, price 2s. 6d.

LORIMER (Peter) D.D.—JOHN KNOX AND THE CHURCH OF ENGLAND. His Work in her Pulpit, and his Influence upon her Liturgy, Articles, and Parties. Demy 8vo. price 12s.
  JOHN WICLIF AND HIS ENGLISH PRECURSORS. By GERHARD VICTOR LECHLER. Translated from the German, with additional Notes. 2 vols. Demy 8vo. price 21s.

MACLACHLAN (Mrs.)—NOTES AND EXTRACTS ON EVERLASTING PUNISHMENT AND ETERNAL LIFE, ACCORDING TO LITERAL INTERPRETATION. Small crown 8vo. cloth, price 3s. 6d.

MACNAUGHT (Rev. John)—CŒNA DOMINI : An Essay on the Lord's Supper, its Primitive Institution, Apostolic Uses, and Subsequent History. Demy 8vo. price 14s.

MAGNUS (Mrs.)—ABOUT THE JEWS SINCE BIBLE TIMES. From the Babylonian Exile till the English Exodus. Small crown 8vo. cloth, price 5s.

MAIR (R. S.) M.D., F.R.C.S.E.—THE MEDICAL GUIDE FOR ANGLO-INDIANS. Being a Compendium of Advice to Europeans in India, relating to the Preservation and Regulation of Health. With a Supplement on the Management of Children in India. Second Edition. Crown 8vo. limp cloth, price 3s. 6d.

MANNING (His Eminence Cardinal)—THE TRUE STORY OF THE VATICAN COUNCIL. Crown 8vo. price 5s.

MARKHAM (Capt. Albert Hastings) R.N.—THE GREAT FROZEN SEA : A Personal Narrative of the Voyage of the *Alert* during the Arctic Expedition of 1875-6. With Six Full-page Illustrations, Two Maps, and Twenty-seven Woodcuts. Fourth and Cheaper Edition. Crown 8vo. cloth, price 6s.

A POLAR RECONNAISSANCE : being the Voyage of the 'Isbjörn' to Novaya Zemlya in 1879. With 10 Illustrations. Demy 8vo. cloth, price 16s.

McGRATH (Terence)—PICTURES FROM IRELAND. New and Cheaper Edition. Crown 8vo. cloth, price 2s.

MERRITT (Henry)—ART-CRITICISM AND ROMANCE. With Recollections and Twenty-three Illustrations in *eau-forte*, by Anna Lea Merritt. Two vols. Large post 8vo. cloth, price 25s.

MILLER (Edward)—THE HISTORY AND DOCTRINES OF IRVINGISM ; or, the so-called Catholic and Apostolic Church. 2 vols. Large post 8vo. price 25s.

THE CHURCH IN RELATION TO THE STATE. Large crown 8vo. cloth, price 7s. 6d.

MILNE (James)—TABLES OF EXCHANGE for the Conversion of Sterling Money into Indian and Ceylon Currency, at Rates from 1s. 8d. to 2s. 3d. per Rupee. Second Edition. Demy 8vo. Cloth, price £2. 2s.

MINCHIN (J. G.)—BULGARIA SINCE THE WAR : Notes of a Tour in the Autumn of 1879. Small crown 8vo. cloth, price 3s. 6d.

MOCKLER (E.)—A GRAMMAR OF THE BALOOCHEE LANGUAGE, as it is spoken in Makran (Ancient Gedrosia), in the Persia-Arabic and Roman characters. Fcap. 8vo. price 5s.

MOFFAT (R. S.)—ECONOMY OF CONSUMPTION : a Study in Political Economy. Demy 8vo. price 18s.

THE PRINCIPLES OF A TIME POLICY : being an Exposition of a Method of Settling Disputes between Employers and Employed in regard to Time and Wages, by a simple Process of Mercantile Barter, without recourse to Strikes or Locks-out. Reprinted from 'The Economy of Consumption,' with a Preface and Appendix containing Observations on some Reviews of that book, and a Re-criticism of the Theories of Ricardo and J. S. Mill on Rent, Value, and Cost of Production. Demy 8vo. price 3s. 6d.

MOLTKE (Field-Marshal Von)—LETTERS FROM RUSSIA. Translated by ROBINA NAPIER. Crown 8vo. price 6s.

NOTES OF TRAVEL. Being Extracts from the Journals of. Crown 8vo. cloth, price 6s.

MORELL (J. R.)—EUCLID SIMPLIFIED IN METHOD AND LANGUAGE. Being a Manual of Geometry. Compiled from the most important French Works, approved by the University of Paris and the Minister of Public Instruction. Fcap. 8vo. price 2s. 6d.

MORSE (E. S.) Ph.D.—FIRST BOOK OF ZOOLOGY. With numerous Illustrations. New and Cheaper Edition. Crown 8vo. price 2s. 6d.

NEWMAN (J. H.) D.D.—CHARACTERISTICS FROM THE WRITINGS OF. Being Selections from his various Works. Arranged with the Author's personal Approval. Third Edition. With Portrait. Crown 8vo. price 6s.

*** A Portrait of the Rev. Dr. J. H. Newman, mounted for framing, can be had price 2s. 6d.

NEW WERTHER. By LOKI. Small crown 8vo. cloth, 2s. 6d.

NICHOLAS (T.)—THE PEDIGREE OF THE ENGLISH PEOPLE. Fifth Edition. Demy 8vo. price 16s.

NICHOLSON (Edward Byron)—THE GOSPEL ACCORDING TO THE HEBREWS. Its Fragments Translated and Annotated with a Critical Analysis of the External and Internal Evidence relating to it. Demy 8vo. cloth, price 9s. 6d.

THE RIGHTS OF AN ANIMAL. Crown 8vo. cloth, price 3s. 6d.

NICOLS (Arthur) F.G.S., F.R.G.S.—CHAPTERS FROM THE PHYSICAL HISTORY OF THE EARTH : an Introduction to Geology and Palæontology. With numerous Illustrations. Crown 8vo. cloth, price 5s.

NORMAN PEOPLE (THE), and their Existing Descendants in the British Dominions and the United States of America. Demy 8vo. price 21s.

NUCES : EXERCISES ON THE SYNTAX OF THE PUBLIC SCHOOL LATIN PRIMER. New Edition in Three Parts. Crown 8vo. each 1s.

*** The Three Parts can also be had bound together in cloth, price 3s.

O'MEARA (Kathleen)—FREDERIC OZANAM, Professor of the Sorbonne: His Life and Work. Second Edition. Crown 8vo. cloth, price 7s. 6d.

OUR PUBLIC SCHOOLS—ETON, HARROW, WINCHESTER, RUGBY, WESTMINSTER, MARLBOROUGH, THE CHARTERHOUSE. Crown 8vo. cloth, price 6s.

OWEN (F. M.)—JOHN KEATS : a Study. Crown 8vo. cloth, price 6s.

OWEN (Rev. Robert) B.D.—SANCTORALE CATHOLICUM; or, Book of Saints. With Notes, Critical, Exegetical, and Historical. Demy 8vo. cloth, price 18s.

AN ESSAY ON THE COMMUNION OF SAINTS. Including an Examination of the Cultus Sanctorum. Price 2s.

PARKER (Joseph) D.D.—THE PARACLETE : An Essay on the Personality and Ministry of the Holy Ghost, with some reference to current discussions. Second Edition. Demy 8vo. price 12s.

PARR (Capt. H. Hallam, C. M. G.)—A SKETCH OF THE KAFIR AND ZULU WARS : Guadana to Isandhlwana. With Maps. Small Crown 8vo. cloth, price 5s.

PARSLOE (Joseph) — OUR RAILWAYS. Sketches, Historical and Descriptive. With Practical Information as to Fares and Rates, &c., and a Chapter on Railway Reform. Crown 8vo. price 6s.

PATTISON (Mrs. Mark)—THE RENAISSANCE OF ART IN FRANCE. With Nineteen Steel Engravings. 2 vols. demy 8vo. cloth, price 32*s*.

PAUL (C. Kegan)—WILLIAM GODWIN: HIS FRIENDS AND CONTEMPORARIES. With Portraits and Facsimiles of the Handwriting of Godwin and his Wife. 2 vols. Square post 8vo. price 28*s*.

THE GENIUS OF CHRISTIANITY UNVEILED. Being Essays by William Godwin never before published. Edited, with a Preface, by C. Kegan Paul. Crown 8vo. price 7*s*. 6*d*.

MARY WOLLSTONECRAFT. Letters to Imlay. New Edition with Prefatory Memoir by. Two Portraits in *eau-forte* by ANNA LEA MERRITT. Crown 8vo. cloth, 6*s*.

PAYNE (Prof. J. F.)—LECTURES ON EDUCATION. Price 6*d*. each.
    II. Fröbel and the Kindergarten System. Second Edition.

A VISIT TO GERMAN SCHOOLS: ELEMENTARY SCHOOLS IN GERMANY. Notes of a Professional Tour to inspect some of the Kindergartens, Primary Schools, Public Girls' Schools, and Schools for Technical Instruction in Hamburgh, Berlin, Dresden, Weimar, Gotha, Eisenach, in the autumn of 1874. With Critical Discussions of the General Principles and Practice of Kindergartens and other Schemes of Elementary Education. Crown 8vo. price 4*s*. 6*d*.

PENRICE (Maj. J.) B.A.—A DICTIONARY AND GLOSSARY OF THE KO-RAN. With Copious Grammatical References and Explanations of the Text. 4to. price 21*s*.

PESCHEL (Dr. Oscar)—THE RACES OF MAN AND THEIR GEOGRAPHICAL DISTRIBUTION. Large crown 8vo. price 9*s*.

PINCHES (Thomas) M.A.—SAMUEL WILBERFORCE: FAITH—SERVICE—RECOMPENSE. Three Sermons. With a Portrait of Bishop Wilberforce (after a Portrait by Charles Watkins). Crown 8vo. cloth, price 4*s*. 6*d*.

PLAYFAIR (Lieut-Col.) Her Britannic Majesty's Consul-General in Algiers.
    TRAVELS IN THE FOOTSTEPS OF BRUCE IN ALGERIA AND TUNIS. Illustrated by facsimiles of Bruce's original Drawings, Photographs, Maps, &c. Royal 4to. cloth, bevelled boards, gilt leaves, price £3. 3*s*.

POLLOCK (Frederick)—SPINOZA, HIS LIFE AND PHILOSOPHY. Demy 8vo. cloth, price 16*s*.

POLLOCK (W. H.)—LECTURES ON FRENCH POETS. Delivered at the Royal Institution. Small crown 8vo. cloth, price 5*s*.

POOR (Laura E.)—SANSKRIT AND ITS KINDRED LITERATURES. Studies in Comparative Mythology. Small crown 8vo. cloth, 5*s*.

POUSHKIN (A. S.)—RUSSIAN ROMANCE. Translated from the Tales of Belkin, &c. By Mrs. J. Buchan Telfer (*née* Mouravieff). New and Cheaper Edition. Crown 8vo. price 3*s*. 6*d*.

PRESBYTER—UNFOLDINGS OF CHRISTIAN HOPE. An Essay shewing that the Doctrine contained in the Damnatory Clauses of the Creed commonly called Athanasian is Unscriptural. Small crown 8vo. price 4*s*. 6*d*.

PRICE (Prof. Bonamy)—CURRENCY AND BANKING. Crown 8vo. Price 6*s*.

CHAPTERS ON PRACTICAL POLITICAL ECONOMY. Being the Substance of Lectures delivered before the University of Oxford. Large post 8vo. price 12*s*.

PROTEUS AND AMADEUS. A Correspondence. Edited by AUBREY DE VERE. Crown 8vo. price 5s.

PULPIT COMMENTARY (THE). Edited by the Rev. J. S. EXELL and the Rev. Canon H. D. M. SPENCE.

> EZRA, NEHEMIAH, AND ESTHER. By Rev. Canon G. RAWLINSON, M.A.; with Homilies by Rev. Prof. J. R. THOMSON, M.A., Rev. Prof. R. A. REDFORD, LL.B., M.A., Rev. W. S. LEWIS, M.A., Rev. J. A. MACDONALD, Rev. A. MACKENNAL, B.A., Rev. W. CLARKSON, B.A., Rev. F. HASTINGS, Rev. W. DINWIDDIE, LL.B., Rev. Prof. ROWLANDS, B.A., Rev. G. WOOD, B.A., Rev. Prof. P. C. BARKER, LL.B., M.A., and Rev. J. S. EXELL. Third Edition. One vol. price 12s. 6d.

> 1 SAMUEL. By the Very Rev. R. P. SMITH, D.D.; with Homilies by Rev. DONALD FRASER, D.D., Rev. Prof. CHAPMAN, and Rev. B. DALE. Third Edition. Price 15s.

> GENESIS. By Rev. T. WHITELAW, M.A.; with Homilies by the Very Rev. J. F. MONTGOMERY, D.D., Rev. Prof. R. A. REDFORD, M.A., LL.B., Rev. F. HASTINGS, Rev. W. ROBERTS, M.A. An Introduction to the Study of the Old Testament by the Rev. Canon FARRAR, D.D., F.R.S.; and Introductions to the Pentateuch by the Right Rev. H. COTTERILL, D.D., and Rev. T. WHITELAW, M.A. Third Edition. One vol. price 15s.

> JUDGES AND RUTH. By the Right Rev. Lord A. C. HERVEY, D.D., and Rev. J. MORRISON, D.D.; with Homilies by Rev. A. F. MUIR, M.A., Rev. W. F. ADENEY, M.A., Rev. W. M. STATHAM, and Rev. Professor J. THOMSON, M.A. Super-royal 8vo. cloth, price 10s. 6d.

> JOSHUA. By Rev. J. J. LIAS, M.A.; with Homilies by Rev. S. R. ALDRIDGE, LL.B., Rev. R. GLOVER, Rev. E. DE PRESSENSÉ, D.D., Rev. J. WAITE, B.A., Rev. F. W. ADENEY, M.A.; and an Introduction by the Rev. A. PLUMMER, M.A. Price 12s. 6d.

PUNJAUB (THE) AND NORTH-WESTERN FRONTIER OF INDIA. By an Old Punjaubee. Crown 8vo. price 5s.

RABBI JESHUA. An Eastern Story. Crown 8vo. cloth, price 3s. 6d.

RAVENSHAW (*John Henry*) *B.C.S.*—GAUR: ITS RUINS AND INSCRIPTIONS. Edited by his Widow. With 44 Photographic Illustrations, and 25 facsimiles of Inscriptions. Royal 4to. cloth, price £3. 13s. 6d.

READ (*Carveth*)—ON THE THEORY OF LOGIC: An Essay. Crown 8vo. price 6s.

REALITIES OF THE FUTURE LIFE. Small crown 8vo. cloth, price 1s. 6d.

RENDELL (*J. M.*)—CONCISE HANDBOOK OF THE ISLAND OF MADEIRA. With Plan of Funchal and Map of the Island. Fcp. 8vo. cloth, 1s. 6d.

REYNOLDS (*Rev. J. W.*)—THE SUPERNATURAL IN NATURE. A Verification by Free Use of Science. Second Edition, revised and enlarged. Demy 8vo. cloth, price 14s.

> THE MYSTERY OF MIRACLES. By the Author of 'The Supernatural in Nature.' Crown 8vo. cloth, price 6s.

RIBOT (*Prof. Th.*)—ENGLISH PSYCHOLOGY. Second Edition. A Revised and Corrected Translation from the latest French Edition. Large post 8vo. price 9s.

> HEREDITY: A Psychological Study on its Phenomena, its Laws, its Causes, and its Consequences. Large crown 8vo. price 9s.

RINK (Chevalier Dr. Henry)—GREENLAND: ITS PEOPLE AND ITS PRODUCTS. By the Chevalier Dr. HENRY RINK, President of the Greenland Board of Trade. With sixteen Illustrations, drawn by the Eskimo, and a Map. Edited by Dr. Robert Brown. Crown 8vo. price 10s. 6d.

ROBERTSON (The late Rev. F. W.) M.A., of Brighton.—LIFE AND LETTERS OF. Edited by the Rev. Stopford Brooke, M.A., Chaplain in Ordinary to the Queen.
- I. Two vols., uniform with the Sermons. With Steel Portrait. Crown 8vo. price 7s. 6d.
- II. Library Edition, in Demy 8vo. with Portrait. Price 12s.
- III. A Popular Edition, in 1 vol. Crown 8vo. price 6s.

SERMONS. Four Series. Small crown 8vo. price 3s. 6d. each.

THE HUMAN RACE, and other Sermons. Preached at Cheltenham, Oxford, and Brighton. Large post 8vo. cloth, price 7s. 6d.

NOTES ON GENESIS. New and Cheaper Edition. Crown 8vo. price 3s. 6d.

EXPOSITORY LECTURES ON ST. PAUL'S EPISTLES TO THE CORINTHIANS. A New Edition. Small crown 8vo. price 5s.

LECTURES AND ADDRESSES, with other Literary Remains. A New Edition. Crown 8vo. price 5s.

AN ANALYSIS OF MR. TENNYSON'S 'IN MEMORIAM.' (Dedicated by Permission to the Poet-Laureate.) Fcp. 8vo. price 2s.

THE EDUCATION OF THE HUMAN RACE. Translated from the German of Gotthold Ephraim Lessing. Fcp. 8vo. price 2s. 6d.

The above Works can also be had, bound in half-morocco.

⁂ A Portrait of the late Rev. F. W. Robertson, mounted for framing, can be had, price 2s. 6d.

RODWELL (G. F.) F.R.A.S., F.C.S.—ETNA: A HISTORY OF THE MOUNTAIN AND ITS ERUPTIONS. With Maps and Illustrations. Square 8vo. cloth, price 9s.

ROSS (Alexander) D.D.—MEMOIR OF ALEXANDER EWING, Bishop of Argyll and the Isles. Second and Cheaper Edition. Demy 8vo. cloth, price 10s. 6d.

SALTS (Rev. Alfred) LL.D.—GODPARENTS AT CONFIRMATION. With a Preface by the Bishop of Manchester. Small crown 8vo. cloth limp, price 2s.

SAMUEL (Sydney M.)—JEWISH LIFE IN THE EAST. Small crown 8vo. cloth, price 3s. 6d.

SAYCE (Rev. Archibald Henry)—INTRODUCTION TO THE SCIENCE OF LANGUAGE. 2 vols. Large post 8vo. cloth, price 25s.

SCIENTIFIC LAYMAN. The New Truth and the Old Faith: are they Incompatible? Demy 8vo. cloth, price 10s. 6d.

SCOONES (W. Baptiste)—FOUR CENTURIES OF ENGLISH LETTERS: A Selection of 350 Letters by 150 Writers, from the Period of the Paston Letters to the Present Time. Second Edition. Large crown 8vo. cloth, price 9s.

SCOTT (Robert H.)—WEATHER CHARTS AND STORM WARNINGS. Second Edition. Illustrated. Crown 8vo. price 3s. 6d.

SCOTT (Leader)—A NOOK IN THE APENNINES : A Summer beneath the Chestnuts. With Frontispiece, and Twenty-seven Illustrations in the Text, chiefly from Original Sketches. Crown 8vo. cloth, price 7s. 6d.

SENIOR (N. W.)—ALEXIS DE TOCQUEVILLE. Correspondence and Conversations with Nassau W. Senior, from 1833 to 1859. Edited by M. C. M Simpson. 2 vols. Large post 8vo. price 21s.

SHAKSPEARE (Charles)—SAINT PAUL AT ATHENS. Spiritual Christianity in relation to some aspects of Modern Thought. Five Sermons preached at St. Stephen's Church, Westbourne Park. With a Preface by the Rev. Canon FARRAR.

SHELLEY (Lady)—SHELLEY MEMORIALS FROM AUTHENTIC SOURCES. With (now first printed) an Essay on Christianity by Percy Bysshe Shelley. With Portrait. Third Edition. Crown 8vo. price 5s.

SHILLITO (Rev. Joseph)—WOMANHOOD : its Duties, Temptations, and Privileges. A Book for Young Women. Third Edition. Crown 8vo. price 3s. 6d.

SHIPLEY (Rev. Orby) M.A.—CHURCH TRACTS : OR, STUDIES IN MODERN PROBLEMS. By various Writers. 2 vols. Crown 8vo. price 5s. each.

PRINCIPLES OF THE FAITH IN RELATION TO SIN. Topics for Thought in Times of Retreat. Eleven Addresses delivered during a Retreat of Three Days to Persons living in the World. Demy 8vo. cloth, price 12s.

SISTER AUGUSTINE, Superior of the Sisters of Charity at the St. Johannis Hospital at Bonn. Authorised Translation by HANS THARAU, from the German 'Memorials of AMALIE VON LASAULX.' Second Edition. Large crown 8vo. cloth, price 7s. 6d.

SMITH (Edward) M.D., LL.B., F.R.S.—HEALTH AND DISEASE, as Influenced by the Daily, Seasonal, and other Cyclical Changes in the Human System. A New Edition. Post 8vo. price 7s. 6d.

PRACTICAL DIETARY FOR FAMILIES, SCHOOLS, AND THE LABOURING CLASSES. A New Edition. Post 8vo. price 3s. 6d.

TUBERCULAR CONSUMPTION IN ITS EARLY AND REMEDIABLE STAGES. Second Edition. Crown 8vo. price 6s.

SPEDDING (James)—REVIEWS AND DISCUSSIONS, LITERARY, POLITICAL, AND HISTORICAL NOT RELATING TO BACON. Demy 8vo. cloth, price 12s. 6d.

STAPFER (Paul)—SHAKSPEARE AND CLASSICAL ANTIQUITY : Greek and Latin Antiquity as presented in Shakspeare's Plays. Translated by EMILY J. CAREY. Large post 8vo. cloth, price 12s.

ST. BERNARD. A Little Book on the Love of God. Translated by MARIANNE CAROLINE and COVENTRY PATMORE. Cloth extra, gilt tops, 4s. 6d.

STEPHENS (Archibald John) LL.D.—THE FOLKESTONE RITUAL CASE. The Substance of the Argument delivered before the Judicial Committee of the Privy Council on behalf of the Respondents. Demy 8vo. cloth, price 6s.

STEVENSON (Rev. W. F.)—HYMNS FOR THE CHURCH AND HOME. Selected and Edited by the Rev. W. Fleming Stevenson.

The most complete Hymn Book published.

The Hymn Book consists of Three Parts :—I. For Public Worship.—II. For Family and Private Worship.—III. For Children.

⁎ Published in various forms and prices, the latter ranging from 8d. to 6s. Lists and full particulars will be furnished on application to the Publishers.

STEVENSON (Robert Louis)—AN INLAND VOYAGE. With Frontispiece by Walter Crane. Crown 8vo. price 7s. 6d.
 TRAVELS WITH A DONKEY IN THE CEVENNES. With Frontispiece by Walter Crane. Crown 8vo. cloth, price 7s. 6d.
 VIRGINIBUS PUERISQUE, and other Papers. Crown 8vo. cloth 6s.

SULLY (James) M.A. — SENSATION AND INTUITION. Demy 8vo. price 10s. 6d.
 PESSIMISM: a History and a Criticism. Second Edition. Demy 8vo. price 14s.

SYME (David)—OUTLINES OF AN INDUSTRIAL SCIENCE. Second Edition. Crown 8vo. price 6s.

TAYLOR (Algernon)—GUIENNE. Notes of an Autumn Tour. Crown 8vo. cloth, price 4s. 6d.

THOMSON (J. Turnbull)—SOCIAL PROBLEMS; OR, AN INQUIRY INTO THE LAWS OF INFLUENCE. With Diagrams. Demy 8vo. cloth, price 10s. 6d.

TODHUNTER (Dr. J.)—A STUDY OF SHELLEY. Crown 8vo. cloth, price 7s.

TWINING (Louisa)—WORKHOUSE VISITING AND MANAGEMENT DURING TWENTY-FIVE YEARS. Small crown 8vo. cloth, price 3s. 6d.

VAUGHAN (H. Halford)—NEW READINGS AND RENDERINGS OF SHAKESPEARE'S TRAGEDIES. 2 vols. demy 8vo. cloth, price 25s.

VILLARI (Professor)—NICCOLO MACHIAVELLI AND HIS TIMES. Translated by Linda Villari. 2 vols. Large post 8vo. price 24s.

VYNER (Lady Mary)—EVERY DAY A PORTION. Adapted from the Bible and the Prayer Book, for the Private Devotions of those living in Widowhood. Collected and Edited by Lady Mary Vyner. Square crown 8vo. extra, price 5s.

WALDSTEIN (Charles) Ph.D.—THE BALANCE OF EMOTION AND INTELLECT; an Introductory Essay to the Study of Philosophy. Crown 8vo. cloth, price 6s.

WALLER (Rev. C. B.)—THE APOCALYPSE, reviewed under the Light of the Doctrine of the Unfolding Ages, and the Relation of All Things. Demy 8vo. price 12s.

WATSON (Sir Thomas) Bart., M.D.—THE ABOLITION OF ZYMOTIC DISEASES, and of other similar Enemies of Mankind. Small crown 8vo. cloth, price 3s. 6d.

WEDMORE (Frederick)—THE MASTERS OF GENRE PAINTING. With Sixteen Illustrations. Crown 8vo. cloth, price 7s. 6d.

WELLS (Capt. John C.) R.N.—SPITZBERGEN—THE GATEWAY TO THE POLYNIA; or, a Voyage to Spitzbergen. With numerous Illustrations by Whymper and others, and Map. New and Cheaper Edition. Demy 8vo. price 6s.

WETMORE (W. S.)—COMMERCIAL TELEGRAPHIC CODE. Second Edition. Post 4to. boards, price 42s.

WHITE (A. D.) LL.D.—WARFARE OF SCIENCE. With Prefatory Note by Professor Tyndall. Second Edition. Crown 8vo. price 3s. 6d.

WHITNEY (Prof. William Dwight)—ESSENTIALS OF ENGLISH GRAMMAR, for the Use of Schools. Crown 8vo. price 3s. 6d.

WICKSTEED (P. H.)—DANTE: Six Sermons. Crown 8vo. cloth, price 5s.

WILLIAMS (Rowland) D.D.—LIFE AND LETTERS OF; with Extracts from his Note-Books. Edited by Mrs. Rowland Williams. With a Photographic Portrait. 2 vols. large post 8vo. price 24s.

 PSALMS, LITANIES, COUNSELS, AND COLLECTS FOR DEVOUT PERSONS. Edited by his Widow. New and Popular Edition. Crown 8vo. price 3s. 6d.

 STRAY THOUGHTS COLLECTED FROM THE WRITINGS OF THE LATE ROWLAND WILLIAMS, D.D. Edited by his Widow. Crown 8vo. cloth, price 3s. 6d.

WILLIS (R.) M.D.—SERVETUS AND CALVIN: a Study of an Important Epoch in the Early History of the Reformation. 8vo. price 16s.

 WILLIAM HARVEY. A History of the Discovery of the Circulation of the Blood: with a Portrait of Harvey after Faithorne. Demy 8vo. cloth, price 14s. Portrait separate.

WILSON (H. Schütz)—THE TOWER AND SCAFFOLD. A Miniature Monograph. Large fcap. 8vo. price 1s.

WOLLSTONECRAFT (Mary)—LETTERS TO IMLAY. New Edition with Prefatory Memoir by C. KEGAN PAUL, author of 'William Godwin: His Friends and Contemporaries,' &c. Two Portraits in *eau-forte* by Anna Lea Merritt. Crown 8vo. cloth, price 6s.

WOLTMANN (Dr. Alfred), and WOERMANN (Dr. Karl)—HISTORY OF PAINTING. Edited by Sidney Colvin. Vol. I. Painting in Antiquity and the Middle Ages. With numerous Illustrations. Medium 8vo. cloth, price 28s.; bevelled boards, gilt leaves, price 30s.

WOOD (Major-General J. Creighton)—DOUBLING THE CONSONANT. Small crown 8vo. cloth, price 1s. 6d.

WORD WAS MADE FLESH. Short Family Readings on the Epistles for each Sunday of the Christian Year. Demy 8vo. cloth, price 10s. 6d.

WRIGHT (Rev. David) M.A.—WAITING FOR THE LIGHT, AND OTHER SERMONS. Crown 8vo. price 6s.

YOUMANS (Eliza A.)—AN ESSAY ON THE CULTURE OF THE OBSERVING POWERS OF CHILDREN, especially in connection with the Study of Botany. Edited, with Notes and a Supplement, by Joseph Payne, F.C.P., Author of 'Lectures on the Science and Art of Education,' &c. Crown 8vo. price 2s. 6d.

 FIRST BOOK OF BOTANY. Designed to Cultivate the Observing Powers of Children. With 300 Engravings. New and Cheaper Edition. Crown 8vo. price 2s. 6d.

YOUMANS (Edward L.) M.D.—A CLASS BOOK OF CHEMISTRY, on the Basis of the New System. With 200 Illustrations. Crown 8vo. price 5s.

THE INTERNATIONAL SCIENTIFIC SERIES.

I. FORMS OF WATER: a Familiar Exposition of the Origin and Phenomena of Glaciers. By J. Tyndall, LL.D., F.R.S. With 25 Illustrations. Seventh Edition. Crown 8vo. price 5s.

II. PHYSICS AND POLITICS; or, Thoughts on the Application of the Principles of 'Natural Selection' and 'Inheritance' to Political Society. By Walter Bagehot. Fifth Edition. Crown 8vo. price 4s.

III. FOODS. By Edward Smith, M.D., LL.B., F.R.S. With numerous Illustrations. Seventh Edition. Crown 8vo. price 5s.

IV. MIND AND BODY: the Theories of their Relation. By Alexander Bain, LL.D. With Four Illustrations. Seventh Edition. Crown 8vo. price 4s.

V. THE STUDY OF SOCIOLOGY. By Herbert Spencer. Tenth Edition. Crown 8vo. price 5s.

VI. ON THE CONSERVATION OF ENERGY. By Balfour Stewart, M.A., LL.D., F.R.S. With 14 Illustrations. Fifth Edition. Crown 8vo. price 5s.

VII. ANIMAL LOCOMOTION; or, Walking, Swimming, and Flying. By J. B. Pettigrew, M.D., F.R.S., &c. With 130 Illustrations. Second Edition. Crown 8vo. price 5s.

VIII. RESPONSIBILITY IN MENTAL DISEASE. By Henry Maudsley, M.D. Third Edition. Crown 8vo. price 5s.

IX. THE NEW CHEMISTRY. By Professor J. P. Cooke, of the Harvard University. With 31 Illustrations. Fifth Edition. Crown 8vo. price 5s.

X. THE SCIENCE OF LAW. By Professor Sheldon Amos. Fourth Edition. Crown 8vo. price 5s.

XI. ANIMAL MECHANISM: a Treatise on Terrestrial and Aerial Locomotion. By Professor E. J. Marey. With 117 Illustrations. Second Edition. Crown 8vo. price 5s.

XII. THE DOCTRINE OF DESCENT AND DARWINISM. By Professor Oscar Schmidt (Strasburg University). With 26 Illustrations. Fourth Edit. Crown 8vo. price 5s.

XIII. THE HISTORY OF THE CONFLICT BETWEEN RELIGION AND SCIENCE. By J. W. Draper, M.D., LL.D. Fourteenth Edition. Crown 8vo. price 5s.

XIV. FUNGI: their Nature, Influences, Uses, &c. By M. C. Cooke, M.D., LL.D. Edited by the Rev. M. J. Berkeley, M.A., F.L.S. With numerous Illustrations. Second Edition. Crown 8vo. price 5s.

XV. THE CHEMICAL EFFECTS OF LIGHT AND PHOTOGRAPHY. By Dr. Hermann Vogel (Polytechnic Academy of Berlin). Translation thoroughly revised. With 100 Illustrations. Third Edition. Crown 8vo. price 5s.

XVI. THE LIFE AND GROWTH OF LANGUAGE. By William Dwight Whitney, Professor of Sanscrit and Comparative Philology in Yale College, Newhaven. Second Edition. Crown 8vo. price 5s.

XVII. MONEY AND THE MECHANISM OF EXCHANGE. By W. Stanley Jevons, M.A., F.R.S. Fourth Edition. Crown 8vo. price 5s.

XVIII. THE NATURE OF LIGHT. With a General Account of Physical Optics. By Dr. Eugene Lommel, Professor of Physics in the University of Erlangen. With 188 Illustrations and a Table of Spectra in Chromo-lithography. Third Edition. Crown 8vo. price 5s.

XIX. ANIMAL PARASITES AND MESSMATES. By Monsieur Van Beneden, Professor of the University of Louvain, Correspondent of the Institute of France. With 83 Illustrations. Second Edition. Crown 8vo. price 5s.

XX. FERMENTATION. By Professor Schützenberger, Director of the Chemical Laboratory at the Sorbonne. With 28 Illustrations. Third Edition. Crown 8vo. price 5s.

XXI. THE FIVE SENSES OF MAN. By Professor Bernstein, of the University of Halle. With 91 Illustrations. Second Edition. Crown 8vo. price 5s.

XXII. THE THEORY OF SOUND IN ITS RELATION TO MUSIC. By Professor Pietro Blaserna, of the Royal University of Rome. With numerous Illustrations. Second Edition. Crown 8vo. price 5s.

XXIII. STUDIES IN SPECTRUM ANALYSIS. By J. Norman Lockyer, F.R.S. With six photographic Illustrations of Spectra, and numerous engravings on Wood. Crown 8vo. Second Edition. Price 6s. 6d.

XXIV. A HISTORY OF THE GROWTH OF THE STEAM ENGINE. By Professor R. H. Thurston. With numerous Illustrations. Second Edition. Crown 8vo. cloth, price 6s. 6d.

XXV. EDUCATION AS A SCIENCE. By Alexander Bain, LL.D. Third Edition. Crown 8vo. cloth, price 5s.

XXVI. THE HUMAN SPECIES. By Prof. A. de Quatrefages. Third Edition. Crown 8vo. cloth, price 5s.

XXVII. MODERN CHROMATICS. With Applications to Art and Industry. By Ogden N. Rood. With 130 original Illustrations. Second Edition. Crown 8vo. cloth, price 5s.

XXVIII. THE CRAYFISH: an Introduction to the Study of Zoology. By Professor T. H. Huxley. With 82 Illustrations. Second Edition. Crown 8vo. cloth, price 5s.

XXIX. THE BRAIN AS AN ORGAN OF MIND. By H. Charlton Bastian, M.D. With numerous Illustrations. Second Edition. Crown 8vo. cloth, price 5s.

XXX. THE ATOMIC THEORY. By Prof. Wurtz. Translated by G. Cleminshaw, F.C.S. Second Edition. Crown 8vo. cloth, price 5s.

XXXI. THE NATURAL CONDITIONS OF EXISTENCE AS THEY AFFECT ANIMAL LIFE. By Karl Semper. With 2 Maps and 106 Woodcuts. Second Edition. Crown 8vo. cloth, price 5s.

XXXII. GENERAL PHYSIOLOGY OF MUSCLES AND NERVES. By Prof. J. Rosenthal. Second Edition. With Illustrations. Crown 8vo. cloth, price 5s.

MILITARY WORKS.

ANDERSON (Col. R. P.)—VICTORIES AND DEFEATS: an Attempt to explain the Causes which have led to them. An Officer's Manual. Demy 8vo. price 14s.

ARMY OF THE NORTH GERMAN CONFEDERATION: a Brief Description of its Organisation, of the Different Branches of the Service and their *rôle* in War, of its Mode of Fighting, &c. Translated from the Corrected Edition, by permission of the Author, by Colonel Edward Newdigate. Demy 8vo. price 5s.

BLUME (Maj. W.)—THE OPERATIONS OF THE GERMAN ARMIES IN FRANCE, from Sedan to the end of the War of 1870-71. With Map. From the Journals of the Head-quarters Staff. Translated by the late E. M. Jones, Maj. 20th Foot, Prof. of Mil. Hist., Sandhurst. Demy 8vo. price 9s.

BOGUSLAWSKI (Capt. A. von)—TACTICAL DEDUCTIONS FROM THE WAR OF 1870-1. Translated by Colonel Sir Lumley Graham, Bart., late 18th (Royal Irish) Regiment. Third Edition, Revised and Corrected. Demy 8vo. price 7s.

BRACKENBURY (Lieut.-Col.) C.B., R.A., A.A.G. MILITARY HANDBOOKS FOR REGIMENTAL OFFICERS. I. Military Sketching and Reconnaissance, by Lieut.-Col. F. J. Hutchison, and Capt. H. G. MacGregor. Second Edition. With 15 Plates. Small 8vo. cloth, price 6s. II. The Elements of Modern Tactics Practically applied to English Formations, by Major Wilkinson Shaw. Second and Cheaper Edition. With 25 Plates and Maps. Small cr. 8vo. cloth, price 9s.

BRIALMONT (Col. A.)—HASTY INTRENCHMENTS. Translated by Lieut. Charles A. Empson, R.A. With Nine Plates. Demy 8vo. price 6s.

CLERY (C.) Lieut.-Col.—MINOR TACTICS. With 26 Maps and Plans. Fifth and revised Edition. Demy 8vo. cloth, price 16s.

DU VERNOIS (Col. von Verdy)—STUDIES IN LEADING TROOPS. An authorised and accurate Translation by Lieutenant H. J. T. Hildyard, 71st Foot. Parts I. and II. Demy 8vo. price 7s.

GOETZE (Capt. A. von)—OPERATIONS OF THE GERMAN ENGINEERS DURING THE WAR OF 1870-1. Published by Authority, and in accordance with Official Documents. Translated from the German by Colonel G. Graham, V.C., C.B., R.E. With 6 large Maps. Demy 8vo. price 21s.

HARRISON (Lieut.-Col. R.) — THE OFFICER'S MEMORANDUM BOOK FOR PEACE AND WAR. Third Edition. Oblong 32mo. roan, with pencil, price 3s. 6d.

HELVIG (Capt. H.)—THE OPERATIONS OF THE BAVARIAN ARMY CORPS. Translated by Captain G. S. Schwabe. With Five large Maps. In 2 vols. Demy 8vo. price 24s.

TACTICAL EXAMPLES: Vol. I. The Battalion, price 15s. Vol. II. The Regiment and Brigade, price 10s. 6d. Translated from the German by Col. Sir Lumley Graham. With nearly 300 Diagrams. Demy 8vo. cloth.

HOFFBAUER (Capt.)—THE GERMAN ARTILLERY IN THE BATTLES NEAR METZ. Based on the Official Reports of the German Artillery. Translated by Captain E. O. Hollist. With Map and Plans. Demy 8vo. price 21s.

LAYMANN (Capt.)—THE FRONTAL ATTACK OF INFANTRY. Translated by Colonel Edward Newdigate. Crown 8vo. price 2s. 6d.

NOTES ON CAVALRY TACTICS, ORGANISATION, &c. By a Cavalry Officer. With Diagrams. Demy 8vo. cloth, price 12s.

PARR (Capt H. Hallam) C.M.G.—THE DRESS, HORSES, AND EQUIPMENT OF INFANTRY AND STAFF OFFICERS. Crown 8vo. cloth, price 1s.

SCHELL (Maj. von)—THE OPERATIONS OF THE FIRST ARMY UNDER GEN. VON GOEBEN. Translated by Col. C. H. von Wright. Four Maps. demy 8vo. price 9s.

THE OPERATIONS OF THE FIRST ARMY UNDER GEN. VON STEINMETZ. Translated by Captain E. O. Hollist. Demy 8vo. price 10s. 6d.

SCHELLENDORF (Major-Gen. B. von) THE DUTIES OF THE GENERAL STAFF. Translated from the German by Lieutenant Hare. Vol. I. Demy 8vo. cloth, 10s. 6d.

SCHERFF (Maj. W. von)—STUDIES IN THE NEW INFANTRY TACTICS. Parts I. and II. Translated from the German by Colonel Lumley Graham. Demy 8vo. price 7s. 6d.

SHADWELL (Maj.-Gen.) C.B.—MOUNTAIN WARFARE. Illustrated by the Campaign of 1799 in Switzerland. Being a Translation of the Swiss Narrative compiled from the Works of the Archduke Charles, Jomini, and others. Also of Notes by General H. Dufour on the Campaign of the Valtelline in 1635. With Appendix, Maps, and Introductory Remarks. Demy 8vo. price 16s.

SHERMAN (Gen. W. T.)—MEMOIRS OF GENERAL W. T. SHERMAN, Commander of the Federal Forces in the American Civil War. By Himself. 2 vols. With Map. Demy 8vo. price 24s. *Copyright English Edition.*

STUBBS (Lieut.-Col. F. W.) — THE REGIMENT OF BENGAL ARTILLERY. The History of its Organisation, Equipment, and War Services. Compiled from Published Works, Official Records, and various Private Sources. With numerous Maps and Illustrations. 2 vols. demy 8vo. price 32s.

STUMM (Lieut. Hugo), German Military Attaché to the Khivan Expedition.—RUSSIA'S ADVANCE EASTWARD Based on the Official Reports of. Translated by Capt. C. E. H. VINCENT, With Map. Crown 8vo. price 6s.

VINCENT (Capt. C. E. H.)—ELEMENTARY MILITARY GEOGRAPHY, RECONNOITRING, AND SKETCHING. Compiled for Non-commissioned Officers and Soldiers of all Arms. Square crown 8vo. price 2s. 6d.

VOLUNTEER, THE MILITIAMAN, AND THE REGULAR SOLDIER, by a Public Schoolboy. Crown 8vo. cloth, price 5s.

WARTENSLEBEN (Count H. von.)—THE OPERATIONS OF THE SOUTH ARMY IN JANUARY AND FEBRUARY, 1871. Compiled from the Official War Documents of the Head-quarters of the Southern Army. Translated by Colonel C. H. von Wright. With Maps. Demy 8vo. price 6s.

THE OPERATIONS OF THE FIRST ARMY UNDER GEN. VON MANTEUFFEL. Translated by Colonel C. H. von Wright. Uniform with the above. Demy 8vo. price 9s.

WICKHAM (Capt. E. H., R.A.)—INFLUENCE OF FIREARMS UPON TACTICS : Historical and Critical Investigations. By an OFFICER OF SUPERIOR RANK (in the German Army). Translated by Captain E. H. Wickham, R.A. Demy 8vo. price 7s. 6d.

WOINOVITS (Capt. I.) — AUSTRIAN CAVALRY EXERCISE. Translated by Captain W. S. Cooke. Crown 8vo. price 7s.

POETRY.

ADAMS (W. D.—LYRICS OF LOVE, from Shakespeare to Tennyson. Selected and arranged by. Fcp. 8vo. cloth extra, gilt edges, price 3s. 6d.
    Also, a Cheaper Edition. Fcp. 8vo. cloth, 2s. 6d.

AMATEUR—A FEW LYRICS. Small crown 8vo. cloth, price 2s.

ANTILOPE: a Tragedy. Large crown 8vo. cloth, price 6s.

AUBERTIN (J. J.)—CAMOENS' LUSIADS. Portuguese Text, with Translation by. Map and Portraits. 2 vols. Demy 8vo. price 30s.

    SEVENTY SONNETS OF CAMOENS. Portuguese Text and Translation, with some original Poems. Dedicated to Capt. Richard F. Burton. Printed on hand made paper, cloth, bevelled boards, gilt tops, price 7s. 6d.

AVIA—THE ODYSSEY OF HOMER. Done into English Verse by. Fcp. 4to. cloth, price 15s.

BANKS (Mrs. G. L.)—RIPPLES AND BREAKERS: Poems. Square 8vo. cloth, price 5s.

BARNES (William)—POEMS OF RURAL LIFE, IN THE DORSET DIALECT. New Edition, complete in one vol. Crown 8vo. cloth, price 8s. 6d.

BAYNES (Rev. Canon R. H.) M.A.—HOME SONGS FOR QUIET HOURS. Fourth Edition. Fcp. 8vo. price 2s. 6d.
    This may also be had handsomely bound in morocco with gilt edges.

BENNETT (Dr. W. C.)—NARRATIVE POEMS AND BALLADS. Fcp. 8vo. sewed, in Coloured Wrapper, price 1s.

    SONGS FOR SAILORS. Dedicated by Special Request to H.R.H. the Duke of Edinburgh. With Steel Portrait and Illustrations. Crown 8vo. price 3s. 6d.
    An Edition in Illustrated Paper Covers, price 1s.

    SONGS OF A SONG WRITER. Crown 8vo. price 6s.

BEVINGTON (L. S.)—KEY NOTES. Small crown 8vo. cloth, price 5s.

BOWEN (H. C.) M.A.—SIMPLE ENGLISH POEMS. English Literature for Junior Classes. In Four Parts. Parts I. II. and III. price 6d. each, and Part IV. price 1s.

BRYANT (W. C.)—POEMS. Red-line Edition. With 24 Illustrations and Portrait of the Author. Crown 8vo. cloth extra, price 7s. 6d.
    A Cheap Edition, with Frontispiece. Small crown 8vo. price 3s. 6d.

BUTLER (Alfred J.)—AMARANTH AND ASPHODEL. Songs from the Greek Anthology. Small crown 8vo. cloth, price 2s.

CALDERON'S DRAMAS: the Wonder-Working Magician—Life is a Dream—the Purgatory of St. Patrick. Translated by Denis Florence MacCarthy. Post 8vo. price 10s.

COLOMB (Colonel)—THE CARDINAL ARCHBISHOP: a Spanish Legend. In 29 Cancions. Small Crown 8vo. cloth, price 5s.

CONWAY (Hugh)—A LIFE'S IDYLLS. Small crown 8vo. cloth, price 3s. 6d.

COPPÉE (Francois)—L'EXILÉE. Done into English Verse, with the sanction of the Author, by I. O. L. Crown 8vo. vellum, price 5s.

COWAN (Rev. William)—POEMS; chiefly Sacred, including Translations from some Ancient Latin Hymns. [Fcp. 8vo. cloth, price 5s.

CRESSWELL (Mrs. G.)—THE KING'S BANNER: Drama in Four Acts. Five Illustrations. 4to. price 10s. 6d.

DAVIES (T. Hart.)—CATULLUS. Translated into English Verse. Crown 8vo. cloth, price 6s.

DENNIS (J.)—ENGLISH SONNETS. Collected and Arranged. Elegantly bound. New and Cheaper Edition. Fcp. 8vo. price 2s. 6d.

DE VERE (Aubrey)—ALEXANDER THE GREAT: a Dramatic Poem. Small crown 8vo. price 5s.

DE VERE (Aubrey)—con.
  THE INFANT BRIDAL, and other Poems. A New and Enlarged Edition. Fcp. 8vo. price 7s. 6d.
  LEGENDS OF THE SAXON SAINTS Small crown 8vo. cloth, price 6s.
  THE LEGENDS OF ST. PATRICK, and other Poems. Small cr. 8vo. price 5s.
  ST. THOMAS OF CANTERBURY : a Dramatic Poem. Large fcp. 8vo. price 5s.
  ANTAR AND ZARA: an Eastern Romance. INISFAIL, and other Poems, Meditative and Lyrical. Fcp. 8vo. price 6s.
  THE FALL OF RORA, THE SEARCH AFTER PROSERPINE, and other Poems, Meditative and Lyrical. Fcp. 8vo. 6s.

DOBELL (Mrs. Horace)—ETHELSTONE, EVELINE, and other Poems. Crown 8vo. cloth, 6s.

DOBSON (Austin) — VIGNETTES IN RHYME, and Vers de Société. Third Edition. Fcp. 8vo. price 5s.
  PROVERBS IN PORCELAIN. By the Author of 'Vignettes in Rhyme.' Second Edition. Crown 8vo. price 6s.

DOLORES : a Theme with Variations. In Three Parts. Small crown 8vo. cloth, price 5s.

DOROTHY : a Country Story in Elegiac Verse. With Preface. Demy 8vo. cloth, price 5s.

DOWDEN (Edward) LL.D.—POEMS. Second Edition. Fcp. 8vo. price 5s.

DOWNTON (Rev. H.) M.A.—HYMNS AND VERSES. Original and Translated. Small crown 8vo. cloth, price 3s. 6d.

DUTT (Toru)—A SHEAF GLEANED IN FRENCH FIELDS. New Edition, with Portrait. Demy 8vo. cloth, 10s. 6d.

EDWARDS (Rev. Basil) — MINOR CHORDS ; or, Songs for the Suffering ; a Volume of Verse. Fcp. 8vo. cloth, price 3s. 6d.; paper, price 2s. 6d.

ELLIOT (Lady Charlotte)—MEDUSA and other Poems. Crown 8vo. cloth, price 6s.

ELLIOTT (Ebenezer), The Corn Law Rhymer.—POEMS. Edited by his son, the Rev. Edwin Elliott, of St. John's, Antigua. 2 vols. crown 8vo. price 18s.

ENGLISH ODES. Selected, with a Critical Introduction by EDMUND W. GOSSE, and a miniature frontispiece by Hamo Thornycroft, A.R.A. Elzevir 8vo. limp parchment antique, price 6s. ; vellum, 7s. 6d.

EPIC OF HADES (THE). By the Author of 'Songs of Two Worlds.' Twelfth Edition. Fcp. 8vo. price 7s. 6d.
  *** Also an Illustrated Edition, with seventeen full-page designs in photomezzotint by George R. Chapman. 4to. cloth, extra gilt leaves, price 25s. ; and a Large Paper Edition with Portrait, price 10s. 6d.

EVANS (Anne)—POEMS AND MUSIC. With Memorial Preface by ANN THACKERAY RITCHIE. Large crown 8vo. cloth, price 7s.

G. H. T.—VERSES, mostly written in India. Crown 8vo. cloth, price 6s.

GINEVRA AND THE DUKE OF GUISE : Two Tragedies. Crown 8vo. cloth, price 6s.

GOSSE (Edmund W.)—NEW POEMS. Crown 8vo. cloth, price 7s. 6d.

GREENOUGH (Mrs. Richard)—MARY MAGDALENE : a Poem. Large post 8vo. parchment antique, bevelled boards, price 6s.

GWEN : a Drama in Monologue. By the Author of the 'Epic of Hades.' Third Edition. Fcp. 8vo. cloth, price 5s.

HAWKER (Robt. Stephen)—THE POETICAL WORKS OF. Now first collected and arranged. With a Prefatory Notice by J. G. Godwin. With Portrait. Crown 8vo. cloth, price 12s.

HAWTREY (Edward M.)—CORYDALIS : a Story of the Sicilian Expedition. Small crown 8vo. cloth, price 3s. 6d.

HOLMES (E. G. A.)—POEMS. First and Second Series. Fcp. 8vo. price 5s. each.

INCHBOLD (J. W.)—ANNUS AMORIS : Sonnets. Fcp. 8vo. price 4s. 6d.

JENKINS (Rev. Canon)—THE GIRDLE LEGEND OF PRATO. Small crown 8vo. cloth, price 2s.

JEROVEAM'S WIFE, and other Poems. Fcp. 8vo. cloth, price 3s. 6d.

KING (Edward)—ECHOES FROM THE ORIENT. With Miscellaneous Poems. Small crown 8vo. cloth, price 3s. 6d.

KING (Mrs. *Hamilton*)—THE DISCIPLES. Fourth Edition, with Portrait and Notes. Crown 8vo. price 7s. 6d.

ASPROMONTE, and other Poems. Second Edition. Fcp. 8vo. price 4s. 6d.

LAIRD-CLOWES (*W.*)—LOVE'S REBELLION: a Poem. Fcp. 8vo. cloth, price 3s. 6d.

LANG (*A.*)—XXII BALLADES IN BLUE CHINA. Elzevir 8vo. parchment. price 3s. 6d.

LEIGHTON (*Robert*)—RECORDS AND OTHER POEMS. With Portrait. Small crown 8vo. cloth, price 7s. 6d.

LOCKER (*F.*)—LONDON LYRICS. A New and Revised Edition, with Additions and a Portrait of the Author. Crown 8vo. cloth elegant, price 6s.

Also, an Edition for the People. Fcp. 8vo. price 2s. 6d.

LOKI.—THE NEW WERTHER. Small crown 8vo. cloth, price 3s. 6d.

LOVE'S GAMUT and other Poems. Small crown 8vo. cloth, price 3s. 6d.

LOVE SONNETS OF PROTEUS. With Frontispiece by the Author. Elzevir 8vo. cloth, price 5s.

LOWNDES (*Henry*)— POEMS AND TRANSLATIONS. Crown 8vo. cloth, price 6s.

LUMSDEN (*Lieut.-Col. H. W.*)—BEOWULF: an Old English Poem. Translated into Modern Rhymes. Small crown 8vo. cloth, price 5s.

MACLEAN (*Charles Donald*)—LATIN AND GREEK VERSE TRANSLATIONS. Small crown 8vo. cloth, price 2s.

MAGNUSSON (*Eirikr*) *M.A.*, and *PALMER* (*E. H.*) *M.A.*—JOHAN LUDVIG RUNEBERG'S LYRICAL SONGS, IDYLLS, AND EPIGRAMS. Fcp. 8vo. cloth, price 5s.

MARIE ANTIONETTE: a Drama. Small crown 8vo. cloth, price 5s.

MIDDLETON (*The Lady*)—BALLADS. Square 16mo. cloth, price 3s. 6d.

MONMOUTH: a Drama, of which the outline is Historical. (Dedicated, by permission, to Mr. Henry Irving.) Small crown 8vo. cloth, price 5s.

MOORE (*Mrs. Bloomfield*)—GONDALINE'S LESSON: The Warden's Tale, Stories for Children, and other Poems. Crown 8vo. cloth, price 5s.

MORICE (*Rev. F. D.*) *M.A.*—THE OLYMPIAN AND PYTHIAN ODES OF PINDAR. A New Translation in English Verse. Crown 8vo. price 7s. 6d.

MORSHEAD (*E. D. A.*)—THE AGAMEMNON OF ÆSCHYLUS. Translated into English Verse. With an Introductory Essay. Crown 8vo. cloth, price 5s.

MORTERRA (*Felix*)—THE LEGEND OF ALLANDALE, and other Poems. Small crown 8vo. cloth, price 6s.

MY OLD PORTFOLIO. A Volume of Poems. Crown 8vo. cloth, price 4s. 6d.

NICHOLSON (*Edward B.*) *Librarian of the London Institution*—THE CHRIST CHILD, and other Poems. Crown 8vo. cloth, price 4s. 6d.

NOAKE (*Major R. Compton*) — THE BIVOUAC; or, Martial Lyrist. With an Appendix: Advice to the Soldier. Fcp. 8vo. price 5s. 6d.

NOEL (*The Hon Roden*)—A LITTLE CHILD'S MONUMENT. Small crown 8vo. cloth, 3s. 6d.

NORRIS (*Rev. Alfred*) —THE INNER AND OUTER LIFE POEMS. Fcp. 8vo. cloth, price 6s.

ODE OF LIFE (THE). By the Author of 'The Epic of Hades' &c. Third Edition. Crown 8vo. cloth, price 5s.

O'HAGAN (*John*) — THE SONG OF ROLAND. Translated into English Verse. Large post 8vo. parchment antique, price 10s. 6d.

PALACE AND PRISON AND FAIR GERALDINE: two Tragedies. By the Author of 'Ginevra' and the 'Duke of Guise.' Crown 8vo. cloth, price 6s.

PALMER (*Charles Walter*)—THE WEED: a Poem. Small crown 8vo. cloth, price 3s.

PAUL (*C. Kegan*)—GOETHE'S FAUST. A New Translation in Rhyme. Crown 8vo. price 6s.

PAYNE (*John*)—SONGS OF LIFE AND DEATH. Crown 8vo. cloth, price 5s.

PENNELL (*H. Cholmondeley*)—PEGASUS RESADDLED. By the Author of 'Puck on Pegasus,' &c. &c. With Ten Full-page Illustrations by George Du Maurier. Second Edition. Fcp. 4to. cloth elegant, 12s. 6d.

PFEIFFER (Emily)—GLAN ALARCH: His Silence and Song: a Poem. Second Edition. Crown 8vo. price 6s.

GERARD'S MONUMENT and other Poems. Second Edition. Crown 8vo. cloth, price 6s.

QUARTERMAN'S GRACE, and other Poems. Crown 8vo. cloth, price 5s.

POEMS. Second Edition. Crown 8vo. cloth, price 6s.

SONNETS AND SONGS. New Edition. 16mo. handsomely printed and bound in cloth, gilt edges, price 4s.

RHOADES (James).—THE GEORGICS OF VIRGIL. Translated into English Verse. Small crown 8vo. cloth, price 5s.

ROBINSON (A. Mary F.)—A HANDFUL OF HONEYSUCKLE. Fcp. 8vo. cloth, price 3s. 6d.

SAPPHO. A Dream, by the Author of 'Palace and Prison' &c. Crown 8vo. cloth, 3s. 6d.

SHELLEY (Percy Bysshe) — POEMS SELECTED FROM. Dedicated to Lady Shelley. With Preface by Richard Garnett. Printed on hand-made paper, with miniature frontispiece, elzevir 8vo. limp parchment antique, price 6s.; vellum, 7s. 6d.

SKINNER (James)—CŒLESTIA. The Manual of St. Augustine. The Latin Text side by side with an English Interpretation in Thirty-six Odes with Notes, *and a plea for the* study *of* Mystical Theology. Large crown 8vo. cloth, 6s.

SONGS OF TWO WORLDS. By the Author of 'The Epic of Hades.' Fifth Edition. Complete in one Volume, with Portrait. Fcp. 8vo. cloth, 7s. 6.

SONGS FOR MUSIC. By Four Friends. Containing Songs by Reginald A. Gatty, Stephen H. Gatty, Greville J. Chester, and Juliana Ewing. Square crown 8vo. price 5s.

STEDMAN (Edmund Clarence)—LYRICS AND IDYLLS, with other Poems. Crown 8vo. cloth, price 7s. 6d.

STEVENS (William)—THE TRUCE OF GOD, and other Poems. Small crown 8vo. cloth, price 3s. 6d.

SWEET SILVERY SAYINGS OF SHAKESPEARE. Crown 8vo. cloth gilt, 7s. 6d.

TAYLOR (Sir H.)—Works Complete in Five Volumes. Crown 8vo. cloth, price 30s.

TENNYSON (Alfred) — Works Complete:—

THE IMPERIAL LIBRARY EDITION. Complete in 7 vols. demy 8vo. price 10s. 6d. each; in Roxburgh binding, 12s. 6d.

AUTHOR'S EDITION. In Six Volumes. Post 8vo. cloth gilt; or half-morocco. Roxburgh style.

CABINET EDITION. 12 Volumes. Each with Frontispiece. Fcp. 8vo. price 2s. 6d. each.

CABINET EDITION. 12 vols. Complete in handsome Ornamental Case.

POCKET VOLUME EDITION. 13 vols. in neat case, price 36s. Ditto, ditto. Extra cloth gilt, in case, price 42s.

THE ROYAL EDITION. In 1 vol. With 25 Illustrations and Portrait. Cloth extra, bevelled boards, gilt leaves, price 21s.

THE GUINEA EDITION. Complete in 12 vols. neatly bound and enclosed in box. Cloth, price 21s.; French morocco, price 31s. 6d.

SHILLING EDITION. In 12 vols. pocket size, 1s. each, sewed.

THE CROWN EDITION. Complete in 1 vol. strongly bound in cloth, price 6s.; cloth, extra gilt leaves, price 7s. 6d.; Roxburgh, half-morocco, price 8s. 6d.

*** Can also be had in a variety of other bindings.

IN MEMORIAM. Choicely printed on hand-made paper, with a miniature portrait in *eau-forte* by Le Rat, after a photograph by the late Mrs. Cameron. Bound in limp parchment, antique, price 6s.; vellum, 7s. 6d.

THE PRINCESS: A Medley. Choicely printed on hand-made paper, with a miniature frontispiece by H. M. Paget and a tail-piece in outline by Gordon Browne. Limp parchment, antique, price 6s.; vellum, price 7s.

TENNYSON (*Alfred*)—cont.

TENNYSON'S SONGS SET TO MUSIC by various Composers. Edited by W. J. Cusins. Dedicated, by express permission, to Her Majesty the Queen. Royal 4to. cloth extra, gilt leaves, price 21s.; or in half-morocco, price 25s.

Original Editions :—

BALLADS, and other Poems. Fcp. 8vo. cloth, price 5s.

POEMS. Small 8vo. price 6s.

MAUD, and other Poems. Small 8vo. price 3s. 6d.

THE PRINCESS. Small 8vo. price 3s. 6d.

IDYLLS OF THE KING. Small 8vo. price 5s.

IDYLLS OF THE KING. Complete. Small 8vo. price 6s.

THE HOLY GRAIL, and other Poems. Small 8vo. price 4s. 6d.

GARETH AND LYNETTE. Small 8vo. price 3s.

ENOCH ARDEN, &c. Small 8vo. price 3s. 6d.

IN MEMORIAM. Small 8vo. price 4s.

HAROLD : a Drama. New Edition. Crown 8vo. price 6s.

QUEEN MARY : a Drama. New Edition. Crown 8vo. price 6s.

THE LOVER'S TALE. Fcap. 8vo. cloth, 3s. 6d.

SELECTIONS FROM THE ABOVE WORKS. Super royal 16mo. price 3s. 6d. ; cloth gilt extra, price 4s.

SONGS FROM THE ABOVE WORKS. 16mo. cloth, price 2s. 6d.; cloth extra, 3s. 6d.

IDYLLS OF THE KING, and other Poems. Illustrated by Julia Margaret Cameron. 2 vols. folio, half-bound morocco, cloth sides, price £6. 6s. each.

TENNYSON FOR THE YOUNG AND FOR RECITATION. Specially arranged. Fcp. 8vo. 1s. 6d.

THE TENNYSON BIRTHDAY BOOK. Edited by Emily Shakespear. 32mo. cloth limp, 2s. ; cloth extra, 3s.

*** A superior Edition, printed in red and black, on antique paper, specially prepared. Small crown 8vo. cloth, extra gilt leaves, price 5s.; and in various calf and morocco bindings.

THOMPSON (*Alice C.*)—PRELUDES : a Volume of Poems. Illustrated by Elizabeth Thompson (Painter of 'The Roll Call'). 8vo. price 7s. 6d.

THRING (*Rev. Godfrey*), B.A.—HYMNS AND SACRED LYRICS. Fcp. 8vo. price 3s. 6d.

TODHUNTER (*Dr. J.*) — LAURELLA, and other Poems. Crown 8vo. 6s. 6d.

ALCESTIS : a Dramatic Poem. Extra fcp. 8vo. cloth, 5s.

A STUDY OF SHELLEY. Crown 8vo. cloth, price 7s.

TOLINGSBY (*Frere*) — ELNORA : an Indian Mythological Poem. Fcp. 8vo. cloth, price 6s.

TRANSLATIONS FROM DANTE, PETRARCH, MICHAEL ANGELO, AND VITTORIA COLONNA. Fcp. 8vo. cloth, price 7s. 6d.

TURNER (*Rev. C. Tennyson*)—SONNETS, LYRICS, AND TRANSLATIONS. Crown 8vo. cloth, price 4s. 6d.

COLLECTED SONNETS, Old and New. With Preface by ALFRED TENNYSON; also some Marginal Notes by S. T. COLERIDGE, and a Critical Essay by JAMES SPEDDING. Fcp. 8vo cloth, price 7s. 6d.

WALTERS (*Sophia Lydia*)—THE BROOK: a Poem. Small crown 8vo. cloth, price 3s. 6d.

A DREAMER'S SKETCH BOOK. With 21 Illustrations by Percival Skelton, R. P. Leitch, W. H. J. BOOT, and T. R. PRITCHETT. Engraved by J. D. Cooper. Fcp. 4to. cloth, price 12s. 6d.

WATERFIELD (*W.*) — HYMNS FOR HOLY DAYS AND SEASONS. 32mo. cloth, price 1s. 6d.

WATSON (*William*)—THE PRINCE'S QUEST, and other Poems. Crown 8vo. cloth, price 5s.

WAY (*A.*) *M.A.*—THE ODES OF HORACE LITERALLY TRANSLATED IN METRE. Fcp. 8vo. price 2s.

WEBSTER (*Augusta*) — DISGUISES : a Drama. Small crown 8vo. cloth, price 5s.

WET DAYS. By a Farmer. Small crown 8vo. cloth, price 6s.

WILLOUGHBY (The Hon. Mrs.)—ON THE NORTH WIND—THISTLEDOWN: a Volume of Poems. Elegantly bound, small crown 8vo. price 7s. 6d.

WOODS (James Chapman) - A CHILD OF THE PEOPLE, and other Poems. Small crown 8vo. cloth, price 5s.

YOUNG (Wm.)—GOTTLOB, ETCETERA. Small crown 8vo. cloth, price 3s. 6d.

WORKS OF FICTION IN ONE VOLUME.

BANKS (Mrs. G. L.)—GOD'S PROVIDENCE HOUSE. New Edition. Crown 8vo. cloth, price 3s. 6d.

BETHAM-EDWARDS (Miss M.) KITTY. With a Frontispiece. Crown 8vo. price 6s.

BLUE ROSES; or, Helen Malinofska's Marriage. By the Author of 'Véra.' New and Cheaper Edition. With Frontispiece. Crown 8vo. cloth, price 6s.

FRISWELL (J. Hain)—ONE OF TWO; or, The Left-Handed Bride. Crown 8vo. cloth, price 3s. 6d.

GARRETT (E.)—BY STILL WATERS: a Story for Quiet Hours. With Seven Illustrations. Crown 8vo. price 6s.

HARDY (Thomas)—A PAIR OF BLUE EYES. Author of 'Far from the Madding Crowd.' New Edition. Crown 8vo. price 6s.

THE RETURN OF THE NATIVE. New Edition. With Frontispiece. Crown 8vo. cloth, price 6s.

HOOPER (Mrs. G.)—THE HOUSE OF RABY. Crown 8vo. cloth, price 3s. 6d.

INGELOW (Jean)—OFF THE SKELLIGS: a Novel. With Frontispiece. Second Edition. Crown 8vo. cloth, price 6s.

MACDONALD (G.)—MALCOLM. With Portrait of the Author engraved on Steel. Fourth Edition. Crown 8vo. price 6s.

THE MARQUIS OF LOSSIE. Second Edition. With Frontispiece. Crown 8vo. cloth, price 6s.

ST. GEORGE AND ST. MICHAEL. Second Edition. With Frontispiece. Crown 8vo. cloth, 6s.

MASTERMAN (J.)—HALF-A-DOZEN DAUGHTERS. Crown 8vo. cloth, price 3s. 6d.

MEREDITH (George) — ORDEAL OF RICHARD FEVEREL. New Edition. Crown 8vo. cloth, price 6s.

MEREDITH (George)—cont. THE EGOIST: A Comedy in Narrative. New and Cheaper Edition, with Frontispiece. Crown 8vo. cloth, price 6s.

PALGRAVE (W. Gifford)—HERMANN AGHA: an Eastern Narrative. Third Edition. Crown 8vo. cloth, price 6s.

PANDURANG HARI; or, Memoirs of a Hindoo. With an Introductory Preface by Sir H. Bartle E. Frere, G.C.S.I., C.B. Crown 8vo. price 6s.

PAUL (Margaret Agnes)—GENTLE AND SIMPLE: A Story. New and Cheaper Edition, with Frontispiece. Crown 8vo. price 6s.

SAUNDERS (John) — ISRAEL MORT, OVERMAN: a Story of the Mine. Crown 8vo. price 6s.

ABEL DRAKE'S WIFE. Crown 8vo. cloth, price 3s. 6d.

HIRELL. Crown 8vo. cloth, price 3s. 6d.

SHAW (Flora L.)—CASTLE BLAIR; a Story of Youthful Lives. New and Cheaper Edition, with Frontispiece. Crown 8vo. price 6s.

STRETTON (Hesba) — THROUGH A NEEDLE'S EYE: a Story. New and Cheaper Edition, with Frontispiece. Crown 8vo. cloth, price 6s.

TAYLOR (Col. Meadows) C.S.I., M.R.I.A. SEETA: a Novel. New and Cheaper Edition. With Frontispiece. Crown 8vo. cloth, price 6s.

TIPPOO SULTAUN: a Tale of the Mysore War. New Edition, with Frontispiece. Crown 8vo. cloth, price 6s.

RALPH DARNELL. New and Cheaper Edition. With Frontispiece. Crown 8vo. cloth, price 6s.

A NOBLE QUEEN. New and Cheaper Edition. With Frontispiece. Crown 8vo. cloth, price 6s.

TAYLOR (Col. Meadows)—cont.

THE CONFESSIONS OF A THUG. Crown 8vo. price 6s.

TARA: a Mahratta Tale. Crown 8vo. price 6s.

THOMAS (Moy)—A FIGHT FOR LIFE. Crown 8vo. cloth, price 3s. 6d.

WITHIN SOUND OF THE SEA. New and Cheaper Edition, with Frontispiece. Crown 8vo. cloth, price 6s.

BOOKS FOR THE YOUNG.

AUNT MARY'S BRAN PIE. By the Author of 'St. Olave's.' Illustrated. Price 3s. 6d.

BARLEE (Ellen)—LOCKED OUT: a Tale of the Strike. With a Frontispiece. Royal 16mo. price 1s. 6d.

BONWICK (J.) F.R.G.S.—THE TASMANIAN LILY. With Frontispiece. Crown 8vo. price 5s.

MIKE HOWE, the Bushranger of Van Diemen's Land. New and Cheaper Edition. With Frontispiece. Crown 8vo. price 3s. 6d.

BRAVE MEN'S FOOTSTEPS. By the Editor of 'Men who have Risen.' A Book of Example and Anecdote for Young People. With Four Illustrations by C. Doyle. Sixth Edition. Crown 8vo. price 3s. 6d.

CHILDREN'S TOYS, and some Elementary Lessons in General Knowledge which they teach. Illustrated. Crown 8vo. cloth, price 5s.

COLERIDGE (Sara)—PRETTY LESSONS IN VERSE FOR GOOD CHILDREN, with some Lessons in Latin, in Easy Rhyme. A New Edition. Illustrated. Fcp. 8vo. cloth, price 3s. 6d.

D'ANVERS (N. R.)—LITTLE MINNIE'S TROUBLES: an Every-day Chronicle. With 4 Illustrations by W. H. Hughes. Fcp. cloth, price 3s. 6d.

PARTED: a Tale of Clouds and Sunshine. With 4 Illustrations. Extra fcp. 8vo. cloth, price 3s. 6d.

PIXIE'S ADVENTURES; or, the Tale of a Terrier. With 21 Illustrations. 16mo. cloth, price 4s. 6d.

NANNY'S ADVENTURES; or, the Tale of Goat. With 12 Illustrations. 16mo. loth, price 4s. 6d.

DAVIES (G. Christopher)—RAMBLES AND ADVENTURES OF OUR SCHOOL FIELD CLUB. With Four Illustrations. Crown 8vo. price 5s.

DRUMMOND (Miss)—TRIPP'S BUILDINGS. A Study from Life, with Frontispiece. Small crown 8vo. price 3s. 6d.

EDMONDS (Herbert)—WELL SPENT LIVES: a Series of Modern Biographies. Crown 8vo. price 5s.

EVANS (Mark)—THE STORY OF OUR FATHER'S LOVE, told to Children; Fourth and Cheaper Edition of Theology for Children. With Four Illustrations. Fcap. 8vo. price 1s. 6d.

FARQUHARSON (M.)

I. ELSIE DINSMORE. Crown 8vo. price 3s. 6d.

II. ELSIE'S GIRLHOOD. Crown 8vo. price 3s. 6d.

III. ELSIE'S HOLIDAYS AT ROSELANDS. Crown 8vo. price 3s. 6d.

HERFORD (Brooke)—THE STORY OF RELIGION IN ENGLAND: a Book for Young Folk. Cr. 8vo. cloth, price 5s.

INGELOW (Jean)—THE LITTLE WONDER-HORN. With Fifteen Illustrations. Small 8vo. price 2s. 6d.

JOHNSON (Virginia W.)—THE CATSKILL FAIRIES. Illustrated by ALFRED FREDERICKS. Cloth, price 5s.

KER (David)—THE BOY SLAVE IN BOKHARA: a Tale of Central Asia. With Illustrations. New and Cheaper Edition. Crown 8vo. price 3s. 6d.

THE WILD HORSEMAN OF THE PAMPAS. Illustrated. New and Cheaper Edition. Crown 8vo. price 3s. 6d.

LAMONT (Martha MacDonald)—THE GLADIATOR: a Life under the Roman Empire in the beginning of the Third Century. With 4 Illustrations by H. M. Paget. Extra fcp. 8vo. cloth, price 3s. 6d.

LEANDER (*Richard*) — FANTASTIC STORIES. Translated from the German by Paulina B. Granville. With Eight Full-page Illustrations by M. E. Fraser-Tytler. Crown 8vo. price 5*s*.

LEE (*Holme*)—HER TITLE OF HONOUR. A Book for Girls. New Edition. With a Frontispiece. Crown 8vo. price 5*s*.

LEWIS (*Mary A.*)—A RAT WITH THREE TALES. New and Cheaper Edition. With Four Illustrations by Catherine F. Frere. Price 3*s*. 6*d*.

MC CLINTOCK (*L.*)—SIR SPANGLE AND THE DINGY HEN. Illustrated. Square crown 8vo. price 2*s*. 6*d*.

MAC KENNA (*S. J.*)—PLUCKY FELLOWS. A Book for Boys. With Six Illustrations. Fourth Edition. Crown 8vo. price 3*s*. 6*d*.

AT SCHOOL WITH AN OLD DRAGOON. With Six Illustrations. Third Edition. Crown 8vo. price 5*s*.

MALDEN (*H. E.*)—PRINCES AND PRINCESSES: Two Fairy Tales. Illustrated Small crown 8vo. price 2*s*. 6*d*.

MASTER BOBBY. By the Author of 'Christina North.' With Six Illustrations. Fcp. 8vo. cloth, price 3*s*. 6*d*.

NAAKE (*J. T.*) — SLAVONIC FAIRY TALES. From Russian, Servian, Polish, and Bohemian Sources. With Four Illustrations. Crown 8vo. price 5*s*.

PELLETAN (*E.*)—THE DESERT PASTOR. JEAN JAROUSSEAU. Translated from the French. By Colonel E. P. De L'Hoste. With a Frontispiece. New Edition. Fcap. 8vo. price 3*s*. 6*d*.

REANEY (*Mrs. G. S.*)—WAKING AND WORKING; or, From Girlhood to Womanhood. New and Cheaper Edition. With a Frontispiece. Cr. 8vo. price 3*s*. 6*d*.

BLESSING AND BLESSED: a Sketch of Girl Life. New and Cheaper Edition. Crown 8vo. cloth, price 3*s*. 6*d*.

ROSE GURNEY'S DISCOVERY. A Book for Girls. Dedicated to their Mothers. Crown 8vo. cloth, price 3*s*. 6*d*.

ENGLISH GIRLS: Their Place and Power. With Preface by the Rev. R. W. Dale. Third Edition. Fcap. 8vo. cloth, price 2*s*. 6*d*.

REANEY (*Mrs. G. S.*)—cont.

JUST ANYONE, and other Stories. Three Illustrations. Royal 16mo. cloth, price 1*s*. 6*d*.

SUNBEAM WILLIE, and other Stories. Three Illustrations. Royal 16mo. price 1*s*. 6*d*.

SUNSHINE JENNY and other Stories. 3 Illustrations. Royal 16mo. cloth, price 1*s*. 6*d*.

ROSS (*Mrs. E.*), ('Nelsie Brook')—DADDY'S PET. A Sketch from Humble Life. With Six Illustrations. Royal 16mo. price 1*s*.

SADLER (*S. W.*) *R.N.*—THE AFRICAN CRUISER: a Midshipman's Adventures on the West Coast. With Three Illustrations. New and Cheaper Edition. Crown 8vo. price 2*s*. 6*d*.

SEEKING HIS FORTUNE, and other Stories. With Four Illustrations. New and Cheaper Edition. Crown 8vo. 2*s*. 6*d*.

SEVEN AUTUMN LEAVES FROM FAIRY LAND. Illustrated with Nine Etchings. Square crown 8vo. price 3*s*. 6*d*.

STOCKTON (*Frank R.*)—A JOLLY FELLOWSHIP. With 20 Illustrations. Crown 8vo. cloth, price 5*s*.

STORR (*Francis*) *and* TURNER (*Hawes*). —CANTERBURY CHIMES; or, Chaucer Tales retold to Children. With Six Illustrations from the Ellesmere MS. Fcap. 8vo. cloth, price 3*s*. 6*d*.

STRETTON (*Hesba*)—DAVID LLOYD'S LAST WILL. With Four Illustrations. Royal 16 mo. price 2*s*. 6*d*.

THE WONDERFUL LIFE. Thirteenth Thousand. Fcap. 8vo. cloth, price 2*s*. 6*d*.

SUNNYLAND STORIES. By the Author of 'Aunt Mary's Bran Pie.' Illustrated. Small 8vo. price 3*s*. 6*d*.

TALES FROM ARIOSTO RE-TOLD FOR CHILDREN. By a Lady. With 3 Illustrations. Crown 8vo. cloth, price 4*s*. 6*d*.

WHITAKER (*Florence*)—CHRISTY'S INHERITANCE. A London Story. Illustrated. Royal 16mo. price 1*s*. 6*d*.

ZIMMERN (*H.*)—STORIES IN PRECIOUS STONES. With Six Illustrations. Third Edition. Crown 8vo. price 5*s*.

CONTENTS OF THE VARIOUS VOLUMES

IN THE COLLECTED EDITIONS OF

MR. TENNYSON'S WORKS.

THE IMPERIAL LIBRARY EDITION,

IN SEVEN OCTAVO VOLUMES.
Cloth, price 10s. 6d. per vol.; 12s. 6d. Roxburgh binding.

CONTENTS.

Vol. I.—MISCELLANEOUS POEMS.
II.—MISCELLANEOUS POEMS.
III.—PRINCESS, AND OTHER POEMS.

Vol. IV.—IN MEMORIAM and MAUD.
V.—IDYLLS OF THE KING.
VI.—IDYLLS OF THE KING.
VII.—DRAMAS.

Printed in large, clear, old-faced type, with a Steel Engraved Portrait of the Author, the set complete, cloth, price £3. 13s. 6d.; or Roxburgh half-morocco, price £4. 7s. 6d.

*** *The handsomest Edition published.*

THE AUTHOR'S EDITION,

IN SIX VOLUMES. Bound in cloth, 38s. 6d.

CONTENTS.

Vol. I.—EARLY POEMS and ENGLISH IDYLLS. 6s.
II.—LOCKSLEY HALL, LUCRETIUS, and other Poems. 6s.
III.—THE IDYLLS OF THE KING, complete. 7s. 6d.

Vol. IV.—THE PRINCESS and MAUD. 6s.
V.—ENOCH ARDEN and IN MEMORIAM. 6s.
VI.—QUEEN MARY and HAROLD. 7s.

This Edition can also be had bound in half-morocco, Roxburgh, price 1s. 6d. per vol. extra.

THE CABINET EDITION,

IN TWELVE VOLUMES. Price 2s. 6d. each.

CONTENTS.

Vol. I.—EARLY POEMS. Illustrated with a Photographic Portrait of Mr. Tennyson.

II.—ENGLISH IDYLLS, and other POEMS. Containing an Engraving of Mr. Tennyson's Residence at Aldworth.

III.—LOCKSLEY HALL, and other POEMS. With an Engraved Picture of Farringford.

IV.—LUCRETIUS, and other POEMS. Containing an Engraving of a Scene in the Garden at Swainston.

V.—IDYLLS OF THE KING. With an Autotype of the Bust of Mr. Tennyson by T. Woolner, R.A.

Vol. VI.—IDYLLS OF THE KING. Illustrated with an Engraved Portrait of 'Elaine,' from a Photographic Study by Julia M. Cameron.

VII.—IDYLLS OF THE KING. Containing an Engraving of 'Arthur,' from a Photographic Study by Julia M. Cameron.

VIII.—THE PRINCESS. With an Engraved Frontispiece.

IX.—MAUD and ENOCH ARDEN. With a Picture of 'Maud,' taken from a Photographic Study by Julia M. Cameron.

X.—IN MEMORIAM. With a Steel Engraving of Arthur H. Hallam, engraved from a picture in possession of the Author, by J. C. Armytage.

XI.—QUEEN MARY: a Drama. With Frontispiece by Walter Crane.

XII.—HAROLD: a Drama. With Frontispiece by Walter Crane.

*** *These Volumes may be had separately, or the Edition complete, in a handsome ornamental case, price 32s.*

THE MINIATURE EDITION,

IN THIRTEEN VOLUMES.

CONTENTS.

Vol. I.—POEMS.
II.—POEMS.
III.—POEMS.
IV.—IDYLLS OF THE KING.
V.—IDYLLS OF THE KING.
VI.—IDYLLS OF THE KING.

Vol. VII.—IDYLLS OF THE KING.
VIII.—IN MEMORIAM.
IX.—PRINCESS.
X.—MAUD.
XI.—ENOCH ARDEN.
XII.—QUEEN MARY.

Vol. XIII.—HAROLD.

Bound in imitation vellum, ornamented in gilt and gilt edges, in case, price 42s. This Edition can also be had in plain binding and case, price 36s.

Spottiswoode & Co., Printers, New-street Square, London.

www.ingramcontent.com/pod-product-compliance
Lightning Source LLC
Chambersburg PA
CBHW032049230426
43672CB00009B/1537